ENDORSEMENTS
STORIES OF FAITH AND
FROM COPS ON THE STREET

"This devotional book is a vivid display of God's work through His warriors on earth."

John M. Wills, Creator of
The Chicago Warriors Thriller Series.

"Grant Wolf captures the essence of the real stories of real cops."

Sheriff Jim Hammond
Hamilton County, Tennessee, Sheriffs Office
Former President, Fellowship of Christian Peace Officers-USA

This book is a "Must Read" book for anyone in the law enforcement profession. The stories will do much more than simply inspire you; they will change your life!"

Officer Michael Dye
Volusia County, FL, Sheriff's Department
Author of *The PeaceKeepers, A Bible Study for Law Enforcement*

"Grant Wolf has been able to document the memories of several heroes in these short stories that even their own families and friends could not do. Police Officers don't see themselves as heroes, only Servants. They are very private people who seldom speak of their acts of hero- ism that keeps our communities, neighborhoods and cities safe daily."

Chief Jimmie Dotson
Houston, Texas Independent School District Police Department
Former Chief, Chattanooga, Tennessee Police Department

"In his book Grant has been able to point out that often there have been police officers who felt alone until they remembered their Lord had promised, 'I will be with you ALWAYS!' Cops, universally find it hard to 'trust' others. It is comforting to know that our creator can be trusted ALWAYS!"

Henry H. "Hank" Harley
Executive Director, Fellowship of Christian Peace Officers-Canada
Chief of Police/Superintendent, Canada Police Service (Ret.)

"As a former Chief Police Officer, I commend these daily devotionals, recounting first-hand experiences of police colleagues, to both inspire and spur you on in your walk with God to recognise the true value of His presence in every situation. For all who as yet have little or no faith, surely what you read about what God has done for others He also can do for you. These pages are not simply for the days of a year but forever!"

Robin Oake, Chief of Police, Isle of Man
London's Metropolitan & Greater Manchester Police

"The field of emergency service is a unique work environment that tests the soul in a very special way. Grant Wolf is a veteran counselor and man of faith that has answered this calling. For many years, he has provided support to those who must deal with the difficult, demanding and often dangerous job of public safety. I recommend this collection of selected stories that tell of the life that only he and those who follow the path will ever fully know or understand."

Mayor Ron Littlefield
Chattanooga, TN

"God's kingdom is demonstrated powerfully in many situations where police officers are doing their duty. The stories shared here will not only encourage and inspire fellow police officers but also give the general reader a unique insight into this influential calling. Through this book I hope many will be moved to support their local officers, in prayer, kindness and through practical help."

Inspector Fiona Prestidge
Chairperson, Police Christian Support Network
New Zealand Police

"A spiritual kaleidoscope of true police stories rarely shared outside the law enforcement circle—a must read!"

Detective/Sergeant Ingrid Dean, Michigan State Police
Author, *Spirit of the Badge:*
60 True Police Stories of Divine Guidance, Miracles & Intuition
www.spiritofthebadge.com

"An outstanding book for any true warrior seeking to see Christ working in our God-ordained profession. Highly recommended!"

Michael "MC" Williams
Police Detective/State Criminal Investigator
Fellowship of Christian Peace Officers (FCPO) National VP
Chaplain, "The Centurion" Law Enforcement Ministry

Stories OF Faith AND Courage FROM
COPS ON THE STREET

Compiled by
GRANT WOLF

GOD & COUNTRY PRESS

ISBN 978-0-89957112-6
First printing—November 2010
Cover designed by Michael Largent, Indoor Graphics, Inc., Chattanooga, TN
Interior design and typesetting by Reider Publishing Services,
    West Hollywood, California
Edited and proofread by Rich Cairnes and Rick Steele

Printed in Canada
16 15 14 13 12 11 –T– 7 6 5 4 3 2

Dedicated to all the men and women around the world
who ever have taken the oath "to protect and serve."

For he is God's servant to do you good.
But if you do wrong, be afraid,
for he does not bear the sword for nothing.
He is God's servant, an agent of wrath
to bring punishment on the wrongdoer.
Therefore, it is necessary to submit to the authorities,
not only because of possible punishment
but also because of conscience.
Romans 13:4, 5

ONLY A MOMENT

Dedicated to those who lost their lives in the line of duty

Dear Lord,
It was only a moment,
but in that moment of madness our world changed.
In that moment countless lives were changed,
hearts were broken, and names previously unknown
are now spoken with reverence.

In only a moment the Line of Blue stretching out across our nation
was broken—that hard, fast, steady line was breached.
In moments like these all citizens become a part of the Line of Blue.
Momentarily we feel defenseless—but only for a moment.

In only a moment the Line of Blue re-forms,
drawing a circle around us to restore our hope.
Our tears dry, our broken hearts are comforted,
weak knees strengthened and sanity restored—
the Line of Blue—our shield of protection still stands.

The moment passes, but in that moment
we mourn for the life that was taken and grieve for the survivors,
remembering the sacrifice made to protect and serve.

It was only a moment—but they are gone,
a sacrifice made to give us a future.
We pause in our sorrow reflecting what might have been . . .
but then we press on for, by the Grace of God,
the Line of Blue still stands!
Amen!

Chuck Boman, Author
Chaplain for Lake Oswego, OR, Fire and Police,
Milwaukie Police, Oregon City Police, and West Linn Police

ON BEING A MAN

Officer Todd Keilbach

Belleville, IL, Police Department

FATHERS teach us how to be "men," but I grew up without a dad. Perhaps a "manly job" would teach me, so I became a police officer. I cussed a lot, spit tobacco, was angry, and "became a man." I worked hard, held down two jobs, won several awards and commendations, and provided for my family. I also became selfish and developed a hardened heart, causing hardships in our marriage. What I didn't know was that "looking like a man" and "being a man" are two different things.

> When I became a man, I put away childish things.
> 1 Corinthians 13:11

We were on vacation when our daughter Alli woke up sleepy and with a slight droop on the right side of her face. We didn't think much of it and went to the mall in Paducah. There we tried to get her out of the car, but she couldn't walk or use the right side of her body. We needed help *fast*, but didn't know where to go. That's when God took over. At an emergency care center a woman dropped everything to lead us to a good hospital. I crumbled when the doctors said my 5-year-old might have a brain tumor. She was airlifted to St. Louis while the rest of us spent the next three hours driving. I was helpless with the weight of the world on my shoulders; I couldn't even be at her side.

Next day our pastor came to St. Louis to be with us and pray. During our agonizing wait he told me, "You are not in control and can't handle or fix it on your own. You need to pray and turn it over to God." So that's what I did. Later that day we found it was not a brain tumor but a stroke. God had taken control, and suddenly we had hope again. In a few days she was much better, and today there is little effect from the episode. But I still had a major issue to resolve—making our marriage whole.

Belleville, IL, officer's patch

I got involved in a Bible study, *A Measure of a Man*, and my life started to change. I began reading the Bible and wanted to learn so badly I read it in six months! I found that being a man is about spiritual growth, loving

Todd Keilbach family

your wife, and loving your children. It's about sacrifice and responsibility, about being a leader and following Christ. Now I no longer need what the world calls "manly," for I've learned those things are really childish. I've exchanged cussing and chewing for a yielding heart. I didn't have a dad to teach me how to be a man, but I have a heavenly Father who continues to do so every day.

BOARDED BY MY HEART!

Sergeant Randy Poel

Grand Haven, MI, Department of Public Safety

A HOCKEY player since I was a kid, I still skate a couple of times a week and currently play in a Saturday night league. "Boarding" is what happens when an opponent knocks you into the boards surrounding the rink. This night I was "boarded" by my heart!

I was skating and (according to teammates) dropped my stick, lurched forward, and then fell straight backward, hitting my head hard on the ice. I suffered a mild concussion. An off-duty fireman ran out onto the ice to treat the injury, while my friend Nate noticed my breathing changing rapidly. He quickly called for an AED (Automatic External Defibrillator), but my breathing declined so rapidly it stopped before they could hook it up. After the first shock I flatlined and CPR was started. After three or four minutes of CPR, the AED analyzed me again and delivered a second shock. This time it brought me back into a life-sustaining heart rhythm. Paramedics arrived in approximately seven minutes, and rushed me to a local hospital. Once stable, I then was transferred to a heart center thirty miles away.

> Commit to the LORD whatever you do, and your plans will succeed.
> Proverbs 16:3

Two days later, a heart catheterization was performed that showed I had an inch-and-a-half blockage of the left anterior descending artery, sometimes called "the widow maker." It was too large to stent; I needed bypass surgery. Eight days after I collapsed the surgery was performed, and four days later I went home to recover.

There were so many "God moments" throughout this ordeal. Nate was one of the few who knew the rink had an AED, and he knew how to use it. He hadn't planned to stay for my game, but had anyway. Why? He wasn't there when I skated the previous Wednesday. What if it had happened then; could anyone else have helped? With no prior signs or symptoms of blockage and at my age (I turned 48 the day after the surgery), a situation like mine is unusual. The doctors said it had been building up for decades. I had been a high school and college athlete, and could have died as a youth during practice or at a game. I think my being active in sports all these years has helped, but I truly believe God still has plans for me. One is that my wife and I want to raise funds to put AEDs in all the hockey rinks in West Michigan.

Prayer has played a prominent part throughout my ordeal, and will continue to do so. I have been a Christian for a long time and know God is watching over me. Yes, he still has plans for me, and I want to be faithful to his leading.

PUNK OR LOST SOUL?

Sergeant Chuck Gilliland
Dallas/Ft. Worth, TX, Airport Police

ONE COLD night a call came in: "moving domestic disturbance." Dispatch had a caller on the phone behind a vehicle where the driver was beating the passenger. Even the flashing blue lights of our patrol cars didn't deter the driver in his violence. After officers separated the driver and the female passenger, they discovered the two were also in business as pimp and prostitute. He was arrested and taken to our jail.

After a long, tiring shift I headed for my car. Walking out I saw the boyfriend/pimp sitting in the front lobby. He was short, skinny, and dressed skimpily in a tank top and shorts. He had pulled both arms inside the shirt to keep warm. I always have Gospel tracts in the pocket of my uniform and thought to myself, *If anyone needs a tract,*

> I tell you the truth, whatever you did for one of the least of these brothers of mine you did for me. Matthew 25:40

this punk does. I headed toward his chair. When I gave him the tract, my "You need to read this" probably sounded more like a command than a request! I got in my car thinking, *You really are a* good *Christian. Could Jesus have done any better?* Then the reality of my self-righteous actions became clear!

I turned around and returned to the station. I had some clean clothes in my gym bag and a box of Gideon Bibles. I got a tee-shirt and Bible and headed back inside where I immediately gave him the tee-shirt. I told him I was off-duty, not operating in an official police capacity, and asked if I could talk to him. When he said "yes," I reached toward the tract I'd given him and asked if I could read it to him. He nodded agreement, and

DFW Officers Chuck Gilliland and David Hornsby

we read through it. In the process the "punk" began to look more like who he really was—a lost soul desperately trying to find his way home.

After a long conversation and going through the Roman Road to Salvation, he prayed to receive Christ. He told me his grandmother had repeatedly tried to get him to go to church with her, and he would tell her he would go the next Sunday! As I left we hugged, exchanged phone numbers, and promised to pray for each other.

Now I felt a different kind of satisfaction—not *self-righteous* but knowing I serve a God who gives second chances to people like that young man and me—a God who loves me and other sinners with the deepest love possible. God puts people in my path who need me as much as I, unknowingly, need them. Together we serve one another and him.

5

WE'RE JUST LIKE YOU—ALMOST!

Constable Merv Tippe (Ret.)

Regina, Saskatchewan

COPS AND non-cops (we call them "civilians") have a lot in common. Cops get married, have families, fight the battle of the budget, deal with leaky roofs, and fix kids' bikes—in short, just about everything people do everywhere. Oh, yes, we also are called names, get shot at, generally aren't paid as well, and often are on call 24/7. But that's okay—we chose this career.

There are also differences in how we can demonstrate our Christianity. Because of work schedules we sometimes can't attend regular church services, especially if we have permanent Sunday assignments. But we do have the opportunity to witness and be a Christian example to the homeless, wayward juveniles, prostitutes, criminals we catch and put in jail, etc.

Some of us teach Sunday school or lead small-group Bible studies. This story is about an experience my wife and I had leading a group in our home when I was in my late 20s. Our pastor asked if we would lead a group, and we said "yes." I was policing in a small town in the Canadian "boonies" where Christians were in the minority and we didn't know what to expect. Our group started small, but it grew.

> Therefore, go and make disciples of all nations, baptizing them in the name of the Father and of the Son and of the Holy Spirit, and teaching them to obey everything I have commanded you. And surely I am with you always, to the very end of the age.
> Matthew 28:19, 20

One couple had visited our church a few times but their attendance was sporadic. I got acquainted with the husband, and God put it in their hearts to attend. At the end of their first night with us they both made decisions for Christ. What an encouragement! Before they left, the wife asked if she could bring her unsaved parents the next week. Of course we said "yes," and her parents came. After a lengthy question-and-answer session, both her father and mother prayed to receive Christ. The younger couple asked if they could bring still another couple the following week. The wife of that couple was a believer, but the husband was not. They came to the Bible study and, praise the Lord, he, too, committed his life to Jesus before leaving that night. No question about it, God was blessing the seed we planted!

Yes, cops and civilians are alike . . . and different. What we have in common are the same Father and the same Great Commission assignment:

CANCER BROUGHT
THIS COP TO CHRIST!

Patrolman Hetzel (H. D.) See

Elyria, OH, Police Department

"DARLENE HAS cancer and the prognosis is not good!" The doctor's words went through me like a knife. My wife was truly a saved Christian, and I'd often asked her to pray on my behalf. Though I was unsaved and didn't think God would hear me, I got down on my knees and prayed, "Darlene is too good for you to take; she deserves to live."

With her fast-growing cancer, there was little hope for Darlene. Even so, she was amazingly strong, while I felt like I was dying inside. She often encouraged me and calmed my breaking heart. I still wasn't sure my prayers would be heard, but prayed constantly. I was so consumed with grief I got on my knees again and prayed aloud, "God, if you will let her live, you can take my life in exchange." With new experimental treatments, Darlene began slowly to improve. After nearly two years, Darlene was in remission. My relief was indescribable. But, recalling my bargain to offer my life for hers, I was concerned that soon God would be "calling in my marker."

Even though I was only 39, I felt I'd better get ready. I thought the hardest question God would ask was why I hadn't taken time to read the book he wrote—the Bible! I'd made other feeble attempts to read it, but this time God created a hunger in my heart for his Word. I really began to understand the Scriptures, and the more I read, the more God worked on my heart. While still thinking God was going to call in my marker, something compelled me to

> Therefore if any man be in Christ, he is a new creature: old things are passed away; behold, all things are become new.
> 2 Corinthians 5:17

7

read the Gospel of John. It shook my world! God showed me he didn't want to take my life, but instead wanted me to give my old life up to him and be born again (John 3:3). A third time I got down on my knees, this time to ask God to forgive my sins. When I accepted Jesus Christ as my Savior, the old Hetzel died and the life I once knew no longer existed. God had called in my marker, I had become a "new creature" (2 Corinthians 5:17 KJV), and he began to show me a world I had never seen.

My life as an officer, husband, father, and friend was changed forever when I accepted God's offer to be his child. I still agonize over the pain and suffering Darlene had to endure with her cancer. But I never shall regret how it brought me to new life in Christ.

AN ANGEL IN DISGUISE

Sergeant Cameron J. Grysen
Houston, TX, Police Department

UNLESS YOU'VE spent four weeks working through the weekends in a big-city police department dealing with five murders, you probably have no concept of the stress I was under. Instead of recuperation time I got a surprise: a major gang shoot-out with one death and no witnesses. After two more days with almost no rest I received another gift: a man found shot dead on the street with no witnesses. On my way out I prayed, "Lord, I'm tired and just can't take anymore. If nothing else, please give me a witness!"

I realized the probable suspects were in a gang under investigation by a task force for several robberies and murders. I asked the task force leader to come with me, but he was running several warrants and couldn't get away. I worked twenty hours straight until early the next day, but still had no witnesses. I headed for home with sleep in my grasp when my cell phone rang: "Come back to the office."

> Be not forgetful to entertain strangers: for thereby some have entertained angels unawares.
> Hebrews 13:2 (KJV)

The SWAT unit had run their warrants, arrested several suspects, and then gone to breakfast together. Their waitress asked what they were up to, and they told her of the case and their arrests. She replied, "What a coincidence! My best friend witnessed a murder about that same time!" They got her name, picked her up for me, and we all met at the station. We showed her a photo spread of the suspects, put together by the task force. Without hesitation and with great confidence, the witness pointed to three suspects. "I never forget a face," she said.

I thought of James 5:2, 3, which reads, "You have not because you ask not and when you do, you ask amiss." No doubt about it—I had a need, asked the only One who could help, and he answered my prayer. Oh, yes, do you recall the Scripture about "entertain[ing] angels unaware" (Hebrews 13:2 KJV)? Well, my witness's name was—you guessed it— Angel!

PAINTBALL?
I DON'T THINK SO!

Lisa Lerner, wife of Officer Chuck Lerner
Law Enforcement Missionary
El Paso, TX

COPS ARE a strange breed, aren't they? I had just spent the most nerve-wracking 143 minutes of my life when my officer husband called, telling me what he'd just gone through as if it were the most awesome paintball game in his life! God bless him!

We had been married for a year, and I'd only been a born-again believer about three years. It was 1990, and Chuck was an El Paso street patrol officer. I was working at Walgreens on one side of the Franklin Mountains, and Chuck's patrol area was on the other side. The TV in the store was on, when the newscaster interrupted the program with a breaking story: A GI home on leave was shooting at police with a high-powered rifle out the windows of his house. It was in the area where Chuck was working! I remembered that Chuck had volunteered to work undercover on a special residential patrol that day, and he wasn't wearing his body armor vest. Call it "woman's intuition," but I knew he was there!

One of my co-workers was a guy who attended church and believed as I did, so I went to him and told him what was happening. We began to pray. There was no one I could call, and even though I desperately wanted to go to the scene, driving there like a mad woman wouldn't help. All the streets would be blocked off, and I probably couldn't get within blocks of where the incident was happening. Besides, I couldn't change or control the situation, and I wouldn't be walking by faith. Perhaps what happened next was a

definitive moment in my spiritual growth: I realized only God could save my husband's life, and no one could take it from him unless God allowed it. I placed my full trust in the Lord and no one else.

The next 143 minutes were the longest I can remember. I kept on working, made small talk with customers, watched the TV, and prayed. Holding the tears back, I just prayed, trusted, and waited. Then Chuck called! He *was* at the scene, had taken cover in one of the wheel wells of a car parked in front of the house, and heard the bullets going over his head! SWAT had deployed tear gas, captured the subject, and taken him to jail. No officer was injured, and Chuck was okay. God is faithful!

JANUARY 8

A SERVICE CALL

Lieutenant Sean A. Gill

Macomb, MS, Police Department

The radio sounds, a familiar voice, a service call dispatched.
Responding, deep in your heart you know
it is not the same as the last,
and not the same as the first.
It is not the first, and it is not the last.
Again the radio sounds, the familiar voice is God's,
His Holy Spirit dispatched,
prompting you deep in your heart,
to respond to a call for service,
the Service Call of God.

SPEAKING TO a group of men at a local church, I sensed in my heart to share with them a different perspective about law enforcement officers—the perspective that we, as peace officers, have answered a call for service. I quoted from Ezekiel 3:17: "Son of man, I have made you a watchman for the house of Israel." In like manner, those of us in law enforcement are watchmen—watchmen over the communities where God has placed us to serve.

In Romans, chapter 13, we learn, "Everyone must submit to governing authorities. For all authority comes from God, and those in positions of authority have been placed there by God" (v. 1 NLT). Some translations go on to say that officers are God's ministers.

We also are God's "peacekeepers," having answered his call for service. In the position of authority God has given us, we go about our duties as ministers for good, not evil. But, as the Bible says, "If you do evil, be afraid; for he does not bear the sword in vain; for he is God's minister, an avenger to *execute* wrath on him who practices evil!" (Romans 13:4 NKJV). In "doing good," we sometimes have to "bear the sword" against those who practice evil. Matthew 5:9 says, "Blessed are the peacemakers, for they will be called sons of God." We are peacemakers, and we look forward to the same "harvest of righteousness" (James 3:18) as all our Christian brothers and sisters.

> Peacemakers who sow in peace raise a harvest of righteousness. James 3:18

JANUARY 9

ZERO VISIBILITY

Sheriff Jim Hammond

Hamilton County, TN

SNOW HITTING the windshield of the small Cessna and zero visibility made the other two passengers and me more than a little nervous on our final instrument approach to the Chattanooga Airport. However, the controlled voice of our seasoned pilot repeating information from the tower gave us a sense of calm reassurance that we soon would be on the ground. *That's good,* I thought, as I didn't want to be late to teach a criminal justice class at the university. We were returning from a probation officers' program in Memphis, and looked forward to home and families.

Wreckage of plane carrying Sheriff Hammond

Outside was a sea of white, with an occasional snowflake hitting the window. Suddenly a tree branch struck the right wing, followed quickly by another. As the plane shook violently, pieces of debris began hitting me on the head, neck, arms, and chest. Then the noise of the plane breaking apart was followed by an awful silence! I was upside down with a small fire burning to my left and wreckage everywhere. I unbuckled my seatbelt and dropped about three feet to the ground, then freed a co-worker strapped in her seat above me and carried her to safety. As the fire intensified I quickly pulled a second co-worker out. He was badly injured and bleeding from a head wound, so I carried him to the female worker, telling her to hold his head up and put pressure on his wound. The pilot was not to be found; he had been killed instantly and was buried under the wreckage.

> Thou wilt keep *him* in perfect peace, *whose* mind *is* stayed *on thee*: because he trusteth in thee. Isaiah 26:3 (KJV)

We had crashed in a state park about four miles from the airport. I headed toward a light in the distance when the chief park ranger appeared, followed quickly by fire and medical help. I was the least injured, but the other two were hospitalized for several days. We all three recovered, but the memories of that night will last forever.

Reflecting back on the accident and how quickly help arrived, I am reminded of the perfect peace God gave me. It was as if he spoke to my heart and said, "Be calm. I am with you and you will be all right." There was "zero visibility" outside on that dark and cold night, but perfect clarity in my trust that God would see me through. Not one moment did I feel as if I was going to die. In that and many difficult situations since, I know that God gives perfect peace to those who trust in him.

JANUARY 10

"PUT THE GUN AWAY!"

Sergeant William Stevenson
Rogers City, MI, Police Department

ROGERS CITY is not large, and there were only two officers on duty at night, working in one-man cars. About 12:30 a.m. we received a domestic disturbance call. I was about three minutes away, while the other officer, a rookie, was closer. As is my practice, en route I prayed for God's protection and wisdom.

When I arrived, the rookie officer was parked in front of the home, standing outside his car and well-illuminated by the street light. I parked about fifty yards away from the home and instructed the rookie to take cover.

All the family members had left the house, and the wife came over to me. She said her husband was intoxicated and had his hunting rifle. He had told her he was going to shoot the first cop he saw. Miraculously, before long the husband came out of the house without his weapon, but he was pretty shaken up. After we were sure he was under control, we took him back inside to talk with him.

Once in the house, I asked him about the rifle, and he pointed to a .308 rifle with scope in a gun cabinet. He said had taken the rifle out of the cabinet, and confirmed what his wife had told me, that he planned to shoot the first officer who arrived at his home. Then something strange had happened—after getting the rifle out of the cabinet he heard a loud voice inside the house telling him to "put the gun away." The man knew no one else was in the house, and was frightened by a voice he could not explain. In addition to preventing the man from committing a violent act, the "voice" accomplished something else. His wife had said he was drunk, but the "voice" seemed to have sobered him up. And, to my knowledge, he has not consumed any alcohol in the twenty years since the incident.

> The Spirit himself intercedes for us with groans that words cannot express. Romans 8:26

My prayer on the way to the call was just a "general prayer," without asking for anything specific. But the Bible says that when we don't know how to pray, the Holy Spirit will make "yearnings and groanings" (Romans 8:26, AMP) on our behalf. To me, the "voice" the man heard in his house is a good example of the Holy Spirit at work. I didn't know what to pray for, but he did!

JANUARY 11

THE POWER OF THE DOGS

Stuart Nightingale, Senior Sergeant
New Zealand Police

EVEN IN high-stress situations, God takes care of his own. While executing a search warrant, three of us had gone behind a garage. Suddenly, a Brown American Pit Bull, used as a pig-hunting dog, came running at us flat-out, growling, bearing its teeth, and very aggressive. The dog attacked my colleague, knocking him over and fiercely biting at his legs—you could see puncture marks through his torn trousers. Pepper spray and a baton had no effect on the dog. I knew it would take quick action to keep the dog from killing my partner!

I grabbed the dog by his leather collar and pulled him off my colleague, feeling the flesh in his legs tear in the process. Fearing for my colleague's life, I ordered a third man present to take him to the hospital as he was clearly going into shock. Going over a side fence they left in a patrol car for medical help. Then the dog broke free, seized me on my right forearm and bit through to the bone. I thought he had broken it, and was trying to tear the flesh off my arm. I knew I had to stop his biting, but didn't know what to do (I was not trained in dog control and wasn't armed).

I decided to force my free hand into his mouth to make him gag. When I did this he momentarily let go, allowing me a brief opportunity

14

to grab him by two hands around his collar. I knelt down, pulled him toward me with his back to my chest, and kept his head facing forward so he couldn't see me. For about five minutes I held him this way while blood and dog saliva were running down my front. Two pig dogs in nearby cages had become greatly enraged and were trying to break free. I thought that if they got out I might die—I felt all alone and helpless. It took all my weight to hold the dog until other staff finally arrived. Later, a dog ranger said that what I did was exactly the right thing to do, and that it was remarkable I wasn't more seriously injured.

> Deliver my life from the sword, my precious life from the power of the dogs. Psalm 22:20

The event resulted in significant follow-up media coverage that shone a spotlight on 'dangerous' dog breeds and dog ownership in general. The dog owner pleaded guilty to owning a dangerous dog and other matters, and has been prosecuted. For that I am grateful, but I'm most grateful for God's help that day. There is no other way to explain what I did other than the Lord was in charge. I have no doubt about it.

BENCH-PRESSING A CAMARO

Bill Hubbard, Executive Police Officer

Taos, NM, Police Department

LOCAL UNITS, we have a 9-1-1 call of a car having fallen on a man and he's pinned underneath!" Having been a cop for thirty-one years, there's just not a whole lot out there that will still give me a shot of adrenaline and make me want to run with lights and siren in 5 p.m. traffic, but this broadcast did! I was only about a mile away, and I knew I was probably the closest emergency responder. I got to my car, turned on my lights, and navigated my Impala to the address.

As I reached the scene I could see I was the first one there. Legs were sticking out from under a car and all four tires were still on the ground. At least the man didn't get the full weight of the car when it fell off the jack. He was alive and could respond verbally, but was in obvious agony. I had no luck searching for a jack or lever while precious minutes slipped by. What could I do?

My squadmate, Gavin, arrived. "Grab a railroad tie or wooden block," I hollered. "Let's see if we can get this car up." We heard sirens and knew help was on the way, but this was *now* and time was of the essence. Two off-duty firefighters pulled up who had heard the call on the radio in their personal vehicle, and a passerby stopped to help. With the "heft" of one of those firefighters and five of us on the scene, I thought we might have a shot at picking up the back of the Camaro and pulling the guy out.

> It is God who arms me with strength and makes my way perfect.
> 2 Samuel 22:33

Everything was a blur as the five of us moved into position. I yelled, "Let's pick it up!" and we all grabbed hold of the back bumper and lifted at the same time. Incredibly, we succeeded! The firefighter standing by the man pulled him out, and suddenly he was free! Just as we set the car down EMS arrived. We all could rejoice—a life had been saved! What was truly amazing is that the beefed-up, well-muscled firefighter I thought was going to be so much help wasn't—he was still trying to get his gloves on! We three "average-size guys" had picked up that car! Had God sent an angel to assist?

Since I became a Christian years ago God has proved Philippians 4:13 over and over to me: "I can do all things through Christ who strengthens me" (NKJV). Now I see this Scripture verse in an entirely new light!

JANUARY 13

MY EYES WERE BLIND, I COULD NOT SEE!

Patrolman H. D. See

Elyria, OH, Police Department

FOR AT least four years I noticed "Igor." Regardless of the weather, nearly every night he was on a bench near the post office. Nearby was his bicycle with all his worldly possessions in its saddlebags. The bench was "home." We all knew he was homeless and harmless, so no one hassled him for vagrancy. We were told he had a place where he showered and ate, which made me feel better. In time he "faded into the landscape." He was still there, but this unbeliever simply stopped "seeing" him.

One freezing cold winter night—after I received Christ—I truly "saw" Igor for the first time. God had given me a new heart, and the sight of the homeless man in the bitter cold was more than I could take. Immediately I wanted to know who he was and why he was living on the streets. As I left my cruiser and walked toward him, he got off the bench and started to leave with all his belongings. After I yelled several times to get his attention he turned, and in a European accent said, "I'm moving; I don't bother anyone."

I replied, "Wait, you don't understand. God has spoken to my heart and I truly want to help you. What is your name?" He stopped, paused for a moment, and through watery eyes said, "Igor." Our friendship had begun.

We talked about how he had become homeless. The old YMCA where he lived had been torn down to construct a new building, and he and the other residents were given little time to find new housing. He was working at the time, but couldn't even afford a room with his low pay. The bench near the old post office became his home!

Igor was 63 years old when we met, and I helped him obtain benefits for which he was eligible. Shortly after, we got him a very-low income apartment and he was off the streets! As dignity was restored in his life, Igor was able to get a better job. Later, even at his older age he went back to school at our local college. He is still doing well today.

There is no way to describe the joy God brought to my heart by helping Igor. I often think of how long I (and others) had seen him daily on that bench and never did anything. God also saw Igor and waited patiently for me to "see" him with believer's eyes. Even more than that, Igor was the first person to whom I ever testified about Jesus! I thank God for not giving up waiting for me to open my heart in Christian love.

> Then will the eyes of the blind be opened and the ears of the deaf unstopped. Isaiah 35:5

FROM COMMUNIST COP
TO CHRISTIAN "REPENTER"

Lieutenant Colonel Traian Restea

Romanian National Police

LIEUTENANT Colonel Traian Restea was a Romanian police officer from 1983 to 2005. He was raised as a communist and went through police training under the communist regime. After the fall of communist dictator Nicolae Ceauşescu in December 1989, life began to change for Restea. Perhaps the most dramatic of all was that he became a Christian— derisively termed "a repenter" by nonbelievers.

As Restea recalls, "To be a Christian policeman in a formerly communist country was very difficult in the early 1990s. Under the old regime the police were hated and dreaded. People never knew when a policeman came to the door what the charge might be or, if a loved one was arrested, if they'd ever see them again. After years of oppression, the people's mentality toward us was as adversaries. When I became a Christian, many attitudes toward me changed. Even in the official police structure, many felt you couldn't be a Christian and an officer. In more than one instance, Christian police officers were demoted, banished to remote posts, or harassed until they simply left the force.

> For our light affliction, which is but for a moment, is working for us a far more exceeding and eternal weight of glory.
>
> 2 Corinthians 4:17 (NKJV)

"When people learned I had become a Christian many were suspicious and didn't believe me, some shunned me, and some simply didn't know what to think. Gradually, as people observed the way I acted with no hard feelings and my changed attitude, they began to see me in a different light. I was able to share Jesus and his love with them, and many came to love the Lord because of my witness.

"People's confidence in me increased significantly, and many came to me with problems and situations where they needed help or action. When I asked, 'Why?' they said it was because I was a Christian and feared God. I earned a lot of respect and trust because people knew I would not be corrupted or twist what they said. Some of the street gangs even gave me a new name: Instead of 'TOUGH' they called me 'REPENTANT'! They knew that God was on my side and I was on his!

"Even though I faced a lot of criticism and derision both within the force and from civilians, I knew I was at peace with God. Being a 'repenter' and policeman was not easy, but was it worth it? Yes! Any hardship I endured is nothing compared with the joys of being a Christian. Amen!"

JANUARY 15

THE RUNAWAY

Sergeant Chuck Gilliland

Dallas/Ft. Worth, TX, Airport Police

PEOPLE DEAL with their problems in many different ways. These parents had reached the point they no longer could deal with their 15-year-old son's behavior, so they were shipping him off to relatives. He didn't want to leave home, friends, and parents so, when they arrived at the airport and he saw an opportunity to run, he did! The parents contacted us (DFW Police), and we began the search.

After keeping diligent watch at my post for more than an hour, I badly needed to go to the bathroom. As I was returning to my post, who should stick his head out of a stall but the boy. His face fell when he saw me; the game was over! I notified the parents and took him to my patrol car, but there was a tugging at my heart to witness to him. I knew we'd have several minutes before his parents arrived, so I began to ask him about his life. I looked for an opportunity to slip the Gospel into the conversation, and was able to do so within the first two minutes. I learned he had been to church once at Easter, but didn't know or care to learn about God. Even so, he was very polite and allowed me to explain the plan of salvation. He also accepted a Gospel tract and the Gideon Bible I offered him. About then his parents arrived and carted him back to the terminal to rebook his flight.

This happened years ago, but I still wonder about that young man. I made a copy of his ID card and taped it to the inside cover of my Bible. I still think about him and pray for him whenever I notice the card. Did he get his life straightened out in his new envi-

> I planted the seed, Apollos watered it, but God made it grow.
> 1 Corinthians 3:6

19

ronment? Were the relatives who took him in Christians, and did they water the seed I sowed? Is he now a brother in Christ, or still a lost soul? I may never know, for we don't always get to see the fruit of our efforts. But the message is clear: God wants you and me to make Jesus known to all we can. He will take care of the rest!

WHOSE RESPONSIBILITY IS IT?

Sergeant David M. Greenhalgh (Ret.)

Delta (Vancouver, Canada) Police Department

MORE THAN forty years ago at the British Columbia Justice Institute a Canadian judge made this statement: "The first thing you have to know about the justice system is that it is a 'system,' and no one person is responsible for it." This struck me to the core! God established the justice system when he conducted the first trial in Genesis, chapter 3, and he ordained police officers as his ministers in Romans, chapter 13. As a man called by God into police work in 1966, I am responsible to him within his system.

At a men's conference in 1978 I knelt beside my bed and began to pray. I had been reading Psalm 94:15: "Judgment will again be founded on righteousness, and all the upright in heart will follow it." At that point the Holy Spirit challenged me with the question that follows in verse 16: "Who will rise up for me against the wicked? Who will take a stand for me against evildoers?" For me this was a life-changing experience: I was already a Christian, but that day I became "God's policeman." I resolved before the Lord I would take ownership of every aspect of the justice system where I had interaction.

This commitment often put me in conflict and made me unpopular with Crown prosecutors, justice bureaucrats, one or two judges, and a raft of police managers over the next twenty-five years. I had resolved to be an uncompromising cop in ethical standards, productivity, performance, and effectiveness. The Holy Spirit gave me a spirit of workplace excellence and a deep motivation to pursue constant improvement. For the rest of my career this created conflict. Even so, God blessed my ministry in police work. I was often called upon by government to act as a consultant, and became the most contracted-out member in the history of

20

our agency. I retired in 2003 with a list of commendations, awards, medals, plaques, letters, and certificates for outstanding performance. For these I give credit to Jesus and the ongoing wisdom and inspiration I received from the Holy Spirit. Believers must understand we are not of this world, and our

> Be careful to obey all the law my servant Moses gave you; do not turn from it to the right or to the left. Joshua 1:7

spirit frequently is under attack from the spirit of this world. While I no longer am under Crown authority, I always will be God's policeman, standing for what is right.

SHE NEEDED A LOVING FATHER

Sergeant Mark Oliver, Badge No. D745

New Zealand Police

AS A NEW constable, I took a phone call early one morning from a very distressed young lady. She rang up to tell me she was heading down to the railway tracks to throw herself under the next train. From our continued conversation I managed to get a general idea of where she might be, so several officers and a K-9 unit were dispatched to the area. Eventually they found her and brought her back to the police station. In person, she began to tell me more of her story.

The young lady had been both sexually and physically abused by her own father while growing up. Even though I wasn't very old myself and quite new as a constable, I prayed silently, "Lord, you really are the only answer to all this young lady has endured. The two of us come from opposite ends of the spectrum. I was raised in a Christian home with two very loving parents, and she has been brought up in a family where her father chose to abuse and degrade her, and her mother pretended it wasn't happening."

As I shared the fact that I was a Christian, she looked at me for the first time. Up till then, she only had stared at the ground. She told me her doctor was a Christian and, as it turned out, attended a church similar to mine. Jokingly, she mused that perhaps the two of us were conspiring against her! I told her it was no accident I had been working that night, and God definitely had a hand in it. After several hours of conversation she laid aside her suicidal thoughts, and I was able to take the young

lady home. Over the next few months she became friends with my wife and me, and eventually gave her life over to the Lord.

The change in her life was remarkable. She had been wearing dark clothing to avoid notice, walking the streets alone at all hours of the day and night, and not interacting with anyone because she felt so worthless. Now she is an outgoing, bubbly young lady finally beginning to enjoy life. I'm so glad God gave me the opportunity to tell her there was a loving, heavenly Father waiting for her to accept his Son as her Savior. Watching her get baptised was a very special occasion I always will remember. She is a true testament to the power of God being able to change hearts.

JANUARY 18

MY "AH-HA!" MOMENT

Jeffrey P. Rush, Deputy Sheriff
Jefferson County, AL, Sheriff's Office

SOMETIMES it's easy to compartmentalize your life and take on a different persona for each area—job, family, outside activities, church. As a professional I've worn a law enforcement badge for more than thirty years, trying to live in an honorable way. But somehow in the process I hadn't put it all together—policing and being a godly man are one and the same. When I finally did, it was my "ah-ha!" moment, and it changed my life.

As a criminal justice professor I study a lot. In his book *No More Christian Nice Guy*, author Paul Coughlin wrote about *thumos*, a Greek word often translated as "spiritedness" or "passion." He helped me understand that the "passion" I had for my life as a law enforcement professional should be demonstrated with exuberance in all my roles—husband, father, criminal justice professor, and, through all, "Christian."

Policing is God-ordained, and so is my role as a man. God destined me to be a man, and he called me into law enforcement. He never meant for me to separate the two but to manifest godliness in every aspect of my life. What I do and who I am are so intertwined they are inseparable. There can be no division in my life between being on- or off-duty: the same characteristics, principles, values, concerns, passions, and love for God and man could not be compartmentalized.

Policing is a difficult profession with much toxicity: the stuff we see and deal with, the stuff we cannot remove—all are toxic. Being a man of Christ doesn't remove the toxicities, but it does help manage them in a much more positive way. Most police agencies have policy and procedure manuals detailing how personnel are to act and respond in a variety of situations. The Bible is the Christian "policy and procedure manual" for how Christian officers should respond to the toxicities of our work. All we have to do is read it and put God's principles to work. The job may not be any easier, but our lives are when we live "24/7" according to God's "playbook." In times of crisis an officer always wants a caring and capable partner. We have that in Christ; he always has our back!

> For we know, brothers loved by God, that he has chosen you . . . And so you became a model to all the believers in Macedonia and Achaia.
> 1 Thessalonians 1:4, 7

IMPONDERABLE CIRCUMSTANCES

"Anonymous"

A retired state trooper

PICTURE THE situation: winter, severe ice storm, accident between a semi and a car (cars everywhere!), plenty of warning flares, but cars that couldn't stop because of the ice. In one word: trouble! It wasn't until the next summer when the magnitude of all the unlikely circumstances fully sank in: I shouldn't have been where I was, I should have suffered more damage than I did, the doctor shouldn't have been there, I shouldn't have been able to walk back up to the highway, and, why did I hear that voice?

When I saw the accident I stopped to block oncoming traffic, turned on my lights, radioed for county help (I was a state officer), and began checking for injuries. One vehicle was "at risk" of being hit, so I began trying to move the ladies from that car to another stopped car in a safer position. I had to go to a door next to oncoming traffic to help one lady. As I opened the door it was as though someone tapped me on the shoulder and said, "Look back." I did, and have never been so scared in my life. Heading straight toward me was a car sliding out of control through the flares!

Thinking the car was going to be hit, I pushed the lady as far to the other side of the car as possible, slammed the door, and had nowhere to go but the guardrail of the bridge we were on. Bad choice; the driver was going to hit the rail before the car! I let go, tucked into a parachutist's roll and dropped—falling downhill to the railroad tracks below. After I stopped, somehow I made it back up the grade holding my badly broken arm with the other, waited nearly two hours for an ambulance, and was in surgery four hours. My surgery was done by one of the best orthopedists in the world, in town for a seminar and staying at the hospital because of the storm!

> He will cover you with his feathers, and under his wings you will find refuge; his faithfulness will be your shield and rampart. Psalm 91:4

Only God could have orchestrated everything: getting me to the accident in time to move the ladies to a safer place, "being told" to look over my shoulder, the fantastic surgeon who shouldn't have been there, and—get this: I went back to the scene the next summer. I'd fallen forty feet and then walked back up an icy slope without holding on. That summer day I had to "crawl on all fours" to climb the steep incline. God had been my buckler and shield that winter night . . . he always is!

JANUARY 20

THE BADGE

Detective Corporal M. C. Williams
Colorado

LAW ENFORCEMENT *is* my "calling!" From grade school through college I knew I had "the call" to become an officer. I graduated at the top of my academy class, and flew through field training; I had "the gift." I also had a problem. Even though I was raised "in church" and accepted Christ as my Savior in college, my personal and spiritual lives

24

Detective M. C. "Mike" Williams

were out of sync. I lived and breathed police work, and soon "the badge" had become my lord and my god. The end result of my pride, arrogance, and self-righteous attitude about policing resulted in my marriage ending in divorce. My "god" had let me down!

I relocated to a mountain resort community in 1995 where I arrested a local politician for drunk driving. With her political connections, she used the legal system to get even. Ultimately I was forced to resign from that agency and go elsewhere. With my credentials I thought I'd be scooped up quickly by another agency, but that didn't happen. I found myself existing on low-paying security jobs, deeply in debt, miserable and depressed, angry at "the system," angry at my profession, and even angrier at God. It took two years to re-enter full-time law enforcement. Even so my personal sin still was a real problem, my second marriage fell apart, and I felt so alienated I literally "left the country" to serve as a police supervisor on an overseas military post. Utterly broken and crushed, I asked God to forgive me, recommitted my life to Christ, and finally

> You shall have no other gods before me.
> Exodus 20:3

25

made him my true Lord. That was what God had been waiting for.

Soon he placed me in an elite State Police investigations unit, and I immersed myself in a solid Bible-teaching church. I also met weekly for Bible study and fellowship with a great group of Christian officers who held me accountable. I came to understand that God had a special plan for me, as he does for each of us. In due time he brought me home to Colorado and gave me a position that forced me to focus on things other than "the job." In perhaps the biggest miracle of all, God gave me a wonderful wife, ministry partner, and soul mate.

Finally I am where God wants me: ministering to, for, and with my fellow officers. I now am "God's sheepdog," protecting his sheep from the wolves. My confidence is in him, not my profession, and I am stoked about what God has in store for me both now and in the life to come.

GOD SAVED ME TWICE

Deputy Jeff DeGrow
Charleston County, SC, Sheriff's Office

I GAVE MY life to the Lord about a year before the incident. I felt as if being a Christian were something personal between him and me, so I didn't talk about it much around the department. All that changed January 21, 2010.

That morning I responded to a call in an area where there had been a rash of burglaries. This one had just occurred, so we felt the suspect might still be in the vicinity. When I headed back to the station I saw three subjects walking, which seemed odd on a cold, rainy day. I decided to check them out, and they started running when they saw me. Then they split up, with two going one way and the third another. I radioed for backup and went after the lone suspect.

At a certain point I got out of my car and chased him on foot. I had my TASER out and when we were close enough I told him to stop or I'd tase him. I'd just followed him around the corner of a trailer when suddenly I felt a very forceful pressure in my right eye. I fell to the ground— I thought I'd been hit with a baseball bat! Then everything went white and my right ear was ringing—I'd been shot in my right eye! Before he finished he shot me five times more—graze wounds on my head and shoulder and two shots through my right forearm without hitting any major arteries, bones, or ligaments.

As I lay dazed I could feel the presence of God and knew I was hanging between life and death. I had a sense I was going to be all right and was starting to come out of my daze when the shooter came back. He saw I wasn't dead, but he'd used all his bullets and

> O LORD my God, I called to you for help and you healed me. O LORD, you brought me up from the grave; you spared me from going down into the pit. Psalm 30:2, 3

fled. Somehow I got to my feet, radioed that I'd been hit and needed EMS ASAP! As I staggered to the road and waited for backup units, I prayed aloud, "Lord, please spare my life, please spare my life!" Finally help arrived and I was on the way to the hospital; God had answered my prayer! He'd saved me for eternity a year before; that Thursday morning he saved me from death! God had saved me twice!

JANUARY 22

HOW CAN I KEEP FROM PRAISING GOD!

Deputy Jeff DeGrow
Charleston County, SC, Sheriff's Office

WHEN I first became a Christian I kept it pretty personal. For one thing, it's not something usually talked about very actively in the law enforcement community. I tried to live right and read my Bible, finding answers I couldn't find elsewhere. I found a good Bible-based church with an awesome pastor who kept my attention and kept me motivated. I grew closer to the Lord and began to wonder what I could do to spread God's Word. After being shot six times and left for dead, then spending four hours in lifesaving surgery, I had new impetus to share my faith with others.

I am a pretty proactive cop and try to connect with people I encounter—drug dealers, abusers, thieves, carjackers, burglars. I believed these were the ones who needed God the most, so I tried to talk with them about him. Some would blow me off and not listen, but some at "rock bottom" would listen, knowing I was telling them the truth. My hope was to help some of them change their way of living and find the right path, the path to God.

The third day after the shooting—Sunday, January 24—I was in church, on my knees at the altar, thanking God for sparing my life. I talked to my pastor about how I could repay God for his gift of my life. I came to the realization it would be by living in accordance with God's will and spreading his Word. Suddenly the Great Commission—"Go ye into all the world, and preach the gospel to every creature" (Mark 16:15 KJV)—became very personal and meaningful. Since the shooting I have given my testimony at church and spoken at other places, always glorifying God and sharing the Gospel. Even though it was *I* who went through the ordeal, it's not about me; it's about how good God is.

> Praise the LORD. Praise God in his sanctuary; praise him in his mighty heavens. Psalm 150:1

Many have said, "Man, you're so lucky to be alive." Luck had nothing to do with it; it was God's grace and divine intervention that saved me.

JANUARY 23

NEARLY KILLED BY A MAD WOMAN!

Officer James Duke
Metropolitan Nashville, TN, Police Department

FROM THE age of 14, James Duke knew one day he would be a police officer. Even though it is a difficult job, he wanted to serve the Lord by "protecting people." On January 23, 1991, Duke needed protection *"from* the people."

Duke was attempting to arrest a shoplifter who refused to get out of her car. When he reached through the widow to open her locked door and remove her, she rolled up the window, trapping his arms, and drove off at speeds between 45 and 60 miles per hour. The driver told Duke she planned to reach the interstate, force a tractor-trailer against concrete dividers and thrust him between the semi and concrete walls so he would be crushed to death. During the wild and very dangerous ride, Duke managed three times to wrestle the steering wheel to avoid being struck by other vehicles when the shoplifter tried to sideswipe his body between them.

Finally, the woman's car ran into a ditch and was stopped. For the first time since leaving the parking lot, Duke finally could plant his feet firmly on the ground. He pulled hard with his arms, broke the window, and fell to the ground. A Nashville Metro Council member had seen him hanging from the car, and was first on the scene to assist. Duke had suffered a severed artery in his left arm, and underwent surgery that night at Metro General Hospital. It took eleven months before he again could use his left hand, and eighteen months before he could fire his revolver to maintain sworn officer qualification.

> [God] is my shield, the power that saves me, and my place of safety. He is my refuge, my savior, the one who saves me from violence.
> 2 Samuel 22:3 (NLT)

In 1991, few police departments realized that officers involved with trauma or near-death injuries had more than just physical wounds. Duke says: "From 1991 until 1998, I suffered nightmares, sweats, and anxiety attacks. I couldn't even watch action movies that involved car chases!" The Nashville Police Department had a Behavioral Health Service Division, but in 1991 it wasn't mandatory to participate in critical incident stress management debriefing (as it is today). It wasn't until 1998 that Duke "learned the stress I was experiencing was perfectly normal."

Along with being an officer, Duke is coordinator of the Peer Support Program in the Behavioral Health Services Division. He also is a police chaplain and coordinator of the department's volunteer chaplaincy program. Most of all he calls himself "a servant of the Most High God with a shepherd's heart."

MERCY WHERE
MERCY IS DUE

Officer John T. Campbell, I.D. 14716

California Highway Patrol

DRIVERS DO speed! Even police officers have to watch their speed. The lure of the open road can be quite tempting at times. Then there are the occasions when the driver focuses on the road, and his speed creeps up. Working speed enforcement on a county road I stopped a man going well over the 55-mile-per-hour speed limit. I made contact with him and explained the reason for the stop. At that the middle-aged man kindly asked for a verbal warning. There was something in his voice that spoke sincerity; I didn't discern irresponsibility or selfishness.

There are many reasons people ask for a verbal warning: they don't *want* to pay the fine, they *can't afford* to pay the fine (these usually are irresponsible), or they may be *in denial about speeding.* Even in the face of radar and the fact theirs was the only vehicle on the road, they will contend to their grave they weren't speeding because it didn't "feel" as if they were speeding. Others have a genuine need, and an experienced officer can pick up on that if they listen carefully.

> "This is what the Lord Almighty says: 'Administer true justice; show mercy and compassion to one another.'"
> Zechariah 7:9

I took the man's license, registration, and insurance information and asked the Lord as I walked back to my patrol car, "Father, what should I do with this man? The letter of state law and departmental policy says to write the man a ticket for speeding, but the mercy and grace of your Spirit is telling me to let him go."

The Lord spoke into my spirit, "Let him go."

Walking back to the violator's car I told the man, "My Father says, 'You do not have, because you do not ask God' (James 4:2). I don't normally do this, but since you asked I'm going to give you a verbal warning for speeding." At that instant he began to weep uncontrollably.

He responded, "Man, there sure aren't many guys like you out there nowadays. Thank you!" He praised God and went on his way thankful for my act of mercy. At that moment I realized God truly had spoken to me, and I had balanced what the law calls for with God's mercy, grace, and compassion.

Not everyone who asks gets a verbal warning, since many ask for selfish reasons. However, when they do ask, I usually run it past the Spirit of God for the decision. We serve a God of truth, and Jesus says the Holy Spirit will teach us and guide us into all truth. God knows our hearts and those of the people we meet. When we are walking closely with God, he will let us know truth in our heart if we ask him.

I SAW THE LIGHT!

"Officer Randy"
Baltimore, MD

THROUGHOUT my career I have been a Christian. In my early years with the county police department I worked in a low-income section where many of the young adult males were unemployed and casual drug users. So was "Ken."

I made it a point to give folks I arrested an opportunity to talk about their lives, especially their need for Christ. Some would talk, some wouldn't. Ken was always angry, didn't like being held accountable for his behavior, and refused to look at his life. I arrested Ken five different times for drug violations, and the fourth time he tried to destroy the evidence. Then came our final encounter!

I was checking out a loud party in an apartment complex and saw Ken exit the apartment with an open container of alcohol. I suspected he also was carrying drugs. When he took off running, the chase was on! During the chase he ran into a parked car with such force I felt surely both he and the car were hurt. I couldn't help but think, *Serves you right!*

He ran into a nearby field hoping to lose me in the dark, but he ran out of luck! I caught and tackled him to the ground, then decided to teach him a lesson! As he squirmed in my tight grip I reached for my trusty heavy-duty police flashlight. *It's time,* I thought, *to "show him the light"!* While contemplating the justice I was about to administer, out of nowhere appeared a little old lady walking a small dog. She made eye contact with me as if to say, "Don't you dare!" God had sent a guardian angel in human form to keep me from making the biggest mistake of my life! Seeing her stopped me in my tracks, keeping me from doing something in which I didn't believe, which was against the values of my faith in Christ and my agency, and which might have meant the end of my career.

Instead, I simply handcuffed him and called for a transport vehicle. I saw him later in court, but never again. Occasionally I wonder if he ever "saw the light," and pray that God reaches him before it is too late. I also have thanked the Lord many times for his mercy and watchful eye over me, especially for that night when *God showed me the light* in the wee hours of a dark morning!

> Dearly beloved, avenge not yourselves, but rather give place unto wrath: for it is written, Vengeance is mine; I will repay, saith the Lord. Romans 12:19 (KJV)

SPIRITUAL DEBRIEFING HELPED

Sergeant Dace Cochran

Jackson County, OR, Sheriff's Office

JANUARY 26, 2003, was Super Bowl Sunday—the Tampa Bay Buccaneers versus the Oakland Raiders—and everyone was getting ready to enjoy the game, even those of us who had to work and listen to it on the radio. Game time was forty-five minutes away when I got the call of a motor vehicle crash involving injuries. I was very close to the location, and was the first emergency responder to arrive.

A pickup truck was on its side, just off the edge of the road. Under the front corner was an 11-year-old girl, pinned by the truck's weight. Some passersby, neighbors, and I attempted to lift the truck by brute force, or at least rock it while someone tried to pull the girl out from beneath it. Unfortunately, the weight of the truck was too much for us and we were unable to free her. She was pronounced dead by the medics who arrived a short time later.

This was a tough case for me to process emotionally, as I had an 11-year-old son and 9-year-old daughter at home at the time. I felt very guilty that we had been unable to lift the vehicle and free her, and needed to talk with somebody. After finishing my assignment at the scene, I cleared and called my pastor. He was quite understanding of the situation, and agreed to meet with me. We talked about my feelings regarding the case, I shed some tears, and we prayed together. That time with him greatly eased my soul. (As a side note, helping officers deal with situations like this is why so many departments have chaplains and pastors on call 24/7.) Even though I continued to be involved with the case during an extensive amount of follow-up investigation, that "immediate debriefing" helped me feel at peace throughout it all.

As an officer who has done accident reconstruction for more than a decade, I've dealt with many bad and very sad vehicle crashes. They involve death notifications, drunk or careless drivers to prosecute, and witnesses to interview. There are other types of cases where people have done horrific things to other people that should never be done to anyone. But no matter how bad the job gets, I get my sense of peace back when I go to church. It

> What joy for those whose strength comes from the LORD.
> Psalm 84:5 (NLT)

refreshes your soul after having to deal with the cares of this world. For me, it would be hard to keep myself on an even keel for very long without being in God's house with God's people and finding comfort in God's Word.

UNKNOWN TROUBLE

Deputy Nathan Bickerstaff
Ellis County, TX Sheriffs Officer

UNKNOWN trouble" calls are a nightmare! You don't know if it's for murder, arson, robbery, rape, kidnapping, extortion, terrorist bombings, narcotics, shootouts or even grave robbing. After an already trying day I received this "Unknown trouble" call: "Make contact with the woman caller, code two."

I found the caller waving nervously in the front yard. "There's a lady in the house terribly drunk with a new baby," she said. "She dropped that child on the ground last week, and tonight she was staggering on the front porch with it and almost fell. I told my husband I was calling the Law."

33

I walked carefully up the porch steps, stood to the side of the door and knocked. I heard the shuffling of feet and a crash, and then I knocked again. Finally a bleary-eyed woman weaving from side-to-side opened the door and demanded, "What do you want?" My backup had arrived, and I told her we heard she might be having difficulties with her baby. "Mind if we come in, we're here to help you." Sneering she said, "I know how the police help!" We told her that if she could just show us that the baby was OK we'd be on our way."

Once we were inside the drunken woman screamed, "Get out of my house!" She grabbed the baby off the kitchen table and held it tightly to her. As we tried to get the child she fought with us, then jerked backward and fell heavily into a chair, holding the crying infant by one leg in a death grip. Together we pulled the child to safety. It was after midnight when we got the woman booked in, the child admitted to the hospital and under the care of Child Protective Services. What a night! Perhaps now you can understand why most officers hate to hear the dispatcher say, "Unknown trouble!"

> For God hath not given us the spirit of fear; but of power, and of love, and of a sound mind.
> 2 Timothy 1:7

An officer's job is difficult and fraught with danger, and full of surprises. That is why it is so important to walk with the Lord. Jesus told us not to be filled with fear, for he is with us always (Matthew 28:20). That is how we are able to respond to "unknown trouble" calls. An unknown author wrote this: I shall pass this way but once; any good therefore that I can do, or any kindness that I can show - let me not defer nor neglect it, for I shall not pass this way again. These are good words for an officer to live by.

FAITH, HOPE, AND DARLENE

Chaplain David Dickson

Haitian Police Chaplaincy Association

HOPE HAS such an enduring quality in the human spirit. After the devastating January 12, 2010, Haitian earthquake, I was part of a team which ministered to the police, aid workers, and families in Haiti. Pictures can't begin to convey the scale of tragedy caused in thirty-five seconds. Human tragedies included the deaths of 120 members of the Haitian Parliament and three thousand at the university, and the collapse of most major buildings, including Police Headquarters and buildings many stories tall. The awful sights and stench we experienced over many days were mind-boggling.

There are many stories of endurance and courage as people coped with the aftermath of the quake, but a story of hope is what I found most touching. Sixteen-year-old Darlene Etienne had been showering when the earthquake hit, and was trapped in her bathroom. January 28, sixteen days later—a world survival record in these conditions—she was found by someone who thought they saw a leg move. A rescue operation led by the French rescue team swung into action, as all other rescue teams had gone home. (Teams usually stay only until there is very little chance of survival). My group was at the site when Darlene was successfully lifted from the rubble. A police chaplain assisting the team was close enough to hand her his necklace of a cross, which she quickly wrapped in her hand. Spontaneous applause and cheering from the crowd brought many tears of joy that day!

> And now these three remain: faith, hope and love. But the greatest of these is love.
> 1 Corinthians 13:13

Looking at the picture I took just seconds after the rescue gives me a great sense of pride in the power of hope—hope not lost even when buried under a mountain of rubble. The Bible says in Romans 15:13, "May the God of hope fill you with all joy and peace as you trust in him, so that you may overflow with hope by the power of the Holy Spirit." People need hope and will respond to it. As police chaplains, offering people hope is our job and our privilege.

THE POWER OF PRAYER

David Laumatia, Senior Sergeant
New Zealand Police

A MENTAL PATIENT was being violent, and the institution staff were unable to get him to a secure room where he could be controlled and not a danger to himself or anyone else. The police were called, and the information received indicated he was a large male of solid build and approximately six feet, four inches tall.

The last time he had suffered a violent episode, it took several strong men to control him. This time, a team of several police staff came to the hospital armed with batons and pepper spray. In briefing them I said, "We may have to wrestle him to the ground as he is not going to come easily." The apprehensive look of the staff only heightened my fears.

> When they came to Jesus, they saw the man who had been possessed by the legion of demons, sitting there, dressed and in his right mind; and they were afraid. Mark 5:15

I prayed to the Lord for guidance through the situation so no one would get hurt. In the foyer to the secure rooms, approximately 6 meters by 4 meters, three burly staff members stood safely back from the patient. In his hand he grasped a pen, threatening to use it as a weapon on anyone who came near him. Realizing he was under demonic oppression, silently I asked God through Jesus' name for authority over the Enemy. I recalled Luke 10:19, 20, where Jesus says, "I have given you authority to trample on snakes and scorpions and to overcome all the power of the enemy; nothing will harm you. However, do not rejoice that the spirits submit to you, but rejoice that your names are written in heaven."

After praying, I spoke to him calmly, and told him what he was to do. He would not look at me, but followed my every instruction. However, in doing so his tongue flicked in and out of his mouth like a snake. After being asked, he walked into his cell and discarded the pen without anyone getting hurt. It confirmed for me that in the Lord, believers do have authority over a demonically oppressed person. I remember hospital staff members looking at me in bewilderment as to why this person did everything he was told without anyone laying a hand on him.

As we walked out of the building I looked at a fellow Christian officer and whispered to him, "It's amazing what the power of prayer will do!"

THE *AMBER PLAN*

Chaplain Harold Elliott

Arlington, TX, Police Department

IN JANUARY 1996, 9-year-old Amber Hagerman was abducted while playing near her Arlington, Texas, home. She was found murdered a few days later. It was my responsibility to make the death notification to her family. They had hoped for a different ending, but came to realize it probably would not be. When I confirmed their worst fears, they did what most devoted family members do: they wept bitter tears.

Making the notification deepened a painful personal wound. Just a few days short of a year prior, my family had been devastated by the tragic death of our own daughter. The medical examiner ruled her death "Unde-

President G. W. Bush signing Amber Plan into law

termined," and we don't know how she died. Was it an accident, suicide, or homicide? We live with all three possibilities.

Therefore comfort one another with these words. 1 Thessalonians 4:18 (NASB)

While I really didn't know how Amber's family felt when their world was shattered with such horrible news, I know how it feels to lose tragically someone you love. Neither the Hagermans nor the Elliotts were ready to say goodbye to their daughters. Suddenly, we didn't even know how to act. How could you hurt this much and still live? Could we survive? Did we even want to survive?

The nation and much of the world is now familiar with the name "Amber Hagerman." In 2003, President Bush signed into law the *Amber Plan*. Implementation of *Amber Alerts* continues annually to save the lives of children who might otherwise become statistics. Unfortunately, it cannot erase the emotional pain of the survivors of those who are not saved. More than three million American adults have lost a close family member violently. With another three-plus million relatives and close friends, the number is staggering. Those who hurt need a friend, someone who warmly whispers the name of the deceased, wraps a grieving soul with loving arms, and then remains silent. Unfortunately, some survivors simply cannot cope and move on, sometimes even dying from the grief.

As a police chaplain, I sought to comfort Amber Hagerman's family that fateful night in 1996. In the Sermon on the Mount, Jesus says, "Blessed are those who mourn, for they will be comforted" (Matthew 5:4). I believe we both were blessed when I yielded to an impulse to share my own personal story with them. In an instant, we were comforting one another.

WHY STAY?

Anonymous

9-1-1 Dispatcher

After nine years of dispatching I was tired and burned out on my 9-1-1 job. I wanted regular hours like normal folks, and Sundays off to attend church. The atmosphere where I worked was toxic, as were some of my co-workers. Repeatedly I sought other jobs within the department, and couldn't understand why none became available. I begged God to open a door for me elsewhere.

Then one Sunday I was answering 9-1-1 calls when a young boy called frantically to tell me there was "a monster in the bathroom." I asked him who told him this, and he said his sister. The two of them were hiding under the coffee table in the living room, and he wanted a policeman to come to the house soon because he "had to go."

I explained that mommies are great monster killers, and he should run and get Mommy on the phone. He then exclaimed that his Daddy was there and could beat up any old monster. Again I told him, "Run and get Daddy on the phone." I could actually hear his little padded feet running down the hall.

> And if anyone gives even a cup of cold water to one of these little ones because he is my disciple, I tell you the truth, he will certainly not lose his reward
> Matthew 10:42

While I was handling this call, I heard in the background of our dispatch office another dispatcher *yelling*, "Put your mother on the phone!" at a small child who had called. Children are taught at a young age to call 9-1-1 if they need help. We dispatchers are "front-line ambassadors" who are the first to help anyone—no matter their problem or age—and need to understand that. It may not be an emergency to us, but it may seem like one to them. It was at that moment I had an epiphany: If an impatient operator had answered his call, this little boy might have gotten a bad impression of police personnel that he could hold forever.

By the time the boy's very sleepy father came on the line, I was in tears. It was for innocent callers like this that God had me there. In the five additional years I spent as a dispatcher I made it a point daily to understand that God has a reason for where he places his children. Our challenge is simply to understand that and to serve him cheerfully.

REFUGE IN CHRIST

Sergeant Mark Oliver, Badge No. D 745
New Zealand Police

LESS THAN six weeks after the powerful earthquake that triggered the Asian Tsunami of December 26, 2004, I was part of a team that went to help in Thailand. Even though cleanup was under way, devastation from the tsunami was still very evident. Most areas looked as if the waves had just gone through.

We stayed on Phuket Island, but traveled north to a site set up as a mortuary to house thousands of bodies recovered since the tragedy. On the way, I remember quietly staring out the bus window and looking toward the coast. There was practically nothing left standing between the road and the sea. Houses, hotels—buildings of every kind—were gone, washed away by the sheer power of the waves as they crashed inland. I clearly remember coming over the brow of a hill into a coastal community which had experienced massive destruction. Everything had been destroyed: Cars were wrapped around trees like paper, and splintered broken wood and crumbling concrete were scattered everywhere. In the midst of all the destruction and damage, one building sill stood with a cross on its outside wall.

> The eternal God is your refuge, and underneath are the everlasting arms.
> Deuteronomy 33:27

I don't know if it was a church or not, but it was a dramatic illustration that in the midst of all of life's devastation, the one solid, stable thing is Christ.

I was tasked with completing an audit of the refrigeration containers full of the recovered bodies. Some of the containers had forty in them, while others had up to eighty. At one of the temporary mortuary sights there was row upon row of containers. It was overwhelming to deal with the extreme level of death and destruction that had occurred. From time to time, police members working at the sites would break down because of what they saw and had to deal with.

While there, I was able to attend a church service at the hotel where we stayed. The congregation that day was made up of members from police agencies all over the South Pacific. Being able to meet with other Christians and pray for the workers and survivors added to the sense of

God's timelessness. It also was a unique experience to share with others our belief in God. In the midst of so much destruction and suffering, we were able to find peace in the stability only God can give. He is the Alpha and the Omega (Revelation 1:8; 21:6; 22:13), the same yesterday, today, and forever! (Hebrews 13:8).

OFFICER DOWN!
NO SHOTS FIRED!

Chaplain Leonard Grubb

Painesville, OH, Police Department

AT 7 A.M., breakfast hour for most people, I was present for shift-change roll call during my first week as a police chaplain. The topic of discussion: (this was not a Christian gathering!) preserving a fetus as evidence in a rape case—certainly not normal "breakfast table" conversation! That was when my eyes were opened to the awful world in which police officers live.

Few civilians are aware of what officers face, things far more damaging than the business end of a criminal's weapon! They are deep in the middle of the spiritual battle between good and evil, which truly is the great pressure of the job. It is easy to be overcome by discouragement, fatigue, and negativity! Some try to combat it with a macabre sense of humor, while others can't. We usually think of a "line-of-duty death" as one involving a shooting or an accident. Unfortunately, we lose far too many officers through suicide, alcohol and other-drug addictions, extramarital affairs, divorce, family violence, and worse. I refer to these as "the unseen killers."

My third year as a chaplain, a seventeen-year officer came to me for alcohol counseling. Embittered after years of service, he had become an alcoholic, drove while under the influence, was arrested, and lost his job. Now he was deeply depressed. Many in that situation have committed suicide; at least he chose to seek counseling. A good number of departments offer secular counseling, but far too many officers do not have or take advantage of spiritual counseling. Without developing a Biblical viewpoint, it's difficult to develop the well-rounded life and healthy spiritual growth which I believe gives one the greatest opportunity to be healed.

This man came to me in time. In our many hours together he listened, we challenged each other, he found a caring friend, and he began to see that life was worth living—he wasn't a lost cause. I felt early on he was teachable, someone who was willing to change. As the weeks went by, he went from being a pessimist to being an optimist—from feeling self-defeat to overflowing with hope for the future. Faith in God replaced his emptiness, and I was grateful to have been a part in this change. His renewal ultimately led to rehire by another department that knew him only as an experienced officer with a positive attitude.

> He is a dear brother, a faithful minister and fellow servant in the Lord.
> Colossians 4:7

Officers are there "to protect and serve" the public. We police chaplains are there "to protect and serve" our officers. I thank God for the privilege of ministering to them!

DISCIPLINE WITH LOVE

Deputy Nathan Bickerstaff
Ellis County, TX, Sheriff's Office

THE YOUNG boy's heart sank when he saw me drive up in my patrol car. When his mother opened the door he tried to look innocent, but he knew why I was there. After a round of introductions, questions, answers, and denials he finally admitted to his crime—breaking into the schoolhouse. The tears came when I said, "You're going to have to appear in juvenile court."

After I left him and his mother, I thought: *Maybe this fatherless boy needs someone to believe in him besides his mother.* God has given *me* not just a second chance, but third and fourth chances. Could I be the one to give this boy another chance before he got into real trouble? My decision was made: I would talk with the judge about getting him into a mentoring program.

When my son was young I asked if he knew what I did for a living. He said, "Yes, you put bad guys in jail." His answer helped me realize that young kids don't understand all the ways law enforcement officers can help.

43

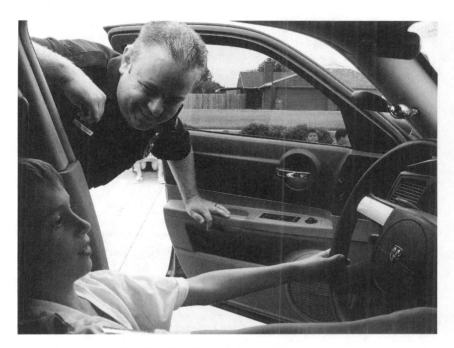

Sheriff's office "Community Day" Open House

Adolescents make many decisions that can affect their whole lives, often not understanding the seriousness of the consequences until a cop is called to settle a problem. As officers we sometimes have the power to make a recommendation: "Throw the book at this punk" or, "Let's help him turn his life around." It's a judgment call. I sensed that this boy would respond favorably to the latter, so I spoke with the judge.

A lot of today's young people are crying out for help and love—someone just to care. Regardless of how independent and carefree they may act on the outside, many are hurting inside. As police we are in a perfect position to partner with parents and caretakers to help kids become responsible adults. Most cops I have met do like kids and generally are sympathetic toward them. But we need parents to tell their children that police don't just "put bad guys in jail"; we also care for all who want to do what is right, and we like to give kids

> Teach them the decrees and laws, and show them the way to live and the duties they are to perform. Exodus 18:20

a second chance. For this young man it paid off; now he is a police officer serving in Juvenile.

Parents, let your children know we are there for them. If they have a positive image toward us, it may pay dividends in the long run. We Christian officers know how sympathetic Jesus is toward us. He can work through us to help you with your children, with your positive support. If we help just one young boy or girl, it's worth the world to us!

FEBRUARY 4

A TROUBLING CALL

Jason J. Everett
Rolling Meadows, IL, Police Department

THE CALLER was frantic: A young female had pushed her way into the caller's home, and was stealing money and refusing to leave. When we arrived I saw a female outside the front door in a nurse's uniform. She told us, "Thank God, you are here; that woman is impossible!"

About that time a "sweet little old lady" came to the screen door and quickly locked it from the inside. She snapped, "It's about time you got here. I didn't know how much longer I was going to be trapped in my house."

The nurse gave me her identification, which confirmed she was a nurse, and explained to me the lady was suffering from Alzheimer's. When I was unable to reason with the lady, the nurse gave me the telephone number of the lady's son. After allowing the woman to speak to her son, she said it could not have been he, as her son never would have "taken the burglar's side!" She continued screaming at us to arrest the nurse! Perplexed as to the next step, we convinced the homeowner to check her paperwork in the bedroom, which gave time for the nurse to come back into the home. As soon as the homeowner saw the nurse, she began to scream, "Get her out! Get her out!" We tried to calm her down, but she would only repeat, "Why are the police helping someone steal? Where is the justice? I need help!" She was still pleading for help when we left.

I was greatly troubled by this call for a number of reasons. First was my frustration at our inability to help her. Then I was troubled by her situation. Because of her Alzheimer's, she truly believed a criminal had broken into her home. When she reached out to the police for help, from her

45

perspective we refused. Even though she was in no danger, she was terrified.

A police officer can be challenged in a variety of situations. Literally every type of problem humans encounter—from the mundane to the grotesque—can involve us. Those calls test me and my faith. I know God has a plan for each life, but things like Alzheimer's and its effects are hard to understand. When I leave a scene like that with my faith in God still firm, I feel I have met the challenge and prevailed. Romans 5:3 states, "We can rejoice, too, when we run into problems and trials, for we know that they help us develop endurance." Daily I am developing endurance.

> We who are strong ought to bear with the failings of the weak and not to please ourselves.
> Romans 15:1

FEBRUARY 5

"POLICING" AN IRAQI ROADSIDE

Sergeant Mark A. Smeltzer, Badge No. 264

Chattanooga, TN, Police Department

LIKE MANY law enforcement officers, I am a military reservist, most recently deployed to Iraq. As a troop commander I was responsible for 218 personnel, many who daily patrolled the roads in our area to keep them clear of IEDs (Improvised Explosive Devices). Basically, we "policed the area." Knowing the danger and wanting God's protection, we began each day by reading from the 91st Psalm.

In military parlance, "policing the area" means walking through a field, parade grounds, encampment site, etc., and picking up all pieces of stray paper, cigarette butts, soda cans, etc., to give it a neat appearance. Ask anyone who went through Army boot camp about "policing an area," and they'll probably tell you it was an unpleasant "make-work" project from an overzealous commander.

The "policing" we did in Iraq was just as unpleasant, but for an important cause: It was necessary to keep the routes clear for both military and civilian personnel. We suffered through heat, long hours, dust, and endless amount of trash: packages, boxes, bags, rocks; it was not a sought-after assignment. It also was humdrum and tedious enough one could become complacent if it weren't for the occasional IED with sniper hidden nearby.

On this particular day I was on patrol with one of my teams. Among all the other debris, my lead scout and I found a burlap sack we suspected might contain an IED. Investigating closer, we opened the bag and discovered a large artillery round with a small "Motorola-type" radio strapped on top. Seeing it from about a foot away, it seemed the size of an M1A1 tank. These types of devices usually are under close observation, so we knew we probably were moments away from manual detonation from a remote location. To say that we ran for our lives is putting it mildly. I suspect I'd have outrun even the speediest sprinter that day!

> I will say of the LORD, *He is* my refuge and my fortress: my God; in him will I trust. Psalm 91:2

That night the enormity of it hit me: Instead of going to bed in a bunk I might have been going home in a body bag! Talk about a sobering thought; God certainly got my attention that day! For as long as I can remember I always have believed in God. I struggle like everyone else to be a "good" Christian and do what is right, but I know I fall far short of the mark. However, this and other experiences in Iraq convinced me how real God is and how much he cares for me. I am grateful for many things he has given me, but I'm especially thankful for God's protection that day.

FEBRUARY 6

GOD'S MESSENGER

Sergeant Dace Cochran

Jackson County, OR, Sheriff's Office

AS A SHERIFF'S deputy, I usually deal with the rougher or maybe just more unfortunate end of the human spectrum. It's hard not to become jaded or cynical over everyone's hard-luck story—or rationalization of why the incident wasn't their fault. We also bear the title "peace officer," which puts us in a unique position of being able to talk with people who may be at the end of their rope. Some are open to considering a path different from the ones they've tried in the past, even to talk about going to church. Of course, as government employees, we are careful not to violate any laws or department rulings while observing the Lord's leading.

The driver of a vehicle I stopped for a traffic violation was driving under the influence and on a suspended license. It turned out he was a long-time alcoholic, but seemed receptive to getting out of his continual pattern of self-defeat. As we waited to process his breath sample at the jail, I told him the answer he was seeking could be found at church by getting into God's Word and receiving a brand new heart. In response to my invitation, lo and behold, he showed up for the next Sunday morning service. Then he came back for the evening service and several times after. During one of these services he went forward during the invitation for salvation. The story isn't perfect so far, for he has not got totally away from alcohol. However, he has continued to come to church on-and-off for several years, and has made a step in the right direction.

Hopefully, the seed that was planted will one day be firmly rooted, and he'll achieve the growth he needs. In law enforcement we sometimes get locked into thinking the only solution to addictions is a twelve-step program, supervised drugs, or jail time. For me, I want people to know there's another alternative: establishing a church relationship and getting to know God. Since most Christians will never meet the segment of population we deal with, we have an unusual opportunity to be God's messengers to people who desperately need him.

> "Go, stand in the temple courts," he said, "and tell the people the full message of this new life." Acts 5:20

FOLLOWING GOD'S PATH

Deputy Marcus Dotson

Hamilton County, TN, Sheriff's Department

I'D BEEN raised in church but had "backslid." To encourage me, my family gave me a Police Officer's Bible for Christmas one year, and I began reading it. Three years later I gave my life to Christ. In the back of the Bible were stories by peace officers, and one officer told how he prayed on the way to answer calls. I decided to adopt that practice.

This particular day we were looking for a suspect who had shot at his girlfriend the previous night. I had been rerouted that morning to work in the general area where we thought the suspect might be, and I had been alerted to that fact. Dispatch radioed to say he might be headed south on the highway with a child in his car. At the time I was making rounds on secondary roads, but headed back to the highway. Since there were several routes I could have taken, I began praying to Jesus asking for guidance and protection. It seemed very clear to me that he was saying "Go this way," and I did. I continued praying that our team could capture the man without harm, for the suspect was armed and dangerous.

As I finished praying I spotted—as plain as day—the suspect's vehicle, but it was headed north instead of south! I radioed other members of the team who already were staged up and waiting—Sergeant McDowell and Deputies Rountree and Nolan—to get into position, as I was behind the vehicle. When all was ready, we turned on our blue lights. At first the driver hesitated, but then pulled into a parking lot. Without further incident we arrested both him and another

> My steps have held to your paths; my feet have not slipped. Psalm 17:5

man (for a narcotics violation) without harm, and rescued the child. I give all the glory to God, for I believe he persuaded the man to pull over because of his child. Our team made the arrest, but God deserved the glory, praise and honor.

I firmly believe the voice I heard was God telling me to "stay on the path you are on." That's what he wants all Christians to do, to follow the path of faith and trust in Jesus. If you know someone who isn't doing that, why not do what my family did for me? Give them a Bible and pray for them!

FEBRUARY 8

"DEPUTY BOB"

"Deputy Bob" Walsh

BEING A jailer isn't a pleasant assignment. Face it, you're "in jail" just like the prisoners. Oh, yes, you are "free" to go home at the end of your shift and you're not in a cell, but jail is jail.

For two years I was assigned to the corrections department, sometimes questioning how God's purpose for my life could be accomplished by working in the jail. There were times when I felt like Moses jousting with Pharaoh (Exodus 5, 7–12), getting nowhere. Sailors describe this experience as "dead in the water." For the most part inmates are mean-spirited school dropouts who have used drugs and made a host of other bad decisions—not what we want for our children when they grow up.

I began thinking about how I could use my creative talents to reach school-age children. I wanted to influence them to make healthy choices that would keep them out of the criminal justice system. Ten years down the road I didn't want to see them inside the same jail walls I found so depressing. I decided to create community outreach lessons that were educational and entertaining at the same time. They would teach the opposite of what I experienced from the inmates: kindness instead of meanness, being a friend instead of bullying, honesty instead of lying, faith instead of godlessness. I created puppets to put my ventriloquist skills to work. I created a deputy sheriff interacting with Inmate Joe, Junior Deputy Matthew, Jeremiah Student, and Grandpa. As my wife made outfits for the dummies, God affirmed in her heart this was the work he was giving us to have a positive effect on our community.

> Jesus said, "Let the little children come to me, and do not hinder them, for the kingdom of heaven belongs to such as these." Matthew 19:14

With approvals secured, I began traveling around the city presenting "Choices with Deputy Bob and Friends" in schools, recreation centers, libraries, and wherever else the opportunity presented itself. The reception and results we received have proved their value for children as well as being a good public relations tool for our sheriff's department.

As word of the program spread I have been able to give my ventriloquist presentations to school-age children many places, including Hong Kong and the People's Republic of China. We now have a video archive available to everyone, which can be found on *YouTube.com* under the subscription "Deputy BobJ479" or at www.deputybob.com. Being in jail is no fun, for the inmate *or* the jailor. But the experience did provide the resource I needed to help steer young people in the right direction—away from my jail!

ARE YOU AVAILABLE?

Chaplain Art Sphar

Sumner and Bonney Lake, WA, Police Departments

CALMLY THE dispatcher told me a man had reported his wife missing a couple of days earlier. The police had found her body stuffed inside the trunk of her car in Tacoma, and they needed a chaplain to notify the man his wife's body had been found. She concluded by asking, "Are you available?"

"Yes, I can do that," I replied. The dispatcher continued, "There is one more thing you need to know: He is the prime suspect, and we want you to observe how he takes the news when you tell him we have found his wife's body."

> Be ready in season and out of season.
> 2 Timothy 4:2 (NKJV)

"Let me see if I understand what you are asking," I said. "You want me, an unarmed chaplain, to call on a man you think has just killed his wife?"

"Yes," she replied, "and we really want you to observe how he reacts to the news."

"Okay, I can do that," I told her, my voice now several octaves higher.

Two Pierce County deputies met me a few blocks away, and I briefed them on the situation. With my portable radio in hand I told them, "If I say "help," I mean *right now!*" They agreed to cover me, so I went to the door and informed the man. He did take the news rather strangely. In the next few days other evidence was gathered proving he had killed his wife. Before they could arrest him, he committed suicide.

I still think about that call and the dispatcher's question. "Are you available?" normally means someone needs a chaplain urgently—*right then!* It doesn't matter whether it's day or night, what else he might be doing or where else he might need to be; if he's going to accept the job of chaplain, he must handle the responsibility.

I think "Are you available?" applies to all Christians. When God makes it clear he needs us in a given circumstance, that should become our first priority. The question "Are you available?" is a moment of truth. How do you answer?

I FINALLY GAVE IN!

Lieutenant Charles Grom

A Central Valley California law enforcement agency

IF YOU THINK it's too late to let God into your life—that you are not worthy of his love—you're sadly mistaken. I went to church as a child, but never developed a real relationship with Christ. When I finally did years later, I found that surrender to him brought endless rewards. Most cops have a hard time with the concept of loving Jesus completely and giving him control of their lives. That's because we tend to rely on one another—or only ourselves—when things get bad. We are trained to make decisions quickly, without a lot of chitchat and contemplation. Rarely do we take time to think through a problem, or even ask for advice.

When I was accused by someone in my own department of misconduct, incompetence, and dishonesty, I did what any seasoned officer and former detective would do: I dug in my heels and prepared for the fight. I knew that the accusations were false, but they challenged and threatened all I felt I had achieved as a twenty-year veteran and senior officer. I was prepared to defend myself with the same professionalism and composure I have used many times when on the witness stand before the opposing attorney. The difference this time was that I was the accused, and preparing my defense was causing serious damage at home as well as at work. It was too much for me; I couldn't handle it alone.

> Come unto me, all ye that labour and are heavy laden, and I will give you rest. Matthew 11:28 (KJV)

With great clarity I recall the day I closed my office door, turned the ringer on my phone down low, and laid it all down at Jesus' feet. I told God he could deal with the accusation, my career, me, and my life. From that point on I was ready to accept whatever he desired. My incredible burden was lifted, and the calm and peace that came over me were overwhelming.

Over the next several weeks my home life regained some stability, and individuals within the department came forward to support me—some even prayed with me. In the night I would awaken with thoughts of things needed to clarify the case, and I knew it was God talking to me. I had never heard things like that so clearly, and I listened. I was cleared of all allegations, and my career and reputation were intact. But the real victory was establishing a firm relationship with Christ and laying my burdens down at his feet. He is always there, he will never desert me, and he has all the answers I need. I had thought I was too old and too far gone for Jesus to accept me—I was wrong!

THE MURDER WEAPON

Sheriff Jim Hammond
Hamilton County, TN

IN MY forty-plus years in law enforcement I have seen the hand of the Lord at work many times; perhaps none was more direct than in the recovery of a gun used to murder a taxi driver in cold blood.

"It was a dark and stormy night" aptly describes the night of the murder—wet, cold, and alternating between freezing rain and light snow showers. I was at home enjoying a toasty fireplace with my wife and children when the phone rang about 9:30 p.m. Homicide detectives were en route to the scene of an apparent shooting near a local marina. A homeowner heard what sounded like gunshots, then saw two individuals running from a vehicle parked near the marina's entrance. Disturbed, she called the sheriff's office.

When officers arrived at the scene they found a white male slumped dead across the front seat of his taxicab with a gunshot wound to the head. Within half an hour two young men who fit the description given by the witness were taken into custody, but we still needed to find the murder weapon!

After learning about the situation I went to the scene to help search for the weapon. It was like looking for the proverbial "needle in a hay stack" in the dark, wet cold. Since school children would be walking these roads the next morning—and because guns rust quickly—we felt a strong sense of urgency. As I drove to my assigned position I remember praying, "Lord, please help us find this weapon so we can wrap up the case and get back to our homes for the rest and warmth we need."

My assigned position was about one hundred feet from where one suspect was apprehended, and I began a sweeping search of the ditches and sides of the road with my flashlight. I have never been so cold or wet before or since in my career! After about thirty steps, my light glinted on a handgun in the grass—about three feet from the pavement. One of the suspects had been walking down the road and panicked when a patrol car passed him. Trying not to draw attention by throwing the weapon away, he simply dropped the gun at his side and continued walking.

> Ask and it will be given to you; seek and you will find; knock and the door will be opened to you.
> Matthew 7:7

Many have been skeptical when I say the Lord led me to the murder weapon. However, the incident enhanced my confidence in God's leadership, and it remains steady some twenty years later.

FEBRUARY 12

CAN YOU LOVE A SCUMBAG?

Officer Jim Salo
Loveland, CO, Police Department (1976)

WITH A few years' experience—a new job in a new department in a new city at the foothills of the Rockies, a new home, and a new baby on the way—I was on top of the world. That is, until God brought me face-to-face with the reality of my own sin—a lack of love and compassion!

One night on midnight shift the drunk I'd arrested vomited all over me and the side of my patrol car. Boy, was I mad! I didn't abuse him, but treated him as roughly as I could legally. On the way to jail, he vomited again, this time in my car and down the barrel of my mounted and locked shotgun! I was furious! After putting him to bed in city jail, I went home to shower and change uniforms. Then I drove back to the jail, literally holding my nose against the stench! I got him up and made him scrub out my car in the middle of the night. It still stunk, so after a time out on patrol I came back and made him do it again: "Scrub out my patrol car, you scumbag!"

Back in the twice-cleaned auto, my shift nearly over, I was sitting in a parking lot working on reports. It was then God spoke to my conscience in a still, small voice: "What a fine Christian you are! Maybe for the first time ever that drunk came across a real Christian, and you treated him badly. What is he going to think about me from what he sees reflected in your life? You may have had opportunities growing up that he didn't have, but I love him just as much as I love you! Yes, I love all the 'scumbags' of the earth!" Ouch—that hurt! In fact it hurt so bad I got out of my patrol car and knelt on the pavement in tears. I pleaded with God to forgive me for my lack of holy love for the people he had created—all people, good or bad. That experience changed my life forever.

> "'Love the Lord your God with all your heart and with all your soul and with all your mind and with all your strength.' The second is this: 'Love your neighbor as yourself.' There is no commandment greater than these."
> Mark 12:30–32

More than thirty-four years have gone by since then, and I've been able to serve the Lord faithfully as an officer, police chaplain, and a minister. Why? I think it's because when God spoke to me in that early morning hour I listened, and was willing to see people through his eyes. Yes, I learned to love people—even scumbags!

FEBRUARY 13

VALENTINE'S DAY GOD'S WAY!

Anonmyous

Houston, TX, Police Department

IT WAS LATE at night, and I had just finished my shift on patrol. I walked through the front door of my home, dropped my equipment bag on the floor, and fell to my knees weeping bitterly. During the previous several weeks a dark, foreboding, and heavy depression had settled on me. It was weighing me down and showed no signs of lifting. As I wept, I prayed in desperation, "God, I don't know if I can take this anymore! Please lift this depression off me. I am so lonely. If it is your will for me to remain single the rest of my life, give me the ability to accept and enjoy it; I cannot do it on my own. Your will, not mine, be done." I was finally a broken man before God. I had no way of knowing this prayer would be an important turning point in my life.

Ten years earlier, my wife took our two children and divorced me. I mourned their loss for several years. My grief was so deep I felt like someone had reached into my chest, pulled my heart out, and left a big, empty hole in its place. I continued backsliding away from God and became angry against his institution of marriage. I did not want to get married again, so I had several intimate relationships with women without the sanctity of marriage. My life was empty.

I asked God's forgiveness and rededicated my life to him. His Holy Spirit began working in my life, and he gave me a new desire to pray, study his Word, and love Jesus. As I did, God gave me a renewed respect for sex within the boundaries of marriage. Moreover, I spent approximately two years without a relationship. I believe God used this difficult time of solitude to teach me how to trust in his love, bringing me through a spiritual "desert wilderness" by giving me his grace.

> For this reason a man will leave his father and mother and be united to his wife, and they will become one flesh.
> Genesis 2:24

As I prayed that night, the empty hole I had felt ten years earlier was replaced by a strong sense of God's presence. Interestingly, God did not take away my depression for another two weeks, but made it bearable by his presence and love. Psalm 147:3 says, "He healeth the broken in heart, and bindeth up their wounds" (KJV). God completed his healing a few months later, just before Valentine's Day. This is when I met and began dating my future wife, another officer in my department. In the years since, we have spent Valentine's Day, which celebrates love and affection between a man and a woman, in the manner God meant it to be, as husband and wife united in holy matrimony.

FEBRUARY 14

MY PRIORITIES WERE ALL MESSED UP

*Deputy Michael Dye**
Volusia County, FL, Sheriff's Department

IT WAS Valentine's Day 1991. A young detective assigned to general crimes, I had decided to propose marriage to my fiancée after a very nice candlelight dinner. We had finished, and the time was right! Down

56

on one knee, I pulled out an engagement ring and asked, "Will you marry me?" Thankfully, she said yes. Everything was going just as planned. Then my pager went off!

Calling the office, I found that a fugitive I had been waiting months to catch would be flying in on a commercial flight that night. The arrival time? Thirty minutes from then! So I left—my newly engaged fiancée, the ring, the valentines and the ambiance. From the standpoint of doing my job, that was the right thing to do. But from the standpoint of getting our relationship "off on the right foot," I'm afraid it was a harbinger of things to come.

> And this is love: that we walk in obedience to his commands. 2 John 1:6

In the early years of our marriage, work generally came first. In trying to get ahead in my career, I didn't set a very good example for our marriage. My priorities were all messed up! When we got engaged, we were not active in church, and we didn't have a strong faith in Jesus as Lord and Savior. I put the job in front of everything else. It took me a few years of headaches and heartaches before I learned the maxim of "God first, family second, and the job third." I thought the purpose of working was a "means to an end," something to pay the bills and to have spending money. There are plenty of verses in the Bible that give other, better purposes, including working in order to share with others in need (Ephesians 4:28). Boy, I had a lot of learning to do!

While I don't always succeed in the "God first, family second, job third" priority system, I try all the time. When those three are in proper balance, I am happier and more satisfied in both my personal and professional lives. Today, we are happily married, blessed with a beautiful daughter, and active in our church. We have a strong faith in God and, together, are praising him and receiving his daily blessings in our lives. Some folks think you can't be in law enforcement and be a Christian. That couldn't be further from the truth. I feel blessed to be a peace officer, actively involved in my family and church, and leading a ministry called The PeaceKeepers. Be assured: When your priorities are straight, God will bless!

*Author of *The Peacekeeper's- A Bible Study for Law Enforcement Officers*

"I WILL HOLD THINE HAND"

Deputy Gloria Williams, No. 2431

Hamilton County, TN, Sheriff's Office

AS SOON as I read Isaiah 42:6 I had my answer—God wanted me to go to jail!

For seventeen years I was employed at a state mental hospital, receiving many "attaboys" (or "attagirls," since I'm a woman) for my work and positive attitude, and enjoying being God's servant there. One of the things I enjoyed about working in the forensic unit was talking with jail deputies who brought prisoners in for mental evaluation. We'd laugh and talk together while they were standing guard, and a couple of officers had strongly suggested, "You ought to come and work with us in the jail." That's something I couldn't imagine, but I know God was preparing the way.

As I drew closer to the Lord, in my final three years at the hospital things changed . . . the Enemy began working through his servants to make my life miserable. After one particularly trying day I was at the end of my rope. I no longer loved going to work and I needed a change. That night I cried out to God asking him to show me the light, and he did! The Holy Spirit led me to Isaiah, chapter 42, verses 6 and 7: "I the LORD have called thee in righteousness, and **will hold thine hand,** and will keep thee, and give thee for a covenant of the people, for a light of the Gentiles; To open the blind eyes, to bring out the prisoners from the prison, *and* them that sit in darkness out of the prison house" (KJV emphasis added).

> Trust in the LORD with all your heart and lean not on your own understanding; in all your ways acknowledge him, and he will make your paths straight. Proverbs 3:5, 6

I began to scream, and tears ran down my face like a waterfall. I felt God was telling me to go to the jail, where he had a new ministry for me. The very next day I applied at the jail, and started working there soon after that. In the sheriff's department I found many other believing officers who looked at their job as ministry, not work, and I'm finding it such a joy to be part of an organization where so many share Jesus with the lost and glorify the Lord in their work. In my own understanding I would never have gone to jail; it took God to open my eyes so I could bring light to those in darkness!

GOD'S WORD IN PRACTICE

Chief Robert W. Lowen

Woodstock, IL, Police Department

WHILE A patrol officer, I responded to a call at a local supermarket. A store security agent had apprehended a 20-year-old female shoplifting groceries. As I handcuffed her, took possession of the stolen items, and prepared to transport her to the station, she was greatly distressed. The amount of the theft was around $30, so she would be charged with misdemeanor retail theft.

Two things caught my attention: First, she did not appear to be the typical "career shoplifter," who steals items like infant formula, cold medicine, or high-priced, easily concealed items to support drug habits. Second, what she had taken were "junk food" items, such as Twinkies, candy bars, cookies, and other high-calorie, high-fat foods. She had no prior criminal record.

When I tried to gain insight into why she had stolen, she told me she had a "splurge and purge" eating disorder. She also said her father was a Chicago police officer and would be greatly embarrassed by her actions. For obvious reasons she didn't want to call her parents, but had no one else to call to post the required $100 bond. She would have to spend the night in the lockup, awaiting a judge who could issue a recognizance bond or lower the dollar amount.

Even though it was against department regulations, I posted bond for her. Knowing what a police dad can be like (having two daughters and experience with dealing with my own "demons"), I had sympathy for her. I took time to impress on her how I had dealt with my own problems by turning my life over to the Lord Jesus Christ. I maintained constant vigilance in prayer, often many times a day. She listened intently, and appeared to have some interest in what I said. I was relatively sure I'd never hear from her again, or be repaid for posting her bond.

> But be doers of the word, and not hearers only. James 1:22 (NKJV)

Some months later, I was pleasantly surprised when she sent me a "thank you" card and returned the money. She wrote that she had taken my advice and was dealing with her issues by renewing her trust in the Lord. She was getting appropriate counseling and following a recovery program. She went on to thank me for sharing my experiences with her, saying they were having a positive impact on her life.

The Golden Rule says we are to "Do unto others as we would have them do unto us." I'm thankful God brought that to my mind in that incident.

POOR CHOICES
BRING BAD RESULTS

Detective Larry A. Napp
Portage, MI, Police Department

IT WAS to be a typical day: up by 4:30 for my morning jog, get cleaned up, have devotions and breakfast, kiss my wife goodbye, then head for the office. My case was the "breaking and entering" of a local pet store (they even stole a snake!). After getting permission I went to check out a good lead in a nearby village.

After spotting the suspect's car I followed him to his house, identified myself as a police officer, and said I'd like to speak with him. He asked me to wait a minute, telling me he had a child in the car (which he did). There was no anger or any indication there might be a problem. He reached into his front seat, then came back shooting at me with a stolen 38-caliber revolver! I was not wearing a bulletproof vest, felt myself being hit with bullets, and realized, *This is not going to be a typical day!* He shot me three times in the abdomen and once in the left ear, during which time I was unholstering my gun and shooting back. After he was down I walked back to my car and radioed for help. Then I lay down on the driveway because "I don't want to get blood in my car!" As I lay there I remembered thinking, *So this is what dying is like,* and saying, "Lord, take me home." When two officers from my department and medical help came, I felt as if the cavalry had arrived!

> If you do wrong, be afraid, for [the officer] does not bear the sword for nothing. He is God's servant, an agent of wrath to bring punishment on the wrongdoer.
> Romans 13:4

For the next three to four weeks I was kept in an induced coma. All three of the bullets went through my abdomenal area, nicking the pancreas, stomach, liver, colon, and the area near the kidney, but then exited again (one of the bullets came out at the hospital and fell on the floor!). People have asked if I experienced much pain, but I don't remember pain—just "things" going in and warm blood coming out.

When I came out of the coma that February 17, I just wished I could talk to the suspect about the investigation. I had never met him previously and had nothing against him. Yet, because I represented law enforcement, I was shot, and in the process he lost his life. Was he saved? I'll never know unless the Lord reveals it to me in heaven. His action makes me think of the saying, "You can choose your sin, but you can't choose the consequences." Unfortunately, his choice led to the consequence of death.

FEBRUARY 18

MAN ON FIRE

Officer William J. Cox

Grand Junction, CO, Police Department

FOR NO apparent reason, something compelled me to stop. I was on patrol in a neighborhood where I'd lived as a child, and had driven by "my old house." Next door lived a family who routinely entertained outside, and several people were gathered around a small fire pit, which had been placed in the driveway. Nothing unusual, I suppose, but the feeling I needed to stop was too strong to ignore; I pulled over and just observed.

Suddenly the situation went from what was a lighthearted gathering of friends to a life-threatening emergency. Not thinking clearly, "Tom" picked up a gas can and poured gasoline into the fire pit. Unintentionally, he had just set himself on fire. There was a fire extinguisher only a few feet away, but in the panic of the moment no one thought to use it. I grabbed my fire extinguisher, was on scene within seconds and doused Tom, who was engulfed in flames. For financial reasons he declined an ambulance, so I took him to the hospital. Both legs were burned, but the right leg sustained the worst injury, with third-degree burns.

As a police officer, the only thing certain when going on shift is the constant uncertainty of exactly what incidents or events will unfold. Foremost, my prayers are for God's protection for me and my fellow officers,

61

but I also ask God to use me for his glory. As a police officer I am a public servant; as a Christian I am God's servant.

It was not coincidence I was sitting in that exact place at that time. I don't believe in coincidence—I believe in God! The overwhelming feeling I had to stop my car was God prompting me into position. He placed me there for quick action and gave me the clear thinking needed to save Tom. I was the Lord's instrument, but it was God who saved Tom's life. When we earnestly pray for God to use us, it shouldn't come as any surprise when he does. Every day is a new opportunity to serve him, whether it's taking someone to an appointment, taking food to someone in need, or anything God asks us to do. All it takes is an open and willing heart.

> Snatch others from the fire and save them.
> Jude 1:23

FEBRUARY 19

APPREHENDED BY PRAYER

Captain Gary Del Greco (Ret.)
West New York, NJ, Police Department

A FEW MONTHS after I accepted Christ as my Savior, my church had a study on prayer, which had a profound effect on my thinking. At the time I was sergeant on the midnight shift, and one night we were briefed on a person wanted for homicide. Not long before, he had entered a home and stabbed a girl several times, and then stabbed her 10-year-old brother, who had come to her aid. He had entered the house through a window and tried to start a fire in the attic. Apparently he had been stalking the family, and I wanted to end the ordeal—*tonight!*

As I set up the night shift lineup I started to pray, "Dear God, please let this man be caught tonight so we can remove him from terrorizing this family." We had detectives stake out the house hoping he would attempt to enter it again, but without success. The suspect lived in New York City, and the last bus back to the cCity left at 3:30 a.m. Since we hadn't caught him by then, we decided he must have taken the bus home. With that I called off the surveillance, but left a post car to keep tabs on the house.

About 3:50 a.m. I decided to take a ride around the town. As I left headquarters I turned toward the main street of town and noticed a man duck into a store's doorway. I decided to check him out. After backup arrived and we approached him, we realized he fit the description of the person we wanted. At headquarters the detectives verified his identity. On his person we found a knife, a toy gun, and a glass cutter, and on his pants were trace evidences of insulation from the attic where he had tried to set the home on fire.

While making out the arrest report I remembered my prayer of several hours earlier, asking that he be caught, never thinking I would be the one to make the capture. Here he had made it through our surveillance, and I caught him only a block away from police headquarters! God had delivered him into my hands! I received an award for the capture and wore it with pride the next twenty years. Whenever asked about it I always gave the credit to the Lord, saying, "God gave it to me!"

> And pray in the Spirit on all occasions with all kinds of prayers and requests. Ephesians 6:18

GOD WON THE ARGUMENT

Sergeant Cameron J. Grysen
Houston, TX, Police Department

GOD, I don't want to talk to him. You can see he's angry, probably hostile, and I'm sure he doesn't want to talk about spiritual things!" I had gotten gone off duty after a long shift; all I wanted was a cup of java at the local "Stop and Rob." It wasn't a nice neighborhood, but the price was right. Now here was this angry young fellow leaning against the building, and the Holy Spirit said, "Talk to him!"

Finally I gave in, said I would do it and be nice, even though he'd probably smart off at me. I said a little prayer and launched into what I hoped would be a short conversation: "How are you doing, my friend?" (I used my "friendly witnessing approach" because it's usually more effective.) There, I'd done it. Now I'll hear his invective, he'll turn away, and I can get my coffee. That didn't happen, so I went on. I asked him how he was doing, his name, what was going on in his life, about school, parents (no father, of course), and the like. I don't think many had taken time to show interest and concern for him, and he started to melt right in front of me. As I turned the conversation to spiritual things he showed a gen-

63

uine interest. After I told him the story of Jesus on the cross, he said his grandmother had told him many times about Jesus but he had never trusted him as his Savior. He did that day, right outside the convenience store. I asked him to go tell his grandmother about his decision, and before he parted, we wept together and hugged (I'll bet that's the first time he ever hugged a cop!).

> The LORD does not look at the things man looks at. Man looks at the outward appearance, but the LORD looks at the heart. 1 Samuel 16:7

That night I had a *big* apology to make to God, who once again had proved me wrong. I recalled the words of the prophet Isaiah: "For My thoughts are not your thoughts nor are your ways My ways, says the Lord. For as the heavens are higher than the earth, so are My ways higher than your ways, and My thoughts than your thoughts" (Isaiah 55:8, 9 NKJV). Sometimes I do get "stinkin' thinkin'." When that happens I'm learning the best thing to do is simply listen and obey God; he never makes a mistake!

FEBRUARY 21

MIKE'S STORY

Chief Michael Marchese
Lakemoor, IL, Police Department

IT'S HARD to sum up thirty years in law enforcement, of seeing everything from the good to the bad—people helping people, fathers murdering their own children, seeing one of our own die in the line of duty, and coming to realize the true meaning of being part of "the police family."

February 22, 2006, I received a call I never wanted: Detective/Officer Jared Scott Jensen of the Colorado Springs Police Department had been shot and killed while trying to apprehend a felon wanted for attempted murder. To make matters worse, Jared's father and stepmother lived in my community. Police protocol calls for death notices to be delivered by members of a local department, and we had the solemn responsibility to notify Jared's parents before they learned it from another source.

One of the most difficult tasks given to law enforcement officers is notifying someone of a loved one's death. This notification was difficult not only because we had to inform a father that his 30-year-old son had been killed in the line of duty, but also because we had lost a brother officer. I felt a strong sense of duty to handle this myself with the assistance of another officer and our police chaplain.

Jared's father, Thomas Jensen, was remarkable. During the two hours we grieved and cried together, Tom shared many wonderful and exceptional stories about all his children, especially Jared. It was humbling and an honor to witness his compassion and understanding that day. He read to us an essay Jared had written as a cadet in training, which said so much about the father and his son who gave his all as a police officer.

> Precious in the sight of the LORD is the death of his saints. Psalm 116:15

In police work you do not let go of friendship, and Tom and I have remained in contact over the years. We share the understanding of how tragic and evil Jared's death was as he paid the ultimate price with his life. As fellow Christians, our love for God has brought us even closer. It was God's love that brought us through that awful day and continues to give us comfort and understanding.

TOM AND JARED'S STORY

Thomas Jensen (Jared's father)
Schaumburg, IL

FROM AGE 8 into his 20s, my son Jared was an actor. He was professionally trained, worked in Hollywood and Chicago, and received many awards. In 2002, disenchanted, he was through with acting, choosing instead policing in Colorado Springs alongside his brother. He served with distinction from July 2002 until February 22, 2006, when he was murdered senselessly in the line of duty. To become a Colorado Springs officer, Jared had to write an essay on why he wanted to be an officer. This is a portion of what he wrote:

> "The traits I feel I already possess to be an effective police officer include keen observation skills, good physical health and sound judgment. However, I think the most important traits I can bring to the Colorado Springs Police Department are my commitment and passion. I have the commitment to do the job as I have been trained to do and to continuously better myself as both a police

officer and as a citizen of the community. I have the commitment to be unwavering in my promise to uphold the law, protect the rights and safety of others, and to defy all forms of corruption. Along with my commitment I have the passion to take all necessary and warranted risks to help others.

> Every morning I will put to silence all the wicked in the land; I will cut off every evildoer from the city of the LORD. Psalm 101:8—"The Policeman's Psalm"

"My father instilled in me the will to always go towards danger to defeat it rather than to simply seek out my own safety. I am willing to face danger simply because I was raised to do all I could to help others.

"The promise to protect and serve is not something I will take lightly. I will be unmitigated in my devotion to my training . . . to continue to seek out all the knowledge available, and continuously improve my effectiveness as a police officer. (Jared S. Jensen—Police Academy Entrance Essay, 2002)

Detective Jared Jensen

In his brief time on the force, Jared fulfilled his desire for a life that mattered and counted. He left an indelible mark with a positive influence on thousands of people. I told the more than five thousand people who attended his funeral service, "His entrance essay is one of my most cherished possessions." Since July 2006 I have maintained a Web site—www.afatherslove.info—in honor of a beloved son whose life made a difference.

THE DEATH OF A SAINT

Lieutenant Chuck Urgo (Ret.)

Chicago, IL, Police Department

ON FEBRUARY 22, 2010, Chicago Police Sergeant Alan Haymaker was en route to a burglary call when his squad car spun into a tree on an icy patch of Chicago's Outer Drive. Even though fire department paramedics were on the scene within minutes, heroic efforts by them and a team of doctors at the hospital were insufficient to save his life. Of the nearly 1,700 police "line-of-duty" deaths nationwide in a recent ten-year period, nearly a third were in auto crashes, surpassed only by shootings.

Lt. Chuck Urgo

The degree of respect for police deaths was manifested by the hundreds of law enforcement officers from Chicago and numerous state, local, and federal agencies who gathered for Al's funeral. Eulogies were offered by the mayor, the police superintendent, family members, friends, and fellow officers. All cited his accomplishments as a police professional, especially his work serving in a high-crime area of the city. For those of us who knew Al personally, we remember him as a husband, father, outstanding officer, and a faithful follower of Jesus Christ. He was a police officer who lived his faith in Christ on and off the job.

Romans 1:7 tells us all Christians are "called to be saints." Al Haymaker was one of those saints. He was a strong Christian who had

67

attended Moody Bible Institute, served as an associate pastor, and was involved in a master's program at Trinity Divinity School. Al considered police work an extension of his ministry.

> Precious in the sight of the LORD is the death of his saints. Psalm 116:15

On one assignment, he and his partner were called to an alley to remove the body of a newborn child. The usual procedure is to place the deceased in a body bag and transport it in the back of a paddy wagon. Instead, Al located a blanket, tenderly wrapped it around the child, and carried the body in his arms to the medical examiner's office.

In his eulogy, Al's brother-in-law told those gathered that Al would "give him no end of grief" in heaven if he didn't tell them about the Jesus he and Al loved and served, and proceeded to explain the plan of salvation. After the twenty-one-gun salute and playing of "Amazing Grace" by a large number of bagpipes, I thought to myself, *Al was a witness for Christ in life; through his funeral service he was a witness for Christ in death.*

FEBRUARY 24

SHOOT OR DON'T SHOOT?

Sergeant Cameron J. Grysen
Houston, TX, Police Department

THE CALL had all the earmarks of trouble: It was night, at an apartment complex in a bad part of town, and a man was shooting a gun "at anything that moves!" Suddenly our "routine patrol" wasn't routine anymore! One more thing: No one was available to back us up!

My partner and I raced to the complex, then drove slowly around the parking lot. We didn't see or hear anything, so we exited the car and started walking around the buildings. We'd just gone past a corner when we heard two loud bangs from a gun. Out of the corner of our eyes we located the source: a second-story balcony about fifty yards away. We dove for cover behind a wall and began moving cautiously toward the suspect, covering each other as we moved. As we got close, we could see it was a man who appeared highly intoxicated. He was holding a pistol, pointing it straight in front of him and staring off into space.

We gave him voice commands to put down the gun in both English and Spanish, which he didn't acknowledge. Finally, after a long while he did lay the pistol on the railing in front of him. I moved out of my covered position, getting as close to the suspect as possible, while my partner ran up the stairs to get him. I needed to be in position to shoot in case he tried to shoot my partner. As it was, we were able to take the suspect down and arrest him with no shots fired.

Unknown to us, a lot of people who were holed up in their apartments for protection were watching through their windows. Relieved that the crisis had ended, they all came out after the arrest. One witness was a young man attending the High School for Law Enforcement. This is a magnet school in Houston for students interested in careers in law enforcement. He thanked us for ending the terror safely, and said he'd just seen a film in class that day about "when and when not to shoot."

> Though I walk in the midst of trouble, you preserve my life.
> Psalm 138:7

From the scenario depicted in the film, he said we should have shot the man. My thoughts on that were, *I'm glad I didn't see the film. I know God was watching over us, and it's far better to save a life than to have blood shed!*

TWISTS AND TURNS

Captain Randy W. Dunn, No. 527

Chattanooga, TN, Police Department

TWISTS AND turns are a part of life, including mine. I was saved as a young teen but by high school was walking my own way. I married at age 22, had a son, divorced when he was 6 months old, remarried a short time later, and divorced again just before joining the police department at age 27. My first assignment was in the inner city, with special projects along the way. Six years later I went to Narcotics—my true police calling!—and became a member of the SWAT team. I also had married Karen. She is my strength and compassionate partner, and a great mother to my son. I thank God for her every day.

Working in Narcotics I spoke to kids at schools, exhorting them to stay off drugs and explaining how drugs affect both their life and the lives of those around them. I also coached sports in my off-time and helped many people, both young and old. Over the years I've touched the lives of many officers and their families as a member of a trained Critical Incident Debriefing Team. Yes, and I helped put in prison criminals who were destroying lives with the drugs they sold. My job was like a game: They tried to stay out of prison, and I tried to put them there for as long as possible.

> In all your ways acknowledge him, and he will make your paths straight. Proverbs 3:6

It is said that adversity tends to bring people back to God. I have been in the path of danger and looked death in the face. I've been involved in police-related shootings and had to take life, been in vehicle accidents, dealt with death and destruction on the job, lost members of my personal and police families, and very good friends. All the while I knew that if God chose to end my life it was his choice and no one else's. As I dealt with all that, plus health problems and family issues, I began what I now know was my path back toward God. I began talking with him and asking for his help. I know he always answered my prayers but because I didn't always get the answer I wanted, sometimes I didn't think he did. But God did, and he brought me back to him.

Would I do this job again? Yes! I was called by God to be a peace-keeper, and through all my "twists and turns" I have remained faithful to that calling.

FEBRUARY 26

OFFICER DOWN!

Chaim Kolodny, NHA, CMC, EMT-I

Senior Bureau Chaplain
Los Angeles, CA, Police Department

IN THE department they've nicknamed me "The White Cloud," because nothing ever happens when I ride along. This wet, wintry Saturday night the name didn't fit after the radio spit out, *"All units . . . officer down . . . officer down . . . shooting in progress . . . 84th and Broadway . . . multiple*

Chaplain Chaim Kolodny

shots fired . . . units to respond!" If you haven't lived through it, you really can't understand the awful urgency in the dispatcher's voice, horrific thoughts by all of how desperate it is, or the desire to get on scene as fast as possible. We were no exception.

All officers not tied up with an incident make certain all their gear is in place, then speed to the scene—a brother or sister has been injured or killed. What makes us the angriest is that the officer was hurt only for doing the right thing—"protecting and serving." En route I recalled King David's words in Psalm 91:4: "He will protect you like a bird spreading its wings over its young" (*Tanakh*) and Psalm 140:7: "You have the power to save me, and you keep me safe in every battle" (*Tanakh*). The scene looked like "total out-of-control" chaos: flashing lights, strobes pulsating, and cars everywhere (black and whites and detective cars), fire engines, etc., for as far as the eye could see. The blades of Air Support added a dizzying chop-chop to the now very cold and pristine night sky. But it actually is a highly disciplined chaotic scene, with each officer there to help, lined up in an orderly manner and going about the job professionally and courageously, most not knowing how the wounded officer is doing. There are no "lookie Lou's" in a situation like this.

At the scene I shielded my chaplain ID card from roving eyes for one simple reason: "Officer Down" and "Chaplain" could send the wrong message, especially when the facts are not yet known. We found that the officer already had been taken to the hospital, so I went, too—my place was there. The officer was "down, but not out"!

TAKE MINE FIRST!

Chaim Kolodny, NHA, CMC, EMT-I

Senior Bureau Chaplain
Los Angeles, CA, Police Department

ARRIVING at Harbor UCLA Hospital, we went immediately to Surgery. The injured officer was just being wheeled in, and we began "the wait." In the eerie quiet we were all on edge. *How badly is he hurt? Was it a head, heart, or belly shot?* With most of the body's "important" organs there, a bullet in the gut is fatal at worst and horribly destructive at best. We talked about life, God, and everything in between. The wounded officer's partner was traumatized by what happened to his partner, in a "tough guy" sort of way. After the shots were fired, he had pulled his partner into the car, used an emergency trauma kit to help stop the blood loss, and radioed for help.

About this time we learned a lot of blood had been lost. Quickly, dozens of officers who had come to the hospital were lining up to donate blood: "Take mine first!" After what seemed like hours, the doctors said our officer would survive; the bullet had caused a deep and bloody flesh wound with no major internal damage. This was the best news we'd heard all night! Meanwhile, Air Support was flying in the officer's wife and young daughter in a chopper; they were about twenty minutes out.

By the time they arrived the officer had been wheeled into a recovery room, the breathing tube and ventilator had been removed, and he was able to speak with them and the LAPD cChief, a welcome comforter in situations like this.

The good doctor took me aside and confided, "That officer is one very lucky kid; someone was watching over him tonight!" His recovery would be swift: first the recovery room, then ICU overnight as a precaution, to a regular room next day, and then "home, sweet home." Several officers turned to me and asked, Could we have a prayer of thanksgiving? Of course I said yes.

I won't attempt to describe the family reunion, as that could not do justice to the true thanksgiving and miracle we witnessed that night. But I will say this about the department: The care, concern, and compassion I witnessed that night is just a glimpse into what I see on a daily basis. Don't get me wrong, police officers are human beings who make mistakes, but they care about the community and do their jobs honorably and courageously. Like the officers who wanted to give their blood "first," they stand the possibility every day of "giving their blood" for us. They are true heroes!

> They were the heroes of old, men of renown.
> Genesis 6:4

"I DIDN'T SAY GOODBYE"

Patrolman Bob Rice (Ret.)

Delaware River Port Authority Police Department and New Jersey CISM Team

HANK, MY stepfather, was a Marine Vietnam vet. After military service, he became a police officer and was named Chief three years later. He remained in that position for twenty-seven years. Hank suffered from meningitis and—due to Agent Orange exposure—diabetes. After a heart attack February 24, 2010, the doctors pronounced him dead. However, a nurse continued to work on him until she got a pulse. He was then put on life support, and given a one-in-a-million chance of survival. After being asked to consider terminating life support, we paid our last respects and prayed.

At the hospital the next day we discovered the vent tube was gone, and he was breathing on his own. By the third day he felt well enough to shave, eat, laugh, and talk about returning home. But later that day, we learned his kidneys had shut down, and there was a good possibility he couldn't survive the dialysis treatments needed.

Several times while talking he told us he had been in water, clinging to little yellow life preservers around him. There were people in front of him waving him to "come on."

73

Henry "Hank" Jefferson

Even though he had a terrible pain in his chest he told them, "I can't come, I didn't say good-bye."

On Sunday I told my mother I needed to speak with Hank alone before I left. I talked with him about what could happen with the planned medical procedure. He again told me about the life preservers, and his belief that God allowed him to "come back" to say good-bye. He cried, and said he was afraid he would die in his sleep. I had shared my testimony with him many times, but did again. I told him that God loved him, and that I needed to know where he was with the Lord. After more conversation we prayed together, and Hank finally accepted Jesus Christ as his personal Savior. I told him I loved him, and we left the hospital.

> Rejoice that your names are written in heaven. Luke 10:20

That was the last conversation any of us had with him, other than my mother telling him "good-bye" when we left. Over the next four hours he suffered a series of heart attacks, and we were summoned back to the hospital. Not long after, he died with me and one of his sons by his side. I thank God every day for the opportunity to pray with Hank and lead him to the Lord. It was a precious blessing I always will cherish!

"THAT IS SO COOL!"

Jason Everett

Rolling Meadows, Illinois, Police Department

WE HAVE a Supervisor who adopted *Star Trek* as his alternate reality. In the *Star Trek: Next Generation* series, the badge on their uniforms is pressed when characters want to talk with one another. The badge then "beeps," and is used as a walkie-talkie. This Supervisor had a replica of that badge.

One night, he placed the sound-effect device from the *Star* Trek badge on the back of his police badge. He then asked our dispatchers to monitor the booking room with their video cameras and microphones. All he needed then was a "victim!"

An offender, arrested for driving while intoxicated, was brought in by a midnight shift officer. He was giving the arresting officer a hard time, complicating the booking process. Enter the supervisor into the booking room. The offender began lecturing the supervisor on what "real police do" and the use of taxpayer money, so the supervisor pressed his badge, making it "beep." When the dispatcher's voice was heard over the intercom: "Go ahead, sir," the supervisor asked dispatch to call for a taxi to take the offender home. The offender was wide-eyed and opened mouthed at this high-tech device! In awe he said: "That is so cool!" The supervisor told him this was a new system we were testing, and that the badge also served as a video camera with images sent straight to dispatch! Disbelieving, the offender asked him to prove it. The Supervisor told the offender to push the badge and when dispatch answered, ask them to describe something on his person. So the offender pressed the badge, put his face up to it, and asked what color shirt he was wearing. The dispatcher looked at the video feed from the camera in booking and told him, "tan." For the rest of the session, the offender carried on a full conversation with the supervisor's chest!

The film director, Alfred Hitchcock, was considered the master at making horror films. He said that when the situation got too tense, he would switch to a scene which made movie-goers laugh and relax. Then he could resume the serious part of his film. I think that is true in policing: so much of our work deals with heart-rending situations that we need to find levity now and then. The supervisor's playfulness did no harm, but it did help lift our spirits that night!

> A happy heart makes the face cheerful, but heartache crushes the spirit. Proverbs 15:13

IS OUR HEARING
THE LAST TO GO?

Justin Zeng, Asian Liaison Officer
Counties Manukau Police District, New Zealand Police

IT IS SAID that as we die our blood pressure drops, saving blood for the brain and heart. Since our ears are close to our brains, they will have a decent blood supply as long as the brain does.

A 39-year-old Asian woman had been run over and left for dead after her purse was snatched at a local mall. As the Asian Liaison Officer for my New Zealand police district, I was called to the hospital where she had been taken. Upon arrival I was told she suffered brain damage with injuries so severe that surgery was not an option. She was not expected to live.

The woman was lying on a bed motionless with a life-support machine connected to her chest. Her heartbroken family was at her bedside, and my heart was gripped with a profound sadness. Her mother was comforting her husband saying, "Sit down, papa. Remember that you have high blood pressure."

I asked the mother, "Does your daughter have any religious beliefs?"

She said, "No, not that I am aware of."

I said, "Aunty, I am a Christian. Would you allow me to pray for your daughter?" With tears in her eyes she said yes, and I poured out my heart to Jesus. "Lord, you are merciful. Please save her life, please. At least she will know you before she leaves this world. Please grant her your salvation." We all waited for a miracle, but unfortunately she died.

> Give attention to your servant's prayer and his plea for mercy, O LORD my God. Hear the cry and the prayer that your servant is praying in your presence.
> 2 Chronicles 6:19

At her funeral service a frail lady, aunt of the deceased, came forward to pay tribute to her niece. What she said next thrilled my heart: "I am her auntie and I live in Hong Kong. I was informed of the tragedy the day she died and I was so very sad. That night, exhausted by sorrow, I finally went to bed. Then I had a dream: My niece suddenly sat up in her hospital bed, resurrected! I asked her what had happened and she said, 'I believed in Jesus.' I can't explain having a dream like that!"

Hearing that, I had to ask myself this question: *Can God reach some-one in a coma?* Whatever the answer, please do not hold back on praying for everyone who comes across your path. You never know what the results may be!

THE LORD IS MY SHEPHERD

David Laumatia, Senior Sergeant
New Zealand Police

AS A SHIFT manager I was called to a domestic disturbance in Mangere. The offender had thrown knives at his wife and children and otherwise threatened to kill them. They managed to escape, but told us he was in the house and would not come out. There was no phone at the address. Police already had been inside, so we were forced to again clear the house to see to whether the offender was there.

I called for Delta (dog and handler) and armed my staff, then followed Delta inside with my firearm drawn. My heart was pounding, as we were told the offender had a knife and was willing to use it. I remember praying, "Lord, protect and be with me." Together Delta, my staff, and I cleared one room at a time. Finding no one, the tension grew with anticipation. Finally, Delta felt he was not in there. We regrouped back at the SFP (Safe Forward Point) and advised the family they should stay elsewhere until we found the offender.

A detective went back to the house with me to lock it up. As we closed the windows and doors, I walked past the first room on the left. There I felt the Lord urging me to look in it again. I knew Delta had cleared, but the Lord's urging was strong. I opened a closet full of clutter and rubbish and saw a sleeping bag covering something. When I kicked the bag it felt like a body, but there was no reaction. I put my hand down and could feel heat coming from his head. My heart was pounding. I drew my Glock pistol and called out to the detective, and still the body did not move. With my pistol poised at the offender's head I yelled for him to show me his hands. When he saw

> Even though I walk through the valley of the shadow of death, I will fear no evil, for you are with me; your rod and your staff, they comfort me. Psalm 23:4

78

my pistol pointed between his eyes he began cowering and shaking uncontrollably. My heart was racing as I forced him to the ground, where we handcuffed him. I was so pumped that I screamed, "I love this job!"

The dog handler was very embarrassed about having missed the offender, and I know God led me back to that room. It could have been very different for the family if he had not. Without a doubt it was the Lord's guidance and protection in that situation that resulted in the man's apprehension. Praise and glory to God's name! The Lord is my Shepherd!

GOD URGED ME ON!

Officer Caleb Williams

Gulfport, MS, Police Department

Grant Wolf, Executive Director (Ret.)

Fellowship of Christian Peace Officers (FCPO)

GRANT: "Caleb's phone call was like dozens I received during my seventeen years as executive director of FCPO—with one difference, the sense of urgency. Many called about starting a ministry chapter in their area, but didn't follow through. I knew Caleb would!"

As Caleb recalls: "Some other officers and I felt as though our work, specifically our shift work, was causing us to slip in our walk with the Lord. Some were struggling with sin; others weren't spending enough time with family and/or going to church. As I sat car-to-car with another officer one night, I wanted to find a way to use our being police officers to get back in touch with Christ. I remembered seeing a shoulder patch on a wall in the Gulfport Airport Police office that had to do with Christian police. I went there and saw that it was for the Fellowship of Christian Peace Officers (FCPO).

"I went on the Internet and compared what FCPO and other ministries stood for. Then I talked with some other officers as to why I felt we needed to get a chapter going in Gulfport. Everyone had the same question: 'How will taking more time away from my family help in my walk with Christ and my family life?' This was a good point, which needed a good answer. As I prayed about it, there were times when I wanted to give up on the idea, but had a feeling I needed to push the issue. I finally realized God could not work in us if we did not give him the opportunity. If we expected him to be there in our struggles, we needed to give a portion of our time back over to him. God was already there; we didn't need to find him, just bow before him. This is a hard thing for police officers to do.

> The LORD loves the just and will not forsake his faithful ones. They will be protected forever.
> Psalm 37:28

"I called Grant to get the process started, and found a restaurant where we could meet. A local pastor said he would be our chaplain and help us get started. Over the next few months we met several times, always inviting officers from other agencies. Again, officers asked what we were going to do with our chapter when we got it up and running. All I could say was, 'I guess that's up to God. He will let us know when the time is right.' We had our answer loud and clear August 29!"

MARCH 4

CHAPLAIN TO THE EMERGENCY ROOM!

Chaplain Don Hipple
Virginia Beach, VA, Police Department

IN SPITE of the so-called "separation of church and state" that has crept into our thinking, the courts have recognized that people in high-stress jobs, such as the military, law enforcement, and firemen, need trained personnel to give them "succor and spiritual support" in time of need. As a chaplain I fully agree with that assessment but have one to add of my own—sometimes we chaplains also need "succor and support."

One of my first call-outs after becoming a new police chaplain for the city of Virginia Beach was to an emergency room. The dispatcher informed me there were three fatalities from a vehicle crash and I was needed. Going to the hospital in a driving rain didn't lift my mood as I thought about what I would face there. At the hospital morgue a fellow officer ushered me in to where lay three 18-year-old high school students. I was asked to stand by, as their families were on their way; I would be needed to comfort them.

Through a long and emotional night, one by one, families arrived to identify their sons. There were many tears, and I cannot begin to remember the number of times I heard the anguished question, "Why?" As a parent myself I strongly felt their sense of loss and devastation.

When I finally left for the night and got to my vehicle I started kicking the tires and asking the same question, "Why? God, why did this happen? Why did these three young men leave school in a hurry looking forward to a weekend out of school, only to have their lives snuffed out in an instant?" They were gone, the lives of three families were changed forever, and so was mine. Thus was my introduction to being a police chaplain.

> Why, you do not even know what will happen tomorrow. What is your life? You are a mist that appears for a little while and then vanishes.
> James 4:14

The week that followed was long for our community: three memorial services, three burials, and at school three debriefing sessions where students could talk things out. And the question kept coming up, "Why?" There really is no answer, for most of us will never fully understand in this lifetime the "why" of things like that.

Perhaps the closest we can get is found in Isaiah 57:1, 2. In this passage the question is raised as to why the good die young. God's answer: "To be spared from evil," and, "Those who walk uprightly enter into peace; they find rest as they lie in death" (NLT). Since that November day I've taken many calls and am grateful to be a police chaplain. While many of those calls are a blur, I will never forget that heart-wrenching night.

MARCH 5

AS IRON SHARPENS IRON

Sergeant Dino Heckermann, Badge No. 3537

Streamwood, IL, Police Department

IT'S GREAT to be 22 years old, living out a childhood dream, in top physical shape, wearing a shiny police badge, and feeling invincible. I believed in God and the historical Jesus, but I was lost spiritually. At the department I met a senior juvenile police detective, Darwin Adams. An imposing man in stature with a vise-grip handshake from years of milking cows, he had a gentle heart. Detective Adams seemed very old to me at the time (I heard that when he began his police career he only earned fifty cents an hour!), but he was who I needed—a wise, older mentor.

Streamwood P.D. patch

Three years later at 25 I felt burned out spiritually. I asked myself, *Can you survive a twenty-plus-year police career, dealing with the stress of the job?* Chasing women and drinking beer after shift was not cutting the mustard for me. But then there was Detective Adams . . . his quiet strength and peaceful heart had grabbed my attention. I wanted what he had, so I took up his invitation to attend a men's breakfast at Moody Church. Even though I grew up in Chicago I had never heard of Moody. In fact, I thought he meant "Moonie Church," but being at the end of my spiritual rope I was willing to try anything.

We attended a Moody Church men's breakfast. It was a life-changing experience to hear fifteen hundred men singing praises to God. Though strange to me at first, it captured my heart. I do not remember the message, but my spiritual taste buds thirsted for God.

> Whatever happens, conduct yourselves in a manner worthy of the gospel of Christ. Philippians 1:27

Shortly thereafter, I accepted an invitation from Detective Adams and Officer Tom Cooper to attend a Promise Keepers conference in Texas with other police officers and firefighters. Until the opening session I didn't understand what Promise Keepers was all about, but I discovered then. When the invitation was given after Coach Tom Landry's powerful Gospel message, I gave my life to Jesus Christ in front of seventy thousand men!

I am so thankful for the obedience of those police officers who have mentored me—"Christian Oaks," I call them. They walk worthy of the Lord, giving me and others opportunities to hear the Good News of Jesus Christ. My prayer is that God will give me similar opportunities to mentor others for his kingdom.

> As iron sharpens iron, so one man sharpens another. Proverbs 27:17

AN OFFICER SAVED MY LIFE

Anonymous

I WAS A troubled young man of 17 whose life was saved by the kindness of a police officer. I had grown up in the interior of British Columbia in the 60s, and got caught up in the counterculture of that era. A ward of the government, after being molested several times in foster homes, they just cut me a cheque each month and let me live alone anywhere I wished. So, in the eleventh grade I rented a room in a flop house, kept going to school, and walked the streets, high on LSD. It was not yet categorized and still legal.

My night meanderings were noticed by RCMP Officer Mike Hewitt. He would pick me up, buy me food and coffee, and just talk. A kind man, he would let me sit in the back of his car while he drove around doing his job. If he got busy he would drop me off, but every night he looked for me on the streets, and a friendship grew. In spite of his friendship, I was very troubled and depressed. I decided I didn't want to live any longer, overdosed on LSD, fell into a coma, and disappeared. No one cared if I was alive or dead . . . except Mike. He became quite concerned for my well-being and began asking around

> 'I needed clothes and you clothed me, I was sick and you looked after me, I was in prison and you came to visit me."
> Matthew 25:36

for me. Later he told me he had an urgent feeling I was in danger and needed to be found. Finally, he located me on a cot in a place nicknamed "The Dirty Dozen," a heartbeat away from death. After two weeks in a hospital I woke up to an "Alice in Wonderland" world, and spent 18 months in a state mental institution. The only person who came to see me during all that time was Mike, and he had to drive 250 miles to do it!

The result of his efforts is that I got well, and am now one of God's servants. Through Mike's caring and God's grace, I reached responsible adulthood and founded the Argentine Children's Missions. The past six years I spent in Argentina working with, providing food for, and giving hope to children there. For all who think cops are tough guys to be feared, you are wrong. Mike taught me how to love and care for those who can't care for themselves, and I'm just passing on to others what I learned. To Mike and all the other caring cops of this world, thank you and God bless you!

INTEGRITY IN THE FACE OF ADVERSITY

Sergeant Trace Wedel, Badge No. 35123
California Department of Corrections

THE DICTIONARY definition of *integrity* is "adherence to moral and ethical principles; soundness of moral character; honesty; wholeness or completeness." As a peace officer I took an oath, which includes being honest and ethical. My obligation as a Christian is to be of sound moral character.

In 2000, I was a witness in an Internal Affairs investigation of possible sexual harassment. A female lieutenant, married to an administrator, was found guilty and suspended for sixty days. Afterward, the lieutenant regularly subjected me to retaliation, harassment, and a hostile work environment, while she was protected by the administration. After bogus write-ups and a punitive job change, I was passed over for promotion. I lodged a complaint with the inspector general. Thirty-seven of my forty-three allegations were sustained. Even so, no action was taken because the investigation exceeded time constraints. So our supervisors' organization filed a civil lawsuit on my behalf. After three years of this I was physically and mentally exhausted, and feared I would lose my job. Finally I was classified medically as a "stress case," subjected to psychiatric evaluations, and made to see a plethora of Workers' Compensation doctors. My family life was turned upside down, with me becoming "Mr. Mom" and my wife forced to return to full-time nursing. As one who always had received outstanding job reviews and commendations, I couldn't understand why I was subjected to such terrible treatment while the guilty parties got a pass? Why me? Eventually I realized my Christian values were diametrically opposed to the values of my organization.

> For it is commendable if a man bears up under the pain of unjust suffering because he is conscious of God.
> 1 Peter 2:19

Eventually justice prevailed when our governor appointed a new agency secretary who implemented sweeping changes. After twenty months without work or pay, I returned to my job. Nine months later, the day before a civil trial was to commence, the state asked to settle the case.

They paid me for my lost time, gave me back my seniority, and my case was accepted by Workers' Compensation. However, it took four more years before Workers' Compensation finally settled. No official action ever was taken against the guilty parties, but I was vindicated.

Throughout the entire nine-year ordeal, I had a lot of time to reflect, meditate on God's Word, pray, and journal. The story of Job's suffering became very meaningful and relevant to me. In the end, my integrity was not compromised, and God sustained me through it all.

THE LEPER

Chaplain Art Sphar

Sumner and Bonney Lake, WA, Police Departments

IN THE movies, death scenes often are portrayed in a moving and poignant manner. However, when law enforcement officers are involved in a death situation, it usually isn't a very pretty picture.

Our fire department medics had made an heroic effort to save a woman's life, but it was too late: She died of a heroin overdose. From the way her body looked, you could tell she had led a very hard life. All we could do now was wait for the medical examiner to take her body away.

Her husband was a slender man with longish, dark hair that stuck out in every direction, bushy dark eyebrows, a thick, full beard and moustache, and flashing eyes, which gave him an especially wild appearance. He was shirtless and clutching a soiled tee shirt in his hands, using it to wipe the tears from his eyes. Until a couple of months ago he had been homeless, living under a bridge. Now he was mourning the death of his wife. I was somewhat surprised that this wild-looking, unkempt man could experience such profound grief. But there he was, weeping into his shirt, and finally lying down on the floor next to her, holding her in his arms.

At long last his tears subsided enough that we moved out to the porch to wait for the medical examiner. While in some other circumstances I might have put my arm around the shoulder of a grieving husband, I

> The LORD is good to all; he has compassion on all he has made.
> Psalm 145:9

was having a profound "approach-avoidance" conflict. I was so repelled by his unwashed appearance and body odor I just couldn't do it.

Then I remembered the incident in which a leper fell at Jesus' feet and said, "Lord, if you are willing, you can make me clean." Jesus reached out his hand, touched the man, and said, "I am willing, . . . Be clean!" Immediately the man was cured of his leprosy (Matthew 8:2, 3).

With shame in my heart I thought, *If Jesus could reach out and touch that leper, with God's help I can touch and comfort this grieving man.* And I did.

ONE OUT OF FIVE

Tanya Stanturf

Independence, MO, Police Department

AS SOON as I saw him I knew something was wrong. It was the middle of the night and I was working at the front desk. He was elderly, stumbling, disoriented, and looking very sleepy. *Could he be intoxicated?* I wondered. He leaned against the protective window that separated us, but couldn't speak. Something about his look told me he wasn't drunk, but something was seriously wrong. Finally he said his lower stomach hurt. Immediately I phoned dispatch to send an ambulance to the department lobby.

He grew paler in color, and my mind kept saying, *He needs help, fast!* I've been trained as an EMT and lifeguard and am certified in CPR and something just "clicked" in my brain. Sitting him down, I pulled on latex gloves just as a precaution if I had to perform CPR. Though only five minutes had elapsed, it seemed like hours for the ambulance to arrive. Without delay they got him on a gurney and into the ambulance. Later I was told that as soon as they got him to the ambulance he "did code" (flat-lined) and the ambulance crew revived him. He coded twice more that night, once on arrival at the hospital and the other during emergency surgery. I was told he had suffered an aortic dissection, the same condition that killed actor John Ritter. Those who have lived through it describe it as the most painful thing that ever happened to them. Blood surges from the heart into the main artery, forcing a tiny rip in the aorta's lining that grows and threatens to burst like a dam in a flood. Only one out of five people survives an aortic dissection; this man did!

> Do you see a man skilled in his work? He will serve before kings.
> Proverbs 22:29

When the gentleman was well enough he asked for a press conference in which he thanked the police department, ambulance crew, and hospital staff for their work in saving his life. He also requested a meeting to thank me in person for my quick action and for listening to my intuition. At the time of this incident I was dissatisfied in my job, wondering if the Lord had a place for me elsewhere. God definitely showed me I was in the right place, serving where he wanted me.

MARCH 10

THE NIGHTMARE

Officer Quentin Wilson

Houston, TX, Independent School District Police Department

Award Citation for Officer Wilson

THE NIGHTMARE started March 10, 2007, when Officer Quentin Wilson was working a funeral procession on his motorcycle. A driver of a pickup truck cut into the procession in front of him, braked the vehicle, and caused Wilson to slam into the back of the truck. Wilson suffered blunt trauma, including thirteen broken ribs, two punctured lungs, a broken femur and humerus, and a broken back. His chest cavity was caving in. At the hospital he went into cardiac arrest, then was hooked up to a high-frequency oscillator breathing machine and put into a drug-induced paralytic coma. He spent 106 days in hospitals before transferring to rehab. Over the next few months he had to learn how to function all over again—starting with walking.

On the first day in rehab the therapist put him between parallel bars and told him, "You're going to walk today." While shocked at the aggressiveness of rehab, he poured his heart into everything he was asked to do.

When discouraged, he looked at a photo of his daughter on the wall to have something to fight for. Thirty-two months and twenty-four operations later, he was back in uniform.

Says Wilson, "I'm still pinching myself, I can't believe it's all happened. It went from doctors telling my wife, 'We don't think he's going to make it; it's up to God now' to, 'He'll probably never sit up in bed again without help.'" However, he progressed from sitting up to getting into a wheelchair without help to walking with a walker to walking without a walker. He goes on to say, "I couldn't have done this without God. My church had a mission group praying for me

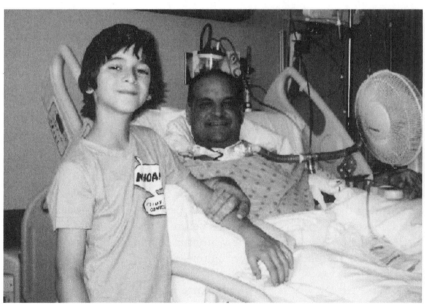

Wilson recuperating from crash (nephew by his side)

88

in Hungary and around the world. Doctors said they prayed for me. My recovery came from the power of prayer and wonderful doctors." When people ask, Wilson says, "I just tell people I know God has a purpose for me. God has a plan. If it's to inspire people who are desperate and don't know if they can make it, that's fine. If it's just simply being here for my wife and daughter, that's fine for me."

> "The blind receive sight, the lame walk, those who have leprosy are cured, the deaf hear, the dead are raised, and the good news is preached to the poor."
> Matthew 11:5

(Reprinted by permission from the *HISDPD* publication, *The Connection*)

"ONE EYEBROW OPEN"

Constable Jackson Shewry
Henderson, New Zealand, Police

MY PASTOR had been teaching on being obedient to God and stepping out in faith, on "walking around with one eyebrow open" expecting a miracle. I decided to give it a try and was being diligent in my prayer life and Bible reading.

While investigating an aggravated robbery I picked up a female suspect ("Crystal") and took her back to the station. My practice is to try to establish good rapport with offenders by showing an interest in their lives rather than focusing on the offense. Then, if the opportunity arises I try to start a conversation about God and religion. It seemed clear to me God wanted me to do that with Crystal.

She began saying that recently she had been taking her kids to church, but, before she got involved, she really wanted to talk to someone about what being a Christian was all about. She told me she wanted what Christians have—inner peace—no matter their life situation. I began telling her about my faith beliefs and, just as we pulled into the station, she said, "It is like we were supposed to meet."

After I finished interviewing her about the robbery, we resumed our conversation about God. Crystal asked me about faith, forgiveness, being

born again, heaven and hell, spiritual warfare, and prayer. Just as it says in John
16:13, it seemed as though the Holy Spirit
was giving me answers upon answers to her
questions. I really sensed progress had been
made with her. She said she didn't have a

> I planted, Apollos watered, but God gave the increase.
> 1 Corinthians 3:6 (NKJV)

Bible but really wanted something to read. I didn't have one with me, but
gave her some Scripture passages to study I'd printed off. She was very
grateful to get them and most appreciative of our conversation.

After I took her home and headed back to the station I realized I'd
done just what the pastor said: been obedient and "kept one eyebrow
open." Then I was given the miracle of sharing God's Word with a soul
who needed it. I turned the radio on to listen, but when I heard what was
playing ("Hell's Bells" by *AC/DC*) I turned it off and worshipped God.
Since our conversation, Crystal has joined a church and small groups and
is reading the Bible. A seed had been planted!

MARCH 12

BE THOU MY VISION

John M. Wills (Ret.)

Federal Bureau of Investigation

AFTER TEACHING a group of officers in West Virginia, I decided to
drive home rather than wait until morning. I left at dusk in a light
rain, and felt some trepidation about the road conditions, but went forward anyway.

The first hour was uneventful, but my faith was soon challenged. West
Virginia is aptly named the Mountaineer State. Ascending one of those
mountains, I saw several electronic warning signs blazing the dire message,
"Slow—Dense Fog Ahead." I've driven foggy roadways all over the United
States, but never experienced anything like I was about to encounter.
Higher up the mountain, the fog enveloped my car like a heavy woolen
blanket. I nervously focused on the taillights of a semi ahead, while trying
to stay within my lane. Near the crest, the fog was so intense that the
lighted lane markers were only visible from a distance of five to ten feet.

The fog was so thick it muffled outside sounds and created an effect
of suspended animation. I couldn't see or hear other vehicles, even though

I knew I was in a formation of several other cars and trucks. My speed had decreased to about 10 miles per hour, but I was fearful of running into a slower vehicle, or that a semi would run over mine. I was so completely detached from reality, it was almost as if I had been taken up to the heavens. Alone and a little terrified, I began to pray. I looked over to the passenger seat and visualized Jesus sitting there, helping me gain the courage I needed that everything would be all right. At that point my isolation chamber became my cathedral—Jesus was there testing me. Would I place my faith completely in his hands?

Miraculously, taillights, lane markers, trucks, and other traffic materialized. The faint, red blurs became full-fledged red beacons as drivers rode their brakes down the descent. The fog finally dissipated, allowing me to see clearly once again. Isaiah wrote about "eyes that cannot see." That's what I had: eyes that couldn't see because of the fog around me. Isn't that what we face each day—the "fog" of this world, which obscures our heavenly vision? Even though I ask God each morning to walk with me, it's up to me

> I will lead the blind by ways they have not known, along unfamiliar paths I will guide them; I will turn the darkness into light before them.
> Isaiah 42:16

to rely on his guidance to stay the course. When Peter tried to walk to the Lord on water, he began to sink when he lost his heavenly vision.

"Lord, help me keep my eyes on you today!"

MARCH 13

MONGREL MOBSTER

Constable Matt Davis, MDAH12

Huntley, New Zealand, Police

A FEW WEEKS before arresting Daniel, I had stopped his wife for having a really "dodgy-looking" car. We started to talk about God, and she told me they had got involved with a cult whose members had been willing to support them. However she wasn't happy with their teachings, so I shared Biblical truth with her. I recall promising to pray for her, and left it at that.

The day of the incident while driving to work (evening shift) I sensed the Holy Spirit saying to me, "Someone will ask you for dinner tonight, feed them!"

91

I attributed this to fatigue on my part, but later that evening I arrested Daniel for an assault on his partner. He is a Mongrel Mob member, which is an ethnic criminal gang made up of mainly Māori and Polynesian men. They are organised similarly to a biker gang, such as *Hell's Angels*, and offer the support and brotherhood that many displaced men desperately seek, unfortunately

> Therefore, as God's chosen people, holy and dearly loved, clothe yourselves with compassion, kindness, humility, gentleness and patience.
> Colossians 3:12

through crime and violence. Daniel had called me at the station to say he was turning himself in. Then without warning he asked, "Will I get dinner tonight?" I was completely floored!

As I processed him, he again asked about dinner, so I got him takeaway. As we talked that night he told me about his hard life and that he had accepted Christ years ago, but never found the love or acceptance he needed in a church. Even so, he felt God had changed him radically. We sat in an interview room for an hour just talking about his struggles with anger and how he had never been offered help. Sadly, he had gotten involved with the cult his wife had told me about, simply because they showed him love. I showed him from the Bible various Scripture passages that refuted what he had been taught, and then I prayed for him. After the legalities relating to the assault were cleared up he was released, but he moved away because he could not get the support he wanted.

Much of what we do in police work is mundane and not earth-shattering. Through our testimony and lives we Christian cops do our best to impact our communities with the love of our mighty, eternal, and loving Savior, Jesus. We simply can't determine what the outcome will be.

APOLOGY IN ORDER!

Lieutenant Dennis E. Nail

Martinsville, IN, Police Department

IT WAS March 14, and the funeral service for my aunt—who always had treated me as if I were her own son—was over. Family and friends had left our church, and were crossing a narrow street to the church parking lot. Suddenly, from out of nowhere, came a small pickup truck being driven quite recklessly.

All eyes were on me at this point, with that questioning look that conveyed, "Well, you're a policeman. What are you going to do?" I ran across the street, jumped into my unmarked cruiser, notified Dispatch, and took off. Within minutes, other units responded, and three young males were apprehended. My emotion meter already was on "high" from the funeral and the fact family members had been endangered. The fact these were local troublemakers who knew cops better than members of their own family didn't help. The driver was cuffed and being placed in one of the marked cars when I yelled at him. You might say I "let him have it with both barrels"!

> "Anyone who is angry with his brother will be subject to judgment . . . anyone who says, 'You fool!' will be in danger of the fire of hell."
> Matthew 5:22

Just then the Holy Spirit placed me in check. "There's no need to yell. He's been caught and is going to jail." That took the wind out of my sails, and nothing could ease the grief I felt. I certainly had not been a good witness to the driver.

The next morning I was back on duty, and the Holy Spirit refused to leave me alone. I wrestled with my conscience and asked God, "Do you really want me to go to the jail and apologize to this guy?" (That was the direction I was being led.) In spite of my stubbornness, the burden in my heart kept getting heavier. Finally I gave in and went to the jail.

At the jail, I asked the jailer to bring the prisoner to a small conference room; I needed to speak to him. The man greeted me by name when he arrived (like I said, he knows us)! When we were alone, I looked him in the eye and apologized for yelling at him. I said it was uncalled for, and would he forgive me? In shock, he told me I didn't need to apologize. I said, "Yes, I do, because God sent me to ask if I can pray with you as well."

As I left the jail my burden lifted. I could almost hear my aunt whisper in my ear, "Now *that's* the Christian boy I know!"

DOWN FOR THE COUNT
(BUT NOT OUT)!

Sergeant Adams
North Carolina Police Officer

AFTER WRESTLING professionally for ten years I was "down for the count!" My "over the rope leg drop" ended in disaster when my opponent slammed me hard. Next day in the ER they said the "explosion" I heard and felt in my left ear and left side of my neck was what is called a "stunner." That pretty well ended my wrestling career.

I shouldn't have been wrestling anyway. I was and am a law enforcement professional, and should have been concentrating on my job. To supplement my police income I'd bought a gym, got into body building and wrestling, and liked the results, both personal and financial. I'd also forsaken my Christian roots, savored "the pleasures of sin for a season," and was living it up.

Even before the accident, things had "started to go south." My gym co-owner left the gym and signed everything over to me, including a mountain of debt. My rent jumped 300 percent. I'd moved to smaller quarters, lost customers, couldn't keep up my payments, and was on the brink of bankruptcy. With the accident I had bulging disks, couldn't move my neck, and was told to do nothing physical for six months. Then I got a call from New York for a lucrative deal to wrestle there and didn't know whether to laugh or cry . . . so I went for a drive.

> This is what the LORD says: "Stand at the crossroads and look; ask for the ancient paths, ask where the good way is, and walk in it, and you will find rest for your souls." Jeremiah 6:16

Pushing buttons on the car radio I came across a Christian station and heard a sermon. Listening to it, I first laughed and then I cried. Stopping the car I said this prayer: "God, if you are real, show me and I will give myself to you." I invited Jesus into my heart to live as I never had before. I drove home and told my wife we needed to start going to church, and she agreed. Next day as I was going to sign bankruptcy papers I received a call from an out-of-town police agency, offering me a $10,000-a-year salary increase. I said yes, realizing at once this was the answer to my prayer, and canceled the bankruptcy proceedings. We got a second mortgage, refinanced our home, and took care of the debts.

It took almost breaking my neck for me to realize wrestling had become my god. Then the God of the universe got my attention and showed me in a mighty way that his path is better. Since my "wake-up call" ten years ago, life has just kept getting sweeter. I'm sorry I almost had to break my neck in the process, but I'm glad God got my attention!

MARCH 16

AFTER THE MOUNTAIN COMES THE VALLEY

Sergeant Adams

North Carolina Police Officer

MY YEARS of dissipation and turning my back on God were over, and I'd finally found my way "back home." The life-changing injury I'd suffered in wrestling changed both my life and Renee's. We'd been told we couldn't have children but now had two. We went through Dave Ramsey's "Financial Peace University" and were getting our financial affairs in order. I was happy in the new police position I'd taken, and life was good.

One day I was sitting in my office and talking out loud to God (sometimes I find that more satisfactory than simply saying a silent prayer). I had been reading about the "mountaintop experience" Moses had and was envious. I asked God for one. Let me say here that I've always been skeptical when people say, "God told me this" or, "I heard God say that." Not anymore!

As I was talking out loud I felt a hand on my right shoulder. No one else was in the room but then I distinctly heard a voice say, "I am here." The voice didn't seem to come from an outside source but came from within my own being. It was as the Scripture says in Jeremiah 4:19: "My heart makes a noise in me; I cannot hold my peace, because you have heard, O my soul" (NKJV). I realized God had spoken and given me my mountaintop experience. Then I thought, *You didn't have the faith to believe that God could give you what you asked, so he did it to prove you wrong.* The experience left me shaking and in tears.

Two weeks later I learned the reason God had revealed himself to me that day. During an exam the doctor told me I had multiple myeloma

95

(MM), a type of incurable (but in some cases manageable) cancer that starts in the plasma cells, a type of white blood cell found in the bone marrow. He said I was in the first, or MGUS (Monoclonal Gammopathy of Undetermined Significance), stage. For some reason I had no fear; my calm was unbelievable. God has kept the disease in check. I still am in the benign stage, but have my bone marrow tested every six months. As the saying goes, "I don't know what to expect in the future, but I know who holds it." My life is a gift and the MM is not a death sentence. It simply helps to serve as a reminder of who God is and his wonderful grace toward me.

> The LORD was not in the wind; and after the wind an earthquake, but the LORD was not in the earthquake, and after the earthquake a fire, but the LORD was not in the fire; and after the fire a still small voice.
> 1 Kings 19:11, 12 (NKJV)

AN EMERALD GREEN FORD!

Sergeant David M. Greenhalgh (Ret.)

Delta (Vancouver, Canada) Police Department

OVER THE course of a police career an officer drives many cars. My favorite was a '78 emerald green Ford sedan equipped with a dash-mounted fireball and siren. I felt that God had given it to me, and I kept it immaculate. I had acquired several good habits in the three years I worked plainclothes: keeping my vehicle up, working afternoon shifts (most detectives prefer day shift), continuing to arrest DUIs, backing up patrol officers when needed, and keeping a good relationship with them.

One day Dale, a Christian officer assigned to the Tswassen District, called for backup to deal with an uncooperative DUI suspect he had stopped on a four-lane undivided highway. On my arrival two other marked units were stopped facing north, and Dale was arguing with a long-haired, tattooed biker type. I nosed the Ford up on the shoulder headed the wrong way.

The driver was huge, about 6'7", more than 300 pounds—drunk, belligerent, profane, totally uncooperative and refusing to exit the car—and accompanied by a female. He was truly a scary person, making my colleagues quite apprehensive that he might start a fight.

I had gotten out of my car and made this quick evaluation when the suspect jammed his car into gear, drove around mine, and took off north-bound. I don't know how, but I was back in my car and turned around so fast that I became the primary pursuit unit, followed by the three marked units already facing the right way. The suspect made multiple attempts to ram me broadside as we swerved over all four lanes of the highway, which fortunately was traffic-free. After a couple of miles he suddenly pulled over and stopped. I was out of the car in an instant, dragged him out of the driver's seat, forced him over the hood and handcuffed him.

> For he will command his angels concerning you to guard you in all your ways. Psalm 91:11

Breathing a sigh of relief I looked up. My three uniformed colleagues were standing there, legs apart, guns drawn in two-handed stance, all pointing their guns in our general direction. The driver had freaked them out that much.

At the station I walked around my beautiful green Ford—there wasn't a scratch on it! God gave me a mental image of an angel sitting on every corner of my unit. I'm positive it wasn't my skillful driving or my strength and ability that overcame and allowed me to cuff the suspect. In this encounter between angels and demons, the angels won!

MARCH 18

"THROW THAT #&*@# THING AWAY!"

Sergeant Brian Cain, Badge No. 713

Holly Springs, GA, Police Department

WHEN THE assistant chief said that, I couldn't believe my ears! How could anyone make a remark like that about the Bible—God's Word?

We had a brand-new mayor, new chief, and new assistant chief. The chief had been promoted from within, but the assistant chief (AC) had been hired from outside the department. The AC, another sergeant, and I were walking into a room when the AC saw a Bible lying on a credenza. He picked it up and said, "What the h-ll is this?" We use inmates to help during the day, and I told him it was probably a Bible an inmate had been given by the jail chaplaincy staff. It was then the AC said, "Throw that #%&@ thing away!"

To make matters worse, he asked the sergeant to do his dirty work. The sergeant responded, "No, sir, I don't throw Bibles away."

At that the AC grabbed the Bible and said, "I'll throw it away myself. I don't read fiction anyway." I thought, *Surely he won't,* but he did. (Note: Numbers 15:31 talks about what happens to those who "have treated the LORD's word with contempt" (NLT).)

I retrieved the Bible from the trash can, went to the chief, and recounted the events. He said he would look into the matter. (I learned soon after that the AC was an atheist and had made his views well known at his last department.) The next day the AC called me into his office and apologized. He said it was out of character for him to behave in such a manner, and apologized for offending me. I told him that what he did was not only offensive, but also violated department policy. I also told him that friendship and working relationships within the department were never based on religious views, but on character and mutual respect. It was the only time in my law enforcement career that I got to "dress down" an assistant chief. Reflecting on the incident later I was reminded of Matthew 10:22: "All men will hate you because of me, but he who stands firm to the end will be saved."

> But they will have to give account to him who is ready to judge the living and the dead. 1 Peter 4:5

MARCH 19

MY BROTHER, MY HERO

Donna Marquez

Sister of slain Chicago, IL, Officer Donald. J. Marquez
Star No. 8620

ON MARCH 18, 2002, the 10 p.m. news ended with "Officer Shot!" Later that night we learned it was my brother, Donald. How could that be!

"Henry's" house needed repairs, and neighbors wanted the city to tear it down. An elderly recluse, Henry had lived there all his life, and said he'd die in it before anyone could take it away. My brother and his partner were

98

assigned to serve a warrant on him. After Don and his partner knocked on the door, Henry opened fire on the officers, striking Don in the head.

As my brother lay dying, his partner sent out the call, "Officer Down!" Though a myriad of officers came, Henry kept firing with two guns, preventing them from rescuing my brother. After an intensive gun battle, Henry was also killed. As one police chaplain said, it was one of the department's greatest acts of courage and heroism. With so many bullets flying, God protected the officers from further bloodshed. Later I went to the crime scene. As I looked at my brother's shed blood, all I could think of was Jesus and how he shed his blood for us. I told those present Donnie had not died in vain; his death was a part of God's plan but difficult to understand.

> In all things God works for the good of those who love him, who have been called according to his purpose. Romans 8:28

Donnie and I were raised in a Christian home, but I became very angry at God and questioned, "Why?" It's something I had to work through, and still do not fully understand. Even so, on the fourth anniversary of my brother's death, I became a police chaplain. What a joy God has given me to share my faith! And if an officer is contemplating suicide or needs hope for any reason, it is wonderful to tell that person not to give up—there is hope in Jesus.

My parents were never the same after Donnie's sudden and violent death. When mother died in June 2009, in her final hours she remembered my brother Don and called out his name. I couldn't help but think that God had rejoined my mother and brother in heaven. And I look forward to the day when our entire family is there, together again!

MARCH 20

BEAUTIFUL FEET!

David Laumatia, Senior Sergeant
New Zealand Police

I NEED TO leave work now," our typist said. "My mother-in-law has been rushed to the hospital and is dying!" While driving her there, I spoke to her about the blessed hope Christians have in Christ Jesus. After dropping her off at the hospital entrance I started to leave, but felt like God was asking me to return and pray for her mother-in-law.

The typist was in the Emergency Department and very glad to see me. I asked if a pastor was present to pray for her mother-in-law, and she said no. I looked into the woman's room, and saw a frail older lady breathing what appeared to be her last breaths. The doctor felt she would die any moment, and went to get some morphine to ease her pain. I was in full uniform and knew only the typist, so she introduced me to her family. When I told them I was a Christian and asked if I could pray for her, they gave their consent.

Compassion filled my heart and tears welled in my eyes as I put my hand on her and began to pray. She had an oxygen mask over her face, and was breathing heavily and gasping for her breath. As I looked into her eyes and began to pray a prayer of faith, her breathing slowed and her vital signs began to normalize. When the doctor returned, expecting the worst, he asked what had happened. A family member said, "That cop prayed for her and she is healed." Then I said my good-byes and left.

> He commanded us to preach to the people and to testify. . . . Acts 10:42

Over the next couple of weeks I was invited back to pray with the family, and was able to tell them of the blessed hope in Christ Jesus. The elderly lady eventually went to be with the Lord, and I was invited to speak at her funeral. There, I was able to testify about the grace of God and the hope we have in Jesus, in both this life and the next.

In reflecting on the incident I can't help but think about Romans 10:14, 15: "How, then, can they call on the one they have not believed in? And how can they believe in the one of whom they have not heard? And how can they hear without someone preaching to them? And how can they preach unless they are sent? As it is written, 'How beautiful are the feet of those who bring good news!'"

MARCH 21

NOT A RESPECTER OF PERSONS

Officer John T. Campbell, I.D. 14716
California Highway Patrol

IN LAW enforcement we have to know when to be tough, when to be lenient, when to be gentle, and when to strike with the force of a sledgehammer. It's a task difficult for man, but with God at the helm, it's a walk in the park. If we let God's Word ring true in our spirits, his wisdom ultimately will filter into our minds.

I was working freeway speed enforcement when a southbound vehicle approached my location at a speed confirmed by radar at about 100 miles per hour. I initiated an enforcement stop in short order. I contacted the driver, explained the reason for the stop, and asked for the required documentation. When the driver gave me the documents, he identified himself as a pastor. Instantly I became uneasy, as I have great respect for the servants of God.

I went back to my patrol car and began to pray, "Father, do you want me to give one of your pastors a ticket for speeding?" Ringing through my spirit was 1 Chronicles 16:22: "Touch not mine anointed, and do my prophets no harm." I didn't want to give a ticket to one of the Lord's anointed!

As I searched the Spirit of God for my answer the Lord brought Acts 10:34 to my remembrance: "God is no respecter of persons" (KJV). I also felt that the pastor was attempting to use his position to gain favor. Consequently, I gave him a ticket for driving 100 miles an hour.

> Is [God] not the One . . . who shows no partiality to princes and does not favor the rich over the poor, for they are all the work of his hands?
> Job 34:18, 19

You may be thinking, *"You didn't!"* Yes, I did, but not until I had lifted the matter up in prayer to God. Not only did the Holy Spirit tell me what to do, but he also uncovered the intent and heart of the pastor.

Back in my car making notes of the stop I remember thinking, *A person never knows when the hand of the Lord is going to chastise him*. The position a man holds—regardless of how high it may be in his eyes—is not going to alter the consequences. If we need a spanking, God is going to give it to us *no matter who we are*. The Lord has people everywhere in positions with the authority to exercise his will. This knowledge should keep each of us humble. As I go about my work I try to stay in constant communion with God. I highly recommend that to all. Do that and your mind will be calm, your steps sure, and your spirit at peace.

BECAUSE HE FIRST LOVED ME

David, No. 625

South Dakota municipal law enforcement

I FIRST MET Jesus at Bible camp when I was about 7 years old. One night during a dramatic presentation the Lord spoke to my heart and I accepted Jesus as the Truth. When I was 10 my dad, who was a police officer, divorced Mom, which hurt, but really didn't make much of a change in my life, as he was often gone anyway.

I completed obligatory religion classes at our church, but didn't attend regularly on Sundays. Around that time I began questioning the truth of the Bible and the existence of God. I was trying to prove I was right (which I wasn't) by reading my Bible more. At every step God tried to show me how much he loved me and wanted me as his son, but I didn't listen. My rebellion continued through high school and into college, with all the usual thirst for instant gratification.

> As a prisoner for the Lord, then, I urge you to live a life worthy of the calling you have received. Ephesians 4:1

For as long as I could remember I had wanted to go into law enforcement, and became a recruit in early 1993. I earned the honor graduate award, and worked hard my first probationary year to be the best officer I could. When my probation ended I went back to the frivolity of my high school and college days: drinking too much and leaving my wife home alone. We split and nearly divorced until she told me she was pregnant with our first child. I tried to pull it together on my own but couldn't—I lacked a relationship with my Savior. Facing the loss of my wife, my unborn daughter, and my job, I finally recognized God's claim on my life. He used some truly amazing people to free me from the chains that had bound me so long.

Now I love Jesus because he first loved me. I love my wife, my daughter, and my son. I wish I could tell you I walk in complete obedience to my Master's call every day, but I don't. However, I am working out my salvation daily with fear and trembling through the power of the Holy Spirit. At age 7 I made Jesus my Savior; today he also is my Lord.

I have come to know that without Christ I am nothing and could not face each day. To all believers, please remember we must reach out to those near us, shining our light for all to see. Don't leave your brothers and sisters in the dark! Tell them how much Jesus has done for both you and them. Walk the walk, talk the talk, repent when you miss the mark, and make amends to those you've hurt!

KINDNESS BEGETS KINDNESS

Chaplain Jim Nichols
Omaha, NE, Police Department

I WAS AT work when my wife called me frantically from an ambulance. She and our 8- and 10-year-old children had been involved in an accident. When I reached the hospital the sergeant who had been at the scene told me what happened. Two plainclothes Omaha police officers had pulled over a known meth dealer. As they approached his car he sped away, running two stop signs at 58 miles per hour. At the second one he slammed into my family's van, pinning our son between the seat and door. At first he was unresponsive, but by the time they extracted him from the van he was conscious with slurred speech.

> "Teacher, which is the greatest commandment in the Law?" Jesus replied: "'Love the Lord your God with all your heart and with all your soul and with all your mind.' And the second is like it: 'Love your neighbor as yourself.'"
>
> Matthew 22:36–40

At the hospital everything checked out normal for my wife and daughter. Our son was sitting up and talking, but complained about a bad headache. Since he appeared to be all right, no special tests or x-rays were performed. A couple of hours after we got home he showed signs of a concussion—head pain and vomiting. Quickly we rushed him to the hospital, where they gave him a CAT scan. There the ER doctor told us our son had fractured his skull and severed an artery, causing bleeding in his brain. He was dying and needed lifesaving surgery as soon as possible! As I explained this to my son, we prayed and asked God to save his life and to forgive the man who was responsible for his injuries.

Our son was rushed into surgery around midnight while my wife, daughter, many friends, and I prayed together for his life. An agonizing three hours later the surgery was over; our son had made it through and was taken to ICU. Miraculously, he was moved to a regular room later that day.

When the police department learned about our son's condition, several officers visited us in the hospital. They even checked up on us after we went home. We were so overwhelmed by the support they gave that I volunteered to be a department chaplain. By God's grace they accepted me. Because of the Lord's goodness the only reminder of that horrific event is a long scar on our son's head. When I see this scar it reminds me of two things: first, of the miracle God performed and how much he loves us; and second, of the reality and danger associated with the war on drugs.

MARCH 24

YOU'VE GOT CANCER

Officer Craig Phinney
Ankeny, IA, Police Department

NO MORE chasing bad guys for you, Craig; you're going to have to give up your job! You have the onset of cancer, and the best way to proceed is to remove the whole colon." He'd been treating me seven years for ulcers of the colon and should have known better than to call my career a *job*! Policing is my *career*, and I wasn't going to let anything stop me, not even colon cancer!

That five-minute conversation was followed by a week of depression. But after positive support from my supervisors, I met with a specialist. He was much more encouraging, so I made my decision: "Game on, Doc!" The complete colon removal was done March 24, 2009. I spent two weeks in the hospital with complications, then six weeks at home with an ostomy bag. In May, a second surgery was performed to reconnect. After being home for one day, it was back to the hospital for another week—more complications.

Cancer does funny things with time. First, it surprises you because you don't expect it. Second, you're caught between time moving ever so slowly, giving you too much time to think, and time moving so fast you can't live the life you want to live. During my stay in the hospital, I had time to think (whether after the drug haze or because of it, I don't know). I found myself asking these questions: What would I do if God gave me an extra, twenty-fifth hour each day? How could I use it to benefit myself or someone else? As I thought about that "extra hour," I made some commitments:

First, cancer changes your lifestyle, but it shouldn't end the joy of living.

> The LORD is my strength and my shield; my heart trusts in him, and I am helped. Psalm 28:7

Your cancer affects those around you. My wife and I talked it through and tried to face it together, head-on in a positive way. We have regular "date nights."

We got involved with a cancer support group.

We welcomed and accepted friends who wanted to encourage us, and stayed involved with social activities. Don't shut yourself up and become a recluse.

Finally, we kept our faith in God. Whether you're at church or fishing, *talk to him!* God listens, and he cares.

On July 01, 2009, I suited up for the first time in four months, 44 pounds lighter. I kissed my wife, thanked her for everything she had done, promised to be safe, and went back to a profession *I love.* Do you remember that the first doctor said my *job* would be over? Well I'm back in my *career, chasing bad guys!* God is good!

MARCH 25

HE WANTED TO KNOW THE TRUTH

Leilani Napp, Wife of Detective Larry A. Napp

Portage, MI

IT WAS a question I had wanted to avoid: Larry wanted to know what had happened to the man he'd shot five weeks before. (See *Devotion* on February 17.)

After Larry left for work February 17, I settled into my daily routine, which included homeschooling our two teens. Then Lt. Hudeck from Larry's department came to our house with the news Larry had been shot. Our neighbor quickly came to the house so I could go to the hospital. Later, another detective brought the children there. Knowing the seriousness of his wounds, we didn't know what to expect.

During the lengthy time he was kept in a medical coma, the house felt so empty and I felt so alone, even with family and friends coming and going. Many times all I could do was cry. When Larry was well enough I would go to the hospital and do what I could to help him feel comfortable—putting pieces of ice in his mouth, wiping his head with a damp cloth, turning the fan on and then off, and so on. I wanted him well and home so badly I'd have done anything to help speed up the process. The time came for the question I was told Larry might ask, the one I wanted to avoid. I asked Larry if it mattered, but he pressed the issue—was the man dead? When I finally told him yes, it greatly troubled Larry: What had been the man's standing with the Lord, considering the circumstances? If the man was a believer, why did he do what he did?

> Indeed, in our hearts we felt the sentence of death. But this happened that we might not rely on ourselves but on God, who raises the dead.
> 2 Corinthians 1:9

Larry received so many cards and notes that we made albums. One card that really stood out came from the man's widow. In spite of her own grief and difficult time she sent flowers and wished the best for Larry in her card. It took Larry about fourteen months to recover, giving us both a lot of time to reflect on God's grace and mercy. Not only did we experience his grace and mercy, but we felt the many prayers lifted up on our behalf.

MARCH 26

NEVER ALONE

Chaplain

Medford, OR, Police Department

IT WAS 2:30 a.m. on a Saturday morning. I had just dropped off my "ride-along" after a fairly quiet and uneventful evening. As he got out of my patrol car I said, "You know, five minutes after you leave, something big will happen and you'll miss it!" A few minutes later I found myself right in the middle of that prediction.

A vehicle, occupied by three persons, sped through a construction zone at over 100 miles an hour. Peering through a blinding dust cloud, all I could see was two small headlights as the vehicle raced passed me and headed recklessly into the night. I notified Dispatch and turned to follow the vehicle. I was familiar with the road and knew instinctively the vehicle could not make the "S" turn waiting ominously ahead. Moments later I came upon a horrific crash scene. Smoke and dust filled the darkness as did a sweet yet sickening and obnoxious odor caused by a natural gas leak, fuel from the vehicle, and a small fire. I notified Dispatch and began the search for survivors, but there was none. Bodies and body parts lay as mute testimony to the unbelievable and surreal impact of the shredded vehicle. The traffic team estimated impact speed to be near 130 miles per hour.

For a period of time, which seemed like an ageless eternity, I was alone in the quiet eeriness of the scene. Then, local residents began to appear through the surrounding trees. Moving as timid, shadowy figures, they looked in disbelief at their front lawns, slowly comprehending the devastating carnage in the wreckage strewn there.

> For he hath said, I will never leave thee, nor forsake thee. So that we may boldly say, The Lord is my helper, and I will not fear what man shall do unto me.
> Hebrews 13:5, 6 (NKJV)

Law, Fire, and Medical arrived. Their first question to me was, "Are you all right? How did you handle the initial discovery of such a horrifying tragedy?" The officers were concerned their chaplain had been alone at such a gruesome scene. Though isolated on a dark stretch of rural highway, faced with a scene forever etched in my mind, at no time was I alone. God's presence and grace had kept me calm and controlled, and his strength overwhelmed any fear or weakness I might have experienced.

That night God once again proved to me and to all who were concerned for me that he is indeed "a refuge . . . in times of trouble" (Psalm 9:9).

MARCH 27

WHAT'S INSIDE THE PACKAGE?

Sergeant Dino Heckermann
Streamwood, IL, Police Department

(Editor's Note: An officer's job is 24/365. Working holidays is not always pleasant, it is necessary in order to provide safety for the citizens served. The following was written by Detective Heckermann in relationship to Easter, and is based in part on a eulogy given by his chief, Alan V. Popp.)

Sgt. Heckermann and Chief Popp

*My experience has taught me: Police officers today come in many
different packages.
We are somewhat similar to the chocolate confectionery rabbits
that are available during Easter.
We are wrapped up in a real nice package on the outside
and look pretty much the same
with neat-appearing pressed uniforms, shinny badges and shoes.
It's not until you get us home that you discover what is on the
inside.
Are we* SOLID *or hollow?*

*For me there is no greater joy than to bite into a solid chocolate
    rabbit;*
*no greater disappointment than to feel the crumble of a hollow
    one.*
Police Officers are like that also.

*When our hearts are committed to the **Truth of Jesus**,*
everyone will notice that we are SOLID TO THE CORE.
*When we are faced with adversity; it will be the **Solid Truth of
    Jesus**,*
that will define us.

"The LORD said to Samuel, 'Do not consider his appearance or his
height, for I have rejected him. The LORD does not look at the things man
looks at. Man looks at the outward appearance, but the LORD looks at
the heart'" (1 Samuel 16:7).

"Who has believed our message and to whom has the arm of the
LORD been revealed? He grew up before him like a tender shoot, and like
a root out of dry ground. He had no beauty or majesty to attract us to
him, nothing in his appearance that we should desire him. He was
despised and rejected by men, a man of sorrows, and familiar with suffering. Like one from whom men hide their faces he was despised, and we
esteemed him not" (Isaiah 53:1–3).

This Easter I pray that you have placed your trust in Jesus—he is *solid
to the core!*

APPEARANCES CAN BE DECEIVING

Susan Skov, Parking Enforcement Officer
Independence, MO, Police Department

THE CAR was in the middle of a driving lane on a busy highway. The
flashers weren't on, and the obviously abandoned car was causing

major traffic problems. I was on my way to another call but activated my emergency lights and stopped to investigate. After checking the license and asking the dispatcher to find a phone number for the owner I got out to inspect the car. I had been thinking how careless it was to dump a car in the middle of the road, but this vehicle didn't fit the normal description of an abandoned car. It was clean, obviously well-used, and had a child's carseat in the back. As a parking enforcement officer I've seen every sort of car, in various conditions, dumped nearly every imaginable place, but not in the middle of the road. This had to be something different. But then Dispatch said the owner's phone had been disconnected. *Great,* I thought, *another dumped car!*

> The LORD is compassionate and gracious, slow to anger, abounding in love.
> Psalm 103:8

With a tow truck on the scene and my paperwork completed—including filling out citations—we were ready to clear the road. Just then I saw a man and young woman jump out of a car on the other side of the road, frantically running in my direction with a gas can in hand! There was fear in the young woman's eyes as she pleaded with me not to tow the car. Both she and her husband were wearing the uniforms of restaurant waitpersons, and I begin to "see the bigger picture."

It was then I realized that not everything is as it appears to be. As law enforcement officers it is easy to go through our days with tunnel vision, thinking everyone is a "bad guy." We forget that folks are just like us—struggling to make it through until the next day, hoping we won't run out of gas before payday, or worrying some unexpected problem may rear its ugly head and leave us in a bind.

That day helped open my eyes, to make me realize that first appearances can be deceiving. Now each day I ask God to remind me of that truth, to show me people the way he sees them, and—most importantly—to open the eyes of my heart.

A STRUGGLE WITH THE FORCES OF DARKNESS

Drucilla Wells, JD, Supervisory Special Agent (Ret.)

Federal Bureau of Investigation

*S*ANTERIA IS an African-Caribbean religion that involves worship of multiple gods, animal sacrifices, and spells. It is quite common in the Caribbean and some places in the United States. While assigned to a narcotics squad investigating a Colombian cocaine distribution ring, we found that several of the key subjects were involved in Santeria.

We arrested ten men and "Miguel," the key subject. At his court appearance the prosecutor requested no bail for Miguel, who had previously stabbed a man, fled to avoid prosecution, was a licensed pilot, and had no legitimate source of income. Imagine my dismay when the judge granted bail of $150,000, and said 10 percent of that amount would be sufficient to insure Miguel's appearance for trial! Within a few days the $15,000 was raised, Miguel was out of jail, and—no surprise—failed to appear for trial! At that the judge issued a warrant for unlawful flight to avoid prosecution, and the fugitive hunt was on!

Drucilla Wells

We learned that in jail Miguel had begun to practice Santeria rituals, including one designed to keep him out of jail. At that point God impressed upon me this was not just a fugitive investigation but a spiritual battle. In prayer I asked God to overcome the demonic forces Miguel was relying on to defeat justice and to keep him out of jail. We learned Miguel frequented a nightclub near his

111

former residence, so we set up surveillance and sent Hispanic agents into the club. They confirmed he was inside, and we began getting into position. Before we were ready, our lookout radioed that Miguel had left the club and was walking toward our location. As he rounded the corner out of view of the club we converged on him. A teammate and I started to handcuff him but he began a struggle, and we ended up on the ground wrestling with an armed subject. After we prevailed, it was off to jail!

> Ye are of God, little children, and have overcome them: because greater is he that is in you, than he that is in the world. 1 John 4:4 (NKJV)

On the way there I sat in the backseat with Miguel, who assured me he wouldn't have used his gun on me. Then he said, "I should've known things would go wrong, because a couple of days ago the spirits told me something bad was going to happen."

With his admission I realized God had used his power to overcome the forces of darkness, the so-called "gods" of Santeria that had admitted to Miguel they were powerless in the face of God. I was reminded of Ephesians 6:12: "For our struggle is not against flesh and blood, but against the rulers, against the powers, against the world forces of this darkness, against the spiritual forces of wickedness in the heavenly places" (NASB). God alone is sovereign.

"FORGIVE AND COMFORT"

Detective Corporal M. C. Williams

Colorado

WE THINK of cell phones and texting as major driving issues, but there are many others to distract motorists from their driving. Changing radio or temperature controls, eating a burger or french fries, or even reading with a book on the steering wheel—all have caused problems. Cody was distracted trying to retrieve a packet of sunflower seeds that had fallen, and the teen lost control of his pickup. He careened off the highway and struck two Colorado State Patrol troopers.

It was the afternoon of October 11, 2007. Troopers Zach Templeton and Scott "Scotty" Hinshaw had stopped to assist a motorist off I-76, northeast of Denver. Moments later, their "routine motorist assist call" became a nightmare. They were pinned under Cody's out-of-control truck, killing Zach and leaving Scotty with horrific injuries. Thinking he was dying, too, Scott cried out to God and asked Christ into his heart. A "preacher's kid," he previously had rejected the Savior's lordship. But God answered his call and, in nothing short of a miracle, spared his life. In his perfect will and mercy, God spared Scotty for greater work.

In the months to follow, Scotty endured unimaginable pain, excruciating rehab, and numerous surgeries. Throughout it all, Scotty "stayed the course," understanding he had been spared for a reason. In an incredible sense of revelation, God made it clear Scott

> Now instead, you ought to forgive and comfort him, so that he will not be overwhelmed by excessive sorrow.
> 2 Corinthians 2:7

was to forgive Cody and reach out to him. Still in tremendous pain, Scotty came alongside the young man at his trial and sentencing. He told Cody and the judge that he would "be there" to help the young man stay on track. During this process Scott—a former Marine and quintessential "cop's cop"—also responded to a new call on his life: to use the October 11 incident as a vehicle to reach others with the Gospel of Christ.

Over the next two years, Scott and his devoted wife, Susan, continued to reach out to Cody. They even brought him with them when—still very much in pain from the accident—Scott spoke to a packed house at a Centurion Law Enforcement Ministry service in Littleton, Colorado. He continued to mentor Cody, ultimately leading him to Christ. In March of 2010, Scott baptized Cody and preached both services at the young man's church.

A testament to God's grace and mercy, Scott Hinshaw is still a Colorado State Patrol trooper. At the same time, he is being used more and more to teach the Lord's message of forgiveness and salvation.

MURDER, JUSTICE, OR PEACE?

Officer/Chaplain J. R. McNeil, Badge No. 279

Pinellas Park, FL, Police Department

THE CONTROVERSY was immense: Her parents thought it would be murder, and her husband said it would bring her peace. Finally, the justice system stepped in: Terry Schiavo's long years of a wakeful unconscious state would end.

For seven years Terry had been fed through a tube. Her parents thought she would come out of her coma, while her husband felt it more humane to remove the tube. Who had legal authority to make a decision? Many—from the president to well-known celebrities—offered opinions. Because the controversy had grown strong and rowdy and she was in a

Scene outside Terry Schiavo's hospice facility

Chaplain McNeil with officers

hospice facility in our city, it became our task to provide round-the-clock security.

The situation grew quite serious. Public clamor brought the news media, traffic jams, threats of fights between opposing factions, and celebrities with their own agendas. The celebrities and national news anchors greatly increased our security problem. So many came from around the world that we deployed the SWAT Team and utilized plain-clothes detectives to blend with the crowd and take its pulse. Most of our officers were stationed outside, but I was one of a few inside. On two occasions I accompanied the attending nurse as she cared for Terry. Terry never spoke to us or, in my estimation, did she seem as if she was trying to. As a chaplain and an officer, I well understood the concerns over removing her feeding tube. There were ethical and spiritual ramifications, as well as unanswered questions about keeping her alive or letting her die. Since life is created by God, shouldn't he end it? As did many others, I wrestled with those questions as I kept watch. I couldn't help but ponder, *Is a life without apparent meaning any life at all?*

Officers around me also had their feelings and thoughts. For some it just meant overtime pay, but others were forced to think about their own mortality and end-of-life decisions. Stress appeared to be affecting every-

115

one: the parents, the husband, the crowds, and the officers. Long-forgotten moral and religious convictions surfaced. I tried to remain neutral as I listened to and comforted those who were uneasy and needed to vent

> Thy will be done in earth, as it is in heaven.
> Matthew 6:10 (KJV)

about the life-or-death scenario that absorbed us. As for me, my observation is that making life-or-death decisions about a loved one is not easy. The decision needs to be bathed in prayer, with all participants feeling a strong sense of God's leading.

PRAYED INTO CONFUSION

Sergeant David M. Greenhalgh (Ret.)

Delta (Vancouver, Canada) Police Department

ABOUT 1980, I was a detective with a suburban Vancouver (BC) area police department. One morning the whole unit was called upon to investigate the kidnapping of a Vancouver bank manager's wife. The kidnappers forced their way into her house after her husband left for work, overpowered her, stuffed her in a large box, and carried her out to a van. They then made a $200,000 ransom demand to the bank manager by phone, and he quickly called the Vancouver Police. We were very concerned for the safety of the victim, as there was reason to believe she had seen her kidnappers.

At the scene of the kidnapping I called my wife at home and asked her to start a prayer chain at our local church. For some reason I felt led to tell her to ask people to pray for God to bring confusion to the crooks. Within minutes many people were praying in agreement.

The criminals called the bank manager and gave as a drop point a garbage can location at the intersection of two streets. However, the two streets did not intersect but ran parallel. The crooks became so confused that they released the victim unharmed onto the streets. There was superb cooperation with the Vancouver City Police, and one of their alert officers stopped a suspicious-looking van. It belonged to the criminals, who were arrested and charged.

> But the LORD your God will deliver them over to you, throwing them into great confusion until they are destroyed.
> Deuteronomy 7:23

The story ran next day in the *Vancouver Sun*. I don't recall the entire front page headline except that it began "Confused crooks." I did receive some derision for giving credit to the Christian prayer chain, but that's all right: We did our job, God did his!

THE SATURDAY BEFORE EASTER

Lieutenant Chuck Urgo (Ret.)

Chicago, IL, Police Department

ONE OF the most difficult tasks assigned an officer or police chaplain is the delivery of a death notice. This was the responsibility of my department's detective division when I was assigned to it.

On the Saturday between Good Friday and Easter Sunday, my partner and I had the sorrowful task of notifying a family that a man had been involved in a fatal highway accident between Chicago and Milwaukee. We located the home in a north side Chicago neighborhood and walked toward the front porch. There we saw two little girls about 8 and 10 years of age, dressed in what appeared to be their Easter dresses. We introduced ourselves to the lady of the house, went inside, and then asked her to be seated. In making a death notice, we try to gather all members present in the house to give them the information. Of course, when the wife learned what had happened to her husband, her outcry of disbelief was to be expected. Unfortunately, I have heard that outcry too many times in my career.

> He is not here; he has risen, just as he said . . . go quickly and tell his disciples: "He has risen from the dead and is going ahead of you into Galilee. There you will see him."
> Matthew 28:6, 7

We waited until the awful news had begun to sink in and her immediate grief had subsided, and then gave her the information she needed to contact the appropriate law enforcement officials in Wisconsin. According to protocol we offered to stay with her and the children until family or friends could arrive. When we left the house I was struck by the impact our job would have on people's lives. Instantly they went from being a happy family looking forward to Easter, to being a family who would never be the same again—Daddy would not be coming home. For this family, that Saturday between Good Friday and Easter Sunday was as black as it was for Jesus' followers when he was in the tomb.

Chicago Skyline

As I pondered that thought, the Lord reminded me of the many lives that have been changed for eternity by that Passover weekend. With Jesus' death, burial, and resurrection, sorrow turned to joy, not just for his disciples but for all who receive him as their Lord and Savior. That news is so wonderful we need to share it over and over with all who will listen. *He is alive!*

APRIL 3

HIS EYE IS ON THE SPARROW

Bill Hubbard, Executive Police Officer

Taos, NM, Police Department

AS I WATCHED the small sparrow on the wire-spiked courthouse ledge tenderly care for her brood of four I thought of the song "His Eye Is on the Sparrow." Her loving care was in great contrast to why I had traveled to California from New Mexico. Another "sparrow," a young blue-eyed boy in my state had been sexually abused. To make matters worse the abuser—a so-called "family friend"—was a pedophile into child pornography.

This was the second trial—the first ended in a mistrial, which was *not* good news. Seventeen agents from as far away as Moscow, Russia, had flown in to testify, and we had to do it all over again. The only upside was that the case had gone well for the prosecution the first time.

> Do you want to be free from fear of the one in authority? Then do what is right and he will commend you. . . . But if you do wrong, be afraid, for he does not bear the sword for nothing. He is God's servant.
> Romans 13:3, 4

Even in a "best case" scenario, a case like this is a nightmare. Real children had been sexually abused to produce photos and videos shown on the Internet. The man on trial had befriended a family and abused their 7-year-old son. Then he had the audacity to brag about his conquest on "chat lines" with fellow pedophiles. While busting those men, Customs agents had come across the online "chats" that mentioned my town and the little boy's unique first name. That allowed me to find the boy and his family, who had no clue their "friend" had abused their son. I swore out a warrant for his arrest and pursued him for five months before he was found and arrested. I thank God he has not been free a single day since!

My state laws only allowed for a three-year prison term, but that gave federal investigators time to crack the codes and encryptions he had built into his computer. However, it wasn't until they intercepted his online "chats" with fellow pedophiles that the investigators were able to bring federal charges.

After five years of hard work my day in court finally came. "Please raise your right hand. Do you swear to tell the truth, the whole truth, and nothing but the truth, so help you God?" I replied, "I do."

The government's case proved overwhelming; in less than ninety minutes the verdict came: "Guilty on all counts." For ruining so many lives the pedophile was put away for life. In stark contrast to him, the sparrow went to great lengths to protect her young. God's eye is also on "sparrows" such as that little boy, and we exist to help protect them for him.

GOING UP?

Vinse J. Gilliam, Deputy Chief Investigator (Ret.)
Bureau of Investigation
Ventura County, CA, District Attorney's Office

THE THREE of us were crammed into an undersized, out-of-the-way elevator, headed for the third floor of the building, when the chief investigator led us in prayer. This was one of my first political corruption investigations, and I was undeniably nervous. What should I ask staff members as I probed for the truth? The Chief's explicit prayer, asking God to direct our interviews, gave me a renewed sense of confidence that truth would be revealed.

> Send forth your light and your truth, let them guide me. Psalm 43:3

Information had come to our office that the planning director of a city in our jurisdiction was providing favorable treatment for certain contractors in exchange for financial kickbacks. A special investigation was opened, and two of us were assigned to assist the chief investigator. All three were Christian peace officers. We decided on the strategy of an "unannounced visit" to interview the six or so employees in that department; hence, the ride on the back elevator! We anticipated interviewing two or three witnesses apiece that morning, but my interview took so long I only did one! However, this turned out to be the crucial witness who gave us the information we were seeking. The Chief's prayer had been answered, and we collected sufficient information for the planning director to be terminated.

Over my thirty-eight-year law enforcement career, I conducted countless numbers of interviews. Without a doubt, every time I sought the Lord's intervention prior to the interview, the quality of the interview and amount of information gained was substantially greater. Eventually, every interviewer learns to probe for as much information and detail as possible in the interview process. To the extent that is achieved, the more able we are to obtain unmitigated truth and a clearer picture of what actually happened in a given situation. With full and complete facts openly identified, justice can be served.

As a committed Christian, my goal always was to seek the truth and see justice applied fairly across the board. Prayer might not be considered as a standard part of an investigator's training process, but I am grateful it was part of mine. As Alfred, Lord Tennyson, wrote, "More things are wrought by prayer than this world ever dreamt of." Tennyson was right!

DEATH FROM A RATTLER, LIFE FROM GOD

Officer Randy Rich
Columbus, OH, Police Department

THE STORY of my relationship with God is like far too many: went to church as a kid; in my teens wanted to know "what can I get away with"; by my 20s replaced God with *more:* more sex, more beer, more money, motorcycles, and cars—*more!*

My dad was a good cop and a good father. He did everything possible to help us have a good life. One night when I was 21 he called me from work to see how things were going and to say he loved me. That was our last conversation. About 1 a.m. he pulled a traffic violator over. While dad was doing a computer check on his license, the man wrestled his gun away from him and shot him three times. Dad lived long enough to call for help, but died en route to the hospital. Some civilians followed the suspect, and officers arrested the killer—James Rattler—within minutes.

> Man's anger does not bring about the righteous life that God desires.
> James 1:20

Mom used to say, "God does everything for a reason." But I couldn't figure out a reason for this, and I was angry at God—*if there* was *a God!* I wanted Rattler dead, even if I had to do it myself. Through a plea bargain, he was sentenced to life in prison, with no chance of parole for thirty-three years. I hoped he would be truly miserable in prison.

I went on with my life, became a police officer, got married, and had a family . . . but nothing gave me satisfaction. I struggled with whether God was real. Finally my stepfather said, "Randy, you can be the best person you know how to be, and still not make it to heaven." He told me Jesus was God, and he held the answer to all my questions. He gave me a New Testament with Jesus' words printed in red, and I loved reading those "red" words.

Then I got to Mark 4:37–41, where Jesus and his disciples were on a boat and in a bad storm. Afraid, they woke him up, and he asked, "Why are you so fearful, how is it that you have no faith?" (NKJV) It was as if he was speaking to me: "I work in other people's lives; when are you going to trust me to work in yours?"

At that point I made the conscious decision to trust Christ with my life. My first thought was, "I need to tell others about this," but then I thought no. I'm basically a shy person and didn't want to be a pushy Christian: *I'll just share it with my family and a few friends.* However, God had other plans . . . but that's another story!

EVEN COPS CRASH!

Lieutenant Charles Grom

A Central Valley California law enforcement agency

ASK A COP why he or she gets in the business and almost always they will tell you "to help people." Ask them what they like most about the job, and it's because they get to "drive a fast car and carry a gun." All this is cool stuff, and the most fun is the car . . . that is, until you have your first accident!

After about sixteen months on the job, I was working swing shift in one of the outlying beats of the county, where I see more cows than cars. It's a great area to work if you're burned out and need a break. Usually there are few calls for service, and the traffic is so light you even have to hunt to make a car stop. It was close to 7 p.m., just as the sun was beginning to set over the hills.

A call came that a woman had taken an overdose of prescription medications, and she was fighting with the EMS personnel who had come to take her to the hospital. Not knowing what to expect I hit the lights and started my run down that old country road.

About three or four minutes later something happened, and I have no idea what it was. What I do remember was crawling out of my patrol car, standing in a field, and hearing the familiar voice of my dispatcher as he frantically maneuvered responding units to

> With one heart and mouth you may glorify the God and Father of our Lord Jesus Christ.
> Romans 15:6

123

my location. A short time later I saw lights over the ridge, and soon was airlifted to a local hospital. Based on a recording of radio traffic, which I listened to later, I had survived a very serious accident and lost consciousness for at least ten minutes. After seeing photos of the car and the damage to the farmer's fence, which had to be replaced, to say I'm lucky to be alive is an understatement!

Over the years I have wondered how I survived that crash. Many might say either it was "the luck of the draw" or because of my seat belt. I, too, have attempted to rationalize why I'm still alive. But I believe the simple truth is that God was with me that night. His plan for my life on this earth hadn't ended, and he wanted to give me even more reasons to glorify him in my life and share his Word with others.

APRIL 7

COLOR MEANT NOTHING

Reverend Dean Kavouras, Chaplain

Cleveland Division Safety Forces
Federal Bureau of Investigation

DEATH IS no respecter of persons, regardless of race, color, or creed. At dinner one evening I received a page to call on the family of a 15-year-old black girl who had taken her own life the night before. The fire and police officers who had attended asked that I go to represent them. At first I felt no urgency since the death took place nearly 24 hours earlier, but something told me I shouldn't wait.

The first people I met at the home were in the driveway. I explained why I had come, and asked if they could take me to the victim's mother. Inside were about forty people crowded into the small home. I introduced myself to the mother, telling her that the officers from last night asked me to offer my condolences and pray for the family. She sincerely was overjoyed and appreciative of their kind gesture, and immediately took me into the front room. There she told everyone to quiet down because "the Reverend is here to pray."

> It is better to go to a house of mourning than to go to a house of feasting, for death is the destiny of every man; the living should take this to heart. Ecclesiastes 7:2

Though I was the lone white face in a sea of black, we all felt the sorrow of death and the sense of God's presence.

In introducing myself, I told them the police and fire officers who attended the previous night extended their sympathies. Handling a death wasn't just a job to them, for they truly care about the people they serve. I had come at the request of those officers to pray with the family and friends, to offer comfort, and do whatever else I could. With that said, I opened the Scripture to the Twenty-third Psalm, reading in a reverent yet deliberate voice. Then I read the New Testament counterpart in John 10:1–5, 7–18, 25–30. Finally, I concluded with a prayer from the *Lutheran Prayer Book*, which reads in part, "Amid our tears O Lord, we praise you as you have received our loved one to yourself in glory for all eternity. Comfort us with the glorious hope of the resurrection and the life eternal. Grant us grace to say with a believing heart: Thy will be done. Comfort us through your Gospel, which promises strength and help to the troubled and weary. O Lord, forsake us not in this hour."

I concluded with The Lord's Prayer and the Apostolic blessing and left. As I did, a young lady said, "God bless you, Sir. You came at the right time." I thanked the Lord I had listened to his urgings and had not delayed.

APRIL 8

THE MARIJUANA USER

Brian Blumenberg
Chattanooga, TN, Police Department

ONE EVENING, while I was working on second shift, my wife was riding with me, and I was called to direct traffic at a house fire. During the blaze, several vehicles had to be redirected so they would not run over the fire hoses.

During my watch a man drove his car right up to a fire hose. When I stopped him and he rolled down the window, I could smell marijuana. In answer to my question as to whether he had any marijuana in the vehicle, he said he had smoked some earlier. I had him get out of the vehicle and got permission to search it, finding marijuana. A check of his identification revealed that his driver's license had been revoked for driving under the influence. At that point I knew I was going to have to seize his vehicle and take him to jail.

I handcuffed and placed him in the back of my cruiser, then finished all the paperwork relating to his vehicle. As I got into the car for the trip to jail, he said he was going through a rough time in his life and asked if I would pray with him. I was grateful he recognized his need for prayer, but also dismayed at the mistakes he had made that had brought him to this point. My wife and I prayed for him, then I took him to jail and booked him. Of course, when the case went to court he was found guilty.

> Confess your trespasses to one another, and pray for one another, that you may be healed. The effective, fervent prayer of a righteous man avails much. James 5:16

Later that year I had to make a call at the man's address. His wife answered the door, and I asked how her husband was doing. She told me that my arresting him and praying for him was a turning point, that he had turned his life around and was doing much better.

Many times people feel that the worst thing that could happen to them is to be arrested and spend time in jail. Yet I've heard other officers say that God sometimes uses "wake-up calls" like that to put his wayward children on the right path. Romans 13 is right: we *are* God's ordained ministering servants!

"END OF WATCH"

Linda Figgins, Widow of Sergeant Daniel P. Figgins

St. Charles, IL, Police Department

DAN FIGGINS' "end of watch" occurred April 9, 2005, when he suffered a heart attack while chasing four suspects. At two o'clock that morning, the doorbell rang and I opened the door to the St. Charles chief of police and the chaplain. I knew immediately my old life had ended and a new one begun. For a while I had a delusional belief I would wake up and the nightmare would be over. Each day brought a new pain, a new memory, a new realization I needed to adjust to "a new normal." Fortunately, my treasury of memories with Dan helped paint the picture of what God wanted me to do next.

Dan had been my "rock" for thirty-three years. He encouraged me through my bachelor's and master's degrees, then to begin teaching at the university level. He followed his own dream by changing jobs from being a grocery store produce manager to becoming a police officer. We had two daughters and expected life as we had known it would continue indefinitely. Instead, suddenly it was over.

Two days after Dan's burial I received an award from the president. The following May, I met the president a second time when Dan's name was placed in the National Police Memorial in Washington, DC. With a scholarship from the Fraternal Order of Police I was able to begin my doctoral studies. In Dan's memory we built a new home on the family farm, then had to rebuild two more times in three years—once after a flood and again a month later after it was struck by lightning and burned to the ground. Through all of this I have had to deal with a potentially deadly form of breast cancer and many months of chemotherapy and radiation.

> Love each other as I have loved you.
> John 15:12

Too often the story of police marriages is of couples growing apart, infidelities, other major family problems, and divorce. Ours was not like that. We had a strong faith in God and complete trust in each other. Dan's greatest gift to me was allowing and encouraging me to change. Together we accepted change, weaving it into a beautiful tapestry created through the process of loving one another. Dan was a brave police officer who died in the line of duty. Even more, he was a precious husband who loved me and our family.

(For information on the Foundation established in Dan's memory to help prevent police heart attacks, go to www.dpfigginsmemorialfoundation.org)

A MOTHER-IN-LAW'S PRAYERS

Constable Merv Tippe (Ret.)

Regina, Saskatchewan

WHEN YOU'RE a law enforcement officer and a guy's mother-in-law calls and asks to meet you for coffee, you really don't know what to expect. Two weeks before, I had met her daughter and son-in-law through a home Bible study, and had the privilege of seeing him commit his life to the Lord. Was the mother-in-law going to tell me some dreaded secret about his past, or chastise me for meddling in their lives? Needless to say, I was both curious and a little bit on edge!

We agreed on a time at a local coffee shop and met (if I'm going to meet with a woman alone, it will be in a public place!). After placing our orders and exchanging pleasantries, this is what she told me:

When her daughter had married seventeen years earlier she was beside herself because her son-in-law-to-be was unsaved. Greatly distraught she had fasted and prayed for ten days, beseeching God for his mercy. During that time the Lord told her that one day a Christian police officer would come to town and lead the son-in-law to Christ.

Years—and police officers—had come and gone, and she had just about given up hope. Had she truly received a message from the Lord, or was it just her imagination? Now I had come to town and led him to Christ, and she wanted me to know I was the answer to her seventeen years of prayers!

Now, none of us can argue the fact there are a number of miracles in this story—the faithfulness of the mother-in-law for being steadfast in prayer for seventeen years, her belief that a police officer would one day lead him to Christ, the fact that her prayers ended in fruition, and the miracle that God permitted me to be the officer he had identified so many years earlier.

> As soon as you began to pray, an answer was given, which I have come to tell you, for you are highly esteemed. Therefore, consider the message and understand the vision.
> Daniel 9:23

One more thing: Seventeen years earlier I was a 9-year-old boy playing with dump trucks on my father's driveway. I wasn't raised in a Christian home and had only come to know the Lord about four-and-a-half years before she called me. Was it possible God chose me all those years before to be the answer to her prayers? You be the judge!

REBELLION BROUGHT DEATH*

Sergeant Cameron J. Grysen

Houston, TX, Police Department

FIVE DAYS earlier my friend Bruno, a fellow officer, had been shot, and I was concerned. Before going to my nightside job at a restaurant/bar, I called to check on his condition, which had been critical but stable. The news that he was not expected to make it through the night left me in shock. While I was reflecting on that news, a customer told me there was a man looking into cars with a flashlight in the back parking lot. A second report came that he might have a gun. My partner was late that night, so I'd have to go it alone.

With Bruno on my mind I ran toward the back lot, determined I wasn't going to be the next officer in the department to get shot. As I drew nearer I heard glass breaking and saw the suspect. I took my pistol off "safe" and started shouting, "Police! Halt!" (From that distance he'd have a hard time shooting at me.) The suspect ran toward a getaway car, but his friends took off without him. He caught up, but couldn't get in, so the foot chase was on!

Unfortunately, he was faster than I. I'd about decided to give up when a fellow officer happened by. "Cameron, what are you doing?" I told him what was happening, but in the dark without a flashlight I was about to give up. He had a flashlight and said, "Let's go look for him."

We found him hiding under a car. My partner yelled, "Show us your hands to prove you don't have a gun!" The suspect didn't comply, so I knelt down and began pulling on his upper arm. As I pulled him out, the suspect jerked away and I fell forward. Then my pistol—in my other hand and pointed parallel to the ground—discharged! Unbelieving, I looked at my partner, who said it wasn't his. Since my safety was still off I knew it had been mine! When I asked if he was hit, my partner said no, but the suspect said yes. EMS came quickly, but the man passed away at the hospital. We found he didn't have a gun but was an ex-con, wanted, and high on cocaine. I have relived this incident

> If you do wrong, be afraid, for he does not bear the sword for nothing. He is God's servant.
> Romans 13:4

many times trying to figure out what went wrong, for I wouldn't have had it happen to my worst enemy. They say that time heals, but it doesn't—only Jesus can heal.

*Romans 13:1, 2

"YOU DON'T CARE ABOUT MY LIFE!"

Officer/Chaplain J. R .McNeil, Badge No. 279

Pinellas Park, FL, Police Department

THE YOUNG lady was driving erratically, as if sick or having car problems. When I pulled her over, her speech was slurred and she wasn't making much sense. You couldn't smell alcohol on her breath or detect it in her eyes, but I knew something was wrong. She did admit to taking medications which I knew could cause driving difficulties, so I called for backup. She agreed to exit her car, talk to me away from traffic, and take a field sobriety test. The results were positive, so I arrested her for driving under the influence.

> Listen to my prayer, O God, do not ignore my plea; hear me and answer me. My thoughts trouble me and I am distraught. Psalm 55:1, 2

In the twenty minutes it took to transport the young woman to Central Breath Testing I invited her to tell me what was going on in her life. As she talked about difficult things she was facing she began to calm down because I was actively listening to her. Then she stopped suddenly and said, "Listen to me! Here I am rambling on and you don't even care about my life!" She hinted at having a personal faith, so I mentioned I was the department chaplain, a minister, and I *did* care about her problems. She wanted proof I was a chaplain, so I gave her my business card. At that she brightened up, asked a few questions, and asked if she could call me for spiritual advice. I said she could call, but was careful to let her know I had been married forever. The tests we gave her proved she had both alcohol and controlled substances in her body, so I booked her into jail and figured I'd never hear from her again unless her case went to court.

I thought that was it, but I was wrong—the young lady did call me for advice. When her case was scheduled before Department of Highway Safety officials to see if her license should be suspended, her attorney asked if I remembered his client. I told him yes, that we had some common interests. He then said, "She said you are a minister who talked to her about her faith and getting back on track." I said yes, that I am the department chaplain and had taken a genuine interest in her situation.

When the hearing officer asked the attorney if he had any questions for me (that's their turn to punch holes in the case against his client), the attorney said no and thanked me for being so kind to his client. That just doesn't happen in cases like this! Silently I thanked God I was "more than just a cop" in this situation.

THE MORLEY STATE BANK ROBBERY

*Angie Grysen**

Widow of Bud Grysen
Sheriff of Ottawa County, MI, for twenty years

ON GOOD FRIDAY, April 13, 1963, a lone gunman robbed the Morley State Bank in Morley, Michigan. The robber drove off in his getaway car, but bank employees got a description of the vehicle along with the license plate.

The information was broadcast over statewide police radio channels, and roadblocks were set up throughout western Michigan. The state police were able to trace the license plate back to a man in Holland, Michigan, about sixty miles from the bank. Thinking the suspect might have bought gas in the area that day, Ottawa County detectives checked with gas stations, and found the suspect had purchased gas. Knowing there was a good chance the suspect might return to the area, Detective John Hemple and Sheriff Bud Grysen set up surveillance on the two roadways that led to the suspect's home. Even though he took back roads and was able to avoid the blocks, he did not

> The angel of the LORD encamps around those who fear him, and he delivers them. Psalm 34:7

131

know the police had his license number. Sheriff Grysen spotted a vehicle matching the description, drove behind it in his unmarked police vehicle, and was able to verify from the plate that this was the bank robber's vehicle. He radioed Detective Hemple for assistance and activated his emergency lights and siren.

A wild chase ensued down secondary gravel roads, reaching speeds of 90 miles an hour on streets designed for no more than 30. The suspect tried to stay on secondary roads, but eventually had to turn onto a major thoroughfare. Sheriff Grysen pulled alongside the suspect vehicle, pointing his service revolver at the suspect. It was then the suspect, Bernie West, decided to give up and pulled over. A pistol was found on his front seat, along with money from the bank totaling $9,519. He was on parole after serving time for an earlier bank robbery. For the Morley robbery, he would receive fifteen years in federal prison.

When Sheriff Grysen attempted to slow down after the chase ended, he found his brakes had deteriorated to the point only shreds of the brake linings were left. Had the chase lasted any longer the brakes could have failed, resulting in a major accident for the sheriff! As he told me that night, Sheriff Grysen believed he had been protected that day by his guardian angel.

*Mrs. Grysen has written a book about her husband's life entitled *The Sheriff*.

APRIL 14

THE MINISTRY OF PRESENCE

Steven R. Spruill

Federal Bureau of Investigation

WE HAD word a cop killer was coming to Washington, DC, to kill his girlfriend, who had been assisting the police in a "locate-and-arrest" effort. We were utilizing a specialized electronic intercept that triangulated on his cell phone signal. He had only activated his phone once the previous night, but we knew he was in the area. Word on this guy was, "If he makes you, he will run. If you corner him, he will shoot."

He made us, but he didn't run. I was the night team leader, and about 2 a.m. my telephone rang. "Send out a group page. Tell your guys to stand down; we got him. He's dead . . . but he got Billy."

Bill Christian was an old-time FBI agent everybody liked. Now he was dead! The caller went on, "I know you want to come out here, but don't. There are too many at the scene already. You probably won't go back to sleep, but just tell your guys we'll meet later this afternoon."

> Blessed are those who mourn for they will be comforted. Matthew 5:4

After he hung up I stood there silently in the dark until my wife asked, "Honey, what's the matter?"

"Babe, one of my buddies is dead."

I did the only thing I could—I drove to Billy's house. It was 4:30 a.m. The police had cut off the street to keep the news media away, and there was a bureau car in the driveway. Before walking up and knocking on the door, I prayed. Many family members were there—wife, children, sisters, and in-laws. The grief was very intense and personal. I couldn't fix anything or make the pain go away. There was no place for empty phrases designed to alleviate stress or discomfort. But I learned a great lesson there—the value of "the ministry of presence." They just needed me; they hung on to me and wept. There's a saying attributed to Mary Kay Ash: "God does not ask for your ability, or your inability, he asks for only your availability." I made myself available.

Five years later I was assigned to the FBI Academy. The anniversary week of Bill's death I got another call. Bill's youngest son had died at Bill's house, a possible suicide. Several members of our old squad and I met at Billy's house. They just needed us . . . again.

"RENDER UNTO CAESAR"

Bill Hubbard, Executive Police Officer

Taos, NM, Police Department

WHEN THE Chief says, "More traffic enforcement," it means just that. The intersection I was monitoring was the scene of frequent terrible crashes, and we needed to put an end to that. The light had turned red while the blue car was about 30 feet from the crosswalk, but the driver paid no heed. Instantly my overhead lights were on and so was the chase!

As I pulled the car over about a block later I couldn't help but notice the bumper sticker: "In case of rapture, this car will be unoccupied." This

133

was a university town, and the driver was a college-age guy, impatiently drumming his fingers on the steering wheel. Unsure of his motives, I maintained a position just behind his doorpost and asked for his driver's license and proof of insurance. "Fine!" he said. "Whatever you want; you're just an agent of Caesar, so do what you will!"

> If you do wrong, be afraid, for he does not bear the sword for nothing. He is God's servant, an agent of wrath to bring punishment on the wrongdoer. Romans 13:4

"I'm a what?" I asked.

"An agent of Caesar," he replied. "'Render unto Caesar,' the Bible says. Just do whatever you are going to do, but be quick about it." On the seat next to him was a huge, well-worn Bible, and a cross dangled from the rearview mirror.

I said, "Sir, I work for this town, not Caesar, and you deliberately ran a red light. You'll need to wait while I check the status of your driver's license and write a citation."

"Whatever," he replied impatiently. His license was clear so I wrote the ticket and returned to my young friend. When I handed him the citation I asked, "Isn't that a Bible there beside you?"

"Yes, why?"

"Well, Caesar was a Roman, wasn't he?"

"Yes."

"Well, isn't Romans a book in the Bible?"

"It is," he answered, sounding bored.

"Well, my badge number is 13, and just for fun, let's see what Romans 13 says!" Thoroughly perplexed he opened his Bible to Romans 13:1 and read, "Everyone must submit to governing authorities. For all authority comes from God, and those in positions of authority have been placed there by God" (NLT).

"Wow, how about that?" I mused. "You have thirty days to appear at Municipal Court to take care of this ticket. Please sign at the bottom and I will give you a copy." The moral of this story is: Don't play "Bible" with the cops; the one who stops you just might be a seminary graduate!

A COP AND A KID

Martin Smith, Authorised Officer (Jailer)

New Zealand Police

WHILE WORKING in South Auckland, New Zealand, as an Enquiry-car member, I was approached by an English teacher from a religious secondary school I had attended. He asked if I would do something sort of "semi-police-related, but off the record."

Seems as though there was a boy in his class who continually was *wagging* (skipping) school. The school was at a loss as to what to do; the parents apparently had tried everything they knew, all to no success. "Would you talk to him?" the teacher asked. Since both parents and teachers had run out of ideas, I agreed to talk to the boy.

One evening a few weeks later I called at the address. They were a lovely family of Mum, Dad, and five, soon to be six, kids. The father was a bus driver working split shifts, and the mother was a full-time at-home Mum. The father had found the boy

> The prayer of a righteous man is powerful and effective. James 5:16

several times sitting at various bus stops when he had been returning home from work in the late morning. The father had punished him, including corporal punishment, but the wagging continued. I began to talk to the lad but he was a bit "difficult" and I wasn't making much headway with him. I "growled at him" in my most ferocious police voice and told him there could be dire consequences from wagging school.

He started to cry, which so touched my heart I backtracked a bit. I asked him if he learned about Jesus at school, and he said he had. With his dad nearby, I asked the boy if he knew that Jesus loved him and died for him. He said yes. I thought, *In for a penny, in for a pound,* and asked Dad if I could pray for his son. He agreed to this, and the entire family was hurriedly summoned to the lounge. I cannot remember exactly what I prayed, but it somewhat was on the lines of asking God to "overshadow this boy and his family" and show them his love. As I finished praying and prepared to leave I saw tears in Dad's eyes. I couldn't help but wonder if this was the first time they'd considered prayer as an answer to their problem! A few months later I again ran into the English teacher and asked about the boy. He had not missed a day of school since!

THE BOY IN THE WELL

Sheriff Bud Grysen (Deceased)*

Sheriff of Ottawa County, MI, for twenty years

APRIL 17, 1971, is a date Sheriff Bud Grysen would never forget. A 3-year-old boy had fallen down a fifteen-foot well hole while playing with friends. The eight-inch-wide hole was newly dug, and not yet been shored up. He fell into it headfirst with his hands over his head.

Both the sheriff's department and volunteer fire department rescue unit were at the scene when Sheriff Grysen arrived. No one was sure what to do, but the firemen had started digging a hole parallel to the well just a few feet away. Sheriff Grysen did not like the looks of that, and told them to stop. The firemen were not very happy with his order, but knew better than to argue with the sheriff. Not only was he the highest-ranking law official in the county, but he also was known as both a godly and wise man. When they asked him what they should do, the sheriff said, "We'll get Bill." Bill was a friend from church and owned a construction company that dug

> He gives wisdom to the wise and knowledge to the discerning.
> Daniel 2:21

sewers. The sheriff felt Bill would have better instincts on what to do, so they sent a patrol car and got him to the site fast! Bill confirmed the Sheriff's suspicions; the rescue hole was way too close!

Bill got a backhoe and started digging a hole at an angle from several feet away. While he was doing that, the volunteers found some 55-gallon drums and cut out both ends. As the rescue hole took shape, the drums were put in place like a culvert to hold back the loose soil. When all was ready, a fire captain crawled down the hole and dug out the last few feet of sand and gravel with his bare hands. This was passed back up the line to firemen behind him. Finally he spotted the back of the boy's head and was able to rescue him. It had been a little over three hours since the first call had come in, and was a very happy ending!

When it was over, Bill told the sheriff the original tunnel probably would have caused both holes to collapse, costing the lives of both the boy and the fireman. God had been gracious in giving the sheriff wisdom to seek professional help before proceeding.

*Submitted by his son, Sergeant Cameron Grysen, Houston, TX, Police Department

LOOK UP!

Sergeant Paul
Northwest Chicago suburbs

IF YOU think you're safe from traffic in a median strip, take a tip from me—think again! It was around 1 a.m., and I'd been working a busy intersection looking for impaired drivers. For good or for bad, they weren't showing up. My assignment was to end in one hour, and I was pressuring myself to get at least one drunk off the road before then. I had made a traffic stop—a female "designated driver"—sober, but simply driving too fast. I gave her a verbal warning and sent her on her way. Then I had to complete a "stop data card," required in my state after each stop to see if racial profiling is involved (analysis continually shows it is not).

To be out of the way while completing the card, I pulled my marked squad car onto a raised median. At this intersection there are two lanes of traffic in each direction with left-turn lanes for all ways as well. This night

> But you are a shield around me, O LORD; you bestow glory on me and lift up my head. Psalm 3:3

there also were traffic barricades set up along one corner due to resurfacing being done. While filling out the stop card my head was down; I wanted to complete it quickly so there'd still be time to find a drunk before my shift was over. Abruptly, something seemed to be saying, "Look up," and I did. Headlights were coming rapidly toward me right in the median!

Quickly I threw the car into gear and accelerated into the northbound lane of traffic; I don't even recall checking to see if the lane was clear. Just as I made my move the dispatchers said an off-duty officer had called in and was following the driver. I made the arrest (got my DUI for the night!) and took a motorist off the road before he could kill someone (like he almost did me!). Video shows he was going at least 45 miles per hour, and I surely would have been dead. Watching it is surreal, as this drunk only missed me by about ten feet!

I have followed Jesus for some time, and know he called me into this profession. God has blessed me with the gift and skills to perform well. On my way to work almost every day I ask the Lord to use me to help someone: victim or offender. That morning the person he chose to help was me, and God told me to "lift up my head!"

Officer McClung with his Chief, J mmie Dotson

MY THREE ANGELS

Officer Michael D. McClung

Houston, TX, Independent School District Police Department

APRIL 19, 2010, I was responding to a school bus accident on the streets of Houston. Over the radio I heard that a fire truck responding to the accident had crashed, and firemen were ejected from their truck. I was to help with traffic control there. On my way, something happened when I came around a corner. I don't remember an impact or anything. What I do remember was being out of my body, looking down, and seeing my foot pointed left while my leg was bent to the right. After being shown this, it was as though an angel took my soul and reunited it with my body. When I came to and tried to get out of the car, I heard a very loud roar! Someone had run me off the road, my car had hit a gas main, and the line had ruptured! I was able to turn the engine off and call on the radio, but the gas was taking its toll—I was losing consciousness.

138

Through my side window, I saw a Houston Fire Department ambulance, and firemen putting on their suits. They, too, were on their way to the accident, and had seen my smashed car. There is no doubt

angels of the Lord were at work. I tried to smash the window with my baton, but could not get any strength in my swings. When I grabbed my right leg in an effort to get more leverage, there was a warm, wet feeling in my hand—it was covered in blood. I cried out, "I can do all things through Christ Jesus who strengthens me!" As I took one last swing with my baton, I must have keyed up my microphone. The last thing I told the fireman—"I can't feel my legs"—ended up being broadcast over the entire police network! Then I woke up in the emergency room. I was in surgery four hours and hospitalized four days, my leg was fractured in three places, and it would be a long time before I could return to work.

Even so, speaking later with another officer, we talked about how good God is. What he said fits best: "The angels woke you up when you needed to be conscious, and took you away in their wings at the moment you needed their comfort."

My wife later told me that my first words as I was waking up from surgery were, "I saw three angels." I have no doubt I did, for God and his angels truly looked after me that day!

APRIL 20

MAKING IT THROUGH THE DAY

Chief Robert W. Lowen
Woodstock, IL, Police Department

"How do you do it, Commander?"

"Do what?" I asked.

"How do you go on day in and day out facing setbacks, enduring the criticisms, putting up with all the garbage, and still appearing to be unfazed by it all?"

This question from my community service officer (CSO) couldn't have come at a worse time. I was working as a police commander in charge of the detectives and juvenile officers of our department. It was a typical "nonsensical day" dealing with the issues faced by a police department of a mid-size suburb bordering the city of Chicago. To be expected are the usual personnel issues,

> The testing of your faith develops perseverance. Perseverance must finish its work so that you may be mature and complete, not lacking anything. James 1:3, 4

typical citizen complaints, acting as a buffer between those above and below me and, of course, the conflicting and unrealistic expectations of City Hall. But there was one more thing: I recently had been passed over for promotion.

How *do* I do it? How does any police officer put up with a never-ending list of human problems and woes? As one man familiar with police work put it, "Sanitation workers are called 'garbage men' because they deal with people's garbage. Police officers also deal with 'garbage'—the 'garbage' of human tragedy."

I asked the CSO to walk with me over to the local coffee shop. While we walked together I talked about my faith in Christ. I pointed out that whatever we do and whoever we are, everyone is faced with trials in their lives. That being the case, how does anyone make it through? Since dealing with trials is a universal problem, there had to be a universal solution. The Bible makes it clear the solution is Jesus.

It is my trust in Jesus that guides me through each day's trials and tribulations. Colossians 3:23 says, "Whatever you do, work at it with all your heart, as working for the Lord, not for men." I told him I work for a Power higher than men, and can trust the Lord to be "a lamp to my feet and a light for my path" (Psalm 119:105). No, I don't succeed in taking all of life's curveballs as well as I'd like, but I do my best to follow the Lord's Word and make him my mainstay.

ALCATRAZ CHANGED ME!

Officer Randy Rich

Columbus, OH, Police Department

NOT LONG after I accepted Christ, my family and I were on vacation and toured Alcatraz—the prison for the "worst of the worst." A former prisoner, Leon "Whitey" Thompson, had written a book about his life. He had turned it around after prison—a U.S. president even offered to clear his record after Whitey had served all his time—but Whitey declined. In his book, he never asked for sympathy; he just wrote about his life in and out of prison. After he had been in prison several years, the guards told him one day, "Come out, you've got a visitor."

Whitey answered, "No, I don't, you've got the wrong man. *There isn't a person on this earth who would come to visit me.*"

They told him, "Yes, you do. Now come on out!" Whitey was right, it was a mistake. He had been in prison fifteen years straight without a single visitor or letter.

From his book I learned that Whitey had grown up in a family with no love. His father was an abusive alcoholic, and his mother abandoned the family when he was four years old. *He made a decision at an early age to never trust another person.* That struck deep in my heart. It didn't matter whose fault it was—his, his parents, society's, or whoever's. But to think someone could be that alone in life bothered me. My thoughts quickly turned to my father's killer, James Rattler. I began to wonder how he grew up and what prison was like for him. I couldn't hate him anymore—Christ had taken the hate away. I actually cared about Mr. Rattler. (See April 5 devotion.)

Late one night the Holy Spirit led me to write him a letter. I mailed it in faith, but I didn't tell anyone about it—not even my wife or mother. In my heart I knew it was the right thing to do, and I knew it was right in God's eyes. I figured no one would understand, especially the police officers I work with. Some were with the department the night dad was killed, and I thought perhaps they would think like I used to, that all killers should be executed, especially a cop killer.

> For if you forgive men when they sin against you, your heavenly Father will also forgive you. But if you do not forgive men their sins, your Father will not forgive your sins.
> Matthew 6:14, 15

My letter began, "To James Lumpkin-Rattler, You've never met me but we have a connection. You killed my father."

LETTER TO A COP KILLER

Officer Randy Rich
Columbus, OH, Police Department

"To: James Lumpkin-Rattler

"You've never met me but we have a connection. You killed my father. You need to know that I am a Christian. I believe in God, I believe in Jesus, and I believe that Jesus died for all sinners. I have sinned and am not a perfect person. You have sinned and are not perfect. No one and nothing on Earth will ever be perfect, but the Lord forgives. *He loves you.* He can answer any question you have about life. But you have to ask. To do this you just need to talk to him by praying.

"You and I probably grew up in very different ways. I was born into a family full of love. My dad worked very hard, and did the best he could at being a father. He spent time with me, took me places, taught me, punished me when I needed it, told me he was proud of me when I did something good, and often told me he loved me. If you did not have this kind of relationship with your family, I'm sorry. You may feel that nobody loves you. That is wrong—God loves you. He made you, and God does not make junk. *You have done some terrible things, but that is the past. If God forgives you, so can I.* You may have to spend years and years in prison for what you have done, but faith can get you through it."

I told him my dad had wanted to see his grandchildren, but Rattler had murdered him two-and-a-half years before my first child was born. Until heaven, my dad would never meet his four grandsons. That was the hardest thing for me to deal with, and the reason it had been so hard for me to forgive Rattler. I went on to tell him what God had saved me from—and what he could save Rattler from: hate, sin, greed, and temptation, and that God had replaced these with hope. I told him how to learn about God: to pray, to ask a chaplain for answers to questions, and to read about Jesus in the New Testament (that's what turned *my* life around). I closed by saying, "I wish you Peace and Happiness (it can be found inside prison walls). Here is a prayer, given to us by God, which I say several times a week":

Randy Rich

> Our Father which art in heaven, Hallowed be thy name. Thy kingdom come, Thy will be done in earth, as it is in heaven. Give us this day our daily bread. And forgive us our debts as, we forgive our debtors. And lead us not into temptation, but deliver us from evil: For thine is the kingdom, and the power, and the glory, for ever. Amen.
> Matthew 6:9–14 (KJV)

APRIL 23

RATTLER WRITES BACK

Officer Randy Rich
Columbus, OH, Police Department

RATTLER WROTE me back. Before I read it I was scared and excited at the same time. I was afraid he might say, "*Screw you, I didn't kill your dad!*" or, "*Yeah, I killed your dad and I enjoyed it!*" Or would he make a lot of excuses and blame my dad? He didn't do any of that. He said he wept when he read my letter. He said he didn't know how I could forgive him after all the pain he'd put me through, that he couldn't stand to see himself in the mirror, and he wished he could end his life. We've written back and forth for several years now, and I truly think he's come to the Lord. However, my correspondence with Rattler is only a small part of the story. It was the start of a life-changing process. I thought I'd written Rattler to help him know God better, but God used it to open *my* eyes and to grow *my* faith.

> I was in prison and you came to visit me.
> Matthew 25:36

When I showed the letter to my wife and my mom, several things happened: Neither thought I was crazy; my wife said it helped her understand

143

me better; and our marriage was strengthened. She talked me into giving a copy of my letter to a friend who hated his mother, and hadn't spoken to her in years. After a lot of persuading I did. After reading the letter he called his mom, told her he forgave her, and they patched things up. Now she comes to visit him and her grandchildren. Wow! All because I handed a guy a piece of paper. I liked this feeling of being used by God!

That began the process of sharing my story with others and following God's lead, even if it led me out of my comfort zone. Friends told me there is an ongoing prison ministry team in our area, and suggested I join. I now work SWAT, but was in undercover narcotics for years. The thought of my going into prison to interact with inmates might not be a good idea. What might an inmate do if he found out I had worked undercover? Worse yet, what if I ran into one I'd locked up? I've always heard you cannot trust any prisoner, but I was learning you can trust God. I had the "joy of the Lord," and I wanted to share it. Though I felt like "a lamb being led to slaughter," I didn't care. All the negative thoughts trying to keep me from going into prison could not outweigh my desire to tell others how much God loves them. I accepted, and became part of the team.

"NO FEAR IN LOVE"*

James L. Day, Senior Chaplain
Manteca, CA, Police Department

ONE OF President Franklin Roosevelt's most-quoted sayings is, "The only thing we have to fear is fear itself." Quite often we find that truth played out in everyday life.

One of our female officers was assigned to notify a young wife of her estranged husband's death, and I was asked to accompany the officer. The separation was not the wife's desire; she had wanted to make her marriage work. To compound the hurt, her husband drowned on an outing with "another woman."

The officer and I met with the young widow, trying to console her while she dealt with grief, anger, and fear. She would be responsible to bury her husband, but had no money. Her only hope was her father-in-law, who, according to her own testimony, "hated [her] guts." How might he respond? In talking it through, she agreed for me to call the father-in-law to discuss the situation. He had been notified of the death by another law enforcement agency, so was dealing with the tragedy himself. He agreed to a meeting with his daughter-in-law and me, so we made plans to meet the next morning at his home.

The wife was so fearful about things, she didn't know whether her husband's dad would pay for the funeral. She wasn't even certain he would allow her to attend. However, before the meeting was over he agreed to both. As we prepared to leave we saw the hand of God working in the man's heart. He placed his arms around his son's wife and said, "I'm sorry for what you are going through. I know you loved my son and I know that, like me, you must be hurting terribly." He then kissed her on the cheek and we departed.

> If it is possible, as far as it depends on you, live at peace with everyone.
> Romans 12:18

It brought to my mind 2 Corinthians 5:19: "God was reconciling the world to himself in Christ, not counting men's sins against them. And he has committed to us the message of reconciliation." While the clear context of this passage refers to reconciliation with God, we know it is well within the will of God that we be reconciled with one another. In this situation, God accomplished his purpose of reconciliation, and healing had begun.

*1 John 4:18

FOUR TWENTY-THREE A.M.

Chris Wilson, Crime Analyst

IT WAS early in the morning—4:23 a.m.—when I was awakened. There wasn't a lot of sleep time left before I had to get up, and I really wanted to go back to sleep . . . but I couldn't. I kept hearing the word "Pray" being whispered softly, so I did. God showed me a police officer whose face was not clear, but I knew he was from my own department. He was kneeling with weapon drawn from a cover position in front of a house. I had no idea what was going on, but could see he was in a residential neighborhood with dawn breaking behind him. I knew he needed help and began to pray fervently. Finally I started to drift back to sleep. It was 4:55 a.m.

When I walked into the Gang Crimes office at 7:30 a.m. one of our sergeants was talking to a clerical staff member. He asked, "Did you hear about the officer-involved shooting this morning?"

> I will praise the LORD, who counsels me; even at night my heart instructs me. Psalm 16:7

I don't listen to the news on my way to work, so I asked. "What shooting?" They told me a woman's boyfriend in a southwest Las Vegas neighborhood had taken her and her children hostage. Officers convinced him to walk outside the residence. When they commanded him to lay face down on the lawn, he turned away from them and reached for a gun in his waistband. The officers had no choice but to fire, killing him instantly. When I learned who the suspect was I recognized his name—he was a gang member who had been extremely violent with officers in the past and continually in and out of jail.

Recalling my early morning "wake-up call" I asked, "What time did the call come in?"

The clerk pulled up the record and answered, "The call originated just after 4 a.m., but it looks like the shooting occurred at 4:57."

A shiver started at the base of my neck and continued down my spine: *So that's why God woke me up when he did!* It was then the sergeant asked me, "Do you still pray for us?"

I told him, "Of course, every day."

After reflecting on that for a moment he smiled and said, "I'm sure glad someone does—we need all the protection we can get on these mean streets!"

Since that day I have never doubted that if you are open to God's leading to pray for others, he will call on you when needed—even in the middle of the night!

GOD MADE THE DIFFERENCE!

Sergeant Mark Oliver, Badge No. D 745

New Zealand Police

I HAVE A friend in the States who once asked the local chief of police how it would affect their workload if there were no domestic disturbances. The chief said it would be cut by two-thirds. Our experience in New Zealand is similar.

One problem the police have with domestic incidents is getting a statement from the injured party. I remember one incident involving a woman's former partner. He had come around to her house and, when she refused to open the door, broke into it and assaulted her son. He tried to assault her as well, but fled when he realised the police had been called. The woman herself had been on the wrong side of the law several times, and was frightened about talking to us. Because she was so nervous, it was difficult getting a statement from her as to exactly what had happened. She looked like she had lived a hard life, having been raised in a gang environment and exposed to the harsher things of this world. I had a real sense of needing to tell her I was a Christian.

> For we are to God the aroma of Christ among those who are being saved. 2 Corinthians 2:15

I don't remember why, but the feeling of need was very strong, probably coming from a leading by the Holy Spirit. A sense of relief came over her when I told her I was a believer. She recently had become a Christian, and that was part of the issue with her ex-partner. She was trying to remove destructive influences from her life, and he was one of them. I then suggested that before she gave her statement, we should pray and seek God's guidance and peace over her and the situation. There in the station's interview room we bowed our heads and prayed. As a result she was able to calmly and methodically explain what had taken place. Once again, God made a difference in a place where her previous interactions had been strained. This time she felt at ease talking to a police officer, and it was a positive experience for me as well.

THE HANDSHAKE

*Detective/Sergeant Ingrid Dean**
Michigan State Police

POLICE OFFICERS are taught many techniques in perfecting our skills. My specialty is interviewing and interrogation, so I've become quite proficient in observing small details. One of those that has affected my career in a spiritually significant manner is the common handshake. I believe handshakes have protected me, warned me, informed me, and relieved me. I think God speaks to me through handshakes. Just like a polygraph is used to detect false statements, a handshake often communicates to me whether a suspect is guilty or innocent.

There's more to a handshake than simply grasping another's hand. In high school a teacher taught my class how to shake hands. We were to grip firmly; not too tight, but not too loose. In the process of shaking hands we were always to look the other person in the eye. That tells you a great deal about them. He taught us that from your handshake the other person is able to determine your sincerity, your attitude, your level of confidence, and your personality. He used to say, "You'll never be unemployed if you know how to do this." My personal experience is that he was right!

> I will give thanks to the LORD because of his righteousness.
> Psalm 7:17

One of the things police often do when wrapping up a case, leaving a scene, or parting company in any situation is to congratulate each other, perhaps with a slap on the back, shaking hands, or some other similar gesture. When policemen are doing that, sometimes we forget others may be watching: family or friends of someone killed in an accident, bystanders who can't understand our need for emotional relief, or a suspect seething with rage. We are public figures, always on display, and can greatly affect how the community feels about us by how we comport ourselves in public.

Why have a story about handshakes in a book like this? First, as a detective, I wanted you to be aware of how observant and aware police officers must be all the time, and the toll it takes on us psychologically. The range and intensity of emotions we experience in any given day is more than the average person feels in a month. One moment we're at peace, the next moment quite excited. Our heart rate increases and decreases quite dramatically. I think that is why many officers die of heart attacks not long after retiring. Second, as a Christian, I realize I am hypersensitive to clues given off by those I interrogate, and I believe that is a gift from God. While a handshake may be small in the scheme of things, it has helped bring closure and fair justice in many cases . . . and I praise and thank the Lord for this gift.

*Sergeant Dean is the author of *Spirit of the Badge.*

APRIL 28

THE INTERROGATION

Detective/Sergeant Ingrid Dean
Michigan State Police

WHEN I first shook his hand, I knew something was wrong. He was a nice-looking, 30-year-old man, with soft, brown eyes. However, I felt his appearance belied the truth. I could feel it; it left me very uneasy; God was saying, "Be careful," and I called on him for guidance.

A small police department asked me to interrogate him. A 13-year-old girl was missing with no explanation other than foul play. She was an all-A student, loved her friends and teachers, and had no reason to run away. The man had been at her house a week prior, after having met the girl's mother at a bar. Just out of prison after a ten-year sentence, he had befriended the family, helped repair their car, and spent Saturday night at their house. A week later, after partying all night, the mother returned home and found that her daughter was missing. Police found a corner of the suspect's prison ID card stuck in the latch of the door. He said that the weekend he was there, he had demonstrated to the mother how to break into her own house if she lost her keys. I thought, *His explanation might be plausible to a jury, but not to me.* I could tell by his handshake that something was wrong.

> In my distress I called to the LORD; I cried to my God for help. Psalm 18:6

After hours of talking, I finally gained his trust by "getting inside his head," and he confessed to his horrific crime. He had been bar hopping, looking for the mother. When he couldn't find her he got mad, broke into the house, and convinced the girl her mother needed her. The little girl didn't seem surprised, put on her shoes, and went with him wearing only her pajamas.

After he bought her a Coke at a convenience store, he wondered what he should do. He said, "I broke into the house, I am on parole, and I didn't want the little girl to tell. I had to do something to her." Eventually he took her into the woods and killed her in ways not fit to describe. He seemed to be without feelings and totally dissociated from the event. However, he agreed to take the police to the scene.

As I was leaving, the local officers shook my hand in congratulation. Then the thought came to me, *You'd better shake his hand, too, or you could lose his trust!* It had to be God, telling me the job wasn't complete until he led the police to her body. Though just touching him and looking again into his eyes gave me great distress, I responded to God's voice. I reached for his hand and told him very sincerely, "You're doing the right thing." I had also done the right thing.

WAS I TOO LATE?

Lieutenant Kyle Harris

Norman, OK, Police Department

SUICIDE IS hard to take. Everyone involved wants to know what went wrong; could we have done more to prevent it? This is especially true when you're involved with the person at the point when they're halfway between life and death.

This suicide took place during the day in an apartment complex parking lot. An ex-husband, against whom a protective order had been filed, was spotted by the maintenance man. By the time police arrived, the "ex" had piped exhaust into his car through one of the windows and duct-taped all the vents. When he knew he had been spotted, he left the parking lot for another area. Other officers were called, and we began searching for the vehicle. Within ten minutes it was found - parked in front of a business about three blocks away. As I pulled up, the officer who found it had reached the vehicle and begun to break out the window

> Preach the word! Be ready in season and out of season. Convince, rebuke, exhort, with all longsuffering and teaching. 2 Timothy 4:2

with his ASP (trade name) baton. By the time I reached the car, the ex-husband had taken two razor blades and severed both jugular veins. He also had lacerated his trachea. I later learned he was a registered nurse, so knew exactly where to cut. Having prior paramedic training, I knew the situation was grave. We already had called for the fire department and an ambulance to respond "code 3." I relayed my observations to Dispatch, and asked them to tell EMS to hurry—the ex-husband was moments from death.

After other officers had taken the razors from him, I entered the car and attempted to stop the bleeding. He turned to me, our eyes meeting, and said he would not hurt anybody. I knew he was dying. Even though I was concerned that my peers might make fun of me for doing it, I knew I needed to witness to the man. I told him about the Lord, and asked him to accept Jesus as his Savior. He never answered me, and died seconds later. In my heart I know God led me to that call to be there with that dying man. While I won't know until heaven, I pray that in those few moments before entering eternity he did take that final, saving step.

Yes, suicide is hard, and one can't help but wonder what the results might have been if someone had taken time to witness to the person before that day. We never should be too busy to neglect that!

HER TESTIMONY CHANGED ME!

David Laumatia, Senior Sergeant
New Zealand Police

BECOMING a detective was going to be the highlight of my life, but instead it resulted in sin that eventually led to separation from my wife. Even though we got back together, the trust in our marriage had gone. During that hard time I began to feel there had to be more to life than what I was experiencing.

One night the partner of one of my officers phoned in sick, so I worked with the officer in his place. I knew Carika was a Christian, and thought I was, too. But as we cruised and she shared her faith, I knew I didn't have the kind of relationship with God that she did. One thing she said that really hit home was that if she did not speak to God every day, she felt miserable. This bothered me, for I said grace before meals and prayed when I was in big trouble, but that was it. I remember asking God if he was real and, if so, could he make himself known to me?

A year later a police friend who knew I was seeking God recommended I go down to a local church, so I did. I listened intently as the preacher spoke powerfully from the Bible. When he finished, he said that if anyone wanted to receive Jesus as their Lord and Savior they should come to the front. A swarm of people rushed forward, but the cop in me held me back at first. Eventually I went forward, and an older man came and prayed with me. Right then I knew I was a sinner, repented in my heart, and received Christ into my life. That night changed me forever!

> So do not be ashamed to testify about our Lord.
> 2 Timothy 1:8

After being touched so powerfully by God, I went home and told my family, "God is real, God is real!" They looked at me as if I had lost my mind, but over the next several months they saw good changes in me. In time God changed all of us and restored our family, and now my wife and two sons also serve the Lord with all their hearts. I am so thankful to Carika for sharing her faith with me. Everywhere I go I tell people that if I don't speak to God every day I feel miserable! Prayer *does* change things.

PRAY, BARB! PRAY!!

Detective James H. Keller, Badge No. 4682

Des Moines, IA, Police Department

WHEN MY wife got home from Wednesday night church, she asked if anything had happened "last Tuesday morning" while I was on shift. I asked, "Why?"

She said her friend Barb had told her this: "About 2:40 a.m., God woke me telling me there was danger and I needed to pray. I did, then fell back asleep. About 2:55, God woke me again and said, '*Now pray, really pray*!' I prayed for ten to fifteen minutes, then felt a peace come over me and I went back to sleep."

My wife continued, "Jim, tell me what happened!"

At that time I was working in uniformed patrol from 10:30 p.m. to 6:30 a.m. in the inner city. We would park in strategic locations near known drug houses, and stop everyone coming or going from those houses. In the process we wrote any and every ticket we could, checked people for warrants, and made many arrests. This made us very unpopular with the occupants! In one three-unit apartment building, at least two were dealing drugs, and a female informant told us they *really* wanted us dead. We turned up the heat, sometimes sitting in their own backyard on lawn chairs!

> I urge, then, first of all, that requests, prayers, intercession and thanksgiving be made for everyone. 1 Timothy 2:1

The night in question, for safety we were slumped down in our car in the alley, barely seeing over the dash. The sideview mirror was turned so I could see down the side of the squad car, and I saw someone crawling on the ground. I yelled, we bailed out, and a known dealer/user started to run. When we caught up to him he was sweating profusely, shaking, and begging us not to kill him. I had a shotgun pointed at him, and he crawled up and tried to put his mouth over the end of it. I pulled it away and asked, "What are you doing, man? What's the matter with you?" We patted him down—no dope, no weapons—ran him for warrants, then kicked him loose. This doper always acted strange, but this time he was stranger than usual.

By now it was about 3:10 a.m. We went back to our spot in the alley, and about 5:30 saw the female informant in her car. We pulled her over and she told us, "Oh, my gosh, you're alive; I can't believe it!" Then she said the doper had been sent out with a handgun to kill us!

Later, when I told my partner about Barb's experience, he replied, "Tell Barb that when God tells her to pray, *pray!*" And I did!

MAY 2

IT HAPPENED
IN AN INSTANT!

Deputy Andrew McIntosh
Crawford County, AR, Sheriff's Department

JUST THREE weeks past graduation from academy, my dream of a career in law enforcement ended when I became the victim of a careless driver. A detention deputy was riding with me, and we had been talking about "religion." I carried a Peace Officer's Bible in my car, but never read it and didn't go to church. I had a nagging feeling God was trying to get my attention, but, like the prophet Jonah, I ran.

At a major intersection, a car approached from the side at a high rate of speed. Before I could get his attention with my lights, he ran the stop sign and hit me. The crash knocked my car onto an embankment, and I felt a sting in my back and a sharp pain down my right leg. I knew I should remain still, but I felt responsible as an officer. I checked on my passenger, who also was injured, then got out of my car. The driver of the other vehicle got out of

> Consider it pure joy, my brothers, whenever you face trials of many kinds.
> James 1:2

his car, and told me his hand was hurt. I asked bystanders to move down the road and stop traffic, then notified Dispatch. The radio lit up with chatter when they heard an officer had been in a collision and was down. The pain became more intense, and I collapsed into my seat when backup arrived.

As they were running tests at the hospital, a fellow deputy called my wife to tell her what had happened. When she arrived and burst into tears I told her, "I'm fine; just a few scratches!" However, the pain persisted after I returned to work, and I went in for more tests. My lower lumbar discs—L-5 and S-1—were herniated into the spinal cord, and I needed surgery. Thus began a year where I had two surgeries with two metal cages, two metal rods, and ten screws installed in my back. My career was over.

I realize that sometimes God uses our worst times to get our attention. As devastating as this has been, I have returned to the Lord and become closer to him. I also have become closer to my wife and children. Though the accident caused much pain, God has eased it with his peace. Through my hurt I rejoice, for now I am free from what kept me from God, and realize how blessed I am. I know God will continue walking with me as I try to honor him in my life.

WALKING WORTHY

Bill Hubbard, Executive Police Officer
Taos, NM, Police Department

IN EPHESIANS 4:1, the Apostle Paul writes, "I, therefore, the prisoner of the Lord, beseech you to walk worthy of the calling with which you were called" (NKJV). Therein lies the reason many Christian officers don't let it be known they are Christians—they aren't walking worthy of their calling.

One thing the law enforcement world has learned—or *should have learned*—from the Rodney King incident is that the whole world is watching. In this day of photo/video-taking cell phones, not to mention our own dashcams and digital pocket recorders, if *we* aren't recording an incident on the street, odds are *someone* is! As an instructor and field training officer, I tell officers not to do or say anything on (or off) duty they'd be ashamed for their mom to see or hear. If they can't order a felon out of his car at gunpoint without dropping the F-bomb, they need to rethink what they are doing. I will always remember a high-ranking, churchgoing officer in our department testifying in court about a foot pursuit and drug arrest. The jury loved him; he was every mother's son . . . until his dashcam video was played. The jury was visibly set back by it. When the court recessed for a break right after the video had been played, the embarrassed officer told me, "I guarantee you *that* will never happen again!"

The whole world *is* watching. As *Christian* police officers, we need to realize that not only the whole world is watching, but other cops are

155

watching, too. I have heard that St. Francis of Assisi said, "Preach the Gospel at all times and, when necessary, use words." In my book, Christian officers should choose to be physically fit, clean-talking, nondrinking, non-tobacco-using, spouse-loving Christian men or women.

And, since the Bible says we are "working for the Lord, not for men" (Colossians 3:23), shouldn't we be the first-on-the-scene, take-down-the-bad-guy, make-the-best-arrest, and make-it-stick-on-paper *best* police officer we possibly can be? We should be role models for those around us.

The Bible calls us many things. We are the *ecclesia*, or "called-out ones." We are "priests" who are "living stones" being built into a spiritual house (1 Peter 2:5 NLT), we are "followers of this Way" (Acts 22:4). With all this, shouldn't it be the goal of every Christian—regardless of our occupation—to walk worthy of our calling?

M A Y   4

WHEN IT'S YOUR OWN CHILD!

Herbert Cropp (Ret.)
McHenry County, IL, Sheriff's Department

AS A SHERIFF'S deputy I've made many calls. Some of the most frantic calls have come from anxious parents, and too often the situation has not turned out well.

On this particular day I was training a new officer, letting him drive the squad car for the first time. Most new officers have "mixed emotions" about that experience. On the one hand they're quite proud to be driving a high-powered car equipped with all the "bells and whistles." On the other, they're not yet familiar with all the controls, and their training officer is by their side. It's a little like taking your first driving test as a teen. We were patrolling on the opposite side of the county from my home when Dispatch radioed me, "The rescue squad is en route to your home because your two-year old daughter isn't breathing." I was in shock, not

Herb Cropp (2nd from right) in retirement photo

knowing what to do next when another officer radioed and told me he would cover my patrol area. With that "go ahead," I told the trainee we would switch places so I could drive. Red lights flashing and "the pedal to the metal," away we went! Looking over at my trainee I said, "Let's pray!" He kind of slid down in his seat, either out of fear for his life or ashamed of my reckless driving. I know we went too fast, but it was *my* child!

> I will proclaim the name of the Lord. Oh, praise the greatness of our God! Deuteronomy 32:3

By the time we'd covered the miles to my house, the rescue squad was pulling away with my daughter in the ambulance. My wife was in tears and planning to follow it. She said rescue had gotten our daughter to breathe sporadically, and she seemed to be getting better. Our daughter did get better, was kept in the hospital overnight, and we brought her home the next day. That was a long time ago, and she now has daughters of her own. Interestingly enough, when one of *her* daughters was two, they went through the same thing and had to call the rescue squad!

Throughout our scare, I kept our daughter before the Lord in prayer. I still thank and praise him daily for all the ways he protected me in my policing career and watched over our family. As for the trainee, he survived the ordeal and we rode together again. But from that point on, I don't think my observations of his driving bothered him—he already knew mine was far from perfect!

THIS NINJA WAS
NO TURTLE!

Sergeant Cameron J. Grysen
Houston, TX, Police Department

VROOM, VROOM! Looking in the side mirror of my patrol car I saw a blue Kawasaki Ninja motorcycle coming. I was on evening shift and waiting at a red light, wondering if this was the guy who'd run from officers five times in the last week.

When he popped a big wheelie and ran through the red light wide-open, my wondering was over! I hit my emergency equipment and put the pedal to the metal, but he left me like I was standing still. I put the information out on the radio and saw another unit pull in behind him about a half-mile ahead. However, I stayed in the chase.

Over the radio the other unit said the Ninja had turned at the next major intersection. When I got to there, traffic was backed up because the light was red, so I decided to cut the corner through a gas station. I was going to head past the pumps, but saw a young gal gassing her car; she had the biggest "deer in the headlights" look I'd ever seen, so I thought I'd just "slide around" the back of the station. About this time the other unit put out

> Though he flees from an iron weapon, a bronze-tipped arrow pierces him. Job 20:24

on the radio he thought we'd lost him. Imagine my surprise when I got to the back of the station to find myself face-to-face with the blue Ninja. I didn't want him to get away again, so I made it clear any action he made would be met with an equal and opposite reaction. He did the right thing and gave himself up!

He said he thought it was "fun to run from the police," but his running days were over. He had become a Slow Ninja Turtle! I was reminded of Psalm 139:8–10: "Where can I go from your Spirit? Where can I flee from your presence? If I go up to the heavens, you are there; if I make my bed in the depths, you are there. If I rise on the wings of the dawn, if I settle on the far side of the sea, even there your hand will guide me; your right hand will hold me fast." What a great thing to know!

HE DIDN'T SEND ME HOME!

*Deputy Michael Davenport, Badge No. 496**

Oklahoma County, OK, Sheriff's Office

"THANK YOU for not sending me home to my Mom and Dad." Those few words—spoken by a child for whom Davenport had served as a court-appointed special advocate (CASA)—will be forever etched in the memory of Michael Davenport. A reserve deputy for the Oklahoma County Sheriff's Office, Davenport joined the CASA program near the end of 2001, and quickly established himself as a very strong voice for the children. Unfortunately, Oklahoma led the nation in the number of children harmed or killed by their caregivers when the courts unwittingly returned them home. A strong Christian and a defender of home and family, Officer Davenport wanted to make a difference.

As Davenport says, "When I became aware of the tremendous need for child advocates and mentors, I decided to reorder my priorities. I wanted to do my part to assure that at least some children could have their best interests represented." Due in part to his training as an officer, Davenport's court reports were so well prepared that the first judge who received one showed it off to the other judges. Later, Davenport was asked to teach an advanced court-report-writing class at the state level and subsequently was honored as "Rookie of the Year."

> "Let the little children come to me, and do not hinder them, for the kingdom of God belongs to such as these."
> Mark 10:14

CASA volunteers can choose their cases, and Mike told them to give him the toughest ones they had. Not satisfied simply with being an advocate, Davenport has obtained free tickets to local sporting events, and has sponsored a free bowling night for all children in the state-run youth shelter. For the past several years he has organized a gift drive to hold a Christmas Eve party for all children who must spend the holiday in the shelter. For all his efforts, Officer Davenport was recognized as the Reserve Deputy of the Year 2008 by the Oklahoma Sheriff's Association.

*Reprinted with permission from *Oklahoma Men* magazine, March 2008

"JUST FOLLOW THE POWER LINES"

*Sheriff Bud Grysen (Deceased)**
Sheriff of Ottawa County, MI, for 20 years

MAY 7, 1962, five-year old Tommy vanished around 4:45 p.m. while playing with friends behind his home. It was a scrub-covered, swampy area with many sinkholes, not far from the *Grand River*. They were playing hide-and-seek, and it was Tommy's turn to hide. When he didn't respond to repeated calls to "come out," his friends told Tommy's parents he was missing, and they called Sheriff Grysen.

At the scene, the Sheriff organized the search effort. Ultimately, nearly a thousand volunteers scoured the swamps and woods throughout the night and the next day. They found one of Tommy's shoes, but no sign of the boy. His mother said all he had on was a sweater, little protection against nighttime temperatures in the low 40s. The chances of finding him alive diminished by the hour.

> Jesus said, "Whoever follows me will never walk in darkness..."
> John 8:12

Next morning the Coast Guard sent in a helicopter and a search plane. Several area factories shut down so workers could help in the search. One worker, Henry Vanderwall, stayed out till 2:30 a.m. looking for Tommy. After a little sleep, Henry went to work at his regular time, but couldn't get little Tommy off his mind. When he asked his boss to let him rejoin the search, the boss let him go.

Back at the scene, Henry searched again in an area that had been covered before. There, he heard the voice of a small boy hollering: "Dear Lord Jesus, get me out of here!" Henry headed toward the voice and found Tommy stuck knee deep in the swampy backwaters of the *Grand*. When Tommy asked Henry what he was doing there, Henry said: "I'm looking for you!" He freed Tommy from the muck, and the boy jumped into his arms. Henry wrapped Tommy in his leather jacket and carried him back out to the road. They were spotted by a State Trooper who fired three shots in the air to let everyone know Tommy had been found. Henry stayed with Tommy in the rescue truck on the trip to the hospital, and the boy's parents met them there. They were overjoyed, thanking everyone. Though they had been praying for the best, they were prepared for the worst.

160

Tommy said he had been frightened by hunters, and got lost in the woods when he ran away from them. His grandmother had told him if he ever gotten lost to follow the power lines, and they would lead him home. He did follow them, but had gone the wrong way.

*Submitted by his son, Sgt. Cameron Grysen, *Houston Police Department*

PRISONERS IN OUR OWN PRISON

Deputy Sheriff Eric Haskins
Oklahoma County, OK, Sheriff's Office

IN THE EARLY morning hours of May 8, we were scurrying about making breakfast preparations for the 2,700-plus inmates in the Oklahoma County Detention Center. Unknown to us, three inmates from the Special Housing Unit (SHU) were making preparations of their own. Two were awaiting trial for first-degree murder, and the third for several other serious charges. They had taken two guards, their clothing, and duty belts. Using the guards' keys they tried to access the unsecure side of the jail in the basement, but could not. When they forced an officer to call over his radio for the door to be opened, the officer gave subtle clues that something was wrong.

The inmates took their hostages back to the second floor, where they captured two more guards. When I arrived I saw a man in a uniform like mine, but when I was within an arm's length he pulled a homemade knife ("shank"), and forced me into a hallway. There I saw four co-workers handcuffed and kneeling on the floor. My lieutenant had a shank to his neck, and soon we both were handcuffed. Then two more guards were taken. So many thoughts race through your head at such a time. My lieutenant and I shared a moment of "We can take these guys," but when you see your co-workers handcuffed and defenseless, guarded by a man with a shank, you set your bravado aside and do what you can to ensure the safety of your fellow officers.

> You gave me life and showed me kindness, and in your providence watched over my spirit.
> Job 10:12

161

Two more friends were taken by surprise, and one was stripped of his uniform and duty gear. Six of us were locked in a visitation room, and my lieutenant and another officer were taken downstairs as a human shield. Though the inmates were just a few feet away from a waiting ride, civilian clothing, weapons, and the freedom they craved so much, so, too, was an armed deputy sheriff. He drew down on the first two inmates as they tried to reach freedom, and drew again when the last inmate made it downstairs. Soon these three very dangerous criminals were back in custody.

It was by the grace of God no one was injured or killed. I believe that if the hand of God had not covered us that night, the whole situation would have gone a lot worse. I praise him for his providence!

MAY 9

SIXTEEN AND PREGNANT

Herbert Cropp (Ret.)

McHenry County, IL, Sheriff's Department

WHILE I was a patrolman I really enjoyed cruising the unincorporated subdivisions of McHenry County, especially stopping and talking to the young people. I became friends with many, and when they would see me patrolling they would come running up to me—all ages, from children through teenagers. We would talk about a lot of different things, such as what was happening in their lives, at school, etc. Trying not to be too bold or overpowering, I would give them friendly advice about working hard in school, not dropping out, listening to their parents and teachers, being truthful, and never being afraid to ask for help or advice.

One day a 16-year-old girl I'd talked with several times came up to me in tears. She said she was pregnant and did not know what to do. She had not yet told her parents.

"We gave you strict orders not to teach in this name," he said. Peter and the other apostles replied: "We must obey God rather than men!" Acts 5:28, 29

We had a long talk and I told her that God loves her, we would pray together, and she should tell her parents. When she asked about an abortion, I responded, "No. God loves all children including the unborn. Tell your parents and seek help from your friends and church. After the baby is born try to finish high school.

Thank God it all worked out. She kept the baby, and we talked several times after that. Over the years and with promotions that moved me into other areas I am sorry to say we lost track of each other. But I will always be thankful God gave me words to say that saved the life of an unborn child and put a pregnant teen on the right track.

In today's environment of so-called "separation of church and state" many jurisdictions tend to frown on conversations between officers and civilians where God or Jesus is mentioned. While such "gag orders" are unconstitutional, many officers feel too intimidated to say what needs to be said. I am so thankful that, when this took place 35 years ago, that feeling wasn't so prevalent.

BROKEN AND BLESSED

Deputy Eric Haskins
Oklahoma County, OK, Sheriff's Office

ONE OF the more difficult passages in the Bible may be James 1:2, 3: "Consider it pure joy, my brothers, whenever you face trials of many kinds, because you know that the testing of your faith develops perseverance." Not too long ago, several events gave me a lot more "pure joy" than I'd ever expected in my life!

My "joy" began when I was taken hostage in the jail where I work, then had to confront the three guilty career criminals face-to-face in a courtroom. Less than a month after that, the doctor told me I was a candidate for the same type of cancer that had claimed my mom's life. We were into the Thanksgiving and Christmas season, and my "joy" wasn't very joyful! As I began to sink into terrible depression, my relationship with my wife deteriorated rapidly, and we separated.

While I struggled with all this, I wasn't able to find many blessings or much "joy" in my life. I struggled daily looking for "highs" among the "lows," but they didn't appear. The problem was simple: I wasn't walking with God. As a kid, my mom forced me to go to church with her whenever the doors were open. But when I turned 18, I rebelled and quit going. I considered myself a Christian, but it was not evident in my daily life.

One day I wandered into a bookstore in the mall. There I saw a title that struck deep into my soul—*Battlefield of the Mind* by Joyce Meyer. Based on 2 Corinthians 10:4, 5, it summarized everything about my life that was wrong. I had to "take captive every thought to make it obedient to Christ" (v. 5). The instant I saw the book, I had to have it. As I began to read, it was clear to me God had a plan for my life (Jeremiah 29:11), and I needed to follow it. I took the Lord as my companion, and the pain and sadness slowly began to subside. There was a lot of growing to do, but I was beginning to find the "joy" James writes about.

> Through faith (you) are shielded by God's power. 1 Peter 1:5

When I made the conscious decision to have a relationship with God, I found out firsthand he is the great Comforter. As my Christian walk grew stronger, I was reunited with my wife and family, and began to see God's blessings in my personal life and my work. Like the Prodigal Son, I was welcomed home into the open arms and heart of God. The trials were rough and my faith was tested, but the adversity brought me where I needed to be—safe in the arms of Jesus!

CODE 444—OFFICER NEEDS HELP!

Chris Wilson, Crime Analyst

HENRY PRENDES was an experienced officer who hadn't worn his vest that February morning because he expected to be in the office all day. When a call for a domestic disturbance came about 10 a.m. Henry didn't give his vest a second thought.

A young woman's boyfriend was beating her, but she had escaped to the front lawn when the first officers got there. When Henry arrived he started for the door, disregarding advice not to go in. None of them knew the boyfriend was an aspiring gangster rap artist with a song, "I'm waitin' for the police to come to my door with my AK-47 and I'm gonna shoot 'em." When Henry walked through the door, the boyfriend did just that—

he shot him! The force spun Henry around, and he collapsed just outside the door. The other officers took cover and tried to locate the shooter, who appeared moments later in a second-story window and began firing at them. They were hopelessly outgunned. A Code 444 (officer needs help ASAP) had gone out as soon as the first shots were fired, and both the Metro helicopter and every officer on duty in the valley was called. Officers in the helicopter could see the dire situation, but they didn't have a rifle. Finally a gang officer arrived with his AR-15, hoping to engage the suspect in a diversionary gun battle while officers pulled Henry to safety. Seeing this, the suspect came to the doorway and shot Henry twice point-blank in the head, killing him instantly! We all were devastated!

It was the first "line-of-duty shooting death" in Las Vegas in eighteen years, and more than fourteen thousand friends and officers from around the United States and Canada attended Henry's funeral. At the close of the two-hour ceremony the pastor spoke of Henry's relationship with Christ and gave an altar call. More than four hundred in the auditorium and 150 listening outside raised their hands and were given confirmation cards. More than 90 percent of those cards went to uniformed officers.

> "Where, O death, is your victory? Where, O death, is your sting?"
> 1 Corinthians 15:55

Later an additional two hundred police officers and firefighters indicated they had prayed to receive Christ. Believers who worked at Metro met daily to pray for more to come to Christ, and many did. We won't know until heaven how many made that decision, but we know Henry's testimony and his violent death pointed many in that direction.

THE WINDOW AND THE BUTTON!

Officer Dan Wolke

Berkeley, CA, Police Department

YOU WOULDN'T normally think of a car window and a metal button as being much protection against a bullet, but it sure worked for me! As a 22-year-old Berkeley police officer I was ambushed and shot after a routine car stop. Later I learned that the three in the car were members of a militant group. Others of that group had shot two Oakland officers a few weeks earlier, killing one and seriously wounding another.

On that dreary November night, just after midnight, I approached a car being driven erratically. Before reaching the driver I felt the leading of the Holy Spirit warning me of danger, so I began walking backward toward my patrol car. Just then, the passenger in the back seat fired several times through the side window about three feet from me. One of the bullets struck me in my stomach as it passed through a metal snap in my jacket. My face and eyes were covered with blood and glass from the shattered window. Standing behind my patrol car, I heard their car doors open and one of the shooters say, "Let's finish him off." I returned fire, striking the driver in the chest. He drove a few blocks before hitting a telephone pole. The car overturned, and the three were arrested a few moments later.

> Love the LORD your God, listen to his voice, and hold fast to him. For the LORD is your life.
> Deuteronomy 30:20

Lying on the ground bleeding, I wondered if I would survive, and prayed that God would save me. I held on to that prayer as I was rushed to the hospital. As it turned out, I was not seriously wounded. God used the car window and my jacket button to slow the bullet down and save my life! This was years before bulletproof vests.

That incident taught me two things: To pay attention when I sense God is telling me something; and remember the power of prayer. I asked God to bring a special godly woman into my life, and he did. I daily asked for his protection over me and my family, and the Lord took me safely through 33 years as a police officer. Two years after retirement, God called me to minister to the Benicia Police Department as a chaplain, and I gladly answered the call. Now I use my being shot and other experiences to share how important it is to be a Christian, and to seek the Lord's guidance and protection in all we do!

I WAS FOREWARNED BY GOD!

Officer Karyl Moore

Traverse City, MI, Police Department

THERE WAS no reason for my anxiety, but the Holy Spirit inside me seemed to say, "Use caution, this is no ordinary traffic stop." The truck's sole occupant, a male, pulled over. With my stomach churning and the hair on my neck bristling, I took a "police-academy-trained position," well behind the doorpost with a good view of the driver's movements through the rear window. As he twisted his body around to show his license, he appeared uncomfortable through his dark glasses. As I told him I'd stopped him for speeding, I kept the conversation brief because he terrified me so much!

Back in my car, the computer system confirmed his identity, but said his record was clean. In astonishment I thought, *If that is so, why do I feel so afraid?*

I was only going to give him a warning to cut things short, but the Holy Spirit seemed to say, "Do not fear; I am with you always." So, I completed the ticket and went back to his truck. He took the ticket and then began a delusional conversation about the Mafia, which seemed very real to him. When he asked if I'd seen *The Godfather* or *Copland*, with Sylvester Stallone, I said no and concluded the conversation.

> Listen to his voice, and hold fast to him. For the LORD is your life.
> Deuteronomy 30:20

Immediately I went back to the station to search for information on him. There was none! Next day at roll call I asked others about him, telling them of his delusional state and my feeling he was "a trigger waiting to go off!" He remained so heavy on my mind that I rented and watched *Copland*, still wondering why. Three days later when I returned to work, I found out why. We received a "man with a gun" call just two blocks from the department while I was on assignment to locate a man walking and carrying a child. They were passengers in a car accident and left the scene. And where did I find them? Two houses away from the man with the gun. And who was the man with the gun? It was the man I had stopped for speeding!

Isaiah 30:21 says, "Whether you turn to the right or to the left, your ears will hear a voice behind you, saying, "This is the way; walk in it." I know that's what happened at the traffic stop: God gave me the alertness I would need a few days later. Who knows what might have happened if I had not listened to his voice? My personal belief is that my preparedness may have saved the lives of the man and the child I had been seeking, and my life (as well as the life of the "man with a gun").

TRAVERSE CITY ISN'T *COPLAND*

Officer Karyl Moore

Traverse City, MI, Police Department

THE DELUSIONAL speeder I'd stopped a few days earlier frightened me into watching the movie *Copland*, a story of police corruption in New York City. In it, Sylvester Stallone takes on the NYPD to triumph over evil. Now, standing with a gun in his hand on the porch of his house, the speeder had become Stallone.

My assignment had been to find a man and child who'd left an accident scene, and I found them two doors down from the gunman. After directing them to safety, I took up a position across the street from the gunman and drew my weapon. One of our sergeants was on the sidewalk, engaged in conversation with the gunman. I felt as if I knew this man well after my prior contact and seeing the movie. I knew what to expect: He'd begin a gun battle, and I might have to shoot him! With that in mind, I began to think through such facts as the weapon I was carrying, the caliber of bullet, and the trajectory it would probably take.

Eventually a shootout did occur, and our sergeant lay wounded and bleeding on the gunman's front porch. After the shooting I started negotiating with the man to allow us to help our officer. The gunman moved inside his house and fired several more shots. I prayed, "Lord, let my voice be that of an angel to his ears." I started speaking again. I told him I was the officer who'd stopped him last week,

> The LORD is on my side; I will not fear: what can man do unto me?
> Psalm 118:6 (KJV)

168

and that Traverse City wasn't *Copland*—that we're good people here and didn't want to hurt him. He remained silent. I continued to negotiate with him, praying for him, our wounded officer, the neighbors and officers around me. Suddenly, a sheriff's deputy rushed the porch and pulled our sergeant to safety. For a long time I continued negotiating with the shooter, repeatedly asking God for the right words to say, and for an angelic voice to say them. Later, SWAT arrived and after a nine-hour standoff, the gunman was taken. Our sergeant had been shot multiple times. Unfortunately, he lost his struggle for life the next day.

From the time I stopped the speeder until he was taken into custody, I know that the Lord was watching over me. I thank God for the Holy Spirit living within to protect, guide, and comfort me through life's toughest challenges. I constantly listen for his voice and reassurance: "Do not fear, Karyl; I am with you always."

MAY 15

PEACE OFFICERS' MEMORIAL DAY

Kristi Neace*, wife of Officer Richard Neace

Union, MO, Police Department

IN 1962, President John F. Kennedy signed Public Law 87-726 designating May 15 as Peace Officers' Memorial Day, and the week in which May 15 falls as National Police Week. President Bill Clinton amended the law with the Violent Crime Control and Law Enforcement Act of 1994, which directs that the American flag be displayed at half-staff on all government buildings on May 15 each year. This is a tribute to the more than 16,000 law enforcement officers who have died in the line of duty, and is the rarest of all honors. The only other regularly scheduled day when flags fly at half-staff is Memorial Day.

National Police Week is recognition by our government that fallen law enforcement officers, as did members of our armed services, died while protecting the lives and freedom of others. As a further reminder, the national Concerns of Police Survivors (COPS) organization distributes more than one-and-a-half million blue ribbons for display on cruiser and private auto antennas during Police Week. While the actual dates

169

change from year to year, National Police Week is always the calendar week, beginning on Sunday, that includes May 15.

> "How the mighty have fallen! The weapons of war have perished!"
> 2 Samuel 1:27

One year on May 15, my sons and I sat at Busch Stadium in St. Louis in anticipation of a special ceremony honoring peace officers in the region. When the sea of blue and black uniforms marched into sight, my eyes suddenly welled up with tears as I thought of how these brave men and women watch over us day and night. Romans 13 tells us they are God's representatives for justice, and they are a visible reminder of God's constant love and care for us. How honored I felt to be part of the police family! Some in the stands may not have had the same highly charged sense of pride I felt that day, but the crowd's genuine respect for our officers was quite evident in the thunderous applause. It was a time when we remembered those who had fallen, and celebrated the courage of those still in service.

*Author, *Lives behind the Badge*

MAY 16

"THAT NONE MAY DIE IN VAIN"

Chaplain C. Grant Wolf (Ret.)
Chattanooga, TN, Police Department

THE SETTING was serene and the mood somber: Citizens of Hamilton County, Tennessee, had unveiled a permanent law enforcement memorial to honor local officers killed in the line of duty. That beautiful May morning in 2003, an impressive memorial was dedicated to show grateful appreciation for those who had made the supreme sacrifice to "serve and protect" their fellow citizens. The five-and-one-half-ton bronze memorial is impressive, but its real significance is in what it represents. Within niches on three sides are life-size bronze figures: a grieving man, a grieving woman, and St. Michael, the patron saint of police. The fourth niche, facing a timeless marble wall, is empty, symbolizing the loss of slain officers to the community.

Plans for the memorial had been set in motion fifteen years before. In 1988, then chief deputy, Jim Hammond (later sheriff), persuaded county commissioners to designate a site near the new courthouse where a fitting memorial could be erected. Later, the chief and his staff initiated a countywide effort to raise funds for the memorial. But ten years before it was completed, annual services began on the site, where a "pocket park" had been created.

Now a tradition, the morning service is "always the same, yet different." Local, state, and national law enforcement agencies are represented, as well as many dignitaries. On the opposite side of the wide street where the memorial is located, a long row of police cars are parked side-by-side. The service begins and ends with prayer, and the "The Star-Spangled Banner" is sung. Chairs are placed to the side of the memorial for dignitaries, and in front—facing it—for family members of the deceased. There are brief speeches, but the main emphasis is a ceremony honoring the dead. As the name of each deceased officer is called, a uniformed officer from his or her agency comes forward, places a rose at the base of the memorial, salutes, and retreats. All is silent except for the rustle of leaves and songs of birds. This is a time and place where the dead are honored. At the close of the service the blue lights on the cars are turned on, symbolizing the "thin blue line."

> "How the mighty
> have fallen in battle!"
> 2 Samuel 1:25

Daily, the memorial reminds us there is a price for freedom, and that price may demand lives. And once a year, during National Police Week, we honor those who have paid the price—"that none may have died in vain."

THE LITTLE BOY

Detective/Sergeant Ingrid P. Dean

Michigan State Police

THE ONE-CAR accident had happened only minutes before, and I was the first officer on the scene. It was the middle of the night and, except for my red patrol lights going 'round and 'round, the road was dark and lonely. Even whoever had called in the accident was nowhere to be seen.

171

A woman had rolled her SUV and was dead, squashed between the driver's seat and steering wheel. The silence gave a false sense of peace—until I heard the whimpering of a child. The vehicle was lying on its side, and when I walked around it I saw a little boy laying half in and half out beneath it. The roof covered and pinned his legs and torso, while his head and arms were free. I felt helpless: There was no way I could lift that vehicle! I phoned to make sure help was on the way, and prayed that just one car with a bunch of people in it would drive by. But nobody came.

The child was conscious and in a surprised voice asked, "Are you a *real* state trooper?"

I couldn't help but chuckle and said, "Of course I am, silly! I know, I'm just a girl, huh?"

He gave a half-smile and then blurted out, "I want my mom! Where's my mom?" Marble-size tears fell down his cheeks, and I saw no reason to tell him she had died.

Instead, I tried to reassure him. "My friends are helping her; they're going to take her to the hospital. But, you know what? I don't have any children. Could I be your mom just for a while?"

> "But now that he is dead . . . Can I bring him back again? I will go to him, but he will not return to me." 2 Samuel 12:23

He nodded his head and said, "Okay . . ." I took his hand in mine.

He was a sweet-faced boy with brown, curly locks, and the most beautiful, big eyes I'd ever seen. He looked up at me seriously. "Am I going to die?" For a split second, I choked. He had obvious internal bleeding, and things didn't look too good.

Regaining my composure and without hesitation I said, "No, you won't die. Whether you decide to live in heaven or choose to stay right here on Earth, you will still be you. Either way, you will still be alive. Nobody ever dies. We all live forever."

He looked into my eyes and I felt he understood. With the hint of a smile, trustingly he squeezed my hand. Then, after what seemed like an eternal moment, he took his last breath and gently passed away.

WE GET ACCUSED!

Sergeant Cameron J. Grysen
Houston, TX, Police Department

EVEN THOUGH we are warned about it in the academy, "being accused" is something we don't expect. "He used foul language when he arrested my innocent little boy!" "He's racist!" "She tricked me into thinking she was a prostitute and I was 'set up.'" The list is endless. You least expect it when you do a good deed for a neighbor, and they lie!

We were living in an apartment when one evening my wife let out a blood-chilling scream: "Cam, help! Get out here!"

She and our daughters were playing outside when the lady next door came dragging her two-year-old by the arm, yelling "She's dead!" When I got there, the lady literally hurled the child—who was limp as a rag doll—at me! The little girl was not breathing and turning blue, and the mother ran back to her door crying out of control. The child still had a faint heartbeat, and my wife thought the little girl might have something stuck in her throat. After the Heimlich maneuver didn't work, I held her upside down and thumped on her back. There were no results from that or from trying to breathe air into her lungs.

> May integrity and uprightness protect me, because my hope is in [God]. Psalm 25:21

Not knowing what else to do, I slowly moved my finger down her throat. I almost had my whole hand in when I felt part of a corncob. By pushing my finger to the side and using my fingernail, I was able to pull it out. Simultaneously, she started sucking in air and convulsing, and her jaw locked down on my finger. When she finally came to her senses I was able to get my finger and the corncob out of her mouth.

What do you suppose the end result of my good deed was? After her daughter started breathing, the mother took her to the ER, where they found the child had a broken arm. The mother told them I did it, and the next day Child Protective Services paid me a visit! My version of what happened seemed to satisfy them, and I never heard from them again.

Most officers learn to be pretty "thick-skinned" about the accusations we receive, but those accusations still hurt. As God's ordained ministers, we do our best to follow The Golden Rule as we "protect and serve." But for our protection, we depend on him!

FROM BULLETS
TO WALMART

Sergeant Dino Heckermann, Badge No. 3537

Streamwood, IL, Police Department

A FEW SUMMERS ago in a gang-related shooting, someone shot at a residence on three separate occasions. Once, a bullet lodged in the wall right above a four-year-old girl's headboard while she was sleeping. The child's father, "Pete," was a gang member, and though he lived elsewhere, the residence had been targeted by a rival gang. I knew "Pete" and his gang very well and had arrested Pete on several occasions. His identifying facial tattoos and other facts left no doubt—Pete definitely was an active gang member.

As time passed the mother and little girl moved away and faded from my memory. My family and I had also moved to a new home and were shopping one day at the local Walmart. It was there I saw Pete with his wife and daughter. Our eyes locked, and I instinctively put my hand in my pocket where I always carry my off-duty firearm. My family was busy shopping, oblivious to Pete, but he never left my sight. They had no idea who Pete was. I had hoped we would pass without incident, but it turned out our daughters were friends and attended the same elementary school. Our families struck up a conversation when it struck me: *Here I am with one hand on my off-duty weapon, while I am greeting Pete's wife and daughter with the other hand!*

During that school year I often saw and spoke with Pete at recitals and school activities, even holding each other's video camera to record our daughters' performances during musicals. God tugged at my heart to talk with him about spiritual matters, and soon we were greeting each other with hugs. My wife and daughters became aware of how I knew Pete and they began to pray for him and his family. We also shared with them how Jesus has transformed our lives.

> And we know that God causes everything to work together for the good of those who love God and are called according to his purpose for them.
> Romans 8:28 (NLT)

As summer approached, my daughter suggested we invite Pete's daughter to attend vacation Bible camp at our church. When we asked her parents they said yes, so I spent a week that summer taking the two girls to and from vacation Bible camp, thanking and praising God. It was amazing for me to realize how God had spared a gang member's little girl to become my daughter's friend, and that he had allowed me to be a witness to Pete and his family. Yes, God is good!

A NEEDLE IN A HAYSTACK!

Officer Chuck Lerner
Cleburne, TX, Police Department

DID YOU ever look for "a needle in a haystack?" That's what it's like when you're trying to find a specific car among hundreds of thousands in your area, especially when it's the border towns of El Paso, Texas, and Ciudad Juárez, Mexico.

An elderly woman had been carjacked at a mall, and the thief threatened to kill her. I had a radioed description of the suspect and stolen vehicle, and diligently began searching the area. With no idea where to begin my search, I earnestly prayed and asked God to be my guide. I was quite concerned the suspect might strike again, this time actually assaulting or killing his victim! God literally directed me to get on the freeway!

As I entered the on-ramp the suspect in the stolen vehicle passed directly in front of me! After radioing other officers for backup, we safely stopped the vehicle and arrested the carjacker without any injuries. Incredibly, the suspect did not attempt to flee or fight. He actually "thanked" me for arresting him, because he said he knew he would have continued carjacking and robbing people. We later learned

> Therefore I tell you, whatever you ask for in prayer, believe that you have received it, and it will be yours. Mark 11:24

he recently had been paroled from prison, and had committed a similar carjacking the previous day. With his arrest we recovered both of the vehicles and other stolen property, and were led to three additional suspects involved in the case.

With my adrenaline lowered and time to reflect, I was amazed at and strengthened by the way in which God answered my prayer. If I had entered the freeway even a minute or two before or after the time God directed me there, I might never have seen the stolen vehicle and the suspect might not have been caught so quickly. As I've learned many times, God's timing is always perfect!

There have been numerous instances when God has helped me do my job as a police officer, but this case stands out as a clear example of what an awesome God we serve, how much he loves and cares for us, and how much he hates sin and evildoers. Most importantly I know for certain He does answer prayer!

PLANTING AND WATERING

Officer Steve Gilmour

Chicago, IL, Police Department

MOST CHRISTIANS have an opportunity every day to work and/or converse with nonbelievers. This is especially true in policing, where believers and nonbelievers often work alongside one another. That pairing, together with the "craziness" of our work, is a good reason Christian officers really need to stand out and be an example.

One otherwise uneventful night I was on patrol with another officer. We were talking and getting acquainted with each other. The conversation finally turned to a point I could share my faith with him. I explained that my life is based on my belief in God, and that Jesus died on the cross for our sins. The officer expressed admiration for my life built on faith, but said he really wasn't on the same page. After that, any effort on my part to further the conversation about the Lord and faith just didn't get anywhere.

> I planted the seed, Apollos watered it, but God made it grow.
> 1 Corinthians 3:6

Though outwardly he didn't seem interested, I sensed that inwardly he did want God in his life. The Lord had allowed me to plant seeds in his heart, and the Holy Spirit seemed to be calling me to pray for this officer daily. I had to keep in mind that it takes time for fruit to grow from a seed!

For more than a year I prayed for this officer each day. Through that period we only worked together a few times and, to be honest, I didn't go much further in discussing the Gospel with him. Then one night I was walking through the station's parking lot, and spotted him in his squad car. He was looking up songs on his "I-Pod" that he had downloaded from a Christian station. When I asked about this new interest in Christian music, he replied, "I don't know why, but recently I've just felt really moved to read the Bible and listen to this type of music. I think I'm becoming a born-again Christian." With "the table set," God opened the door for me to openly share the Lord and offer my help in advancing his faith. Since that night the officer has proclaimed his faith in Christ, has been diligent in reading the Word, and is living a life radically transformed through the saving grace Christ offers.

Most Christians have loved ones we hope someday will accept the gift of salvation. From firsthand experience, let me assure you prayer works. We may not immediately see the fruit, but if we plant the seed and water it faithfully with our prayers, God will give the increase!

MAY 22

TWO CHANGED HEARTS

Anonymous

Sheriff's Deputy, Florida

A LONG-TIME law enforcement officer, my many years of dealing with felons and ex-cons had left me cynical and suspicious as to whether they could truly change . . . until I met Eric.

One of our members had invited him to church, and we got acquainted. After greetings he said, "You don't remember me, do you?" When I told him I was sorry but I didn't, he went on, "When I was 15, you arrested me for burglary!" He said that arrest was one of many that finally put him into the Florida State Prison system at age 21. By then he had become an avowed Satan-worshipper with satanic tattoos covering his hands and arms. He flaunted them to show others how wicked he was.

Then something dramatic happened: in prison he went to a Bible study with another inmate. The teacher explained the Gospel; he was intrigued to know more, and took the free Bible offered. He read and read, and soon realized Jesus is truly God. He turned to Christ in saving faith, repented of his sin, and trusted Christ alone for his salvation. Dur-

177

ing his three years in prison, Eric attended a weekly Bible study and spent much time reading and studying the Scriptures. Released from prison just before his 25th birthday, he returned home and looked for a good Bible-teaching church. That's when we met.

Eric and I established and nurtured a friendship that should not have been. He was a convicted felon, and I was a suspicious cop. Unlike many "jailhouse repenters" I'd met, Eric truly had a changed heart. He even spent thousands of dollars on laser treatments to remove the satanic tattoos. Though his father had mistreated him as a boy, Eric wanted to obey Scripture by showing him honor and respect. Because his father was in bad health from years of alcohol abuse, Eric moved to his area to help care for him and to share the Gospel. However, before he moved he made certain there was a solid, Bible-teaching church there.

> I will give you a new heart and put a new spirit within you.
> Ezekiel 36:26 (NKJV)

As I look back, I realize our friendship was made possible only through Jesus Christ. In prison, Eric's heart had been changed. In our friendship, Christ changed *my* heart also. He gave me strength to overcome my cynicism and dislike for individuals in Eric's position and to see Eric for who he had become—"in Christ . . . a new creation." Too often we fail to see that Christ really can change hearts, whether criminal or cop. But he can, if we are willing to allow it!

MAY 23

IT WAS NOT TO BE

Officer Mark Dennis
Franklin, LA, Police Department

AS A POLICEMAN I witness many things in my work, some of which are very unfortunate. One of those, working crowd control at a hospital where many friends and family members of a patient have gathered, is a somber and sacred responsibility. It doesn't take long to identify the believers and the unbelievers. While both are tearful, the quiet calm demonstrated by believers is in great contrast to the loud, fearful wails, often accompanied by cursing, that come from unbelievers.

Officer Dennis on a mission trip to Kenya

On this day in May, I was called to the hospital after 5½-month-old Thomas had been rushed unresponsive to the emergency room. When the child was taken from the ambulance, he appeared to be a normal little boy, but he was fighting for his life. As doctors and nurses worked to save the life of this child, my mind raced back to my son at that age and the anxiety I would have had in the same circumstance.

> [Jesus said,] "Everything is possible for him who believes." Immediately the boy's father exclaimed, "I do believe; help me overcome my unbelief!" Mark 9:23, 24

The body language of nurses going in and out of the room where Thomas lay told the story—things were not going well. The desperate father kept asking them to "do something!" Unfortunately, the "something" Thomas' father wanted was in God's hands, not theirs. I had been asking the same thing of the Lord, knowing that only our infinite God could accomplish what Thomas needed.

A little after 10 o'clock that evening the nurse brought the sad news Thomas had died. I couldn't help but think of the incident in the Gospel of Mark when Jesus' disciples could not drive an evil spirit out of a man's son. Realizing the situation Jesus said, "'O unbelieving generation, . . .

179

how long shall I stay with you? How long shall I put up with you? Bring the boy to me.' So they brought him" (Mark 9:19, 20). When the disciples asked Jesus why they had been unsuccessful, he said, "This kind can come out only by prayer" (Mark 9:29).

Leaving the hospital I thought to myself, *I am part of that faithless generation.* I don't mean to be, but too often I walk by sight and not by faith. "Oh, God, forgive me and allow me to walk in faith each day."

CHARM SCHOOL FOR OFFICERS

John T. Campbell – I.D. 14716
California Highway Patrol

WHEN THINGS turn out contrary to an officer's expectations, that officer can exhibit emotions such as disappointment, anger, and frustration. Since such emotions can affect our behavior toward people with whom we come in contact, many departments have initiated "Charm School" for officers who get a lot of citizen complaints.

An illustration of the need for Charm School is the thin line between *truth* and *judgment. Truth* is when an officer stops a suspected violator for driving under the influence. When alcohol impairment seems above the legal limits the officer should arrest the driver by saying, "You're under arrest for driving under the influence of alcohol." This is a truth that can be verified by investigation. *Judgment* enters in when the officer says (in so many words), "You're under arrest for driving under the influence of alcohol, *you piece of garbage.*" By the addition of a comment like that, the officer has crossed the line between truth and judgment. Because the officer is angry at the violator's words or actions, the result can be that he charges the citizen with more violations to teach him a lesson.

> . . . in truthful speech and in the power of God; with weapons of righteousness in the right hand and in the left . . .
> 2 Corinthians 6:7

Christian officers shouldn't need Charm School. Instead, we should let God order our steps and reflect Bible truths in all we do. The problem is that many Christian law enforcement officers, like far too many Christians in all walks of life, have not yet matured. In 1 Corinthians, chapter 3, the apostle Paul lamented that instead of being able to handle life like mature adults, the Corinthian believers were still acting like infants. For officers who are not believers, the situation is even worse.

As long as there are citizen complaints, departments will need "Charm School." Unfortunately, these secular schools won't accomplish as much as they should because they're not tackling the real issues: unsaved officers and "baby Christian" officers. Without a "heart understanding" of how God wants us to act in relationship with others, their behavior won't change much. God said in the book of Romans he has "ordained" officers as his ministers of justice. Some officers—even Christians—may need "Charm School." But to be true to their ordination, what officers really need is Christ.

GOD VERSUS GPS

Tanya Stanturf

Independence, MO, Police Department

ALTHOUGH 9-1-1 operators hear a lot of things, something they don't want to hear is a father saying, "I think my son is going to kill himself tonight!" Obviously we have to remain calm and think fast when a call such as that comes in. I got as much information from the father as I could—the son's name, address, landline and cell phone numbers, make and type of vehicle he drove, etc. I also asked for the name of the cell phone carrier, in case we had to track the son down through the GPS (Global Positioning System) in his cell phone.

The father lived out of state, unavailable to help us in person. He told me his son was despondent over a breakup with his girlfriend, and the father had no idea where his son might be. We sent officers to the address where the son lived, but found no one there. The cell phone company was asked to trace the longitude and latitude location of the phone, which we hoped was with the son. We sent officers to that area, but they did not find him. When an officer on the opposite side of town asked

> Be pleased, O LORD, to save me; O LORD, come quickly to help me. You are my help and my deliverer; O my God, do not delay. Psalm 40:13, 17

181

for a description of the son's vehicle, we radioed the information to him. The officer then said he believed he had the vehicle in sight.

At first the young man refused to pull over. However, after the officer followed him for a short distance, he finally did. When the officer walked up to the vehicle he found a hose attached to the tailpipe and stuck through the window. The officer immediately called for an emergency ambulance as the son was disoriented, not very alert, and not breathing very well. But we had found him in time.

I felt very bad for the parents, as I had talked to them numerous times throughout the many hours it took to find their son. Considering we couldn't locate him through GPS (the cell phone company had given us incorrect latitude and longitude information) and the son was actually on the opposite side of town, you'd have to say we found him by "pure luck"—or through God's guidance. There's no question on my part: God triumphed over GPS that night and saved the young man's life!

MAY 26

LAWRENCE GETS A NEW HAT!

Jason J. Everett
Rolling Meadows, IL, Police Department

WHETHER LARGE or small, head wounds are "bleeders," and can cause panic. This was the case with Lawrence.

When I got to his home I could hear hysterical screaming all the way outside. Lawrence's mother had a towel wrapped around the 6-year-old's head while tears streamed down her face. She was nearly incoherent trying to explain what happened, and I could see why the child was screaming so. When a parent is scared, so is the child. His mother's fears panicked Lawrence, and his screaming and thrashing was deepening the wound.

I sat Lawrence—still screaming—down with me on the couch. Uncovering the wound, I could see it was deep enough to expose a small bit of bone. Looking into his eyes, in my best authoritative voice I said, "Lawrence, look at me . . . in my eyes!" When I asked if he was hurt, with a sniffle he nodded yes.

Did he know who I was? "A policeman."

How many policemen were there? "Four!" As a phalanx of firefighters and paramedics burst through the door I asked how he could be so sad with so many of us there to help him. A smile slowly crept across his face, and he even forgot he was injured. However, he clutched at me tightly and began to cry and pull back whenever the medic tried to treat his wound.

The frustrated paramedic said if I couldn't calm the boy down, he'd have to strap him in a stretcher. To avoid that I told Lawrence that if he'd be still, the medic would make him a new hat! In spite of his fears, the boy finally consented. With that, the paramedic wrapped gauze bandaging around his head until he looked like a lobotomy patient! Lawrence had a new hat! By then his brother had come into the room, and wanted one, too. Soon, both boys were showing off their "hats." As Lawrence was put into the ambulance and leaving for the hospital, he was smiling and waving goodbye. Before his mother and brother left in their car to follow him, she gave me a quick hug and said, "Thank you. I don't know what I would have done if you hadn't come." As law enforcement professionals, we are proud to fulfill this requirement:

> "'When did we see you sick or in prison and go to visit you?' The King will reply, 'I tell you the truth, whatever you did for one of the least of these brothers of mine, you did for me.'"
>
> Matthew 25:39, 40

THE AFTERMATH—PART I

Thomas A. Peoples

Texas State Trooper

THROUGH THE dust all I could see was the huge collision of two vehicles, almost as if in slow motion. Law enforcement had been monitoring the intoxicated driver for many miles before he came into my sector. As calls had come in along the way, officers had been too far away to stop him. At each leg of his journey he had managed to elude law enforcement.

I knew he was coming and was waiting for him. Even so, it took me awhile to gain the momentum needed to reach and pull him over. After a

183

high-speed chase, before I could stop him, he crossed the median and crashed into another vehicle head-on. He was killed, and the couple he hit critically injured. In the couple's back seat was a six-year-old boy. A paramedic (who had been right behind me) and I tried to save him—but we couldn't. Then I found out it was Brady!

His mother, Jennifer, worked at a restaurant I frequented, and often brought Brady to work with her. A favorite of many customers, Brady had been sitting on my lap only a week prior. I was devastated: If only I could have stopped the drunk, this innocent young child would still be alive!

> When I was in distress, I sought the Lord . . . and my soul refused to be comforted. Psalm 77:2

I was so upset that management took me off the job for a few days and mandated that I visit the department psychologist. Like we all do, I told the psychologist what he wanted to hear so I could return to work, but I was torn to shreds inside. I shut everyone out of my life, sat home drinking large amounts of alcohol to kill my pain, and cried myself to sleep. I couldn't let anyone know how much the accident had affected me, especially my supervisor. My "cop mentality" had gotten the best of me; I was slowly dying on the inside with nowhere to turn.

My job performance dropped so low, I was called before my patrol sergeant. As I tried to justify my reasons, I broke down in his office. At that point he removed me from patrol duties until cleared by the department psychologist. I went home and parked my unit. Clearly I had to take action.

THE AFTERMATH—PART II

Thomas A. Peoples

Texas State Trooper

TO BE PLACED on administrative leave for psychological reasons is very troubling for most officers. Those who work with you may shun you and view you as unstable for a long time after, and it can affect the remainder of your career. I didn't want that!

After being told I couldn't work again until I'd seen the psychologist, I drove home and parked the patrol unit, jumped in my truck and headed straight to the liquor store. Feeling my career was ruined, I decided what I was going to do. I started drinking at about 2 p.m., and continued into the night. The phone rang several times, but I didn't answer it. At some point I got my duty weapon and began to clean it, planning to end my life. After cleaning the gun I took a stiff drink, picked up my empty weapon, placed the barrel in my mouth and, in tears, pulled the trigger—sort of a "practice run." Then I placed the magazine in the pistol, chambered a round, and prepared to do the unthinkable. With the weapon on the table, I prayed for God's forgiveness, and asked the Lord to give my family strength and understanding.

As I was about to place the barrel in my mouth, someone knocked on my front door. After the third knock, I recognized the voice of my former patrol captain. Realizing he wasn't going to leave, I hid my weapon and opened the door. He had gone through a similar shocking experience, and knew where I was headed. I was too drunk to remember our conversation, but whatever he said worked. He did say it was the "thin blue line" that brought him to my house, and that the road I'd planned to travel was the wrong one. To this day we have never talked about that night, but I owe my life to him for being my guardian angel.

> Cast all your anxiety on him because he cares for you. 1 Peter 5:7

One reason I believe God allowed me to live was so I could tell my story to others. With the right set of conditions and circumstances, too many either have taken or considered taking that wrong path. My goal is to help everyone see there is a better solution and to realize there is someone who cares about them. Above all, Jesus cares!

REACH OUT FOR HIS HAND!

Anonymous
Police Officer, Tennessee

So here you are going through this life,
with feelings of grief and strife,
trying to make it through another day,
but pain continues to build that words cannot portray.

Everything in this world seems to knock you down,
Not letting you get back up—seems like you are going to drown.
You hear about other people's wrongs and their pains,
But your own struggles leave you bound by chains.

Reach out for His hand, reach out for His hand,
His power is amazing, and His blood is cleansing!
He has been there every time you cried,
Holding you tight by His side.
Jesus' love was so great, He stretched His arms out and died.
Trust in Him, He will always provide.

Give Him your burdens,
He will take them to the heavens.
He is knocking on your door:
Accept Jesus, He will be your Savior!

Ask Him for mercy in His name.
He will cleanse you from all your guilt and shame.
He will break the chains that kept you in strife,
Only in Jesus will you have everlasting life.

Reach out for His hand, Reach out for His hand.
His power is amazing, and His blood is cleansing.
He has been there every time you cried,
Holding you ever so tight by His side.
Reach out for His hand, Reach out for His hand!

Immediately Jesus reached out his hand and caught him. "You of little faith," he said, "why did you doubt?" Matthew 14:31

FIGHT-FLIGHT-FRIGHT

Officer Mark Dennis

Franklin, LA, Police Department

A HIGH-SPEED car chase is always frightening: it can jeopardize the lives and well-being of many. That was the case one spring afternoon for Indiana travelers on I-70 after one man's domestic fight turned into a flight many would never forget, including me!

Indiana State Trooper Andy Lohrmen and I had stopped for lunch when a call came over the radio that a man involved in a domestic fight had taken flight and tried to run over an officer in Terre Haute. Shots were fired but the suspect kept on going—headed toward I-70 about twenty miles east of Terre Haute. We quit eating and jumped into our patrol car. Subsequent calls confirmed that the suspect was headed in our direction on I-70, so Andy and I sped to the interstate, found a crossover, and pulled over to set up spike strips.

Though heavy traffic that afternoon, at times the suspect drove more than 100 miles per hour during the chase! We were very concerned innocent civilians might be hurt during the chase, so Andy pulled me aside and began to pray. He asked God to intervene, protecting civilians, officers in the pursuit, and also the suspect. There are a lot of officers like Andy, going to God for wisdom and protection in situations like this. I was very proud of Andy's decision to turn the situation over to God.

In a few minutes we could see the suspect's vehicle approaching. We were preparing to put out the spike strips to slow him down when suddenly—about a quarter-mile

> Whoever flees from the terror will fall into a pit, whoever climbs out of the pit will be caught in a snare. Jeremiah 48:44

west of us—we saw his vehicle pull onto the grass median and roll to a stop. We got in Andy's cruiser and were the first on the scene. After Andy put the situation in God's hands, the Lord had taken action. As the suspect roared through heavy traffic without regard for others' safety, he blew out a tire. This made his car slam into the back of an 18-wheeler. It caused only a small dent to the truck's trailer but disabled the suspect's car. The danger to all was over.

187

With weapons drawn we opened the driver's door. The suspect was dazed and gave us no trouble as we pulled him from the vehicle and cuffed him. God was at work, protecting both us and the public, allowing a very dangerous situation to end peacefully. As other police vehicles arrived and officers took the suspect into custody, our job was done. Andy and I nodded at each other and thanked God for being a God who hears, cares, and acts.

HIS HANDS ARE SO COLD!

Chaplain Don Hipple

Virginia Beach, VA, Police Department

IT IS RARELY good news when your phone rings in the middle of the night (1:45 Sunday morning). That's especially true when you're a police chaplain. Since I lived near the crash scene, 9-1-1 asked me to go. At the scene I saw a small car crushed against a tree. Two high school youngsters—friends and on the baseball team—were trying to beat curfew. Instead, the alcohol they had consumed and one's erratic driving had brought them to that tree—one killed and the other seriously injured. They were only two blocks from home!

As I have done on similar occasions, another officer and I went to the dead youth's home. Responding to our knock, "Joey's" father came to the door: "Is Joey in trouble; out past curfew?"

> "But now that he is dead, why should I fast? Can I bring him back again? I will go to him, but he will not return to me." 2 Samuel 12:23

After making sure he was Joey's father, it was my sad responsibility to say, "I'm very sorry, but your son was killed in an auto accident earlier this morning." The devastated father got the boy's mother out of bed, and there was a time of great grief, disbelief, anger, and other emotions.

Around 4 a.m. I drove the parents to the morgue to make the identification. The walk down that hall at the trauma center seemed endless. Finally we were at their son's dead body; another grim scene. I thought my heart would break when his mother remarked, "His hands are so cold."

188

The sun was coming up on a beautiful Sunday morning as I returned the parents to their home—a sunrise they saw through tears, and one their son never would see. Family members had arrived, and preliminary funeral planning had begun. With their support team in place, I left about 8:30 a.m. When I returned later in the afternoon, members of the baseball team—greatly shaken—were there with other school friends and neighbors. The initial shock was over, but the sadness had just begun. I believe it is the same with parents everywhere: Our children are supposed to bury us, not we bury them. We can get over the loss of parents who die at an advanced age, but the death of a child in the prime of life stays with us forever.

I wish I would never have to go through this again but, as a police chaplain, I will. As long as there are cars, exuberant youth, and the distractions of life, it will happen again—somewhere, sometime, somehow.

DOES IT HAVE TO BE DRAMATIC TO COUNT?

Officer Tiffany Haston

Indianapolis, IN, Metropolitan Police Department

THIS STORY isn't dramatic compared with those of many police officers. In the course of my duties, I have arrested violent felons, chased bad guys down dark alleys, and driven 110 miles per hour to reach partners who were fighting for their lives in a gun battle. I don't have that one story that shocks people, but I do have the belief that every day there is an opportunity to change or save someone's life. A victim I helped years ago recently nominated me for a major award. To my recollection there was nothing special about that case, but it had impacted her in a way that made her remember me years later.

Drive time is prayer time. "Lord, I need your wisdom today." I ask God to watch over police officers, firefighters, paramedics, and soldiers who potentially are in the line of fire every time they go to work. Decisions must be made quickly, so I ask God to help me make good decisions.

One of those might be to take someone's life. In spite of what some think, that decision is not taken lightly. People often ask, "Have you ever shot anyone?"

My response? "No, thank God! If I had, that would mean the person had been trying to kill me or someone else."

> Make it your ambition to lead a quiet life, to mind your own business and to work with your hands, just as we told you.
> 1 Thessalonians 4:11

When I go to work or simply drive my police car off-duty down the street, I have no idea what I will encounter. I have been kicked in the face, spat on, cursed at, and called names, all while trying to do the job I took an oath to do. The relationship many people have with the police is similar to what some people have with the Lord: They like us only when they need us. When I find my relationship with God slacking off, I try to remember how that feels.

Whether we push someone's car out of the snow or save twenty hostages from a robbery, we can and do make a difference every day. As police officers, we see the worst of the worst parts of society every day. It is easy to become frustrated and forget that something we do could affect

191

someone for the rest of their lives. So, when I put that badge on day after day I pray, "Lord, please guide me today in all I do. Let the beauty of Jesus be seen in me."

PRAYER FOR REAL!

Officer Mike Dye[*]
Volusia County, FL, Sheriff's Department

THERE'S PRAYER, and then there's *prayer!* This is about *real prayer!*

My career began as a deputy sheriff in Florida. For a while, it took me to the West Coast before God brought me back to Florida where I belong. While in Patrol, I was assigned to the rough and tough neighborhood of Spring Hill. It was depressed and filled with druggies, alcohol, and hopelessness. God had given me a fresh revelation on the power of prayer, and I decided to put it to use. I prayed up and down the streets of that neighborhood, and for specific buildings. I even asked God to send a Bible-teaching pastor to that neighborhood.

One night a burglar alarm went off at a bar, and I answered the call. It was an ugly, concrete block building, painted black with barred windows. While I was there, God spoke to me and said, "Pray for this building." In obedience, I laid hands on that sin-filled building as I was pulling on doors and windows to check for entry, and asked God to convert it according to his purposes. A short time later and now on day shift, I passed by and saw a lady unloading paint and decorating supplies. When I spoke to her, she said her husband was a pastor, and God had sent them to Florida from New York to start a church. She told me the bar had gone out of business, and God had supplied the building! A few weeks later, I pulled up one day in my patrol car and she was crying. She told me that local thieves were stealing their supplies. I asked the men's group of a large church if they could help, and they did! They took on the entire project, transforming that ugly, sinful bar into a clean house of hope and worship. It went from

> Seek the peace and prosperity of the city to which I have carried you . . . Pray to the LORD for it, because if it prospers, you too will prosper.
> Jeremiah 29:7

"blight to light." Before long the bar across the street also went out of business, and God gave the Pastor the keys to that building at no cost!

Spring Hill is a changed community. It's not perfect, and still has problems with drugs, thefts, and all the other crimes of today's society—but it is changed. Other faithful believers had been crying out to God for help, and he used me as a catalyst. Like I said, there's prayer, and then there's *prayer!* Oh, that more of God's people—especially police officers—would pray over their cities for change. If it can work in Spring Hill, it can work anywhere!

*Author of *The PeaceKeepers: A Bible Study for Law Enforcement Officers*

JUNE 3

NO TERRORIST ATTACKS ON MY WATCH

Colonel Mike Angley (Ret.)

Special Agent, United States Air Force

WHEN I took command of the Middle East operation my mandate was clear: "Make sure no terrorist attacks take place on your watch!" For 25 years I was a special agent with the Air Force Office of Special Investigations (OSI), the "FBI of the Air Force." From 1996–98, in the aftermath of the Khobar Towers terrorist attack, I was commander of all OSI operations in the region. We had lost nineteen USAF airmen in that attack, and were not going to lose any more!

It was an entirely alien culture and region, and I had to learn "on the fly." We set in place counterterrorism teams and operations quite different from how we'd done business before. My territory covered twenty-three countries, so I traveled

Colonel Mike Angley

a great deal. However, most of my time was in Saudi Arabia, since it was a base of operations and the nexus of the terror threat in the region.

> When they cry out to the LORD because of their oppressors, he will send them a savior and defender, and he will rescue them. Isaiah 19:20

My faith guided me considerably. A committed follower of the Lord, I often was surrounded by people who despised Christianity (and any other faith that was not Muslim). Christian religious symbols were forbidden, so we worshipped in Quonset hut military base chapels. Strangely enough, the more that outside forces tried to suppress my faith, the more I seemed to find and feel God around me. Because I went on very dangerous operations, I approached each with the real knowledge it might be my last, and always made peace with God. Then came the time I was in Riyadh during Ramadan. Under Islamic law *(sharia)*, nothing may touch the lips, not even water, and everyone in the country was subject to extra scrutiny. Enforcers, known as the *Mutawa,* or religious police, were easily identified by their purple-stained beards and caning sticks.

I was heading to a restaurant with a Saudi Intelligence Service counterpart, nicknamed Zeki, when the call to prayer rang out. He left me standing alone, scrambling for the nearest mosque. Suddenly two *Mutawa* came at me with their sticks, screaming in Arabic. They were ready to beat me and haul me away to jail, so I shouted, "Jesus! Where is Zeki when I need him?" Hearing the name of Jesus angered them even more! As if in answer to my prayers, Zeki appeared; the mosque doors had closed before he got there. After some spirited dialogue in Arabic, the men drove off, leaving Zeki and me alone, marveling at my close call. By the way, no terrorist attacks took place on my watch—thank you, God!

JUNE 4

BECAUSE GOD LOVED ME

Deputy Jim Landles (Ret.)
Clackamas County, OR, Sheriff's Office

DISPATCH HAD sent me to a residential burglary in progress. Intent on reaching the house before the burglars left, I didn't pay too much attention to an approaching van. But as I was about to wave it by, Dispatch gave a description of a vehicle used in the burglary—it fit the van!

As I approached the van I recognized "Ricky," a known prolific burglar, with his teenage brother. They had just burgled their own parent's home! After making the arrest, I discovered that the van had been taken from Nevada and contained stolen property. I took the suspects to jail and began making inquiries with Nevada law enforcement officials.

I learned that Ricky, a male friend, and a girlfriend had been hitchhiking when a California pastor gave them a lift. Almost immediately, the trio hijacked the van at knifepoint and kidnapped the pastor. Openly, they discussed ways to kill him, and drove far out into the isolated Nevada desert. The pastor had a serious heart condition, and his body began to stress. They stopped the van and took him outside, planning to kill him. He asked if he could pray before they did. Then he fell to his knees and prayed for the hoodlums. At that, Ricky's companion persuaded him not to kill the pastor. Instead, they abandoned him twenty miles off the highway, reasoning he would not survive. However, he did, and eventually contacted the police.

> This is love: not that we loved God, but that he loved us. 1 John 4:10

With this information I interviewed Ricky, who admitted everything. He also said he had a weapon in his possession when I stopped him, and slid it down beside the driver's seat. Ricky told me he had planned to shoot me, but, "Something strongly told me not to!" After the interview I went to the auto compound and sure enough, the loaded weapon was right where he had hidden it. For his criminal acts, Ricky was sentenced to 25 years in a Nevada prison.

On that day I was not a believer. But I knew "someone" or "something" had intervened to save my life and that of the pastor. In time I came to know it was God's love for me; he had saved my life for a purpose. I didn't want to miss out on whatever that was, so I received Jesus as my Savior and now live my life for him.

BROTHERS IN BLUE

Adam Lopez

Abilene, TX, Police Department

IN 2006 I decided to make being "brothers in blue" a reality and begin a ministry by that name. I had been an Abilene police officer for ten years, living as "one of the guys" and doing things of which I'm not proud. When I gave my life to Christ in 2005 my life changed, and I made a covenant of service with God. My best friend, Officer Jeff McCoy, and I started to study the Bible together; he invited me to his church and I began attending with my whole family. I didn't want others in my department wasting their lives as I had, so I started Brothers in Blue.

> And let us consider how we may spur one another on toward love and good deeds. Let us not give up meeting together, as some are in the habit of doing, but let us encourage one another—and all the more as you see the Day approaching.
> Hebrews 10:24, 25

At our first meeting only Jeff and I were there reading our Bibles, praying, and communing together. I invited others to come, saying our meetings would be a place where they could share their hurts, concerns, and needs, and—most important—realize they didn't have to deal with their problems alone. Gradually our meetings grew, and I made and distributed a brochure throughout the department entitled "Ten-64, who's got your back?" (Ten-64 is police code for "I need backup.") More and more officers joined us, and we truly became "Brothers in Blue." We sponsored fellow officers to participate in the Walk to Emmaus ministry, and Jeff and I even worked a prison ministry, Kairos Walk.

Toward the end of May 2007 I wrote another brochure, "T50 major/minor," which is a code for major or minor accidents. Before it could be printed and distributed tragedy struck: Jeff was killed in his patrol car by a drunk driver! I was home on June 5, 2007, with a knee injury when an officer came to my house with the news. I had never before felt pain like that: I had lost my best friend, someone who worked the streets together with me on the same shift, and a brother in Christ. For his funeral our church printed 1,000 copies of the brochure with his picture on it, and I had the solemn honor of speaking. The pain of losing Jeff

Fatal crash of Officer Jeff McCoy

was great, but his legacy of Christian faith and encouragement lives on in the Brothers in Blue. We meet twice a month, encouraging one another, sharing what God is doing in our lives, and reaching out to those who are lost and hurting—doing what we can to glorify Christ in our lives.

TRUSTING IN THE LORD

Henry E. "Hank" Harley (Ret.)

Chief of Police/Superintendent, Canadian Police Service

LIFE WAS good. After 40 years in policing, the last five as superintendent in a large Ontario police service, I had a big retirement party. Then my wife said, "Now you're a has-been!" But that's what wives are for, right?

With time on our hands and a pension, our plan was to travel and spend winters in Florida away from the snow of Canada. But a month before we were to return home, I noticed blood in my stool. Not good! I didn't say anything then so as not to ruin our last month in Florida. But I did pray, "Lord, please don't let this be anything serious." For years I'd heard that a police officer doesn't live long past retirement, and that's all I could think about.

Then I remembered a verse my wife had written in the flyleaf of my Bible: "Trust in the LORD with all your heart and lean not on your own understanding" (Proverbs 3:5). One thing for sure, I was not very understanding; all I had left was trust.

Still I couldn't help but question, "Why me? Why after working all those years and finally reaching retirement does this happen? Lord, I surrendered my life to you, why aren't you taking care of me? Why, why, why?" Straightening up I said to myself: *You've been telling others why you believe and trust in God. Now it's time to put your money where your mouth is!*

> Trust in the LORD with all your heart and lean not on your own understanding. Proverbs 3:5

After the tests my surgeon said, "You have colon cancer but you have a choice: surgery or die!" It didn't take me long to make my choice! Then he said, "We cannot remove the tumor without leaving you with a permanent colostomy"!

Having promised the Lord I would trust him completely—and thinking positively—I replied, "Well, I'd rather have a bag above ground than be in a box underground!"

He laughed and said, "You'll go a long way with an attitude like that."

It wasn't a "walk in the park." There was chemo, radiation, the surgery, infection in the wounds, and "Nurse Cratchit" (my loving wife, again!). She constantly nagged at me, "Follow doctor's orders!" But, since I had been rendered helpless and needed someone else, she also tended to all my needs. I married a winner! The end result: It appears I have beaten the cancer, I'm not suffering from the colostomy, I have a deeper love and appreciation for my wife, and, as the song goes, it feels so good to be "safe in the arms of Jesus." A guy can't beat that, eh? God is so good!

BY COINCIDENCE?
I THINK NOT!

Dwight G. Garretson (Ret.)

Federal Bureau of Investigation

WOULD YOU tell the General that Dwight Garretson is here to see him? I'm with the FBI!" Though I'd already retired at the time, it took the letters "FBI" to get his attention!

I was in Bolivia with the International Justice Mission (IJM), a faith-based, nonprofit, nongovernmental human rights organization that seeks justice for the most abused throughout the world. IJM is best-known for freeing those enslaved in human trafficking, often underage girls forced into prostitution, but we were in La Paz because of abuse of street children by the police.

For 12 years I had been an FBI legal attaché and police instructor in South America. I had heard about IJM and the situation in Bolivia, so I went to their offices to learn more. The organization agreed I was a "fit," so I was recruited as a volunteer to go to Bolivia with an IJM attorney. We met with many of the "appropriate groups" there, but were unable to gain access to the National Police until in desperation I took the "chutz-pah" approach. At Police Headquarters I immediately was ushered in to see the commanding general of the National Police. After meeting us, he referred us to the colonel in charge of Public Affairs. Success at last! Together we agreed the best way to deal with the abuse was to train the La Paz police.

We returned to the United States to flesh out a plan when, by coincidence (?), a recently retired trainer and curriculum developer from the Federal Law Enforcement Training Center (FLETC) had asked about volunteering with IJM. He was fluent in Spanish and familiar with Bolivia. He couldn't travel then, but he studied pertinent Bolivian laws and developed the course materials we needed. About the same time ("by coincidence"), a female officer from California—fluent in Spanish and with extensive experience in crimes against minors—became available as a volunteer. When all was ready the three of us went to La Paz, initially to "train trainers." We

> Plans fail for lack of counsel, but with many advisers they succeed.
> Proverbs 15:22

selected the ten best, and assisted them in presenting the material to all the police officers in La Paz. On a later trip, we helped them present it in other major Bolivian cities.

Our official report to IJM emphasized that, from start to finish, God had orchestrated the plan, bringing together the exact expertise at just the time it was needed. By coincidence? I think not. God at work? No doubt about it!

MISSIONARY COP?

Anonymous female

YOU'RE GOING to be a cop? I thought you wanted to be a missionary!" I'm the only cop in my family, and they knew I'd always wanted to be a missionary—perhaps to South America or Africa, but God chose the streets of Chicago as my mission field.

I was about 25 years old but easily could pass for 16. One day a Narcotics sergeant "discovered" me and thought I would work well in Narcotics. Not long after he gave me the idea, I completed the paperwork and waited. When the call came I accepted, and spent the next eight years in Narcotics.

> I love you, O LORD, my strength. The LORD is my rock, my fortress and my deliverer; my God is my rock, in whom I take refuge. He is my shield and the horn of my salvation, my stronghold.
> Psalm 18:1, 2

I was a Christian but not living for God. I was wild, in my twenties, and working in Narcotics—probably the worst and best place I could be at the time. While working undercover, after making a drug buy one summer night, we tried to arrest the dealer. After a short chase I found myself stock-still in the middle of the street staring at a gun in the dealer's hands. That's *all* I did—just stood there staring! For some strange reason I wasn't scared, but thought, "If the Lord wants me, I'm ready to go." Well, *He* didn't, and so *I* didn't have to be! Then, without warning, the dealer took off and was gone.

My life changed after that incident. I had to deal with a lot of issues in my life, and only God could deliver me from them. I turned back to him and began to grow in my walk, working in ministry and using my experiences in support groups for women and girls. My heart still is in missions. When I retire my hope is to take what I've learned on the streets of Chicago and put it to work on the streets of some third-world country. I still have dreams about that night, sometimes picturing myself lying dead on that street. However, God is in control of all things and I thank Him for sparing my life that night. I wish I could have heard God's voice another way, but perhaps I needed the prospect of death to bring me back to him. The drug dealer? He was never caught, but he'll have to answer for his sins one day!

THE SAN CARLOS DEMONIAC

Stan Young

Regeneration Reservation Ministries

ONE EVENING another fellow and I headed for the San Carlos (Arizona) Prison to pray with and witness to the inmates. At the jail the guards told us they couldn't open the cells because the inmates were "in a mood." Whenever that happened, we would go down the rows of cells and talk through a small crack in the door. On this night I sat a few feet from our team leader and prayed as he talked with an inmate. That was my task, to pray for clear communication of the Gospel.

While we were there, officers brought in a thin, wiry young man and tossed him into the drunk tank. Since it took three very large guards to handle such a small man, I assumed he was on Glass (methamphetamine). The tank had a large, thick Plexiglas pane, and the man repeatedly slammed himself against it and cried out, "Don't listen to him." After a while it dawned on me he was telling the inmate not to listen to the Gospel. This made me pray harder for the leader.

After several minutes we finished and walked toward the door, having to pass the tank, which was the last cell before the exit. As we did, the man again slammed himself against the pane and in a most piteous voice cried out, "Pray for me!" He was bloody from slamming into the wall, was dressed only in his underpants, and had a distorted face and a look in his eyes I'll never forget.

> The effectual fervent prayer of a righteous man availeth much.
> James 5:16 (KJV)

201

As we left and walked to the car, the man's face stuck in my mind and I prayed for him. I realized I hadn't spoken to a single inmate that night, and I believe it was because God wanted me to pray for that man. He may have been high on alcohol and/or other drugs, but I felt as if he was possessed by a demon like the Gadarene demoniac (Mark 5:1–20). His moment of clarity to ask for prayer instead of money or beer shocked me; he was asking me to pray for his agonized soul! I believe he already knew about Christ, but didn't know how to escape from the demon torturing him.

It made me wonder how many tortured souls there are who know of the power and peace of Christ, but are so ensnared by the devil they can't escape him. We must never forget the power of prayer, or that a single prayer from *me* might make the difference for where a specific person spends eternity. Do you know such a soul? Why not pray for that person right now!

FATHER'S DAY ROUNDUP

Vinse J. Gilliam, Deputy Chief Investigator (Ret.)
Ventura County, CA, District Attorney's Office

MOST FATHERS look forward to June and Father's Day. In California, if you're a "deadbeat dad" behind on child support, watch out—you may get caught in the "Father's Day Roundup"!

Throughout the year, a backlog of active arrest warrants can build up. So, during the first two weeks in June, most of our DA investigators are asked to concentrate our efforts on serving those warrants. Because most of the outstanding arrest warrants were for misdemeanor violations, investigators were partnered in teams of two and given a group of warrants in the same geographical area. During one Father's Day Roundup, I

> Speaking the truth in love . . . Ephesians 4:15

was partnered with a veteran investigator with 20-plus years of law enforcement experience. He also was a Christian peace officer.

Domestic violence calls can be some of the most dangerous and unpredictable calls patrol officers receive. Child support cases fit into this same category because they involve three potentially volatile and explosive components: money, children, and an ex-spouse. All too often, money and children are used as pawns to get even with an ex who feels deeply betrayed and/or denied parental rights.

My partner and I attempted to serve a subject who towered over my partner and me in both weight and height. After he stepped out of his house, he erupted with a verbal barrage about his ex, child visitation, not being behind on his support, and "I'm not going to jail!" An arrest try at that point would have been extremely volatile. My partner, with his years of experience, opted for "love and grace" before the "fist-to-cuffs" approach. He said perhaps there had been mistakes in recording his support payments, and he would make some calls. The fact we were willing to consider the subject's point of view brought an instant calming effect to the tense situation.

While my partner made the calls, I tried to reassure the man we would help him if the data was inaccurate. When my partner presented specific information concerning non- or late payments, the subject slowly began to acknowledge guilt, eventually presenting his hands to be cuffed. While the "love and grace" method was partially for our self-preservation, it was also the right thing to do! Even a modest amount of care and compassion for a subject can accomplish a lot!

JUNE 11

NOT A SUPERHERO

Deputy Nathan Bickerstaff
Ellis County, TX, Sheriff's Office

AFTER NEARLY ninety minutes of tense conversation on a Saturday night I was able to calm down a man threatening to commit suicide on the front porch of his house. As he took the .38 caliber pistol away from his head and lay it aside my first thought was, "The Lord really took charge of that situation. Without his help, we would have lost that man." Let me be the first to play down any idea of being a superhero—I was simply doing my job as a sworn officer.

Those of us in policing have a threefold purpose in counseling others:

> Be on your guard; stand firm in the faith; be men of courage; be strong.
> 1 Corinthians 16:13

203

First, to provide assistance to crime victims and their loved ones and
   to counsel those who are depressed or bereaved;
second, to counsel prisoners and their families; and
third, and perhaps the most important, to provide counsel and support for each other on the force.

Perhaps the most difficult aspect of policing is the responsibility to
deliver death notices. Whether an automobile fatality, homicide, suicide, or
other unexpected death, that news usually brings immediate disbelief followed by deep grief. Another vital role is that of assisting fellow officers
face the tremendous stress that accompanies their jobs.

In contrast, there is great reward when a life is saved, such as the case
above. When we are able to convince someone there is a solution other
than suicide, we rejoice with that person's loved ones. For those of us who
are Christian officers, there is even more rejoicing when someone finds
that Christ's Gospel is the true answer to one's needs, both immediate and
eternal.

Romans, chapter 13, says police officers are called by God to be his
"ministers of justice." God knew that ministry was not limited to inside
the four walls of a church on Sunday morning. He knew we would be
needed 24/365. In fact, temple guards were exempted from the com-
mandment of not working on the Sabbath (2 Kings 11:5). As officers we
are expected to have the wisdom of Solomon, the patience of Job, the
courage of David, the strength of Samson, the leadership of Moses, the
kindness of the Good Samaritan, the faith of Daniel, and the love of Jesus.
That's an impossible assignment without knowing Jesus as our Savior. We
aren't superheroes—we're simply doing our job.

JUNE 12

THE CANYON OF EVIL

Special Agent Jon D. Cromer

VA State Police, Bureau of Criminal Investigation

THEY MAY have come from around the world, but most first-time
visitors to the Grand Canyon stay less than three hours. Few venture
more than a few hundred yards below the rim. Only a small fraction ever
descend the many miles of trail to the canyon floor. From personal expe-

rience I can attest it is difficult, but the journey to the bottom is rewarding.

Eighteen years in police work, mostly spent investigating death, metaphorically has taken me many times deep below the rim of another canyon—the Canyon of Evil. There,

the evidence of the evil that humans do to one another cannot be mistaken. It is unspeakable, senseless, and violent, often perpetrated against the seemingly most innocent of victims. Many times observers ask, "Why? Why would a good and loving God allow this?" I must confess that, after a lifetime of following Christ, I sometimes wonder the same.

I have spent my career along those hot and dusty "canyon walls of evil," working with what remains of someone's child, parent, or friend. I find no fault when someone asks, even demands, to know the sense of it all. It is in those moments I think of lessons from the Book of Job, for they speak so perfectly to the problem of human suffering and injustices.

Job suffered, grieved, reasoned, complained, and cried out to God. Friends with much advice attended him. But in the book of Job, chapter 38, God—whom few of us would dare question—asks Job questions of His own: "Who is this that darkens my counsel with words without knowledge?" (v. 2). I read on, trembling at how infinitely big our God is, and how incredibly small our understanding.

When my duties take me beneath the rim of that "Canyon of Evil," I am thankful God is with me. He understands perfectly our thoughts and questions. It is we who cannot yet understand all his ways. I trust in the fact that God is good, he is in control, he hears our prayers, and he is always faithful.

JUNE 13

THIS CHICKEN GOT PLUCKED!

John M. Wills

Federal Bureau of Investigation

THE WOLVES *are preying on the sheep again,* I thought as we cruised the south side of Chicago. Almost continually the radio gave information on yet another crime in progress. It was Friday night, June 13, and we were working a high-crime mission. We spotted a suspicious-looking vehicle and pulled it over. As we dealt with the vehicle and its occupants, another simulcast caught our ear: "Attention, all units in the 7th District, robbery in progress, Church's Fried Chicken, 63rd and Ashland."

Immediately my partner, Ed, and I made the same decision—"Let's go!"

A few blocks later we eased up to the business and took inventory: no activity, no workers visible, it's after midnight, and it's closed. Stealthily approaching the front windows, I crouched and listened. Voices came from the rear of the fast-food restaurant, and I caught a glimpse of someone holding a gun while ordering workers to open the safe. Three female employees huddled fearfully in a corner, and the manager was locked inside his office, where the safe was located. "Ed, it's bona fide, the offender's still inside." We checked the doors—locked! However, the drive-up window was open. My partner was too large for the opening so I went in while he stayed posted outside.

> In my distress I called to the LORD, and he answered me. Jonah 2:2

There was a hall that connected the front of the store with the office. Creeping along it I caught sight of our bad guy; he was threatening to shoot one of the females if the manager refused to open the safe. Holding my position I trained my weapon on the center mass of the thug. Just then, reinforcements arrived with lights and sirens screaming. Unfortunately, the commotion spooked the thug, who looked down the hallway toward the noise. Seeing me plastered against the wall, he fired immediately, striking me in the chest. I instinctively returned fire, my bullet piercing his sternum. As I slid down the wall into a sitting position, my partner fired at the robber. Incredibly, his round went through my leg. Having been hit by both friend and foe, I thought of Jesus' words: "Forgive them, they know not what they do!"

Immobilized by both wounds, my chances for survival looked bleak. "Father, help me!" I prayed. Then the stickup man fell to the ground, succumbing to his wound. I was saved; God heard my cry for help!

WORDS, WORDS, WORDS!

Mickey Koerner, Chief Instructor
Utah Valley University

I AM A FORMER deputy sheriff whose first love is flying. In the past twenty-three years I've taught hundreds of people to fly, but one deputy almost "got my goat."

"Joe Pilot" was about 40 at the time and I was 25. He was a male and I was just a lowly female. Perhaps that was part of the problem. He also was a sergeant for one of the bigger Iowa counties and very self-confident. We got along well through his instrument training, but he was not ready for the check ride. I urged him to practice more consistently and review his ground (altitude) often, but Joe didn't take my counsel. He grew impatient and signed himself up for a check ride. Growing tired of his arrogance and chauvinist attitude, I swallowed my pride and signed off on him for the check ride. He did not pass. Joe came back humbled. He apologized and listened, and then we completed his training. This time he passed his check ride with flying colors!

> "As you go, preach this message: 'The kingdom of heaven is near.'"
> Matthew 10:7

After I moved from Iowa he started flying twin-engine planes, using his pilot certificate to transport inmates apprehended in other counties and neighboring states back to the county jail where he worked. On one of these trips an engine failed while he was flying close to the ground, leaving him with only one operational motor on the big twin. When Joe told me about it he said all he could hear in his head was my voice saying, "Fly the airplane, fly the airplane!" He did and lived to tell about it.

The most humbling part of our conversation was when he thanked me for my training; my words had helped save his life. But the real lesson I learned was the impact of our words when we tell others about Christ (or when we fail to). I helped save Joe from death in a crash; the Gospel has the power to save folks from "the second death." Of all the words I utter, the message of Jesus supplants them all.

207

WHY?

Anonymous Police Officer

WHY WAS I—a well-decorated and respected police officer—sitting there with a group of alcoholics, drug addicts, and child molesters? Because my Christian marriage counselor had suggested this support group! I felt humiliated and as if everyone was laughing at me. Then one day they put me in my place: "You may be a policeman, but you are self-centered just like the rest of us." That's when the light switched on! Because of my mother's influence I was saved at the age of 12. When she died at the youthful age of 45, I lost my spiritual leader and let policing become my master!

After five years as an Air Force firefighter, I thought firefighting would be my civilian profession. Instead, I became a police officer and have been for twenty-two years. Both in Patrol and with the Arson Division I saw many gruesome things that hardened my heart—bad guys, crack cocaine dealers and users, murderers, suicides, rapists, and robbers. I was told I couldn't be both a Christian and police officer at the same time, and I set out to prove it. My hard-core police buddies became my friends, church attendance became irregular, and for no good reason I left my wife and children for another woman. I had all the earmarks of a great policeman but not a great human!

> "No one can serve two masters. Either he will hate the one and love the other, or he will be devoted to the one and despise the other."
> Matthew 6:24

After seven more years and another divorce I was back on the streets and beginning to ask, "Why?" Why was one killed and another lived? Why had I made it as a policeman while others couldn't cut it? "Why?" was often on my mind. At a crime scene where a man shot and killed his estranged wife, then killed himself, I noticed the woman had her Bible open along with other religious materials. Since she was a Christian, why had he killed her? Why? By this time I was struggling in my third marriage and in "that group." That's when they said I was self-centered, but I knew what my real problem was: I wasn't seeking Christ. My wife wasn't impressed with that solution, so I tried to leave her for another woman. Thankfully that didn't happen, my wife took me back, and we started working things out. At that point I let Christ back into my life and really started to change.

After twenty-two years of policing I still reflect on many incidents that raise the question, "Why?" I realize Jesus Christ is the only answer. I deeply regret the self-centeredness that made policing my master, and I praise God for bringing me back to my senses. To the reader I say, "Christ is real. If you know him, don't push him away. If you don't, find someone who can tell you about the Good News."

HOOKED ON CRIME!

Paul Miller, Constable PMW291
Whanganui, New Zealand, Police

MY FATHER was a British police officer, and I grew up with stories about catching bad guys, standing guard outside the Queen Mother's house, and fascinating details of crime investigations. It didn't take long to decide that fighting crime as a police officer was going to be the career for me! I left school at 18 years of age, began my work career as a courthouse clerk, and was 23 when I became a London policeman. (Now I am a 43-year-old police officer in New Zealand, but that's another story!)

I was still in my first six months of service with London's Metro Police, and my work day began at 6 a.m. Four hours earlier an offender had broken into an old hospital and made off with stolen property. I was asked to go investigate. While a security guard was showing me the crime scene, I looked out the broken window and saw an 18-year old male coming out of some bushes carrying a large computer printer. He saw me as I exited the building, dropped the equipment, and the chase was on. He wore only shorts and sneakers whilst I was in full uniform and the traditional London Bobby helmet, which took flight on its own! I'm sure we must have provided entertainment for anyone watching. Incidentally, an elderly gentleman rang the police to say he was safeguarding the helmet until I could retrieve it! Even though my lungs were burning, my will to keep going and the adrenaline flowing carried me on. While the chase only lasted five minutes, sprinting as hard as I was, it seemed much longer!

With unbelievable luck I caught the thief just four hours after he had burgled the hospital. I received many congratulations from

> I, the LORD, love justice; I hate robbery and iniquity. Isaiah 61:8

209

Paul Miller with car

all my peers, even some who'd been officers many years. They all said I must be "blessed" to be that lucky. I did feel "blessed" that day and ever since, because I know that God is with me. In twenty years of policing, both here and in the U.K., I know that God is by my side as my guide and guard in all situations. Oh, and by-the-by, I'm not so sure I want to take out on foot chasing an 18-year-old at the age I am now; I might not be so "lucky!"

JUNE 17

"WHY DIDN'T I HURT?"

Sergeant Traci Schinnerer

Norman, OK, Police Department

WHAT A beautiful sunrise, Lord!" My night shift was ending, the sky was beautiful, and the warm spring air felt so refreshing. Then I turned a corner. A car was in the street with its headlights off, but occupied.

210

As the driver sped off, a man ran out from a house. "You've got to help; he is trying to kill her!" he cried.

I told him to "go back inside," and the chase was on. We went a few blocks and through a parking lot, and then he headed back to the house! The occupants had come outside to watch, but then the vehicle barreled toward them. I was thinking, *What is he doing; he's just hit a brick house! Headquarters, where is my backup?*

Getting out of my cruiser, weapon drawn, I yelled, "Del City Police— get away from the car—get back from the car!" My mind was saying, "Lord, please let this end right." I saw his tail lights—no, those were head- lights. He was trying to run me down! I fired one shot—BAM!—then he was right on me; then I was on his hood. Four shots were exchanged with a wind- shield inches from each of our faces. My ride on his hood lasted only seconds before I slid to the ground in front of his car. I felt the engine's heat; the front left tire had grabbed the braid down my back. *Turn, girl, turn your body!* My body responded as the vehicle accelerated over my right shoulder, back, and the left side of my ribs. All the air in me was released in one gush. "What have I done to him, Lord?" I prayed. "When will this be over?" He accelerated again: over my shoulder, across my back, and off my left side.

"Lo, I am with you alway, even unto the end of the world." Amen. Matthew 28:20

Then there was a slap in my face; the car had dragged me to the curb. I heard, "Open your eyes, girl," but there's no sight, no light, no smell of spring—just the smell of asphalt and the sight and taste of blood. The man checking on me is asking, "Are you okay?" Then the car approached one more time. The front bumper pulled my right arm behind my head and I could feel the heat from the underside of the engine. Only then did he leave; it was over—but why didn't I hurt?

I "danced with the devil" for five days in ICU with chest tubes and horrible nightmares from the morphine. On the tenth day my sister asked, "Did you think you were going to die?"

I answered, "No, it never crossed my mind. I can't explain it, but I wasn't alone, I never felt alone." It was then I realized, *It is not death that people fear; it is the horror of loneliness.* That morning, I was given "the peace of God, which surpasses all understanding" (Philippians 4:7 NKJV)!

MAKE TODAY COUNT

Bill Hubbard, Executive Police Officer

Taos, NM, Police Department

THE DAY started about like any other. I was concentrating on the tasks ahead as I barreled through the lobby of the police station, head down and full of thought. "Morning, Bill!" came the sarcastic greeting from behind me.

My thoughts interrupted, I turned to see the portly, gray-haired uniformed patrol sergeant standing by the front desk. He was smiling because he knew he had just derailed my serious train of thought. "Oh, hi, K. D.," I croaked. "Sorry, I'm just too busy to talk right now." Little did I know that would be my last conversation with him.

Two hours later I was the first detective supervisor to arrive where a gunman had barricaded himself after the fatal shooting of a police officer, my friend, K. D. ("Daddy" to all of us three-stripers). He was only four months away from retirement, an outstanding officer, my friend, and the guy I had nearly ignored in the lobby that morning. Now he lay dead at my feet after being shot five times.

> Now listen, you who say, "Today or tomorrow we will go to this or that city, spend a year there, carry on business and make money." Why, you do not even know what will happen tomorrow. What is your life? You are a mist that appears for a little while and then vanishes. James 4:13, 14

Once the killer was in custody, it was my sad assignment to attend K. D.'s autopsy at the county morgue. Removing the badge from his bloody and bullet-riddled uniform shirt was the hardest thing I have ever done. It was awful. Of the dozens of autopsies I have attended, that one is indelibly burned into my brain. I wouldn't wish a situation like that on anyone. I kept asking, *Why did this happen, why did this good man die when he was so close to retiring? Why?* I kept thinking of John 15:13: "Greater love has no man than this, than to lay down one's life for his friends" (NKJV).

Anyone who has ever worn the badge for any length of time has come to grips with the fact that officers can get killed. I put on the Kevlar and carry a loaded Glock for protection, but it is God who protects me with his divine hand every day. In thirty-one years of policing I have been shot at thirteen times. I am *very much aware* this job could cost me my life.

The fact of the matter is that no one is guaranteed tomorrow. My family and I have made a conscious decision to make every day *count*. Every moment together is savored, each good-bye is given special notice, and each hello is a joyful reunion. Nothing important to our family's well-being is put off until tomorrow. *Today counts!*

SITTING IN GOD'S CROSSHAIRS

Inspector Dan Wolke (Ret.)

Berkeley, CA, Police Department

Chaplain

Benicia, CA, Police Department

"BILL" ROBBED many times, got shot, and kidnapped a motorist. I learned who he was, and discovered that his father was a Florida deputy. I spoke on the phone with his dad, and he asked me to save Bill's life if possible .We prayed and asked God to bless that request. A few days later, Bill was taken into custody at a local hospital, and I interviewed him there. After he admitted to the armed robberies and kidnapping, I took him to my department and booked him. However, before jailing him, I gave him a Bible and prayed for him. This began a remarkable friendship that lasted nearly 17 years.

Bill wrote me from prison, and we started to correspond. Many times I told him Christ loved him and died for his sins. Bill was a tough sell, saying he wasn't sure God really loved him. This continued for eight years until Bill's release. After his release, Bill said prison had changed him; he never wanted to go back again. Unfortunately, he returned to his heroin habit, and robbed to pay for it. After twenty robberies Bill was arrested, and once again we prayed as he went back to jail. This time I knew Bill probably never would get out of jail. Our correspondence resumed. Then Bill contracted Hepatitis C, and tried to get the prison to treat him. He wanted to get out of

> (The LORD is) not willing that any should perish, but that all should come to repentance.
> 2 Peter 3:9 (NKJV)

213

prison and apologize to his parents for the life he had lived. He said his life was beginning to change, and that he was reading his Bible and praying. I sent him *The Ragamuffin Gospel,* which talks about God's grace and forgiveness to us "Ragamuffins."

After I retired as an officer and became a police chaplain, I visited Bill in prison as his friend and pastor. Then the call came that he was dying and wanted me. During the several hours we talked together, he finally was ready. We bowed and prayed "the sinner's prayer" together, and I asked God to show Bill his love and forgiveness. A few days later, Bill died. In my heart I know Bill will be at the Lord's banquet table as we share together in that remarkable feast!

The remarkable truth is that God had Bill in his crosshairs, and never gave up on him. Even if it takes us to the last minute of life, God will give us every chance to repent and accept his promises. He has us all in his crosshairs!

"I'M ALL RIGHT!"

Emergency Services Chaplain John Harth
Missouri State Highway Patrol and local agencies

AFTER SIX years he still doesn't remember that June day. Witnesses said Missouri State Highway Patrol (they don't use "Patrolman" in MO) Brad Lively flew sixty feet in the air when the car hit him. They thought he was dead. When he came to, he fought with those trying to help him; he wanted to get to his car. The chopper came. His RN wife met it at the landing pad. Inside the hospital he tried to get up; he was all right (he said) . . . but he wasn't! His jaw had hit the windshield, both legs were broken in multiple places, and they weren't certain they could save his right leg—there was no circulation below the knee. For a week he had multiple surgeries. It wasn't until he slowly came out of the drug haze he realized how bad it was.

He had met two vehicles going faster than 100 miles per hour on I-55. He had turned in pursuit, and the second vehicle dropped back. He stopped the first, and the second driver, instead of pulling around the stopped vehicle and patrol car, hit Sergeant Lively! The officer put his arm in front of his head before it hit the windshield, which saved him from head trauma.

His gun absorbed some of the impact to his hip. He had four broken ribs, a collapsed lung, fractured mandible, and his jaw was wired shut. The 6'5" officer had eleven surgeries and lost sixty pounds.

It took eighteen months before he returned to work. He went through denial, anger (with himself and others), and felt isolated—completely alone. Always there was the pain! Friends took him to and from rehab, for his children didn't know how to handle what had happened. He had to deal with the naysayers who thought he couldn't make it, and with the reality of what life would be like if he did. Medically, it's amazing he survived. There were times when he thought he'd be better off dead. As Brad says, "Even though you think you're horribly hurt and disfigured, you'll find people worse off than you." And he did. In the beginning he had mentors; now he is one.

Brad looks at life differently now—friends and family have taken on a new and special meaning. He says he is "less robotic" in dealing with people and more empathetic. He's a better listener, and spends more time with accident victims than before. Oh, yes, there's been another change. Brad Lively had-

> People brought to him all who were . . . suffering severe pain, . . . and he healed them.
> Matthew 4:24

n't been much of a churchgoer. But if you should see him on duty, just ask to see the prayer card over his visor. Some good can come out of every disaster!

EXERCISING MY AUTHORITY!

Martin Smith, Authorised Officer (Jailer)
New Zealand Police

WHEN DISPATCH gives you a call such as, "A lady is running naked down the street because God told her to," you don't know what to expect. But I soon found out!

At the street address given, a neighbor called out, "She's over here with us." Sitting on a sofa in the neighbor's lounge was a woman, mid-30s, wrapped in a blanket. She told me that every time she tried to become more Christ-like, something happened!

I told her that if she was serious about God, he would protect and take care of her. Before we could talk further she started to nod her head and torso up and down so violently, I thought the lady's brains would pop out! Then she rolled off the sofa making a growling noise with the voice of a man. Dumbfounded, inwardly I cried, "Jesus, help me!" I had an idea the problem was satanic, but I'd never seen anything like this before!

> When Jesus had called the Twelve together, he gave them power and authority to drive out all demons and to cure diseases. Luke 9:1

After about twenty seconds I thought, *I'm the policeman here, so it's up to me to sort things out.* I telephoned a local church to see if anyone was available to help. The pastor said a church elder had just been to a seminar on "Freedom for the Saints" (dealing with the occult) and was available that morning. The woman said she hadn't been into occult practices, but then the nodding began again. This time I looked at her and said, *"Demon, in the name of Jesus Christ, be still!"* The woman fell backward with a look of relief and great peace on her face. "Thank you, Lord!" I said.

A few moments later an I-car (incident car) crew arrived and wanted to take her to the station and book her. I said, "No, we're taking her to church!" Fortunately another Christian officer was there who agreed that was the right thing to do. Thereupon we took her to the church and deposited her with the pastor and church elder. Later I phoned the pastor, who said the woman had been harassed by mental illness, and had been a day-patient at a nearby hospital. At the church she had a good "deliverance session," then attended a psychiatric day-clinic later and was given a clean bill of health!

That day I learned from firsthand experience I could exercise authority over the Enemy in the name of Jesus. At the right time and the right place God made it clear Satan may be the prince of demons, but God the King is still in charge!

DON'T JOIN IF YOU'RE NOT CALLED!

Jason J. Everett, M.A.P.P.

Rolling Meadows, IL, Police Department

POLICING IS a "called ministry." Romans 13:4 in the King James Version calls police officers "God's ministers." God wants Christians in police ministry, but only if they are called.

An officer who attended my Bible study asked if we could spend some time just talking. He and his wife had been separated, but she now was agreeable to a possible reunion. Considering their past, I felt something about that was odd, and the officer couldn't give any reason for the change. He then told me he was on temporary paid leave from the department for three weeks. When I asked, "Why?" he said he had called the benefits department for clarification on his insurance policy and pension dispersal terms.

Later that day two high-ranking members of his district took his gun away, and told him to report to the department psychiatrist. Then, with a squad car following, he was sent home to his parents' house. After seeing the psychiatrist, he was cleared to return to work after his three-week paid leave. Up to this point, his story still didn't "connect the dots" for me. When a lull settled into our conversation, I asked outright what he had asked the benefits department. He said, "I asked the benefits specialist, hypothetically, how my pension and life insurance would be impacted if I were to commit suicide." Then I understood the scenario.

> "For I know the plans I have for you," declares the LORD, "plans to prosper you and not to harm you, plans to give you hope and a future."
> Jeremiah 29:11

I assumed his suicidal feelings were what caused his wife to want to reconcile. We talked for quite a while until I felt comfortable he would not kill himself that day. After he left for home I called our church's pastoral staff, and they found a Christian counselor who attempted to contact him. However, he refused to talk further about it to anyone—the pastors, counselor, or me. Finally I managed to get him on his cell phone and ask what the single, largest factor was that led him to this dark place. He stated simply, "When I decided to become a police officer."

I believe each of us is called by God to serve him in a special way—

as teachers, farmers, salesmen—in many different fields. Law enforcement is one of those "callings." If the Lord wants you in law enforcement, he will make it clear. If you force yourself into this uniform, that is an invitation for calamity. It almost was for my friend.

THE RIGHT SEASON

Officer Jonathan Parker

Chattanooga, TN, Police Department

ONE NIGHT while patrolling in my district, I noticed numerous cars and individuals gathered around a house known for gang and narcotics activity. Stopping, I noticed several gang members and associates, some of whom I had arrested previously. I never forget which "side" I am on, but try to establish rapport with these young men and take advantage of every opportunity to share the Gospel.

> [God] wants all men to be saved and to come to a knowledge of the truth.
> 1 Timothy 2:4

When I asked why the crowd was gathered, the spokesmen of the group said they were celebrating the birthday of a 4-year-old. Others said they were just "hanging out and partying."

I jokingly asked when they were going to let me come and hang out with them, that I could "bring diversity to the group."

Raucous laughter erupted, and the spokesman said, "Parker, we need you to come be on our side." More guffaws and laughter!

Without having to think too long, I responded with, "I used to be on that side, but I got saved and God has other plans for me." The mood quickly changed, and you could have heard a pin drop. I said it kindly, so as to not pass judgment on them. However, I sensed the Holy Spirit encouraging me to address the lifestyle they were living. God wanted to use that moment and my testimony as a witness to them. Even though the city where I grew up was nearly four hundred miles away, there were many similarities. Many "associates" from my neighborhood sold drugs, carried guns, burglarized homes, and participated in other criminal activities. The "side" I was on before entering into my relationship with Christ was the side of sin.

218

After another brief word and a "Take care," I drove away. In reflecting on what had occurred, my mind went to Peter's sermons in the book of Acts. Like those of the first century, was any of those young men I had spoken with "pricked in their heart?" (2:37 KJV). Was any of them asking, "What should I do to be saved?" I thought of Paul's instructions to Timothy to "be ready in season *and* out of season" in preaching the gospel (2 Timothy 4:2 NKJV). That house wasn't a church and the time not a Sunday morning worship hour, but I felt I had responded to the call, and it was "the right season."

MY MISSION FIELD

Detective Scott Chamberlain

Portland, OR, Police Bureau

AFTER I went through two divorces and "doing it my way," God finally got my attention. When I began in law enforcement in 1982 I thought I knew Christ, but the world called me by name. My motto was, "If you don't look out for number 1, no one else will." When the truth finally broke through my fog, I realized the truth of the statement, "If you don't use it, you lose it." I was going to use my profession to minister to others.

At a Promise Keepers event, I was performing personal security for Gary, Greg, and Michael Smalley. In an off-moment Gary asked me, "How do you reconcile being a cop and being a Christian?" My immediate reply brought them to a stop.

I told him, "Anytime I arrest someone and put them in the back seat of my patrol car, I have a captive audience. Being in charge, I choose a Christian radio station. This usually calms them down, and provokes a conversation regarding whether hope exists for them. That allows me to share Jesus with them."

There have been instances when arrestees have asked me to pray for them before taking them into the jail. What kind of Christian would I be to deny them prayer? I open the back door and with them in cuffs, kneel and lay hands on them, and pray for the now tearful and sobbing

> Men ought to regard us as servants of Christ.
> 1 Corinthians 4:1

219

arrestees. While only the Lord knows what is going on inside them, my prayer is that their hearts will be opened, and that they will accept Jesus and then be filled with the Holy Spirit.

Do you remember the old *Star Trek* theme of "going where no man has gone before"? To a great extent, Christian officers live out that experience almost daily. We go places and see people who rarely see a pastor or church visitation team, and we have an opportunity to minister in almost every incident. Police work is a mission field, and I have been called to it. My hope and prayer is that others see enough evidence in me to "convict me" of being one who loves and follows Jesus.

9-1-1. WHERE IS YOUR EMERGENCY?

Dispatcher/Chaplain Dave Purdle
Founder, Ministry 9-1-1

9-1-1. Where is your emergency?" It was toward the end of a twelve-hour shift, and the officers on the road were headed back to headquarters. When we received the call that a distraught employee was threatening to kill herself, all thoughts of going home ended. The situation was not good: She was some distance away, as the road officers were near headquarters, and they would have to deal with 5 p.m. rush hour traffic!

I kept the caller on the line for updates until the officers arrived, all the time praying and asking for God's guidance that no one would get hurt, that the incident would end quickly, and that I would have wisdom in handling the situation before officers arrived. I asked the caller if the woman would talk to me on the phone. When she got on the line I told her I was a 9-1-1 dispatcher and a chaplain, and calmly asked about her situation. She still had the knife and said she wanted to end her life. I had three responsibilities: Keep the responders updated, talk to the woman, and pray, "Lord, what shall I ask her? What can I say to keep her on the phone?" When she told me of problems with her marriage, children, and tight finances, I tried to give her hope these could be resolved. Then she began to cry, and barriers started to come down.

When the first unit arrived I asked her to put the knife down, saying, "Someone is there to help you." She began to get defensive again.

The initial officer had not waited for backup, and over the phone and on his radio he said, "Don't hang up; there are other knives in her reach!" While I kept the line open and before help arrived, the officer was able to secure the woman. Praise God, the danger was over, and no one was hurt! The woman then was taken for psychiatric assistance.

As a Christian and a 9-1-1 dispatcher for more than a decade, I have called upon God many times for strength, wisdom, direction in my life, and safety for responders and citizens alike.

> Then you will call upon me, and come and pray to me, and I will listen to you. Jeremiah 29:12

When I've needed cars for an emergency and none was available I've asked God to clear one for me. Many times the words suddenly have come, "I'm clear," and I've said once again, "Thank you, Lord."

Next time you're faced with a personal "9-1-1" situation, God has an emergency number free and clear that you can call with no danger of being put on hold:

JUNE 26

A BOY, HIS MOM, AND A POLICE OFFICER

Officer Joshua Wright, Badge No. 1083

Chattanooga, TN, Police Department

I CRADLED HIS small head in my hands and began to pray, "Lord, please let this little guy live; please let him make it through."

The boy, no match for the big SUV that had struck him, looked up as if to say, "I know you're a police officer and I'm excited to see you, but where am I and why are you here?"

Moments earlier, while patrolling, I had noticed a crowd gathering on a side street, so I turned onto it. Just then the radio crackled, "A child has been struck on North Willow."

As I held him I continued to talk and pray but saw him slip into a coma. All around me I heard whispers that angered me: "He's not gonna

Jaquez and Officer Wright

make it" and, "He's dead!" Why weren't they asking God to let him live?!

The ambulance came and had left for the hospital when a young woman came running. In anguish she asked, "Where's my baby?! Where is Jaquez? Is he alive?" I told her he was when he left my hands. As she left for the hospital I asked God to at least let her see him alive one more time.

After I cleared the scene and finished the investigation I went to the hospital. I told the family I was there not as an officer but as a Christian man concerned for the boy's well-being. I gave Jaquez's mother my personal phone number, something I'd never done before or since, and asked her to keep me updated on any changes in his condition. I also told her my family and church family would be praying for Jaquez.

During the nearly three months he was in a coma, his mother never left his side. I talked to her by phone almost daily and visited the hospital frequently. At his bedside with his family present I led prayer for him,

> For you know that we dealt with each of you as a father deals with his own children, encouraging, comforting and urging you to live lives worthy of God, who calls you into his kingdom and glory.
> 1 Thessalonians 2:11, 12

asking for God's healing and protection. The doctors thought he would never come out of the coma but if he did, he might never move or speak again. God proved them wrong, and long months in rehab began. I promised Jaquez that when he was better he could be my partner for a day, riding in my patrol car and running the lights and sirens. When that day finally came we had a blast—and those lights and sirens never looked and sounded so good! We continue to spend time together, and I thank God for the lasting bond he has allowed between me and this great family, demonstrating what prayer and the power of love can do for complete strangers!

ROLL CALL FOR GOD

Nicholas J. Londino Jr. (Ret.)
Federal Bureau of Investigation

POLICE ROLL calls can become somewhat routine. But for fourteen years as an instructor at the FBI Academy, our very special "Roll Call for God" was anything but "routine!" This weekly Bible study was held for interested officers at 7 a.m., before classes started. We would select in advance an appropriate portion of Scripture, then discuss it and seek God's "orders" through his Word. Psalm 119:105 says, "Thy word *is* a lamp unto my feet, and a light unto my path" (KJV). We used this as encouragement to obey God's "orders" as we "walked our beat" at the Academy. Attendees were sworn and unsworn career personnel from the United States and around the world, representing a wide variety of law enforcement occupations. All were bound together in the body of Christ by the Holy Spirit. Hundreds attended over the years, but no written record ever was taken. The names of those who attended, as well as their relationship with God, were left in his hands.

> Let us consider how we may spur one another on toward love and good deeds. Let us not give up meeting together. . . . but let us encourage one another.
> Hebrews 10:24, 25

Students often said they wondered before coming to the Academy if Christian fellowship would be available. They knew how important it was to stay connected with God while away from their family and home

223

church. Many specifically prayed that it would be, and all expressed gratefulness that it was. It was a great blessing to see how they ministered to one another, and how they encouraged me. They often gave testimonies of how God had protected them in dangerous situations, and how the Lord gave them opportunities to witness to criminals. It also was interesting to hear how many had been asked, "How can you be a Christian and in law enforcement?" I would remind them that in Romans 13, law enforcement officers are termed "God's ministers." The real question is, "How can someone be in law enforcement and *not* be a Christian?"

In the years since my retirement, the "Roll Call for God" has continued under various volunteer leaders. God has brought to the Academy committed Christian law enforcement personnel who delight in, hunger for, and thirst for prayer and Bible study together. What a wonderful day it will be when the heavenly roll is called! Then I will worship again with so many believing law enforcement brothers and sisters who shared with me at our special "roll calls" at the FBI Academy.

NOTHING NEW UNDER THE SUN!

Lieutenant Bucky Eacret

Travis County, TX, Sheriff's Office

I'M HEADED for the FBI National Academy in Quantico, Virginia! Wow! Let's see—I'll need a checklist to prepare for the eleven weeks I'll be gone. The Sheriff will take care of things at work, but I'll have to make certain the family will be safe and well (thank goodness for e-mail, cell phones, Skype, and other modern technologies), find someone to teach my Sunday school class, line up someone to cover me in my church worship responsibilities, etc. Uh-oh! What about Christian fellowship at Quantico? What will I find? Anything?"

Fifteen hundred miles later, I got the wild idea of posting notices around the Academy suggesting a get-together for Christians. In high school I'd been active in the Fellowship of Christian Athletes. I thought that was a "high-sounding name," so I posted a notice of a meeting of the Fellowship of Christian Peace Officers Tuesday night at 7 o'clock. To my joy, nine men showed up, representing seven states and one other country. We shared testimonies of how we came to Christ, fears and concerns for our families back home, and our joy in serving the Lord. We bonded immediately in a way only other Christians can understand. At the end of the meeting a Georgia state trooper asked if we were affiliated with the national Fellowship of Christian Peace Officers (FCPO). I laughed and said, "I just made up the name!" Then I looked on the Internet, and, sure enough, I found there was a national ministry! I sent them an e-mail, telling them the funny story. FCPO Executive Director Grant Wolf and several other godly men responded, supported my efforts, and even sent us challenge coins and other materials. Grant also put me in touch with Nick Londino, who for fourteen years had a weekly Bible study while an instructor at the Academy.

> What has been will be again, what has been done will be done again; there is nothing new under the sun.
> Ecclesiastes 1:9

Throughout our months there we met weekly, prayed together, studied God's Word, discussed pertinent topics, supported one another, and made lifelong friendships. One week Nick met with us, sharing stories of the long tradition of Christians worshipping together as they passed through Quantico. Before it was over, thirteen godly men were meeting from East Timor, Egypt, Liberia, and the United States. We had left our lives and families far behind for a while, but we found Christian fellowship at the FBI National Academy!

FROM FEAR TO JOY!

Paul Miller, Constable PMW291

Whanganui, New Zealand, Police

IT WAS MY first week after leaving the Royal New Zealand Police College, walking along the street on patrol. I received my first-ever assignment, to check on an elderly female who hadn't been seen for three days.

Soon I arrived at her house, calling many times from outside in an attempt to get her attention. Despite these repeated attempts, the only response was silence. I fervently was praying that she was okay inside her house, perhaps fast asleep or even hard of hearing. However, I must admit I was growing uneasy.

Eventually I was able to enter the house by carefully prying open the kitchen window. After checking the kitchen and bathroom I checked her bedroom. She was not there. Lastly, I reached the lounge, where the door was closed. As I opened it I was met with an extremely hot gust of air. Looking in, I saw the lady sitting slumped in an armchair in front of the heater, only two metres away. I walked over to check her vital signs expecting the worst, naturally. As I approached she opened her eyes and smiled! I almost jumped backward in joyful surprise. She told me she hadn't been able to move for three days, but knew now she would be all right. How quickly my emotions changed! I went from nervous fear of the unknown, to sadness at the tragedy I thought I had found, and finally to happiness when I discovered everything was all right! After that experience, we officers on foot patrol made certain to check on her regularly.

> "Acknowledge the God of your father, and serve him with whole-hearted devotion and with a willing mind, for the LORD searches every heart and understands every motive behind the thoughts."
> 1 Chronicles 28:9

As an officer of the law I think often of God's admonition in 1 Timothy 5:1, 2: "Do not rebuke an older man harshly, but exhort him as if he were your father. Treat younger men as brothers, older women as mothers, and younger women as sisters, with absolute purity." I feel privileged to serve our Lord in the unique field of law enforcement.

JUNE 30

CONVERSION BY COP!

Officer Mark Dennis
Franklin, LA, Police Department

THE SITUATION with "KC" took place in a small university town in Louisiana. That June night there was a fight in a college-age bar in which KC's nose was broken. When he left the bar about 2 a.m., two large men who had been drinking heavily followed KC in an attempt to keep the fight going. This alarmed KC, age 25 and small in stature, so when he arrived at his vehicle he pulled a handgun from his trunk and fired several shots at the pavement. Unfortunately, some of the bullets ricocheted and struck two young women, seriously injuring one. Officers arrived quickly on the scene, rushed the injured girl to the hospital, and took KC into custody.

As detective on call that night, I took control of the scene while other detectives set up road units to protect the scene and locate witnesses. I went to the hospital, where I prayed with the injured girl and saw to her needs. KC also was there being treated for injuries from the bar fight. He was very upset, crying about what had taken place and afraid of what would happen to him. I couldn't get a taped statement from him because he kept talking about his drinking and having been in rehab more than once. I finally said, "If you really want to stop drinking, rehab is not the answer. Only Jesus can deliver you if you really want him to." Then I went back to the police station.

> Wine is a mocker and beer a brawler; whoever is led astray by them is not wise. Proverbs 20:1

Five months passed before I saw KC at his trial. He asked if we could speak privately, and out in the hallway he thanked me for telling him about Jesus. He was attending church on a regular basis, had accepted Christ as his Savior, and had not had a drink or desire for one since his conversion. As we prayed and parted company, I couldn't help but be amazed at two things: the ruin alcohol can bring, and God's forgiveness for guys like KC, even after continual drunkenness and having shot two girls.

What was the end result of this incident? First, the girls were not permanently injured and had a good recovery. The judge took into account KC's small stature, the fact his nose had been broken in the bar and that the two men chasing him were twice his size, and that the girls were not injured seriously. Therefore, KC was charged only with neglect and illegal discharge of a weapon, and sentenced to time served. Yes, GOD IS GOOD!

THE ROLE OF THE FATHER

Officer James Alvis

Fishers, IN, Police Department

THE DISTRAUGHT mom had come to the station for help, and I was dispatched to meet with her. The problem was her son in his upper teens. She said he was becoming increasingly willful and disobedient, which was causing her much frustration. She then began to tell me the numerous ways he had become incorrigible.

I asked her if there was a dad in the home, and what he was doing to help. She said there was a dad, and that he agreed with her but did nothing. This only added to her frustration. When I asked about the role of faith in the home, the mother said she was a Christian and actively prayed for her son. Further questioning revealed that Dad didn't take an active role as the spiritual leader of the family. She said he talked about being a Christian but didn't go to church, didn't pray, and didn't read his Bible. It was clear to me the problem was the father, not the son.

As we continued to talk I counseled her that to address the problem with her son, she needed to deal with her husband's problem first. I told her I wasn't being judgmental, but, to walk with God, you have to seek him continually, and we discussed ways she could approach her husband about his role as a Christian father, using the issues with her son to help reel him in. While we didn't solve her problem, at the conclusion of our conversation I believe she felt encouraged by what I had said. I thank God that policing gives me opportunities such as that to share my faith and the Gospel message.

Scripture References

Deuteronomy 4:9 – *Teach [God's laws] to your children and to their children after them.*

Ephesians 6:4 – *Fathers, do not exasperate your children; instead, bring them up in the training and instruction of the Lord.*

Exodus 34:7 – *"He punishes the children and their children for the sin of the fathers to the third and fourth generation."*

Ephesians 5:25 – *Husbands, love your wives, just as Christ loved the church and gave himself up for her.*

THE LIFE SAVING AWARD

Officer Jonathan Parker

Chattanooga, TN, Police Department

EACH YEAR my department gives awards for performance in a variety of areas. In May of 2009 I received a Life Saving Award for an event that had occurred the previous July.

On a Wednesday night a husband and his wife were enjoying the eighth day of their first child's life. Around 11:30 p.m. they were awakened by the baby's cries. When they went to check on the baby, the wife felt her heart racing. Her husband told her he'd check on the baby. "Go back to the bedroom and sit down," he told her. Within moments she collapsed on the bed from a massive heart attack and stopped breathing. Her husband quickly dialed 9-1-1 and began CPR. In the nearly eight minutes he worked on her, the husband cried out for a miracle from God. When the para-

Chaplain Wolf and Officer Parker

medics arrived, they shocked her with a defibrillator nine times—four before she regained a heart rhythm. While the paramedics were working, the husband felt led by the Lord to anoint her with oil, lay his Bible across her feet, and pray for a miracle. The paramedics later testified that was the turning point in the situation.

She then was transported to a local hospital before being airlifted to the regional trauma center. A cardiologist determined she had developed a tear in the left anterior descending artery, which clotted and created a major blockage. A stent was used to

> My heart rejoices in the LORD; in the LORD my horn is lifted high.
> 1 Samuel 2:1

Officer Parker with Tennessee Governor Phil Bredesen

reestablish blood flow while she remained on life support. Doctors said she was not expected to live through the ordeal, and stated categorically she would have brain damage after being clinically dead for at least 15 minutes.

Early Thursday morning, the husband felt directed by the Holy Spirit to read Hosea 6:1–3: "After two days he will revive us; in the third day he will raise us up, and we shall live in his sight" (KJV). He accepted those verses as confirmation that by the third day, Saturday, God would raise his wife to new life.

When he walked into her room that Saturday morning she was sitting up in bed smiling, and greeted him with "Hey, Babe!" Once more, God's Word had proved true.

How do I know the details so well, and what does that have to do with the award I mentioned in the beginning? The lady was my wife, and the award was for saving her life! The real reward is that both she and our daughter are well, and we continue to rejoice in the Lord!

THE CHALICE, SACRED VESSELS, AND KENNY

Detective John Nielson (Ret.)

Chicago, IL, Police Department

AFTER SIX break-ins, the church had begged in its Sunday bulletin for the return of the stolen items. One of my neighbors said it was Kenny, a family member, so I went after him. Here's how the story unfolded:

Kenny was a heroin addict who stole a car, stole two chalices and other sacred objects from the Five Holy Martyrs Parish, sold them to a dope dealer who stashed them with his girlfriend, who gave them back to us. Except for the chalices: One belonged to the Bishop himself; the other had been used by the Pope when he visited Chicago in the seventies. The two chalices had gone to "Snake," a tattoo parlor owner who turned them over to Bob, who took them to Las Vegas to sell at a better price. My role? Sort it all out!

When Bob returned from Vegas, we arrested him for probable cause. He requested an attorney, who didn't know me, but knew Ed, a fellow officer. Ed told him, John's okay; the attorney is a former altar boy and anxious to get the objects back to the parish. We struck a deal: Bob was released from custody; Snake was left in jail.

> "The Philistines have returned the ark of the LORD. Come down and take it up to your place."
> 1 Samuel 6:21

Next day the Bishop called me at home. "Come here right now; the chalices just showed up!" As I pulled into the church parking lot, Bob's Catholic attorney was walking out from confession. I thought, *How ironic!* The Bishop said he didn't know who left the items at the church; I just smiled. Now everything was back, my commanders did cartwheels, and the Bishop took us all to dinner—even the defense attorney.

But what had happened with the chalices in Vegas? It seems that Bob tried to fence the vessels to a mob connection, a Catholic, who told Bob, "You'd better take those cups back to the Church or you might end up in somebody's trunk!"

It truly was an amazing recovery of sacred property. Even more than their actual value, the stolen chalices and other vessels were priceless to the church. Most surprising, a church's prayer was answered within three days of their plea, and God used me as his instrument! When the Bishop asked if he could do anything for me personally, I jokingly said: "Yes, you could change the stripes on my sleeves to silver bars on my collar."

He shared, "When a certain mayor was in office, I could do that. But our current mayor is a devout Baptist, and I have no connections there!" That was all right; I preferred promotions on my own merits! Anyway, that's Chicago!

I HAD TO GET THE TRUCK!

Deputy Dave Evans

Yellowstone County, MT, Sheriff's Office

IT WAS midnight on the Fourth of July, 1984, when a call came from a young man who was one of five in a car that had gone into the Yellowstone River. He had swum to safety, but the other four men were still missing. As night shift commander I was familiar with that stretch of dirt road where several cars had failed to negotiate curves after dark. For reasons I can attribute only to the Holy Spirit, instead of going directly to the scene I went to get my pickup with all my Tactical Response gear.

When I got there, one of the boys was about forty feet out from shore, holding on to a large piece of deadfall for his life. Spring runoff was late that year, and the river was running very high. From the truck I got harness and rappelling ropes, then tied the rope to myself and the truck's roll bar. It took three attempts before I was able to get a foothold on a tree sticking out of the water next to him. He had lost a lot of blood from a large gash on his head, and was too weak to hold onto the life vest I had taken him; it floated downstream. With just one vest for both of us, I threw the rope, which was tied to me, over his shoulders and pulled him from his perch to mine. Then the officers on shore pulled us both to safety. In addition to the head wound, he had a broken collarbone and several broken ribs.

I have responded to several accidents on that road both before and since this incident, but never detoured to pick up additional

> Turn to me and have mercy on me; grant your strength to your servant and save the son of your maidservant. Psalm 86:16

233

gear. Due to the darkness and late hour, options like a helicopter or rescue boat were out. Something inside had told me I needed to get the truck. Without the gear it held, this young man would have drowned like three of the four other young men.

His mother was at the hospital when I visited him a few days later. I explained I wasn't there on business, but had just come to see how her son was doing. When she realized I was the officer who rescued him from the river, both she and the boy started crying, as did I. She stood, hugged me, and said words I will never forget: "Thank you for giving me back my son!" Through all the years since, her words have stayed with me, and I always will thank God for having guided me that night.

WHAT'S AN O.I.C.?

Special Agent Don K. Shreffler
Iowa Division of Criminal Investigation

IT BEGAN innocently enough. I was sitting in the Lieutenant's office over coffee when he got a call from an officer in Des Moines. Both of these guys are my friends, and I knew that each was a born-again, Bible-believing Christian. When their conversation was nearly over, I signaled to the Lieutenant that I wanted to speak to the caller. After hanging up the phone, I asked the Lieutenant if he knew the caller was a believer. His eyebrows answered the question. In all the years they had known each other, apparently Christ's name had never been spoken between them.

It took me back to the early 1980s when I sat in my Ankeny, Iowa, PD patrol car, reading a small, easily concealed Bible. I had wondered if there were any other cops who knew the "burning within" experienced by those on the road to Emmaus (Luke 24:13-32). It wasn't until I was hired by the DPS and transferred to Council Bluffs (CB) that I learned there are. There I met a CB Police officer who wore a tie tac in the shape of a fish! Cool! He introduced me to more officers who were believers, the local chapter of the Fellowship of Christian Peace Officers (FCPO), and a man who would become my spiritual father, FCPO Exec-

> Let us do good to all people, especially to those who belong to the family of believers.
> Galatians 6:10

utive Director Grant Wolf. About the same time the Lord brought me to a church where the pastor preached from *an open Bible!* What a brand-new, heavy-duty concept that was to me!

In my travels around western Iowa as a criminal investigation agent, God began my spiritual growth. He put me in contact with his "other kids in law enforcement," either by allowing them to see God's presence in me, or me to see his presence in them. Sometimes it was a "red-faced experience." I remember how convicted I was when I thought, "I didn't know that person was a believer," and the Holy Spirit would fire back, "Did that person know *you* were?" I finally got it; we were brothers and sisters, and shouldn't be strangers! We spot other cops and are proud of the fact that we are special—the Good Guys! We may work for different agencies, but we are warriors, "the elite" (aw, come on, we all think that way, don't we?). How much more we should be able to ID a brother or sister O.I.C.—Officer-in-Christ?

Eons from now, which will be most important: our professional cop-egos, our rank, or the size of our agency; or that we knew each other and were known as "Officers-in-Christ?"

LEAN NOT ON YOUR OWN UNDERSTANDING

Detective Brycen L. Garner

Indianapolis, IN, Metropolitan Police Department

JULY 6, 2006, began as a normal day. As I prepared for my afternoon shift I recited Proverbs 3:5–8 and was on my way. Just after roll call, we received a dispatch of "There's a man with a gun" in the middle of a major Indianapolis street.

My partner said, "Let's jump on that and let day shift go home." At the time we were not overly concerned.

On arrival we could see this was a very serious call; a male was waving a handgun and yelling to passing cars. My partner notified Dispatch of the situation, and we blocked traffic to keep it away from the suspect, who had walked to a nearby apartment building and sat on the stairs.

Together with other officers we worked at keeping him away from the front door to the building, concerned for the people inside. I went around to the back of the building, and found that the suspect easily could enter there and gain access to the apartments. Going inside, I quietly walked to the front until I was directly behind the suspect. Thinking one of the officers outside would talk the man down, I decided to back off and just contain the scene. As I placed myself behind cover I heard, "I'm going in the f——ing house!"

It was then I pleaded with God, "Please don't make me shoot that man." I knew I was the last line of defense for the citizens inside, and might have to take the man's life.

The suspect entered the hallway with his back toward me, and I yelled twice, "Drop your gun!" Before I could say it a third time, he pointed his handgun directly at me. I then discharged my shotgun, striking the suspect in his right arm. I ordered him several more times to drop his gun, but he refused. Once again he raised his weapon, pointing it at me. I shot him a second time in his lower torso, but he still refused to comply. When he raised his gun a third time to shoot, I had no alternative but to fire again. Two years earlier I had become a sworn officer and vowed "to protect and serve." As an ordained minister of God (Romans 13:1, 6), I was obedient to the Lord and to my community. According to Scripture, he disobeyed and suffered the consequences.

> In all your ways acknowledge him, and he will make your paths straight. Proverbs 3:6

Never had Proverbs 3:5 been more real to me than that day: "Trust in the LORD with all your heart and lean not on your own understanding."

JULY 7

"THEY FLEW THROUGH THE AIR"

Sergeant David M. Greenhalgh (Ret.)
Delta (Vancouver, Canada) Police Department

DO YOU remember the song "The Daring Young Man on the Flying Trapeze?" One line reads: "He flew through the air with the greatest of ease!" The incident described here involved more than one young man and no trapeze . . . but there were "men flying"!

"Woody" was training me for a new-to-me police department. It was summer and my second week of training. Mid-evening we were called to deal with a crowd of drunken youths. I had five years' prior experience, but of a much different sort. Woody was a veteran who lived locally and knew most of the

youths, many from prior arrests. I was a skinny 165 pounds, while Woody was much bigger and stronger. In breaking up the crowd, Woody picked out the two ringleaders, put one in a headlock under each arm, and marched them toward the patrol car. I just stared in awe at this! Then the aerial acrobatics began! From nowhere, eight youths dove at Woody and the drunks, with all three disappearing under the pileup—sort of like in football. I wasn't about to let Woody be harmed, so I began pulling them off two at a time. Shortly, Woody reappeared unharmed and with his two young thugs still in tow!

As we left in the car I noticed the mob had quieted considerably and was now under the control of backup officers, including a reserve named "Roger," who did drywall by trade. A young man was sitting on the curb about thirty-five feet away, cursing and saying I was responsible for his being there. *No way,* I thought. *You had to get there by yourself, lunkhead!*

A year or so later I had Roger do some drywall for me, and over a tea break we talked about that night. He said he had never seen anything like what I did! As I pulled bodies off Woody with a single-handed, left-to-right action, he said they literally went "flying through the air" behind me. Furthermore, I actually *was* responsible for the person lying thirty-five feet away! I remember this incident well, but still find it hard to believe I could have sent husky young drunks flying through the air. I don't recall a particular sense of God's presence that night, but I know my adrenaline was insufficient for the task. To God be the glory: On that day and many more he gave me strength well beyond myself!

"IF GOD CAN SPEAK THROUGH A DONKEY, THEN . . ."

Drucilla Wells, JD, Supervisory Special Agent (Ret.)
Federal Bureau of Investigation

THE SCENE was tense: Investigators were closing in on a fugitive who had kidnapped a teenage girl a week before. My partner and I in the Behavioral Analysis (Profiling) Unit had been working closely with them. Our objective: Get her back alive.

She'd been taken from a parking lot in the Midwest and was being held in a rural cabin in the Northwest. The offender later said he'd hoped to take her into hiding and keep her as his "sex slave." We knew she and her parents were believers and events revealed that God was protecting her. The offender had allowed her to call her parents and he'd caught her calling 9-1-1. He didn't kill her for that, which told me God had clearly given her wisdom in dealing with the offender.

When our profiling coordinator called at 1:30 a.m. to update, he said the sheriff and deputies had surrounded the cabin. "What should the sheriff say? How can we get the fugitive to give up or at least allow the girl to live?" Talk about praying! I wasn't trained as a hostage negotiator; neither was my partner.

> "Do not worry about what to say or how to say it. At that time you will be given what to say." Matthew 10:19

We knew nothing about the sheriff and could only speculate as to the fugitive's state of mind and why he had kept his prisoner alive to this point. We suggested some strategies and "soft" language, but knew the outcome was out of our hands. I sank to my knees praying for God's intervention. There were so many unknowns!

What about the officer doing the negotiating—his demeanor, his ability to be patient and reassuring, his measure of wisdom? I prayed for all those and that the fugitive's heart would be softened. I poured out my concerns, knowing the importance of each word and the manner in which the negotiator said them. Just then God brought to mind the account of Balaam's donkey in Numbers 22:28–30. There, God used a talking donkey to prevent Balaam from falsely prophesying over Israel. God reminded me that if he could talk through a donkey, he certainly could speak through an intelligent man! Shortly thereafter, we learned that the victim had been

238

recovered alive and the fugitive had surrendered peacefully. We also learned that the fugitive had allowed the victim to act as a go-between for him and the sheriff. She had been courageous and influential in the fugitive's decision to surrender. The results aren't always that good, but God reassured me once more that he is sovereign over all and knows no limitations.

"GOD LEADS HIS DEAR CHILDREN ALONG"

Deputy Dave Newell (Ret.)

Sarpy County, NE, Sheriff's Department

THE NIGHT it happened I was working my first twelve-hour shift as a rookie with the Sarpy County Sheriff's Department. I had already worked nine hours and was having trouble staying alert. The next assignment on my shift called for me to go to a location about ten miles to the west. I remember so clearly stopping and praying, "God, I'm new at this job, and I'm asking you to guide me throughout my career. Please put me in places where I'm needed, and lead me to where you want me to be, starting now."

As mystical as it may sound, God clearly impressed on me to go southbound on 36th Street. I remember laughing in my cruiser and thinking, "Wow, Lord, go south to go west? Okay, whatever you say," wondering if it was really the Lord or if I'd had one cup of coffee too many. With that I decided to drive south to the river and take the back roads west to my next assignment.

About a half mile from the river, I observed the underside of an upside-down car in a ditch. People occasionally park near these ditches when their rural neighborhoods have parties, but I thought it might be worth taking a look. When I turned on the side lights on my cruiser to check it out, the first thing I saw was a sheared-off telephone pole with a car wrapped around it. As my lights illuminated the vehicle window I saw the bloodied face of a woman pinned inside; she looked to be in great agony. The hair on my neck stood on end—it's one thing to have advance notice of such a wreck and prepare yourself mentally, but quite another to come across it unexpectedly!

The lady, Tammy, was responsive to my questions, so I hurriedly called for emergency services. The Jaws of Life were used to extricate her from the car, and then she was rushed to the hospital. There, Tammy was told she would not have lived if she'd been found much later. After my sergeant arrived on the scene he patted me on the back and said, "Congratulations, Dave, you saved her life!" Although I tried to explain that it was God, not me, I'm not sure he understood that. Some folks just have trouble understanding that God still leads his children along.

> And this is love: that we walk in obedience to his commands. 2 John 1:6

AN INCREDIBLE COINCIDENCE!

Deputy Dave Newell (Ret.)

Sarpy County, NE, Sheriff's Department

ONE SUNDAY night my brother John, a retired Omaha police officer, called to ask me if I remembered "Tammy." The story he proceeded to tell brought tears to my eyes. This is what happened:

Tammy had given her testimony at John's church, saying it started with a cop more than twenty years ago. She'd been driving home from a party and swerved to avoid a small animal. She ended up in a ditch with her car wrapped around a telephone pole. When she regained consciousness she had glass in her mouth, several broken bones, and was bleeding profusely from a compound fracture on her arm. She sat there for hours believing she was going to die. She didn't want her children left in the care of their abusive father, so she begged God to spare them from him. She then said, "After I prayed, an unexplainable peace came over me, and I knew it would be okay, even though I still thought I was going to die. Shortly thereafter a cop found me, and I was taken to the hospital in critical condition.

"The next day the cop visited me in the hospital. He told me, 'You would have died if God had not led me to you. I had asked God what route to take, and he directed me to 36th Street. Since God went out of his way to save your life, you must believe he has something very special for you . . . but you have to pay attention.'" She went on to say, "I didn't come to Jesus for about twelve years, but what the cop said haunted me. Finally I gave in and surrendered my life to Christ."

Knowing that John was a retired cop, Tammy asked him if there was any way to find out who that officer might have been. After asking Tammy a few questions John told her, "I think it was my brother Dave."

Reflecting back on the incident I recalled thinking in the hospital what a cold fish Tammy was, and that it was a waste of time. However, I was obedient to the Great Commission and shared the Gospel with her. I never suspected the result would take such a strange turn of events.

> Be prepared in season and out of season; correct, rebuke and encourage—with great patience and careful instruction. 2 Timothy 4:2

I got together with Tammy, and the next Sunday we told our story to several hundred people in two church services. We wanted them to know what an amazing God we serve, and how important it is to share the Gospel even when we think it's of no use. Face it! Sometimes we only get one shot at telling someone about Jesus, and we mustn't blow it!

FREEDOM IN CHRIST

Officer Mark Belknap
Atlanta, GA, Police Department

MINE WAS a rough beat with many calls, plagued with drugs and violence of all kinds. Still, I often talked with teens who were hanging out after curfew, probing their lives, and sending them home before trouble found them.

"Banks" and his friends were responsible for many area burglaries and thefts, but usually evaded capture. Their greed got them in trouble when they stole from a violent drug dealer. To get even, the drug dealer and his crew did a forced invasion at Banks's home. They held assault rifles on his mother and siblings until Banks gave back what money was left. When I responded, it was plain he saw the danger he had brought on himself and his family.

Banks was later caught and charged, as were those responsible for the home invasion. At the drug dealer's trial, I saw Banks for the first time

241

since his arrest. We talked outside the courtroom, and he joyfully thanked me for the encouragement I make part of my enforcement responsibilities. He was studying the Bible with a group of inmates, and learning about Jesus. He said he believed what he heard, but had not yet accepted Jesus as his Savior. He asked, "How do I do that?"

I was overjoyed he was so close to freedom in Christ and said, "If you believe that Jesus died to pay for your sins, all you have to do is pray and ask him to come into your life as your Savior. Then you will be forgiven!" We walked to a hallway outside the courtroom, got down on our knees, and prayed. It was a short prayer, but long enough for him to receive his salvation then and there. I was overcome by the Holy Spirit at seeing the Lord save a man many would have thought "unsavable."

> It is for freedom that Christ has set us free.
> Galatians 5:1

We stood up; I grabbed him in a bear hug, then walked back into the waiting area. Attorneys, other civilians, and officers were staring at us. What an odd scene we must have made: one man in full police uniform and the other in shackles and an orange prison jumpsuit, bowing in prayer before embracing and walking together with huge smiles on our faces! Banks did not receive, nor did he desire, forgiveness from man for his crimes. But he did receive what we all need—forgiveness from *God* for our sins. At the final judgment it will be a privilege to stand with Banks as God announces his final verdict: "Not guilty!"

JULY 12

HENRY'S NEW HEART!

Chris Wilson, Crime Analyst

BETWEEN 1996 and 1999, Henry had changed from a hard-partying jokester to "a new man." His second wife had led him to Christ; his ex-wife had softened in her attitude toward him and given him more contact with their two daughters. He got the girls involved in his church's teen ministry and they came to Christ. He now had purpose in his life.

I didn't see Henry often, but kept in touch through briefings and e-mails. After I was transferred to his area, one day he took me on a ride-along for a child welfare check. Thirteen-year-old Robert answered the door. Henry said we wanted to make sure he and his two brothers were okay in the 110-degree heat. The heat inside was stifling. There was no power and no food, and they didn't know where their mother was— "She left a couple of days ago," they said. Each boy had a different father, and none of the dads was in contact with them. Henry explained that until a guardian could be located, they would have to go to Child Haven. Robert's eyes filled with tears, but Henry said he personally would make sure they were cared for.

> I will give you a new heart and put a new spirit in you; I will remove from you your heart of stone and give you a heart of flesh.
> Ezekiel 36:26

As we loaded the boys in the car, we thought the same thing: Their mom was gone, they would likely be separated and placed in foster care, and they were hungry. Henry pulled into a McDonald's to let each boy order just what he wanted. We pooled our money and found God had given us the exact amount needed! We took the boys to a park, Henry prayed, and the boys ate everything we had bought.

At Child Haven I took the younger boys inside while Henry talked with Robert. He told Robert he would do everything he could to keep them together, then reassured all three boys of his promise and gave each one his personal cell phone number.

Back at the station we asked God to lead us to the right people, and spent the rest of the shift making phone calls. After three hours Henry was successful at locating a temporary foster care home, and informed the supervisor at Child Haven. He just couldn't bear to see those three boys separated. Yes, the "old Henry" was dead. It was no longer he who lived but Christ living in him. God truly had given him a new heart!

THE HEART OF MISSIONS!

Jason J. Everett

Rolling Meadows, IL, Police Department

LEAVING YOUR home with a baseball bat doesn't seem like "a big thing," but it is when you're chronically in trouble for criminal activities—and you're on the way to a potential gunfight! In addition to that foolishness, the youth apparently hadn't seen the two of us in our bicycle patrol gear right outside his front door!

We were just about to release this young gang member at the end of our interview when my partner, not a Christian, asked him to sit back down. The two of us had discussed this young man in the past, feeling that if we could somehow reach him, he had the potential to rise above his family and the environment, and become a useful human being. My partner talked earnestly with him about the evils of using alcohol and other, illicit drugs, poor school habits and bad grades, and being led by negative influences. He went on to lay out a scenario of what the future might be if the youngster continued on his current path. I thought my partner was finished until he pointed his finger at the youth and said, "You know what you need? You need to find God; he's the only one who can make your life right." My partner then looked at me and asked if there was any way I could arrange for this kid to attend services at my church! The conversation over; we handed the boy back to his mother. I asked my partner where the idea to get the boy into church had come from? He said he'd heard me say that many times, and the only folks he had seen straighten out their lives were those who "found God"!

> . . . a sweet-smelling aroma, an acceptable sacrifice, well pleasing to God.
> Philippians 4:18 (NKJV)

That experience taught me that police work is the heart of the mission field. We run across so many, both criminals and co-workers alike, who are not believers. Even if I am not sharing the gospel, my very presence as a Christian can have a positive influence. I still am to be a Great Commission "seed sower" (1 Corinthians 3:6), but God is using me in my daily work simply as I "travel steadily along his path" (Psalm 37:34 NLT). I realize "God is working in [me], giving [me] the desire and the power to do what pleases him" (Philippians 2:13).

YOU WHAT? IT'S TWO IN THE MORNING!

Kristi Neace, wife of Officer Richard Neace*

Union, MO, Police Department

A MAJOR PROBLEM in law enforcement marriages is communication. Much of the time, sworn officers either are not able (for legal reasons) or do not want to share (too gruesome) their work stories with their spouses. When they do, for some of us it's a major breakthrough. But at two o'clock in the morning?

I was an exhausted young mother with two toddlers, and needed my sleep. In just a few hours they'd be waking up, and any hopes for rest would be gone until tomorrow night. Then suddenly, the bedroom light was on! Did I say "on?" It was glaring like a klieg light! And there was my husband, full of excitement and dancing around the bed while he announced, "I just helped deliver a baby!" He went on to say that a very pregnant, about-to-deliver woman and her husband pulled into the department's parking lot needing help. Rick and a few other emergency personnel were there in time to help a wriggling little baby girl make her debut in the world. Boy, that's not something an officer does every night . . . and he wanted to share his excitement with me! The problem was, I wasn't interested—I wanted my zzz's!

> Who can find a virtuous woman? for her price is far above rubies.
> Proverbs 31:10 (KJV)

Rick's no dummy, and it didn't take him long to realize I preferred sleep over him. The smile faded from his face and he probably mumbled something like, "Sorry I woke you up" as he turned off the light and left the room. Then it hit me—where was that "Proverbs 31 wife" when he needed her? AWOL! At the moment he wanted to share, I put my needs ahead of his.

Later I would pray, "Lord, help me to be the wife you have called me to be. Help me put his needs before my own, and show him how much he means to me. Help me to listen and rejoice with him during moments such as these." I can't say I've always carried through in meeting the high standards set for a wife in Proverbs 31, but that is my heart's desire.

*Author, *Lives behind the Badge*

245

LAW ENFORCEMENT AND THE NEWS MEDIA

Will Carr

Broadcast News Reporter

THERE SEEMS to be a "love/hate" relationship between all branches of government and the news media. This is often the case between law enforcement and local news bureaus. As a newsman having worked in two metropolitan areas, I have experienced firsthand both sides of the picture.

Few understand the many similarities we share. We each are staffed 24/7, we respond to tragic situations, and we often are the first to talk with people involved in the cases—or stories—that captivate public attention.

Several years ago I covered a story where a beautiful baby girl died under extremely suspicious circumstances. "I love her with all of my heart, I wish I could have seen her grow up," her father told me.

> "Then you will know the truth, and the truth will set you free." John 8:32

Unfortunately, days before her second birthday, she died after suffering severe seizures. Just as detectives began asking questions, answers dried up. Then a local magistrate stepped in, acting as an attorney for the mother's family, advising the mother and stepfather not to talk. His interference significantly altered the case's path, and ultimately forced him to step down. Meanwhile, detectives and I continued pursuing answers. Many missteps took place, including the medical examiner changing his conclusion from "homicide" to "unknown." The lead detective and I shared the same theory, that the girl's mother or stepfather played a role in her death, but a "wall of silence" developed at all levels. Finally, things came to a dead end. There was nothing more I could do; my hands were tied.

Members of the media and law enforcement community have much in common. We share the same frustration at the roadblocks—including bureaucracy—that make finding facts difficult. Members of both professions often are frowned upon or downright hated just for trying to do our jobs. We sometimes find ourselves pitted against each other, but I believe we share the same passion for truth, equality, and justice. The disciples once came to Jesus and asked about a man who was driving out demons in his name. They said, "He is not one of us, what shall we do?". Jesus said, "Do not stop him, for whoever is not against you is for you" (Luke 9:49, 50). We in the news media are "for" our brothers in law enforcement!

MISSING THE MARK

Bill Hubbard, Executive Police Officer

Taos, NM, Police Department

THERE ARE very few officers who don't want to be known as a great marksman. Going to the range twice a year to requalify with our firearms is something most cops really enjoy. We get to "pop some caps," enjoy camaraderie with other officers, and—if we're good—earn "bragging rights," at least temporarily!

Due to a couple of factors I am a good shooter: First, I hadn't done much shooting before going to academy, so I didn't have to "unlearn" bad habits. Second, I had great instructors. When you read the Old Testament you can't help but be impressed by how particular God is about "details." So was my basic academy instructor: He was a stickler for details. Over and over we worked on stance, grip, draw, point, and trigger-pull. We were "rookies" when we went under his tutelage; respectable shooters when we came out. In later years I trained with three "greats" of shooting: Ray Chapman, Masaad Ayoob, and John Farnam. They taught me advanced aspects of cover and concealment, moving and shooting, engaging multiple targets, neutralizing moving targets, and how to use a semi-automatic handgun.

> How great is the love the Father has lavished on us, that we should be called children of God!
> 1 John 3:1

In spite of all this, one thing in the semiannual re-qualification ritual always seems to elude me: The Perfect Score. I'm always near 100—perhaps as low as 96 and often 98—but I haven't reached 100 yet! No matter how hard I try, I always "fall short"—I miss the mark!

In the New Testament, the Greek word translated sin literally means "to miss the mark," and it relates to an archer coming short of his target.

Regardless of how hard we try to lead the Christian life, we always "fall short" (Romans 3:23) and "miss the mark." There's just no way to be "good enough" to be perfect in the Lord's sight. What great assurance to know that while we fall short in life, God demonstrated his love for us by allowing Jesus to die on a cross. I may never achieve a "perfect 100" score in marksmanship, but through Jesus Christ I have a right relationship with God and have become his forever child!

ARE PRISONERS PEOPLE, TOO?

Inspector Fiona Prestidge
New Zealand Police

AS A RECENT police college graduate and rookie cop, I needed guidance and good role models in the learning process. A woman, I also had to learn how to cope with the macho culture in existence at the time. I had to come to terms with aspects of police culture that didn't sit comfortably with my God-centered life. Understandably, a lot of officers hold negative attitudes toward many of the people we deal with. It was not uncommon for my colleagues to make derisive comments, writing people off as criminals rather than seeing them as real people.

While working in the cell block I received Margaret into custody. She was 20, as was I, and faced an arson charge for burning down her father's house. We didn't have a heart-to-heart conversation, but I easily could see she was in a deep pit. "Lost" was written all over her. We were the same age and from the same suburb, but our lives were so different. Margaret was remanded to an addiction rehab centre while awaiting sentence, and I wrote her a letter. The Spirit of Christ within me and the heart of God were leading me to reach out to her in friendship. That began an extraordinary relationship between an upstanding young policewoman and a drug- and alcohol-addicted, sexually abused offender.

> "I was in prison and you visited me. Truly I tell you, just as you did it to one of the least of these . . .,you did it to me."
> Matthew 25: 36, 40 (NRSV)

Until that time, Margaret only had criminals as so-called friends; her life had been a misery from childhood on. She poured out her heart to me, seeing a beacon of hope in my friendship with her. We corresponded frequently and I visited her—first in rehab, and then in prison. "God stuff" began to be woven into our conversations, but I always knew my care for her would demonstrate God's love and grace more than words could do. (In the United States there's a saying, "I'd rather see a sermon than hear one any day!")

My contact with Margaret opened my eyes to the hellhole that imprisonment is, and I'm thankful I got that insight early in my career. It has helped me both to value the prevention of crime, and not be too triumphant in seeing people incarcerated. My small step of obedience to God's prompting enabled me to reach out to Margaret, doing something risky and countercultural. It also helped embed in my policing a godly compassion for people, which I want to be the hallmark of my behavior.

AN UNUSUAL TRAFFIC STOP

Constable Merv Tippe (Ret.)

Regina, Saskatchewan

POLICING IS my dream come true. As a small child I stood on the seat of my dad's car, hands on the steering wheel, making siren noises as I sped to my next imagined police call. At age 22, when I graduated from police college I was on my way!

Four years later I was asked to accept a position with a two-person department in a rough rural Canadian community. I had one personal condition: It had to have a good Bible-teaching church where my wife and I could be productive members. To make a long story short, there *was* a good church there. After I met with its pastor and discussed the matter with my wife, I accepted the post.

It *was* a fairly rough community. Shortly after I arrived, an anonymous letter came to the department suggesting that both the Chief and I should go, or someone might blow up our homes. This was just the first of many challenges, and we were very thankful for our church friends. About a month after my wife and I moved into the community, the pastor asked if we would work with a young couple he felt would respond well to us (we were similar in age). I agreed and asked the type of vehicle they drove, formulating a unique approach to meeting him!

249

Later I saw a truck that matched the pastor's description and pulled it over. We hadn't met, so I asked to see his license. When I saw he was the right person I asked him to take a seat in the front of my patrol car. You could tell he was nervous, certain he had broken some law and was about to receive a summons. Wanting to have a little fun with him I said, "It appears you are feeling guilty about something. Are you?" He said he might have been speeding, so just go ahead and give him a ticket. I began to laugh and told him my true mission. I asked if he and his wife would attend a Bible study I was teaching at my home. I don't know whether it was because I was a police officer, but he agreed and said they would come. That began a warm relationship that included him and his wife becoming Christians. I haven't made many "traffic stops" like that, but it's one neither he nor I ever will forget!

> Do your best to present yourself to God as one approved, a workman who does not need to be ashamed and who correctly handles the word of truth. 2 Timothy 2:15

THE UNLIKELY NEGOTIATOR

Sergeant Jonathan Milne

New Zealand Police

HAVING A creative, spontaneous personality may not seem like what a person would expect in a police negotiator. Despite at times my having an unorthodox approach to work, God consistently uses my empathy and willingness to resolve critical incidents and help others.

It was July 19, 2008, and I wasn't meant to be the on-call negotiator (I was relieving another team member who had worked four days straight on a baby kidnapping). When my pager went off, it revealed I'd have to deal with a suicidal person on a fifteenth-floor balcony. He'd released a female hostage, was threatening suicide, and was in possession of a long-bladed knife. After I got there I found he'd already killed two innocent victims. When I first saw him, both hands were wrapped around a large knife pushed against his chest, and his face was contorted with anguish and despair. I was to be primary negotiator.

Jonathan Milne (bottom right) and team members

I introduced myself to Baseem as "John from the police." I told him I would not use any tactical options to apprehend him, and that speaking to me could guarantee his safety. Experience has proved we are more likely to resolve a situation by laying a calm, solid foundation of trust.

> Each time he said, "My grace is all you need. My power works best in weakness."
> 2 Corinthians 12:9 (NLT)

Baseem told me the devil had caused him to kill, and was telling him to kill himself. He was in extreme anguish at having killed the two men and said he deserved to die, as he couldn't "undo" what he had done. He wanted the police to assassinate him, which we call "suicide by cop." I made it clear my purpose was to help *prevent* further loss of life, as I was conscious that Emergency Services had already dealt with two dead victims. I tried to identify what negotiators call "hooks," things Baseem valued that would prevent him from taking his own life. For him these seemed to be the relationship with his father in Iraq, his dreams of diving in New Zealand, and his desire to speak to the girlfriend who had rejected him just prior to the incident.

After two-and-a-half hours of negotiation, Baseem placed his knife down and walked with me from the balcony into the apartment. He subsequently received eighteen years' imprisonment for the murder of the two male victims. One of the victims' families thanked me for saving Baseem's life and for making sure he was held accountable for his actions. In turn, I thank God for the opportunity to serve in such a critical position in spite of my human frailties.

THEY TOOK THE BULLETS FOR US

Chaplain Peter Hansen

Chico, CA, Police Department

WHEN A chaplain's phone rings near midnight, it's never good. Two sheriff's deputies had been murdered in the remote town of Inskip, and my SWAT team had been called. I was to drive the Salvation Army Emergency Canteen uphill to the crime scene so officers could refresh themselves during the long hours ahead. Water, coffee, snack items, and a place for officers to relax during an unsolved mystery are welcome, and I was glad to help.

I'd never driven the huge rig, the size of a UPS truck, and it took an hour of intense driving in the pitch dark on narrowing roads. Finally we arrived at our destination, a lodge with a tiny cabin at a distance. Inside the cabin lay the bodies of the two Butte County deputies, a young man in his 20s and a 61-year-old. They had responded to the lodgekeeper's urgent call for help after a tenant had pistol-whipped the lodgekeeper with his own gun to take the gun the lodgekeeper had.

The eerie night dragged on like a slow, strange dream. Our SWAT team manned the perimeter for the Butte County Sheriff's Department, whose officers entered the cabin, carefully preserving evidence of the violent shootout. Spent gun shells were everywhere, as were the bodies of the two deputies and their killer, shot by the senior deputy.

It is hard to understand why anyone would massacre another human, especially two innocent law enforcement officers simply doing their job.

Peter Hansen

One had hardly begun his career; the other could have retired any time. The officers came as peacemakers, never expecting an ambush. Blinded when entering the pitch-dark cabin from the blazing sun outside, they never saw the man who took their lives. He was a time bomb waiting to explode, and the deputies took his wrath at the cost of their lives. They "took the bullet" for us, just as Jesus did at Calvary, where he willingly "took the bullet" for you and for me.

At 7:15 a.m., as the Chico unit was to descend, we gathered to debrief. I was asked to close with prayer: "Father, we thank you for officers like these two men and their fel-low soldiers who come to our defense. Please be with their families from this day forward, and cause us to remember how fleeting life is. Just as your son died for an eternal purpose, help us to find purpose in these deaths—to know they did not die in vain. Amen."

> Why, you do not even know what will happen tomorrow. What is your life? You are a mist that appears for a little while and then vanishes.
> James 4:14

THE RED DOT

Chaplain Glenn Stone
St. Clair, MI, Police Department

HIS WHOLE demeanor changed after he saw "the red dot." It was on his chest where an officer had aimed his TASER in case it was needed. Then the young man began to weep, and we learned the whole story.

It was a busy weekend—a carnival, offshore boat race, and a rock concert in the park. It brought thousands of people into our community, and called for a plentiful "police presence." As department chaplain, my responsibility was to be on foot patrol with a junior officer. It was nearly 3 a.m. and my shift about to end, when we were called to an argument between two men. It clearly had the potential to become explosive. When we asked the more hostile of the two for identification, he gave us his driver's license and military ID—he was an MP. He continued his belligerence, so our officer unholstered his TASER and shined the red dot. Seeing the dot, the young MP broke down, backed off, knelt down, and began to cry. I knelt with him, and he told me he'd only been home from Iraq 15 days. He couldn't quit thinking about seven people he'd seen killed there. As we talked, I noticed a cross around his neck and asked if he knew a military chaplain. He said yes, and he had the chaplain's number. I suggested we contact him, so he dialed the number right then and left a message for the chaplain to call him back.

> "Hear my prayer, O LORD, listen to my cry for help; be not deaf to my weeping." Psalm 39:12

It was clear both to us and the other man in the argument that the incident had more to do with the soldier's grief than anger. In fact, when my officer and I offered to drive the serviceman home, the other fellow made the same offer! We took him, because I wanted to talk with him. On the way I told him he needed to remember and hold on to four things about the cross around his neck: faith, hope, love, and God. I asked him if he prayed, and he said he did. I told him never to let a day pass without prayer, for that is what would give him the strength he needed in the weeks ahead. The next night he returned to the festivities. He welcomed us as friends, and said the military chaplain had returned the call within the hour! Since then that chaplain and I have discussed ways to help this young man deal with the horror he had experienced.

In reflecting on that incident, I realize that sometimes aggression and anger are a mask for hurt and the need for someone to listen and understand. There are many people like him who need to "see the cross" instead of "the red dot."

BESIEGED BY A DEMON!

Constable Jackson Shewry
Henderson, New Zealand, Police

THERE ARE those who say demons no longer exist—that they were a first-century phenomenon. This goes contrary to Scripture (Ephesians 6:12), and many officers will tell you they have seen Satan in the eyes of more than one drug-crazed person. I did in this man!

It was a Saturday late shift and I was parked doing speed enforcement on a ramp to the motorway between Albany and Whangarei. A motorist told me someone was sitting on the wrong side of the safety rail on an overpass just to the south of me, so I flicked on my lights and sirens for the three-to-four minute drive. On the way, Dispatch said many callers said a man was hanging his legs over the motorway. I felt God telling me this was going to be different from similar situations.

I saw a vehicle parked at the end of the bridge nearest me, and a male leaning on the rail in the middle of the bridge. I parked my car and appealed to him to come to me. As he turned, I saw he had cut his wrists, and there was a trail of blood from his car to him. I caught up with him as he was about to jump, and dragged him off the rail by his tee-shirt. He mumbled, "Leave me alone, I need to do this." And in a matter of seconds he broke my grasp and began running back and forth across the bridge—I couldn't keep up with him because of my safety vest. During the chase the neighbors tried to help . . . but he again reached the rail, put one hand on it, and launched himself onto the motorway below. I honestly thought I saw a demon jump with him . . . I could feel it!

When I got down to his body I saw how badly he was cut, his blood got all over me, and my mind was spinning. Over and over I prayed,

255

"Lord, give me the strength to get through this," for I was fully dependent on God's strength. I needed him. Finally I was relieved from the scene, debriefed, and able to go home. Lying in bed I felt uncomfortable and struggled to get to sleep. So I began to sing worship songs and pray for my peace. Finally God gave it to me, and I fell asleep.

> In my anguish I cried to the LORD, and he answered by setting me free. Psalm 118:5

Most civilians do not realize the stress that situations like this place on police officers. In the United States I understand the average life expectancy of police officers is only 57, far short of what most Americans live. Without God I couldn't make it; even *with* him it can be hard in a situation such as this one.

JULY 23

THE LORD WON THE BATTLE!

Constable Jackson Shewry

Henderson, New Zealand, Police

THE MORNING after the suicide I went to church. I felt internal stress, had butterflies, and was really uncomfortable. As I drove, it seemed the nearer I got to church the more the devil was trying to make things difficult for me.

During worship the uncomfortable sensation increased, though when I concentrated harder on worship it seemed to decrease. As worship ended the pastor (without mentioning my name) began praying for me and the incident that had occurred the previous night. The uncomfortable sensation increased again to such a degree that I nearly broke down in tears. Then, when the worship and prayer ended, it was gone—like a battle within a war had been won. I went to church again that evening and experienced much the same thing, only weaker.

The next day, Monday, I went to a counseling session. As I drew near and then drove under the bridge where it all occurred, the feeling of being under spiritual attack became very strong. Once more I prayed, and the more I prayed, the attack diminished. When I would do something relating to the incident, such as writing my report, I felt uncomfortable—as though

I was feeling the young man's pain. To this day I believe I was face-to-face with the devil or one of his demons when the man jumped—the spiritual force was that strong. No doubt the attacks were from the devil trying to unnerve me . . . but with God I won the war.

Through the whole episode I learned what it is like to depend on God and his strength. We are in spiritual warfare, and Christians are the targets. The devil is very powerful and we must keep our spiritual

> Greater is he that is in you, than he that is in the world. 1 John 4:4 (KJV)

armour on (Ephesians 6:10–18)—we cannot face the devil without God, but with God we can get through anything the devil chucks at us.

JULY 24

HIS BOOK WAS CLOSED

Officer John T. Campbell, I.D. 14716

California Highway Patrol

JULY 24, 2002, a car accident took Sergeant Davidson's life. He was one of the first sergeants I served under, and he was kind, easy-going, fair, and simple. He "didn't sweat the small stuff," because he knew what it was like to work the road. He had retired happily four years earlier, knowing he had "run the race" well and earned a time to relax and enjoy life.

As too often is the case, I didn't give too much thought to him until his death. Because the accident was so untimely I couldn't help but ponder how much more living he should have experienced—but that wasn't to be. I'm sure he didn't wake up that morning thinking it would be his last day to live.

After the pastor's eulogy at graveside, an honor guard began playing "Taps." While listening to the music and saluting the flag, I realized the sergeant's book was closed. All events of his physical life were finished, and all the impact he ever would make on this earth was over. It made me ask, "What things do I have planned for the future that may never be accomplished? What might I

> Encourage the young men to be self-controlled. . . . In your teaching show integrity, seriousness and soundness of speech that cannot be condemned. Titus 2:6–8

257

have done differently today if I had awakened *knowing that today would be my last day on Earth*?

Then I stopped to think of the impact Sergeant Davidson had made on my life. Even though I had no contact with him after his retirement, his goodness and patience with me when I was a new officer had made a lasting impression. I thought, *Good comes from God, and Sergeant Davidson was who he was because of his relationship with God.* Reflecting on how significant and powerful his good leadership was for me, I began to ask questions:

> What kind of impact am I making upon the people I am around daily?
>
> Am I doing things that still will be bringing glory to God after I'm gone?
>
> Do I take for granted the people in my life whom I promised to love and cherish?
>
> Is my influence on my son such that he will be a godly influence for his family?

Second Corinthians 3:3 says, "You show that you are a letter from Christ, the result of our ministry, written not with ink but with the Spirit of the living God, not on tablets of stone but on tablets of human hearts." I want those around me to see that Spirit flowing from my heart!

THE RAPE

Tanya Stanturf
Independence, MO, Police Department

LATE ONE night a 9-1-1 call came in. At first the only thing I could hear on the line was a female screaming, "Stop, please don't, you're hurting me!" My initial reaction was that a "typical" assault was occurring. I tried to get the female to talk, but she wasn't responding to any of my questions. Since she wasn't answering any questions, I just listened without talking. In the quietness I could hear the unmistakable sounds of a rape taking place.

I yelled to my co-workers what was happening, asking them for assistance. One of my co-workers got the cell phone company on the line so we could trace the victim's number, and another plugged into the line with me so she could listen with me for any audio clues as to the caller's location. At one point we heard her say she was only being nice in giving the male a ride home and asking, "Why are you doing this to me?" This enabled us to identify that the victim was in a vehicle, which was a huge help. With information from the cell phone company, the latitude and longitude was traced, so our dispatcher got on the radio and soon had multiple units in the area. All the officers turned on their sirens, so those of us listening might hear them on the line if they found their way to the incident. An agonizing thirty minutes passed, but still they had not located the vehicle. At last the rape was over, and we could hear the rapist talking in the background. Just then we finally heard sirens as well.

According to the officers, they got there as the rapist stepped out of the vehicle and was adjusting his clothing. They took him into custody, and ordered an emergency ambulance for the female. I truly believe the good Lord was on our side that night, because just a few more minutes and the male would have gotten away. Only the Lord could have coordinated everything that had to come together—our on-the-line detection of what was happening, a cell phone with internal GPS, the cooperative cell phone company, and police personnel available for the search. We weren't able to prevent the rape, but with God's help we did catch the rapist before he could strike again.

> But he refused to listen to her, and since he was stronger than she, he raped her. 2 Samuel 13:14

TOO EARLY IN LIFE

Chaplain Clovis H. Sturdivant
Winnfield, LA, Police Department

AT THE age of 20 my only son had been hired as a police officer in a college town. One night while riding with his field training officer (FTO) they noticed a parked car that raised their suspicions. When they got close to it they saw only a single male passenger. They directed their lights on the vehicle, and the driver began to move toward the street with lights off and in a "jerking" fashion, as if unfamiliar with the vehicle. He turned onto the street and continued slowly without lights in the same manner. Deciding it was time to pull the vehicle over and question the driver, the FTO flicked on his roof lights. When the driver refused to stop, backup was called to get in front of the vehicle to slow it down.

The driver appeared to nearly lie down in the seat while the car continued to move. The front unit tried physically to stop the vehicle, causing it to turn onto the front lawn of a residence. My son and the FTO exited their unit while the front unit turned their floodlights on it. When they did, the driver fired a shotgun, just missing my son. Lacking experience, my son rushed the car, while the seasoned officer took cover behind a tree. My son reached the driver's back-door window with weapon drawn while the driver sat motionless, staring straight ahead with the muzzle of the shotgun pointing in the direction of the passenger side. My son pointed his weapon directly at the driver's head, yelling at him to lay the weapon down and back out of his vehicle. At this the driver slowly pulled the muzzle of the shotgun across his body. The other officers yelled at my son to "take him out," as they were becoming frantic for his life. My son was about to discharge a round when the car interior became aglow with a bright light, and the ground shook from a loud noise. The 16-year-old driver had placed the 12-gauge shotgun in his mouth and pulled the trigger, with "spray" from the blast hitting my son and the back of the car.

> God is not unjust; he will not forget your work and the love you have shown him as you have helped his people and continue to help them. Hebrews 6:10

The incident came too early in life for both young men, bringing great sorrow to one father and trauma to me. As a pastor and Vietnam veteran I was asked to help debrief my son, which I did. Soon after, I decided to become a police chaplain. If law enforcement was to be my son's life, it would be mine as well. I wanted to be there both for officers and civilians in their time of need. It is a decision I have never regretted!

PASSING THE BATON

Deputy Debra K. Morse

Hamilton County, TN, Sheriff's Department

DO YOU recall a moment you could credit as either your "time of valor" or "time of stupid self-discovery?" I'd like to share mine with you.

It was 1986, and I'd just returned to the sheriff's department after coming home from military service. At 6:30 one morning I was dispatched to an OB (obstetrics) call where I planned on "playing the waiting game." On arrival I found the mother already had a child, so felt she probably was expert at this sort of thing. Her husband, packed and prepped for her transport to the hospital, was doing what expectant fathers often do—pacing the floor. Since EMS was en route, I felt confident my relief was only moments away. I did some small tasks to assist the couple and attempted to calm the mother, who at times felt compelled to breathe rapidly and "push." Outwardly, I encouraged her to breathe normally and tried to distract her. Inwardly I was praying, "Please, Jesus, I don't want to be a midwife! Lord, where is that ambulance?"

In the calm before the storm, slow motion kicked in! I begged the poor woman not to push, but soon found that life won't wait on convenience. With a silent prayer for direction, I knelt at the couch prepared to receive the baby, who was attempting to greet me. With the sound of sirens nearing, I maneuvered the baby's head and then the shoulder through the opening. Just then the EMT entered the living room. In a transfer worthy of an Olympic relay race, the hand exchange between me and the EMT was close to perfection! A beautiful baby girl had arrived, and with awe and amazement I had helped welcome her into the world.

> From birth I have relied on you; you brought me forth from my mother's womb. I will ever praise you. Psalm 71:6

As the EMTs, mother, baby, and father left, they asked if I would lock up after them. I waited there in the quietness for a little while stunned, not so much at the chaos, but at the wonder of God's hand and the great crescendo of trumpets blasting out life into the world. The father sent me a photo of the mother and her daughter taken in the ambulance. When I look at it I am reminded of my moment of self discovery: Sometimes God asks us to be available and ready for use when he needs us . . . not always on our terms perhaps, but definitely on his!

"THE FAMILY"

Officer Richard Neil (Ret.)

Huber Heights, OH, Police Division

IN LAW enforcement circles we often talk about "the Police Family"—that, like a family, we look after one another, regardless of the circumstances. After what happened to me, I truly can say "the Family" is real.

During my sixteen-year career, assignments included patrol, criminal, crime scene investigations, and, finally, school resource officer. I received many awards and recognitions, and felt it couldn't get any better. It didn't; it got much worse!

One night I encountered a suspicious person with some outstanding warrants who fled on foot. After tackling him in a parking lot I landed on a concrete block, causing catastrophic nerve damage throughout my left ribs and spine. I spent months in and out of five different hospitals, and had eight surgeries. I became dependent on very strong prescription pain medication and suffered through withdrawal. The pain was so intense I was told I would die. For the first time in my life I gave up. My wife put her faith in God, and forced me to take one last trip to the Cleveland Clinic. They implanted a device in my spinal cord that reduced my pain and helped make life bearable. But the career I cherished as a cop was over.

> If one falls down, his friend can help him up. But pity the man who falls and has no one to help him up!
> Ecclesiastes 4:10

It sounds like nothing good could come from such a story, but we were truly blessed by my brothers and sisters in blue. While I was hospitalized, my fellow officers, along with the community, raised thousands of dollars to cover our bills and medical expenses. We didn't ask—they just did it. They donated thousands of hours of sick time, and my family never went without a paycheck! On Christmas Eve, dozens of students

262

from the school where I served brought gifts for my family. I never would have guessed that teenagers I had cared for would be taking care of a cop's family. God is amazing!

Now I serve as an academy instructor, trying to instill the "family concept" of compassion in the next generation of officers. I try to live my life as a tribute to the compassion tendered me by my "brothers and sisters in blue." They were my source of comfort and strength, and a ray of hope in my time of need. I thank God for his Guardians of Justice and Mercy, his "Knights in Blue."

GLOW OF A CHRISTIAN

Officer Brian Blumenberg

Chattanooga, TN, Police Department

WHEN AN officer is called to an accident scene and is out of citations, it's a predicament . . . especially when the supervisor specifically has said, "You WILL write a citation where there's been an accident!"

So, what to do? At the scene I got all the necessary information, filled it in on the accident report and handed a copy back to both drivers. That task completed, the "not at fault" driver was free to leave the scene, and did.

> In the same way, let your light shine before men, that they may see your good deeds and praise your Father in heaven.
> Matthew 5:16

The "at fault" driver and her husband were preparing to leave when the husband asked, "You are a Christian, aren't you?"

I said, "Yes, Sir, I am." He then told me he could tell because when I showed up to work the accident, he could see a "glow" radiating from me. This left me in shock because I didn't think people could identify other Christians simply by seeing them.

The three of us began to talk about the Lord and how he had helped each of us concerning the incident. The husband then suggested we pray before we went our separate ways. So, there by the side of the road we held hands while the husband prayed. After the prayer was over I had a wonderful feeling about how amazing God is: I didn't have any citations *to give,* but God *gave me* a wonderful blessing from that couple.

The experience reminded me of a passage in the Old Testament concerning Moses. After he came out of the tent of the tabernacle, where he had met with God, the Bible says his face "glowed" (Exodus 34:34, 35 MSG). Certainly I'm no Moses, but I'm glad God still gives believers a radiant glow other believers can recognize!

"I CAN'T DO THIS ANYMORE"

Chaplain Terry Hallman

Law Enforcement Chaplains of Tuscaloosa County, AL

I CAN'T DO this anymore," were the first words out of his mouth. His face contorted with shock, once again he said, "I can't do this anymore, I can't take it." As a police chaplain I've come to expect the unexpected, but this time I could not imagine what had happened. A rush of fear gripped me. Then he asked, "Why is God doing this to me?"

In the past several weeks he'd seen too much heartbreak and carnage: a crazed man on whom he had to perform CPR after he shot himself at the end of a high-speed chase; a young boy who drowned (the officer rescued him from the water but could not resuscitate him); and then this morning! I thought, *It's not even 8 a.m.! What could have happened this morning?* On his way to work on the interstate, the deputy had seen an accident involving an eighteen-wheeler and a pedestrian. He and a state trooper were first on scene and did what they could. As Forensics arrived to take the badly mangled body to the morgue, brain matter fell out. The young lady in charge grabbed a sock that had been knocked off the victim's foot, and scooped it up. At that point he became sick and said to himself, *I can't take this anymore! Why is God doing this to me?*

> Be on your guard; stand firm in the faith; be men of courage; be strong.
> 1 Corinthians 16:13

With my mind and heart churning I began to pray. "God, what do I say to him? What kind of answer can I give him? What are you doing?"

In what seemed to be many minutes the Lord spoke to my heart with this thought: "I am not doing this to punish him; I'm using him because he is my child and he has my heart. When he was giving CPR to the man by the train tracks, I was teaching him about LIFE. When he was trying to save the drowning boy, I was teaching him about LOVE. When he was with the pedestrian who was killed, I was teaching him about DEATH."

When I told this broken man what God had said to me, it was a revelation to him. As we sat and talked it was like a breath of fresh air for him, and renewed life rushed into his soul. We prayed together, and I thanked God for helping this deputy understand the great need for officers such as him to help others. Not many can deal with the awful tragedies of life, and he was too good an officer to lose. Daily I pray for officers like him who suffer along with the victims they assist. Let me encourage you to pray also.

JULY 31

JOY'S SMILE

Officer Mark Dennis
Franklin, LA, Police Department

EVEN THOUGH Franklin isn't a large city, there still are a large number of domestic calls. As I became familiar with the town, it wasn't long before I was making "repeat calls" to "regular customers."

One day I was called to "Joy's" residence. Even before I reached her house, from my car I could hear her screaming. She said she didn't want her kids anymore and would I take them? I asked her to calm down and tell me what the problem was. She kept screaming, saying that her children kept the house a mess and wouldn't listen to her. I told Joy this was her problem, not ours. She did not want to hear that! She said that one day I'd find her with a big knife sticking out of her chest that would have been stuck there by her kids. Trying to keep a straight face I told her, "Then that *would* be a police problem, and you should call me then."

Her "monster kids" were three girls, ages 6, 8, and 10. Speaking in a *deep* voice I told them, "God wants us to obey our parents. Do you want to live a good and long life?" They all nodded their heads, so I continued, "You will if you obey and respect your mother." Then I told Joy I would be back the next day.

My son had some VeggieTales videos, so I took one for Joy's children to watch. After that I took one or two of the videos to them every shift I worked. Soon the girls were glued to the TV, watching the tapes over and over and learning about God. His message was new for both them and Joy, and the mother could hardly believe the change in her children.

Joy moved away, but late one evening I stopped a vehicle with a headlamp burnt out. The driver was Joy. Most driver's license pictures look like mug shots, but Joy's had a big, beautiful smile. When I asked where she got that smile, she said, "From you!" I thanked her and reminded her to walk with Christ. As she drove away I was reminded of God's power to restore, renew, and give hope. I thanked God for the opportunity to minister in the lives of people like Joy and her children, and for how modern methods of teaching, such as VeggieTales, can help make the "old, old story" fresh and new for this generation.

> Faith by itself, if it is not accompanied by action, is dead. But someone will say, "You have faith; I have deeds." Show me your faith without deeds, and I will show you my faith by what I do.
> James 2:17, 18

HOLD ON!

Officer Jamie F. Kopinetz
Hummelstown Borough, PA, Police Department

NIGHT BIKE patrol can be interesting—or should I say *scary*? The smell of marijuana lured my partner and me to a truck in a parking lot. He took the driver's side and I took the passenger's. My flashlight in the passenger's face startled the driver, who took his foot off the brake and the truck started rolling! I grabbed the passenger through the window and yelled, "Stop the truck!" I pulled myself up off the ground but could feel the rear wheels against my feet. I was in fear for my life! I don't know whether I was more mad or scared, but I again yelled at the driver, "Stop the truck or I'll shoot!" I would have shot him if I could have drawn my weapon, but I'd have had to let go to do that and he was going too fast. I'd have been badly hurt.

There are many parts of this incident I cannot remember, but one I'll never forget: It was this feeling I was not alone. I heard a voice say to me, "Hold on just a little longer, you'll be fine." I have no doubt it was God. "Just hang on," he said, and I did for the

> Whether you turn to the right or to the left, your ears will hear a voice behind you, saying, "This is the way; walk in it."
> Isaiah 30:21

564 feet I was dragged before the driver stopped. It had never been so clear in my life I was being protected by God.

When it was over I "popped" the passenger with my TASER while another officer grabbed the driver. When other units arrived I was told to cover the driver, but I was so upset at the time that one of the sergeants had to calm me down. He took over my responsibilities and told me to sit tight for a while. That helped a lot. My knees were banged up and my entire body sore, but at the ER it just turned out to be minor abrasions.

I was never so sure and serious about shooting someone in my life as I was that night. I wanted revenge. How could they do this to me when all I did was my duty as an officer? It took a long time, but I've now forgiven them both for what they did. They will face God on their day of judgment. Besides, the incident renewed my purpose in life and faith in God. He spoke to me that night, guarding me and saving my life. He taught me to trust him even in the bad times, just to "Hold on!"

GOING ABROAD
BROUGHT ME HOME

Sergeant Chuck Gilliland

Dallas/Ft. Worth, TX, Airport Police

IT TOOK a missions trip to Africa to show me my true ministry calling. I had become a Christian at age 9 and knew early on that God had called me into ministry. I wanted to attend a private, Christian university but chose a state school because of cost. While there, my heart also settled for "something less," and I veered "off course." Thinking I no longer was worthy for ministry, I went into policing.

Police work can be a dark place, spiritually speaking, and I believe the love of my Christian wife has helped keep me on track. Over time the Lord used her to bring me back to my relationship with him. In 2005 I rededicated my life to the Lord, and he gave me a second chance. That year I went through the weekend Walk to Emmaus program and met Dave Walters, a past board member of the Fellowship of Christian Peace Officers (FCPO). This ministry trains and encourages believing Christian officers to reach for Christ those in law enforcement who are lost. After that weekend I returned to my department and began putting together an FCPO chapter. It took three years, but God's timing was perfect.

> "And you will be my witnesses in Jerusalem, and in all Judea and Samaria, and to the ends of the earth." Acts 1:8

In August of 2009 my wife and I went to Africa on a missions trip. While there, I visited some police stations and shared Jesus. In a police station in Botswana, God showed me that my specific calling is to reach out to police officers. Even though I was involved in FCPO, I hadn't reached the point of realizing my calling, my duty: My "Jerusalem mission field" was right in my own backyard—in my own agency.

The law enforcement field is "white unto harvest" (John 4:35 NKJV). What better place to be "Christ's ambassadors" (2 Corinthians 5:20) than in our own agencies, encouraging officers to have an effective witness to the lost around them! For one reason or another, many officers don't or can't attend church. Departmental Bible studies, fellowship, discipleship, and mentoring cannot take the place of a local congregation, but they do help fulfill the Great Commission.

We may be "the only Bible many of our associates read," and my prayer is that the Holy Spirit will use us to take the Gospel and Jesus' light into the dark place of police work.

THE POCKET CROSS

Captain Glenn Olson (Ret.)
McHenry County, IL, Sheriff's Department

SON, THIS is for you to carry always." I had just become a sworn officer, and mother gave me a wallet-size, laminated card with a tiny cross and a poem, "The Pocket Cross." Thirty-seven years later I still have it . . . and it saved my life.

The Chicago suburbs where I worked were contested between two major motorcycle gangs. Like most urban areas, we had "biker bars" or hangouts. Early one Sunday, I was working a wreck near one of those bars. EMT had finished with the car's driver when we heard a loud crash. An old jalopy had swerved, skidded into a ditch, and barely missed the ambulance and firemen! The driver and his two buddies were members of a notorious motorcycle club. All had been drinking, and the driver was quite belligerent. I told Dispatch we'd had a second accident and "I really could use another deputy!" Other than empty beer cans, the vehicle seemed "clean." The driver grew so belligerent, it became obvious I'd either have to arrest him or calm him down. His cigarettes were in my line of sight, so I said he could get one, hoping it would calm him. What I didn't know was that he had secreted a 10-inch Bowie knife inside the door trim.

Suddenly I heard a sound like fingernails on a blackboard, and a fireman yelled, "Knife!"

I grabbed my heavy police flashlight to defend myself. The driver screamed, "I'm going to kill you," as he prepared to swipe me again. With a bone-crushing swing I hit his forearm, which fell limp, and the knife

> To us who are being saved [the cross] is the power of God.
> 1 Corinthians 1:18

269

dropped to the ground. A fireman grabbed the biker tightly, and the fight was over. The rescue crew now had to deal with his badly broken forearm. The other two bikers suddenly became cooperative!

With nothing left but paperwork, I headed for some quiet and coffee at the restaurant where my wife worked. When she filled my cup she asked, "What happened to your shirt?" Until then, I didn't know he'd cut it. Unbuttoning my shirt, we found he'd ruined it and my new Kevlar vest. Without the vest, the outcome could have been dramatically and tragically different. Later, opening my wallet, I saw the pocket cross! Instantly I thought of my salvation and my mother's love. Up to that point I'd been a "reluctant Christian," but not anymore. My faithful mother died many years ago, but I still carry that tattered card and small cross as a reminder of her love and of the price Jesus paid for my sins.

AUGUST 4

CASE SOLVED!

Constable Merv Tippe (Ret.)

Regina, Saskatchewan

BEING ONE of two officers in a small, rural Canadian town had its challenges. I knew it was God's hand that took me there, so it was interesting to wonder what his plans were for me. The night I interviewed for the job, the chief of police advised me he was a member of a religious group most Christians view as a cult. I made it clear to him I was a Bible-believing, born-again Christian.

Many things happened the year we were together in which God clearly demonstrated his power and glory. One such incident was a break-in at the local café. After we responded and gathered evidence, the Chief asked what I thought the chances were of apprehending the culprit. I told him, "Very good, but first I want to go home, grab a quick bite to eat, and pray for an hour."

He asked, "Do you really think praying will help?"

My reply? "I know of no other way."

About an hour later the Chief was back at my house. When we got into the patrol car, he asked if I still felt that we would catch the culprit. "Yes," I said. Then he asked if I had prayed, and again I said yes.

He told me, "You better have!" When I asked why he replied, "Because I just got off the phone with the radio station, and told them we would have the culprits in custody by 3:30 this afternoon!" Talk about pressure and demonstrating that God answers prayer! Praise be to him—we had the thieves in custody by 3 o'clock—crime solved!

> I was shown mercy because I acted in ignorance and unbelief
> 1 Timothy 1:13

An observer might say catching them was a miracle, but the true miracle was yet to come. After many conversations and demonstrations of my faith in the one, true God, it was my joy to stand beside the Chief one day outside his garage. There he took the step of setting fire to all the books and materials he had gotten from the cult. He told me, "Merv, I don't yet believe like you do, but I have seen enough to know that what I have believed is not the truth." After more study, prayer, and the influence of other Christians, the true miracle came—three months later a fellow believer led the Chief to Christ—case solved!

AUGUST 5

RESULTS, NOT EXCUSES

Sergeant Trace Wedel, Badge No. 35123

California Department of Corrections

TRAVER HAD never worked Control before, and hoped I'd direct him elsewhere. As the control sergeant at one of California's medium-security prisons, I could have made that call. Instead I said, "No, stay. You have to learn it sometime." Control is intimidating to the uninitiated. I had to set up for that evening's prisonwide inmate count, while Traver was kept busy handling nonstop radio traffic and phone calls, exchanging equipment between employees going home and those coming to work, and remotely opening entrance and exit doors.

About thirty minutes into the shift, I heard him tell a caller, "I'm sorry, I don't normally work this job. They usually redirect me."

After hearing him tell that to three callers I instructed him, "Traver, people don't want excuses. They want results." Though he wasn't too pleased with the conversation, I continued, "People who call for information don't care about your problems. If you don't know the answer, politely put them on hold, and ask me. We'll figure it out together." The rest of the night Traver asked a gazillion questions, but together we got results. During the evening we began to connect (perhaps he reminded me of myself when I first started), and at the end of the shift I told him he did a good job. As we shook hands and parted I gave him my number, and told him to call me if he ever had questions or needed help.

He called me a week later and told me I'd made him angry when I had said, "People don't want excuses. They want results." Then he added, "But, the longer I thought about it, the more I realized you were right. Not just about the job in Control, but about me: I realize my whole life I've been making excuses. I really appreciate what you said." That was the beginning of a fifteen-year friendship. We've both had our trials and tribulations, but remained friends. About three years ago he hit rock bottom with his alcohol addiction and finally turned his life over to Christ. He's been sober and improving ever since.

> He who heeds discipline shows the way to life, but whoever ignores correction leads others astray. Proverbs 10:17

My purpose in keeping Traver in Control that night was not for punishment, but to help him grow in his job. He had looked at it as negative, while I meant it for good. Many times we resent where God has us, but the Lord has a reason for it. If we listen, as Traver did, I firmly believe the end result will be worth it.

MORE THAN I EVER WANTED TO KNOW

Anonymous
California Police Officer

MORE than I ever wanted to know" is the only way to describe this conversation. When I booked "Joe" into jail about 10 p.m. he had all the signs of being a "tweaker" (long-term heroin user)—sickly, weak, pale, thinner than a rail, and sweating like a faucet. When I asked him if he knew what to expect, he politely replied, "Yes, officer." With his politeness, and since I had time on my hands, I asked him if he'd like to talk—and that opened the floodgates. With his head down like a whipped dog, he launched into his story.

Joe had been a normal, hard-working construction worker—married, had a child, a home, good benefits package, caring friends, and loving family. Then he got laid off and became depressed about letting his family down. Joe's "buddy" introduced him to mind-numbing heroin. For a time he got "clean" and secured a retail job, but couldn't stay away from the drug's enticing feeling. Then Joe's wife got hooked. In the process they lost every sense of decency—home, friends, and their son, first to the state and then to Joe's parents. Now they "rented" a substandard room from another heroin addict. I asked him about a typical day in their life. I almost wish he hadn't told me.

> Speaking the truth in love, we will in all things grow up into him who is the Head, that is, Christ.
> Ephesians 4:15

Before getting out of bed they shot heroin. Then Joe's wife would get dolled up and head to a part of town where she could turn tricks—their source of income. I couldn't believe what I was hearing: A total stranger had told me he was pimping his wife for money to buy drugs. Joe said he didn't expect me to understand, that only another user can know how desperate a heroin addict can be. In a twisted way he said that sex and heroin were keeping them alive: Sex earned money to buy heroin, which kept them from getting sick, and paid the rent, which made their heroin-addicted landlord happy.

Joe had revealed himself to his core; now what should I say? I asked Joe if he knew the Lord, telling him only Jesus could free him of his addiction and forgive him of his sins. By then meaningful conversation wasn't possible—his last "fix" was wearing off and Joe was fading fast—so I don't know what he heard. The Scripture makes it plain that God, not men, draws lost souls to Christ. I don't know what Joe may ever do about Jesus, but I know I dealt with him as a Christian police officer should.

AN AMBASSADOR FOR CHRIST

David Laumatia, Senior Sergeant
New Zealand Police

UNFORTUNATELY, too many people reach a point where they have lost all hope, and decide to end their own lives. More often than not, I've found them to be folks who either didn't know the Lord or who had very confused ideas about God.

I responded to a call where a person tried to end his life after deciding he couldn't handle things anymore. His girlfriend and her sister found him hanging in a closet, but cut him down before he succeeded. He had made other attempts in the past, so the girls knew he *was* serious.

After he was taken to the hospital, they said they were at their wits' end trying to figure out what to do. His attempts were affecting their lives as well as his own. They had sought answers to the problem from many sources, but it was apparent to me they were looking in the wrong places.

> We are ambassadors for Christ, as though God were making an appeal through us.
> 2 Corinthians 5:20 (NASB)

It may have seemed peculiar to them a police officer would give his testimony, but I shared the profound effect God had made in my life. I said I understood why bad things were happening in their lives, and that Christ Jesus could do for them what he had done for me—freed me from being a self-centered, sinful person to have new life in him. They were desperate for an answer, and I knew of God's power to change their lives. As I spoke it was apparent they knew intuitively I was telling them the truth, so they asked how they could invite Jesus into their lives. After a short lesson where I explained the plan of salvation, they bowed their heads and prayed to receive Christ.

Police officers have a wide sphere of influence, and often have great opportunities to share the good news of Jesus. We have such a blessed hope through Christ Jesus that it would be a shame in this hurting world not to share that hope with people who need him. When I think of those girls and others with whom I have shared my testimony, I thank God for the wonderful opportunities he has given me through the career of policing.

NO "OPEN DOOR" POLICY HERE!

Sergeant Vito Ancona
Lisbon, ME, Police Department

AN OPEN door on the graveyard shift is not a good sign. You don't expect to find a pot of fresh coffee and donuts. Fact is, you really don't know what you'll discover. Most of the time I step inside and feel a sense of peace, knowing there's a reasonable explanation for what has happened. I always unsnap my holster but never draw my weapon. I know that's against everything we've been taught, but in our small town of 10,000, criminals hiding in buildings just wasn't a usual problem.

One night another officer and I responded to a call where a citizen "thought" they saw someone enter a large three-story-plus-attic old house. We entered the house through a cellar window. For some unexplainable reason I had a strong feeling we'd find someone, and immediately drew my weapon. We only used hand signals during the entire search, even though they weren't taught in any of our training.

We searched from cellar to attic but never heard a single noise. Except for the cellar window we entered, there were no signs anyone had been in the residence. Nothing had been touched, but I still felt that someone was there. As we searched the many rooms we covered each other carefully (it's too bad someone hadn't filmed us for training purposes!).

> Love the LORD your God, listen to his voice, and hold fast to him. For the LORD is your life.
> Deuteronomy 30:20

In the attic we found another door where interior walls had been added to make a room. Directly inside the door was a chimney. The space was too narrow for anyone to be hiding behind it, but to the left and the right I could see a small opening between the interior and exterior walls.

First I peered through the opening on the left, but saw nothing. I let my partner know I was heading to the other opening and went behind the chimney. I crouched, stepped back, and there he was—backed into the corner in the very last place he could hide! When he saw my weapon he raised his hands and went to his knees. It was someone I recognized, so I called him by name and we cuffed and searched him. Then we took him out and arrested him. As I said before, when I entered the building it was as if *someone* was telling me there *was* a person in the building and I needed to draw my weapon. I know it was the voice of God, and I'm glad I listened!

FLASH, BANG, FIZZLE!

Sergeant Michael Keller
Knoxville, TN, Police Department

IT SHOULD have been a routine SWAT call (although SWAT calls probably should never be termed "routine.") Instead, two unexpected events took place: The takedown went awry, and God gave me a loud "wake-up call" that finally got my attention. I had a modest Christian upbringing as a youth, but poor choices in friends and lifestyle had pretty much obliterated that.

The incident took place after I'd been on the SWAT team several years. A truck driver had broken into his girlfriend's condo and threatened to kill everybody—including himself—by blowing up the building. Negotiations had begun and SWAT was called, but things were at a standstill. It was getting dark; things were escalating, and we decided it was time to go in. The first man was to carry the shield and deploy the "flash-bang" (a device which makes a bright flash and shrill sound to temporarily blind and deafen). As "the martial arts guy," I would go second with gun holstered (as did the third man) and take away the knife. I had a strange feeling things might go wrong, which they did. The flash-bang took too long to detonate, taking away our element of surprise. In the melee that followed, he charged me with his upraised knife from a distance of two or three feet and yelled, "Shoot me! Shoot me!" I took a lateral step back and, by the grace of God—there is no other explanation—I was able to draw my gun from my secured, military flap-style holster. The first officer and I fired simultaneously, delivering five rounds, four of which were on target. Even though he was badly wounded (he died in

> He rescued me from my powerful enemy, from my foes, who were too strong for me.
> Psalm 18:17

surgery a few hours later), we still had to fight him to handcuff him. After the incident I was giddy; not because I had taken a life, but because I had stared death in the face and won!

After questioning by Internal Affairs, I called a Christian friend from my office. She helped me see that God places people in positions to do what others cannot, and that it was God's guiding hand that saved my life that fateful day. I knew she was right—there was simply no way to draw a holstered weapon from a distance of two feet and fire before he could stab me. I still marvel in disbelief that I survived that day, but only by the grace of God. After talking to my friend that night, I prayed in tears to receive Christ. The Christian journey I had begun in my teens had come full circle: God began a work in me that day that changed my life for the better—not perfect, but drastically different from before.

AUGUST 10

CAR BURGLARIES MADE US BROTHERS!

Detective Tim Tomisek

Chattanooga, TN, Police Department

FINDING FOLKS who burgle cars may not be my "dream job," but I'm the one who dreamed it up. After seven years in Patrol, including two years as a field-training officer, I became a property crimes detective. At the time our community was suffering five hundred to six hundred car break-ins a month, but the department lacked the man-hours to investigate. After one of our captains expressed great frustration over the problem, I suggested creating a specialized unit dealing just with auto burglaries, and he told me to "write up a plan." I did, it was approved, and I was put in command. I felt sort of like Joseph, who was put in charge after he gave God's plan to Pharaoh for dealing with the upcoming famine!

So far, so good! We had a plan and the go-ahead, but needed manpower. I asked for and got one of the city's finest patrol officers, who was a little apprehensive about coming over (was it because of me?), but finally decided to anyway. In our first month we received an overwhelming twenty to thirty reports a day! A big break was when a perpetrator was "caught in the act" and arrested by Patrol. When we interviewed him he confessed to ten other thefts, and we were on our way. Soon after a "Crime Stoppers" TV broadcast, a grandmother phoned to say that her grandson, a crack cocaine addict, was the

> How good and pleasant it is when brothers live together in unity!
> Psalm 133:1

one whose photo had been shown. He was at her house that very moment, so Patrol went immediately. We seized nearly two trunk loads of stolen goods right there. We drove him around the city, and he took us to thirty confirmed locations where he had broken into vehicles. That month the two of us cleared more than 40 cases, so we needed help! Finally we got our third man, a newcomer to our department but with ten years' experience elsewhere. In spite of the fact we were crowded into a tiny office with only two desks, we became instant friends. We worked hard, spent many long hours together, had great teamwork, and paid good dividends to the city with our efforts.

The real key to our success is the Lord. The three of us are strong Christians, active in our churches and in police Bible studies, and have common goals for our lives and families. When we have problems or concerns, we commiserate and pray together as brothers should. Officers often are called "brothers in blue." We are brothers twice over: "in blue," and "in Christ."

THE DEADLY DRINK

Lisa Lerner, wife of Officer Chuck Lerner
Law Enforcement Missionary
El Paso, TX

MANY PETTY thieves lack the education and background for better employment, and often work in fast-food places. When officers eat someplace where a worker is someone they once arrested, they have to watch out for "revenge" in the way of finding spit, bugs, snot, etc., in their food.

Our daughter was six months old, and Chuck was working second (the "graveyard") shift, training a rookie. This night they ate at a local pizza joint they frequented, and Chuck saw that one of the employees was

278

someone he had arrested once. Not long after they had eaten and left, Chuck started to swell and sweat profusely. He felt really sick, so called me to say he was coming home.

When he came through the front door, his face was nearly unrecognizable because it was swollen so badly. His uniform was soaked with sweat, and he just stumbled past me into the bathroom. Chuck's partner was white as a sheet, and said he didn't know what happened: They had shared the same pizza, but he had tea and Chuck had a soda. Going to the bathroom I found Chuck slumped down in the shower, pale and very listless. I didn't know whether to call 9-1-1 or take him to the ER. In a moment it was as though God was telling me to call 9-1-1. The ambulance arrived within minutes. When the medics began to take Chuck's vitals, they could not get a blood pressure reading. His pulse was so low that the "look" between the two EMTs almost sent me to my knees in prayer. They injected both of his thighs with Epinephrine, started an IV in both arms, and took him code 3 (emergency, use lights and siren) to a local hospital. I called friends to stay with our daughter so I could go with him. Believe me, this was one time when I "pray[ed] without ceasing" (1 Thessalonians 5:17).

> And the prayer offered in faith will make the sick person well. James 5:15

At the ER the doctors determined he had "ingested" something that had sent him into anaphylactic shock. They also said that if I had decided to drive him to the hospital myself, he would not have survived. We never determined exactly what was in his drink, but whatever it was could have killed him. God has been faithful to watch over Chuck all these years, and we're so grateful for his merciful care that night.

AUGUST 12

WHY DIDN'T HE SHOOT?

Sergeant David M. Greenhalgh (Ret.)
Delta (Vancouver, Canada) Police Department

IN 1971 I was working in uniform for the Federal Ports Police in the city of Vancouver, British Columbia. About 4 o'clock one morning, my alert partner spotted a suspicious male in the cab of a tractor-trailer unit. We drove past slowly as if seeing nothing and then maintained surveillance from behind a grain elevator. Eventually the truck moved off,

and we attempted to stop it with the aid of another patrol cruiser. What we didn't know was that the suspect was stealing the rig. He did not stop for our lights and siren, and we were in a low-speed pursuit through the narrow streets of downtown Vancouver.

After a mile or two we got ahead of the rig via a side road and cut it off at a "T" junction. The driver saw us, stopped midblock and bailed out into a vacant lot among old townhouses. At the back of the lot was a dark laneway. In the lot were seven or eight abandoned large cement-truck drums that had been damaged by cement setting up. I was at least 400 feet behind the suspect, and ran past the drums to the dark laneway. I had no sense of which way the suspect had gone. Dispatch had called for backup from the city police K-9 unit, so we secured the area and waited. A canine officer found the suspect hiding inside one of the abandoned cement drums.

> Man's days are determined; you have decreed the number of his months and have set limits he cannot exceed.
> Job 14:5

The Vancouver city officers made the arrest and took the data; they also ended up doing all the paperwork! A few hours later they called us. During the interview the suspect admitted he had a loaded pistol (found later in the drum) and considered shooting me in the back as I ran right past him and stood in the laneway! This is long before body armor was issued. It was inconceivable to me that he had stopped within 75 feet of the stolen truck when he had a 400-foot lead on me, and that he'd forego his opportunity to shoot me.

I forgot all about this event until my retirement function in 2003. I wanted one more opportunity to testify about how the Lord walked with me through my entire career, and the Holy Spirit reminded me of this incident. From before I was formed in the womb, God determined my days. That was not the day!

HOW'S MOM?

Detective/Sergeant Ingrid Dean
Michigan State Police

THE YOUNG minister was concerned: Thelma hadn't been to church in three weeks and wasn't answering her door. Could the police help?

Thinking this might be a job for a female officer, my sergeant dispatched me on this "suspicious situation." When the minister and I arrived, I immediately suspected the problem: Her mailbox was stuffed with mail. Since she had no transportation unless someone picked her up, obviously she was inside and in trouble. I remember full well how young and "innocent" the minister seemed, and couldn't help but wonder how he'd react to what I thought we'd find.

The doors were locked, and she didn't answer the bell. Searching around the house for an unlocked window, we finally found one in the bathroom, through which I entered. As soon as we lifted it up we smelled it—death. Even if you've never smelled it before, you know immediately what it is. There is something unnatural and animalistic about it; even a child recognizes the odor. It was quite apparent Thelma had been dead for a while, as I found her body decomposing on the couch. It was summer, there was no ventilation, and the house was stifling with the heat. I was marshaling my thoughts and about to unlock the door to let the minister in when the telephone rang. *It's probably my sergeant checking up on me,* I thought, so I answered it: "Trooper Dean, State Police."

> Precious in the sight of the LORD is the death of his saints. Psalm 116:15

There was a moment of shocked silence on the other end before a female voice said, "Hello, is my mother there, is she all right, and is this *really* the police?"

What could I say? I couldn't lie. Protocol calls for us to find the woman's relatives, notify the police in their areas, and have local officers notify them in person. Even so, swallowing hard I told her the truth . . . and she broke down over the phone. After a few more questions she quieted down, and asked me if I would pray with her, and I did. Then I remembered, *There's a minister outside the front door! Coming to my senses,* I let him in and handed him the phone to handle *his* business . . . and I set to work handling *mine!*

I've thought about that situation several times. I believe God inspired the daughter to call when she did, because the Lord knew there would be people there who could meet her spiritual needs. God knew I was a Christian and would handle it from a believer's perspective (though it's the first time I ever was asked to pray at a scene). The timing was perfect because God had orchestrated it all!

GOD KNEW BEST

Constable Jesse Weeks, No. 8482

Toronto, Canada, Police Service

PROVERBS 16:9 says, "In his heart a man plans his course, but the LORD determines his steps." In my sixth year with the Toronto Police Service I applied for—and obtained, against all odds—a prestigious full-time plainclothes position. With one week of evening shift left before starting the new job, I planned to stay "off the radar."

During that week, I was concerned about the way another officer handled an arrest, and expressed that to one of my sergeants. I wanted to protect her reputation, but my sergeant saw it as an attack on her integrity. He called my "boss-to-be," suggesting I might not be trustworthy. Under a cloud of doubt and rumors, the next week I entered the Major Crime unit. I worked hard to prove myself and got along well with the team. However, five months later the unit's detective was promoted and replaced by a detective who did not like me.

Shortly after, a friend of mine from high school suffered emotional difficulties over a breakup. My attempts to mediate in settling a property dispute between him and his ex ended up with the ex filing a complaint against me. She said my friend used my position as a police officer to intimidate her.

The complaint made its way to management, with the implication I was a rogue cop not to be trusted. I was not given a chance to explain, and was out and back on the street that week! Rumors swirled again, with everyone wondering why I got the boot. I tried to recover over the next nine months, but was fearful I would make another mistake and be raked over the coals again. I found it hard to make decisions, and began falling into depression. I felt no hope of ever advancing and was strongly motivated to leave policing.

Finally, with God's help, I took a risk and joined a new unit. It wasn't a glamorous position, but it gave me the fresh start I needed. I made some new friends, am enjoying policing again, and have time to pursue personal interests. I relish the quietness of the time I have to be with my wife, and

> Make it your ambition to lead a quiet life . . . so that your daily life may win the respect of outsiders and so that you will not be dependent on anybody.
> 1 Thessalonians 4:11, 12

am much better off not being in a high-pressure position that can consume an officer and destroy one's marriage. After much struggle and loss of self-confidence, the Lord restored my soul and made my path straight.

MY FIRST CALL

Chaplain Mike Cava
Valencia County, NM, Sheriff's Department

IT WASN'T just another August day in 1981: I had graduated from the Reserve Police Academy and reported for work. My first assignment? To notify a mother that her 19-year-old son had died after a motorcycle accident in another state! To make things more difficult, before he died he had written a poem he wanted someone to read to her. Then we discovered that the mother had a heart condition. We made the notification without incident but, like everyone's first call, it always will be in my memory.

During my sixteen years with the San Diego Police Department I had made sergeant, and felt I'd be there many more years. But one day I received a call from a high school friend who called to invite me to the school's thirty-year reunion. (He had never called before!) Could I come? I did, and met a friend now living in New Mexico. Over the next five years we corresponded, my wife and I made several trips to New Mexico, and we fell in love with the state. Though I hadn't planned on retiring or moving away, things "just happened" in such a way we ended up doing both.

> In his heart a man plans his course, but the LORD determines his steps.
> Proverbs 16:9

When we arrived in New Mexico, the church we joined was in the process of establishing a chaplaincy program with the sheriff's office. I completed all the requirements and have been a volunteer chaplain for them ever since. Among my other duties, I assist with death notifications and comfort to trauma victims.

As I think back over my life I am reminded of what God says in Jeremiah 1:5: "Before I formed you in the womb I knew you; Before you were born I sanctified you; I ordained you a prophet to the nations." When I made that scary death notification "first call," it wasn't by chance. I believe God was preparing me for twenty-one years later when I would become a chaplain and make many such calls. I believe he orchestrated the events that led us to New Mexico and my becoming a chaplain. None of this was in my plans, but it was in God's. I firmly believe God has a plan for every man, woman, and child. My counsel: Wait on the Lord (*wait* means "to serve"), and let God reveal his will for you!

I JUMPED OFF THE ZILWAUKEE BRIDGE

Captain Gary McGhee (Deceased)

Michigan State Police

I WAS WORKING on I-75 when told to go to the Zilwaukee Bridge; the captain of a 554-foot ship had suffered a heart attack. Then he lost control of the ship and rammed the drawbridge. The only way for a rescuer to reach him was to jump off the bridge, so I did! It was a long way down, and when I landed—BAM! A huge shock wave, like nothing I had ever experienced, jolted my hips and entire spine when I hit! Crew members had to help me to my feet. I was able to bring the captain to consciousness, but he was unresponsive. I discovered he was a diabetic, so we gave him something sweet to revive him. Then first responders arrived with ladders, and he was removed for treatment. We determined that the ship had damaged the main girders of the bridge, and was supporting the southbound lanes. Though I wasn't sure of my authority, I told them not to move the ship. Fortunately, my commanders agreed, and the ship's company cooperated. I went back to work.

The ship's captain sent a thank you note which simply read, "Thank you for saving my life." If a trooper did something good, it was published in an interdepartmental newsletter. So I sent them a copy of the note and a description of what had happened. That's when the trouble started!

Not long after sending the note up the line, my boss called me into his office.

> "Be careful not to do your 'acts of righteousness' before men, to be seen by them. If you do, you will have no reward from your Father in heaven. Matthew 6:1

"Trooper, the department has initiated a Life Saving Award and you're eligible—but you have to prove that your efforts saved the captain's life!"

I refused. "That would be demeaning. I didn't do it to get an award; it was just part of my job!" We didn't part on friendly terms! Later, he told me emphatically that the higher-ups wanted me to get the proof. Again, I refused, so he did the paperwork himself. When the award came it was unceremoniously left in my mail drawer.

As a result of the jump I've had eight operations on my knees, a spinal fusion, bone spurs removed, broken bones removed from my feet, degenerative arthritis, and a host of other issues. And of course, there was the hassle about the award! Should I have jumped? The Bible says we are to "do to others what [we] would have them do to [us]." The captain needed help, and I responded to the call. He lived, and sent a thank you note. That should have been reward enough!

"OH, SHOOT, HE'S GONNA BE OKAY!"

Captain Mark Edwards (Ret.)
Plainfield, NJ, Police Division

WHEN HE said that, I knew I'd survive—but what damage had been done? That night I was working my regular extra job at Burger King, when a quiet evening turned deadly. An armed robbery had taken place nearby, and the suspect was heading my way. Officers in two marked cars, the suspect, and I converged in the parking lot almost simultaneously. To let the officers know where I was—and hoping to stop the suspect—I yelled "Police! Halt!" With that, he fired in the direction of two officers who had exited their car.

I moved to my left to clear their field, monitoring where I thought the suspect might head, and he did! When he saw me, he raised his gun. I thought, *Here we go!* I went into a squat stance, and we exchanged fire. Suddenly I felt like I'd been struck in the head with a bat and thought, *He hit me, now I'm really mad!* I got off one more round and tried to break my stance to help the others pursue him, but fell to the ground. I felt wet hair on my head, and found my hand dripping with blood. *Not good, I* thought, *a head wound usually ranges from extremely damaging to fatal.*

When I checked my other body parts, they seemed to be in working order. I retrieved my gun from about eight feet away, holstered it, and witnessed the final standoff

> There is no god besides me . . . I have wounded and I will heal.
> Deuteronomy 32:39

from where I lay: The suspect lost! Head wounds really bleed, and the sight of me lying quietly in a pool of blood was not encouraging to my rescuers. A paramedic friend said, "Mark, how many fingers do you see on my hand?

Raising my head and seeing all five fingers, I answered, "One short of a half-dozen."

The medic quipped, "Oh, shoot, he's gonna be okay!"

If you survive, one thing about being an "officer down" is the solicitous treatment by emergency personnel. Once in ER, the doctor found I'd been hit twice. There was a lot of blood but no penetration, and it took a lot of scraping to remove the lead deposit smears on the skull. I was released that night. My wife had been brought to the hospital, and officers sent to the house to watch our two young sons. Our daughter had been babysitting. When she came home and saw the police cars, she was traumatized—refused to discuss it for years. But God is good: I survived, and my frazzled daughter, now a mom, had a daughter born on the ninth anniversary of the shooting.

AUGUST 18

"A WORD FITLY SPOKEN"

Sergeant William C. Bolt

Worthington, MN, Police Department

WHILE TRAINING to become a police officer, I had the opportunity to work on Bike Patrol for a small town in Minnesota. As are many people when they enter the field of law enforcement, I was ambitious and idealistic. I worked hard, volunteered for any assignment, and envisioned a world of bad guys and heroic moments that would demonstrate my character and prove my worth.

One hot summer day I rode my bike all over town, running errands for the Chief, talking to kids, and looking for parking violators. After several hours I returned to the department to take a break in the air-conditioned offices and get a drink of cold water.

As I passed the Chief's office, I noticed he was talking to a lady. After walking on a couple of steps, I felt compelled to turn back. I knocked on his open door and apologized for interrupting him. Then I looked at the lady, complimented her on her dress, and left his office.

The next day the Chief called me into his office. After inviting me to sit down, he told me the lady was a rape victim from an old case, and occasionally came in to talk. He said she continued to have difficulties recovering from the assault and moving on in her life. Then he said my honest and sincere compliment had been greatly appreciated, and meant a great deal to her.

This "early on" incident was a great help in shaping my thinking. Catching bad guys is our job, but it takes something more to make us great. That happens when we take time to care about others, show compassion, demonstrate empathy, and treat people like human beings. "Small moments in time" are often when we make the greatest and longest-lasting impact on others. I try to seek out those opportunities and cherish them when I find them. There's an old saying: "I'd rather see a sermon than hear one any day." It's a good saying!

> A word fitly spoken is like apples of gold in pictures of silver.
> Proverbs 25:11 (KJV)

BOSS, I LIED TO YOU!

Constable Matt Davis—MDAH12

Strategic Traffic Unit—Huntly, New Zealand

ONE EVENING after a short high-speed chase, I caught up with a car and stopped it. Being on my own I quickly prayed for protection, something like *"Help me, Lord!"*

The car had two occupants, and the driver was drunk. After going through the drunk driver process, all seemed fine until I asked for his keys. He suddenly became very violent and anti-police! When his friend tried to calm him down, he only became more angry. I had to fight with him in order to subdue and arrest him.

I had called for backup, so a colleague drove us back to the station. On the way the drunken driver apologized for his behavior. I replied by saying I totally forgave him. When he asked if I really meant it, I said yes,

because I was a Christian. As we were processing him back at the station, I asked God for the opportunity to share the Gospel with him. Immediately I felt impressed that God was telling me to say, "You used to go to church as a young fella." I felt I would be going out on a limb if I did, but "gave it a punt" nevertheless.

He replied, "Nah, boss, not me." I was gutted—perhaps I heard God wrong, so I put it in the back of my mind.

He needed a ride home, so I took him. Partway through the journey he piped up and said, "Boss, I'm really sorry, I lied to you—I used to go to church . . ." and he went on to say he'd spent his youth searching for God but never found him. I shared and explained the Good News of redemption through Jesus, then prayed with him and for him. Before he left my car I felt many of his questions had been answered, and he had received the knowledge he had been searching for. Sadly, I do not know if he ever followed up on what I told him, but I know he heard the truth about God.

AUGUST 20

NOT "BUSINESS AS USUAL!"

Officer M. Kaiser

Concord California Police Department

ANOTHER 'business as usual' day, I thought, wondering where I would get my mid-morning coffee. When my beat officer asked for assistance at the parole office, I groaned, "What now?"

A few days earlier, a registered sex offender on federal parole had been detained on the UC Berkeley campus. Told to report to his parole officer, he brought along his wife and three young girls. The oldest, "Alissa," claimed to be the parent of the other two. Their story didn't pan out, which is why the parole officer asked for our help. The parolee claimed to be her uncle, but we couldn't confirm her real name or any tan-

288

gible reason why she was with him. Since he was a registered sex offender, our main concern was for the minor girls, ages 11 and 15. All of us were very frustrated.

After an irritating hour of inconsistent statements, my beat partner and I decided on one last attempt to ascertain the truth. I was hungry and caffeine deprived, but something wasn't right, and duty pulled me to protect the two minors. I was perplexed by all the lies, and why Alissa wouldn't tell us her true identity? I offered to speak to Alissa alone, giving her a chance to tell the truth before we notified Children and Family Services. We talked for well over two hours and built great rapport, but Alissa remained afraid...she didn't want to get anyone in trouble. Then my sergeant asked me to step out of the room, where he told me the parolee had admitted to kidnapping and raping Alissa a long time ago when she was eleven. I returned to the room, and after another grueling fifteen minutes Alissa finally confirmed his admission. Still, she was too fearful to speak her name. Recalling Jeremiah 29:11, I told her there was a greater purpose in why she and I had been together. I didn't have all the answers, but I believed it was God's plan, and that everything would work alright. I also told Alissa we would inform her family that she was alive, and she could return home to them. Alissa remained quite concerned so I asked, "Would it be easier to write your name instead of saying it?" I gave her my notepad and after much hesitation she scribbled her name, "Jaycee Lee Dugard."

> "For I know the plans I have for you," declares the LORD, "plans to prosper you and not to harm you, plans to give you hope and a future."
> Jeremiah 29:11

I remain amazed at the events of that "not business as usual" morning! God used the experiences of my sergeant and me - two Christian police officers working together - to crack open what would become a worldwide news story. For on that August day, God's orchestrated the coming together of Jaycee, my sergeant, my beat officer and I, to expose the parolee—Phillip Garrido—and secure Jaycee's freedom.

A CUP OF COLD WATER

Anonymous

Houston, TX, Police Department

IT WAS A "forgery in progress" call, and I was the first officer to arrive at the bank. From the description we had received, I immediately recognized the suspect. I ordered him to face away from me and place his hands behind his back so I could handcuff him. At first he complied, then suddenly turned and faced me. Like a football player practicing a drill, he began running in place, moving from side-to-side with his hands open in front of his chest. Without warning he charged and hit me with his body. I was only able to land one good punch to his face before he threw me to the ground and escaped out the front door.

Running to his rental car, he fled the scene. However, I soon caught up to him in my patrol car, and the chase was on! He was driving at a high rate of speed and disregarding traffic signals, making this a dangerous pursuit. Though I'd been involved in many pursuits over the years, for some reason I had never prayed and asked God to intervene. This time I did: I asked the Lord to stop the pursuit! Moments after that prayer, an amazing thing happened: A back tire on his vehicle blew, forcing the car up onto a metal guardrail. With the car no longer usable, he fled the scene on foot. Shortly thereafter, a county deputy and I caught him.

> And if anyone gives even a cup of cold water to one of these . . . he will certainly not lose his reward. Matthew 10:42

After the chase and in his anxiety, the handcuffed suspect told me he was very thirsty. Without removing his handcuffs, I held a cup of cold water to his mouth as he sat in my car. I realized this man also was spiritually thirsty. As Proverbs 25:25 says, "Like cold water to a weary soul is good news from a distant land." After quenching his physical thirst, I shared the Good News of the Living Water available through Jesus Christ. I wondered if he had ever set foot in a church and heard that "good news from a distant land!" One more thing: That was the day I learned to use prayer as a spiritual weapon in the war on crime. I have continued to do so ever since!

THE VIRUS OF SIN

David Laumatia, Senior Sergeant
New Zealand Police

THOUSANDS OF viruses caused my home computer to crash. I looked in the yellow pages, found a person named "Niko," and asked him to come.

He came over, and whilst fixing my computer looked at my wall of police photographs and certificates. He told me he wanted to join the police, so I invited him out on patrol.

While we were driving and when the night grew quiet, we started to talk about God. Niko told me he attended church, so I asked him if he knew God and about any sin in his life. He was a little taken aback by that question, and I felt sure he wanted to get out of my car right then and there. I told him about how I had come to Christ, and invited him over for further discussions.

Even though Niko struggled with contacting me again, he came anyway. As we talked about Jesus and how to make him real in your life, Niko took that step and asked Jesus into his heart. Since then, at least twelve people in his family have given their lives to the Lord. These include his wife and his then-84-year-old-grandmother-in-law, who since has gone on to be with our Lord.

> Therefore go and make disciples of all nations, baptizing them in the name of the Father and of the Son and of the Holy Spirit.
> Matthew 28:19

This incident helped me see that when you reach one person for the Lord, that person can reach a multitude of others!

Niko came to fix the viruses on my computer, but God wanted, through Christ Jesus, to fix the virus of sin in his life. What a privilege it was to be used like that!

As a police officer I have civil authority, but as a Christian I know also that God has given me authority to make disciples.

AMBUSHED WITHOUT HOPE

Corporal James Kariuki, No. 31067
Kenya Police Service, Signals Branch Nyeri

IN JANUARY 1977, I joined the Kenya Police Service in the paramilitary General Service Unit (GSU). In July of 1978 I was deployed to the Eastern Province, Moyale District, a border town between Kenya and Ethiopia (biblically known as Abyssinia). There were 130 men in our company, well-trained to fight the *Shifta* bandits and secessionists based in parts of northern Kenya and Ethiopia. These bandits received training and support from Somalia, which also claimed part of Kenya and the neighboring Ethiopia. A month after my deployment, Kenya lost its founding father and president, Jomo Kenyatta (popularly known as "Mzee"), and the country was left leaderless.

Taking advantage of the nationwide mourning, eight hundred insurgents descended on Moyale and its environs with their powerful Alexander Kalashnikovs (AK-47s), anti-personnel grenades, and mortar bombs. Their aim was to get food, drugs, arms, and ammunition for new recruits who had just finished training in Somalia. We had two platoons of sixty GSU men stationed two kilometers from the town, with another eighty manning the border, so were badly outnumbered. In less than ten minutes we were mobilized and on our way in trucks and Land Rovers. However,

> For the Lord had caused the Arameans to hear the sound of chariots and horses and a great army . . . So they got up and fled in the dusk.
> 2 Kings 7:6, 7

before we could reach the area, we were ambushed! Within minutes, six of our officers were dead and another two seriously injured. We called for reinforcements from Nairobi and the men on the border. Nairobi, six hundred kilometers away, sent the Air Force, but they could not help us. Unfortunately, we had to try to fight our way out of the ambush.

We were running out of ammunition, and it seemed only God could rescue us. For the first time in months I remembered God and cried out to him. I had a religious background, but did not accept Jesus as my Lord and Savior until after this incident. At the same time a friend asked how many bullets I had. We had an unwritten rule that it was better to kill ourselves than become prisoners of war. The four bullets I had left gave me two more shots and two to take our own lives.

Suddenly, without warning and by the grace of God, the enemy retreated, and the ambush was over! Another ten minutes and I might have committed suicide. But just as Jesus saved humankind at just the right time, the Lord saved me and my colleagues when the situation was desperate! Hallelujah!

SUICIDE . . . OR LIFE?

Jason J. Everett

Rolling Meadows, IL, Police Department

SUICIDE IS never the right answer—for the individual, loved ones, the community, or the police. Suicide is the one form of death in which the police always are involved, and it's a heart-wrenching experience.

A local street gang member I've had to deal with since early in my career attempted suicide, and I was one of the officers who responded. We found him naked at the top of the stairs leading to his apartment. He was screaming that he was going to kill all of us, and advanced toward us ignoring all commands. At his mother's request but against his wishes, we were compelled to commit him to the hospital. He had attempted to kill himself with alcohol, marijuana, cocaine, and over-the-counter pain medication.

A couple of days later I picked him up at the hospital to take him to the station for booking. I wanted to talk to him about his destructive behavior, but he refused. My primary concern was not the criminal charges, which were relatively minor, but his mental health. He had a wife and a very young son, and was destroying their lives along with his own. To break the silence I finally told him, "I really got to know way too much of you the other night, and there are some parts of your body you should not be showing off in public." He looked at me, chuckled, and said he was too far out of it that night to remember much.

> "Then you will know the truth, and the truth will set you free." John 8:32

From that point on I was able to speak at length with him about the responsibilities of being a good father for his child and a good husband to his wife, and the need to seek help for his addiction. A week later I confirmed that he had contacted a number of recovery services. I would like to report that today he is clean and sober with a good family life—but he is not. What I can say is that for the first time in eight years he is addressing his problems, and has taken a major step in the right direction. As the old saying goes, "You can lead a horse to water, but you can't make him drink." I did what I could, I "[spoke] the truth in love" (Ephesians 4:15).

JUSTICE FOR ALL

Officer/Chaplain J. R. McNeil, Badge No. 279

Pinellas Park, FL, Police Department

SITTING IN my cruiser toward the end of my shift I heard a rap on my window. It was one of our younger officers. He looked as though he were about to have a heart attack, and motioned for me to follow him. Immediately I sensed this was something he wanted to discuss with me as the departmental chaplain.

As we double-timed it into the building and down a long hallway, my mind raced trying to determine why all the hurry. Finally, when we reached a spot seldom frequented by officers, he stopped and pleaded, "I hope you have the answer I need because I'm desperate!" I listened.

He needed to release a boatload of steam and poured it out. On the job a few nights earlier he was forced to take action against another officer, and it was eating him alive. That is something I had to do one time, and it is something officers pray will never be their task. We take an oath to "protect and serve, no matter what," but when it comes to the "badge family" it's like taking a shot in your heart! I fought to keep back the tears. This young officer figured he had committed the "unpardonable sin," and didn't know what to do. I slapped him on the shoulder and told him I understood because I also had been in that position. I reminded him we take an oath that can feel like a curse when it's one of our own. With tears in our eyes, at that moment we truly became "brothers in blue."

After praying, we agreed the best thing he could do was take a few days off work and away from the situation—let the department deal with

> Do not pervert justice; do not show partiality to the poor or favoritism to the great, but judge your neighbor fairly.
> Leviticus 19:15

the matter. Together we sought out his supervisor for the permission he needed, then parted company. I thanked God for the opportunity to help this young man, and for the young officer who realized coming to me was a good first step. Thank you, Lord, for letting me be a police chaplain!

HALL OF SHAME!

Chaplain Joseph Paluszak
Virginia Beach, VA, Police Department

SECOND Thessalonians 3:5 reads, "May the Lord direct your hearts into God's love and Christ's perseverance." This doesn't always come naturally, and more than once God has had to direct my heart away from darkness and back into his love. The lessons I learn from those incidents end up in my "Hall of Shame," and are much more valuable in teaching others than those in my "Hall of Fame."

In policing and chaplaincy there's a tendency to become cynical. When you see people making irresponsible and downright dangerous choices, it is easy to become cynical. Cynicism quickly can be transformed into anger and harsh judgment, especially when another's thoughtlessness destroys innocent lives.

I responded to a double fatality caused when a drunk driver slammed into the car of an innocent couple. At the accident scene and later at the hospital, I shared in their daughter's anguish over her parents' deaths and her anger toward the perpetrator. When the investigating officer informed her the driver was being charged with manslaughter, I inwardly rejoiced with her.

God called me back to my senses when another department chaplain asked if I had taken the opportunity to minister to the driver. Ouch! Not only had I neglected that but—if truth be known—until that moment I had no desire to. Later, friends and family told me the driver was highly thought of by his co-workers and peers, and his actions were completely out of character. Both he and his family were devastated by the

> "You have heard that it was said, 'Love your neighbor and hate your enemy.' But I tell you: Love your enemies and pray for those who persecute you that you may be sons of your Father in heaven."
> Matthew 5:43–45

tragedy. If that chastisement wasn't enough, the following Sunday one of his co-workers grabbed my arm as I was leaving the sanctuary and told me how deeply she was hurting. She said no one—not family, friends, or priest—had been allowed to visit him in his hospital bed where he was handcuffed and under guard. He was suffering immensely from what had happened.

In my self-righteous judgmentalism I had forgotten that God is there for those who fail, as well as those who succeed. Forgiveness "seventy times seven" times applies to all. God knows I've had to throw myself on his mercy often. Jesus taught, "Blessed are the merciful: for they shall obtain mercy" (Matthew 5:7 KJV). With all my weaknesses and short-comings, no one needs mercy more than I.

AUGUST 27

THE MAN IN WHITE

Lieutenant Michael Gates, Chaplain

Pineville, LA, Police Department

IN MY nineteen years as a police officer and chaplain in Pineville, I have seen God at work more times than I can count. Many times the Lord has saved me or others from harm when it didn't seem possible.

One such case involved a child struck by a car. Accident reconstruction indicated the car had been traveling 55 miles per hour when the child was hit. That alone should have killed him. Witnesses said the child bounced off the hood of the car onto the roof, then to the trunk, and finally onto the highway. I was traveling on the same road about half-a-mile away when the accident occurred, so I got there very quickly.

> "For my thoughts are not your thoughts, neither are your ways my ways," declares the LORD. Isaiah 55:8

What I found was horrifying: The child was lying in a pool of blood but still conscious, reaching up to me. We called for a medical helicopter as quickly as possible to airlift him to a hospital. I knew the results couldn't be good. Yet, when the report came back the child had suffered no internal injuries, no broken bones, and no trauma except superficial wounds on his facial area (a wound on the head can produce a substantial blood loss). After a short stay in the ER he was released without extensive treatment. There just wasn't any logical answer for that.

In my investigation, witnesses reported seeing a man in white go to the child immediately after the accident. They said he appeared to bend down and pray over the boy, and then disappeared into the crowd of onlookers who had gathered. Needless to say, the man could not be located and wasn't seen again.

Situations like that always leave me mystified. Some would say "the man was Jesus," while others scoff at the idea. Some might say it simply was an illusion of the mind. As for me, I simply leave it with the individual. Scripture makes it clear that God's thoughts and ways are not ours (Isaiah 55:8). Who am I to say the One who made the universe is not capable of saving a small child's life in the face of indubitable circumstances? Whatever the reason, I have no doubt it was God's hand at work that saved that small child from certain death!

DID YOU REALLY KILL THOSE PEOPLE?

Officer Jim Salo

Las Animas, CO, Police Department

I WAS A rookie in the Las Animas Police Department in 1973, but I was not a rookie Christian. From the time I received Christ at 7 years old, I took my faith very seriously.

While I was working day shift, we received a BOL ("Be on Lookout") bulletin about a convicted double-murderer from North Carolina who might possibly be heading our way. We took this very seriously. We had been taught to play "what if" mind games as to what we might do in certain scenarios, and after receiving the BOL I did just that. But I never dreamed that convict would ever make it to our small town of 3,000 people!

Later that morning we got a call from a local merchant who said a man just leaving his store "acted weird." My backup partner and I went to the store and when we saw him, he looked just like the man described in the bulletin. Without hesitation we drew down on him and arrested him at gunpoint. When he saw two guns pointed his way from two different positions he didn't make a move! The arrest didn't go the way my mind-game scenario had imagined, but it went very smoothly.

> But the Scripture declares that the whole world is a prisoner of sin, so that what was promised, being given through faith in Jesus Christ, might be given to those who believe.
> Galatians 3:22

We held him until the North Carolina authorities came to pick him up. I happened to be on duty again that day, and was the officer who had to process his transfer to the officers who came to get him. We finished the paperwork about a half-hour early, giving me some time alone with the convict in the interrogation room. God gave me an open opportunity and I took it. I just asked him right out, "Did you really kill those two people you were convicted of killing?"

To my surprise he just blurted out, "Yes!" Over the next few minutes I asked him if he knew he could be forgiven, and he exclaimed, "Really?!" I shared John 3:16 and then 3:17, which says God didn't come into the world to condemn the world, but to save it. I asked him if he wanted to be forgiven right then, and in tears he let out an emphatic "Yes!" We prayed together, he poured his heart out to the Lord, and was forgiven by the grace of God!

I never had contact with him after that and don't even remember his name, but God knows who he is. I've prayed for thirty-seven years now that he grew in his faith, and that God was able to use him even behind prison bars.

"DREAMENTX," FIGHTING KATRINA

Trooper Caleb A. Williams
Texas Department of Public Safety

WHILE WORKING as a Gulfport, Mississippi, policeman, my e-mail address said it all: *"Dreamentx."* In August of 2005 my dream of

298

returning home was about to come true. I had interviewed for a position as a Texas State Trooper, then took my family camping in an area without cell phone coverage.

We had started our return to Gulfport when my phone "came to life," and showed I had a lot of messages from the department. When I called and asked, "What's going on?" the sergeant said a huge hurricane was on the way and would hit that night. We stocked up on food and water, and headed back to Mississippi. As we drove through the night and into the storm, we were stopped several times and told we could not go through. Then I would show my badge and explain that I had to. We got to Gulfport with nearly flat tires just as the storm was dying down.

As soon as I got there I went to work. We had no shifts; we just worked to exhaustion around the clock, got a few hours rest where we could, then were back on the job. I put my family in a shut-down school classroom for a few days. When the water subsided and roads were cleared enough, I went back home. Our house, which had been on 17-foot-high pillars, was gone. We had lost everything—pets, belongings, my vintage truck—everything. All we owned was what we had with us. We weren't the only ones; many first responders suffered heavy losses, but we had to keep on working. Quickly the place was becoming lawless, and we were the law.

> Yet give attention to your servant's prayer and his plea for mercy, O LORD my God.
> 2 Chronicles 6:19

When the main roads cleared and with new tires on the car, I sent my nine-months-pregnant wife and two small children back to my parents in Texas. The Gulfport hospital was swamped and didn't need a pregnancy, and we had no home. When they left, there's no way to describe how lost I felt—no house, no family, familiar surroundings gone—it was enough to break a person. Then I looked around and saw "hurt" everywhere— my brother officers, citizens who needed help, a community in shambles— and knew we had to go on. I remember not knowing how to pray or what to pray for. I just asked God to care for my family, and be a crutch our officers could lean on for a little while. I knew the Lord would answer my prayers; I just didn't know how or when.

SURVIVING KATRINA

Sergeant David M. Greenhalgh (Ret.)

FCPO Reconstruction Coordinator*, Gulf Coast, MS

> I would hurry to my place of shelter, far from the tempest and storm.
> Psalm 55:8

IT WAS inconceivable that Katrina's surging flood waters could reach the Herman house from Biloxi's Back Bay, but it did. Prior to Katrina, the largest hurricane ever to hit the Gulf Coast was Camille in 1969. Until Katrina, builders followed "The Rule of Camille" in deciding where it was safe to build. Camille had not flooded where the Herman's house was built, so it was not in a known flood zone.

When Katrina struck, Lieutenant Greg Herman, his wife, and their three children were at home, with no expectation of danger. A Gulfport police officer, Greg felt his well-built bungalow was more than up to the storm. He was not scheduled for duty that night, so he could be home with his family at this critical time. As the winds grew more fierce, water began lapping against the rear patio doors, and Greg knew they needed to go to a nearby two-story home. Greg is 6'9", and the water was already up to his waist. If he had been working, the family might not have made it through the surging tide.

Once at the neighbors' house, the Hermans, the neighbors, and three dogs quickly went to the second floor. The two families—thirteen people—prayed fervently for God's protection as the wind and water tore savagely at the house. God was all they had to rely on, as no other help was available. They knew they were in trouble; they just didn't know how much. During the eight hours they were upstairs, the storm reduced the bottom floor of the neighbor's house to rubble, and partially caved in the southeast wall. Incredibly the house remained standing, but later examination showed it was close to collapse!

When Greg returned to his house, there was nothing left but sticks holding up a roof. The neighbor's two-story house was for them like Noah's Ark, carrying them safely through the storm. Even though both families lost everything, God answered their prayers and preserved their lives and health. He was their shelter and all they had; he was all they needed!

*After Katrina, retired Canadian police Sergeant David Greenhalgh spent nearly eighteen months on the Gulf Coast, coordinating efforts of the Fellowship of Christian Peace Officers–USA (FCPO) and FCPO–Canada in rebuilding dozens of homes for first responders and support personnel.

"WE COULDN'T GET THROUGH!"

Trooper Caleb A. Williams
Texas Department of Public Safety

Grant Wolf, former executive director
Fellowship of Christian Peace Officers–USA (FCPO)

GRANT: From our first contact the prior March, Caleb and I had been in frequent communication. I knew of his desire to return to Texas, and his even stronger desire to get the FCPO ministry underway before he left. After the hurricane hit August 29, our first thought was for Caleb and the other officers there. We knew the storm was bad, we just didn't know how bad. With phone and e-mail contact impossible, we did what we could: prayed, and sent e-mails to a worldwide chain of Christian peace officers asking them to pray.

Caleb: With my family hundreds of miles away and my home destroyed, I would sleep for a few hours in my patrol car, then go back to work. Our normal police role changed. We took people to get medical attention, handed out water and food, and still tried to keep law and order in Gulfport. The resilience and steadfastness of our officers was incredible. They wore the same clothes for days, and worked long hours day after day without complaining or being selfish. Even though they suffered the same losses as the rest of the community, they didn't even take time to deal with their own needs or losses. They set aside their own personal desires, because they were the only ones who could help others.

> Yours, O LORD, is the greatness and the power and the glory and the victory and the majesty . . . in Your hand is power and might . . . to strengthen everyone.
> 1 Chronicles 29:11, 12 (NASB)

Finally, I found a FEMA truck with satellite Internet and contacted my wife, who contacted Grant. When he asked what we needed, I said, "Everything," especially shirts with Gulfport Police ID . . . and chaplains. We had no way to feed or shelter the chaplains, but we needed them. Officers had seen things a person should never have to witness. The mental stress, personal loss, and lack of nutrition and sleep were starting to catch up with us fast. Grant called the International Conference of Police Chaplains (ICPC) requesting chaplains, and had "Gulfport Police" printed on two hundred T-shirts. The day those came, it was like getting magical Christmas gifts. Officers from other communities began to arrive, and we no longer felt alone. When we learned of the thousands who'd been praying for us around the globe, we were overwhelmed. Those who came and those who prayed were answering a call from the Lord; they also were answering our prayers. He still was in control!

A MODERN-DAY NOAH'S ARK

Sergeant David M. Greenhalgh (Ret.)
FCPO Reconstruction Coordinator, Gulf Coast, MS

AFTER FLOODWATERS from Hurricane Katrina had subsided enough, officers in hard-hit Mississippi Gulf towns began search-and-rescue missions. In Biloxi, an officer came across a large boat that had been deposited in a downtown street. On board were a man and woman. The man told the officer what had happened.

He had felt safe riding out Katrina in his own home, since it hadn't flooded during Hurricane Camille. Prior to *Katrina,* the largest flood in Gulf Coast history had been *Camille.* If property hadn't flooded then, it was considered to be safe from flooding. But when the floodwaters started coming through his door, there was no escape. He thought to himself, *This is it, I'm done for!* He retreated to the second floor, but the waters rapidly followed him. As the second floor filled, he went into the attic. Before long the raging waters and savage winds tore his house apart, and he was afloat in a maelstrom of debris. Once more he thought, *I'm done for!*

> He stilled the storm to a whisper; the waves of the sea were hushed.
> Psalm 107:29

Then he drifted against a massive vertical steel beam that had supported the roof of a huge boathouse. He clung to it, but realized that couldn't last long. When a woman floated by, he reached out and grabbed her so she, too, could cling to the beam. Just as he thought all hope was lost, a large power boat drifted by with a line trailing behind it. He grabbed the line, and somehow managed to get himself and the woman aboard. He couldn't start the boat and thought they were drifting out to sea. Was this modern-day "Noah's Ark" going to end up being their tomb by being pushed out into the Gulf? That was not to be the case. After several more stomach-churning hours, the storm gradually subsided, and the receding waters deposited them safely in the middle of downtown Biloxi!

HE DEFIED ORDERS!

Sergeant David M. Greenhalgh (Ret.)

FCPO Reconstruction Coordinator

AS WERE many homes of Gulf Coast officers, Bay St. Louis, Mississippi, Police Sergeant Robert O'Neal's home was gutted by Hurricane Katrina. He, his wife, and their family waited out the storm at the police building. From there, Robert could see people wading through waist-deep waters carrying babies from a housing project and shouting for help. A general policy in South Mississippi is that emergency vehicle activity ceases when winds exceed 70 miles per hour; Katrina's reached *200 miles per hour!*

A committed Christian, Robert felt strongly that he should help, but was told not to leave the building. His decision was reminiscent of the fifth chapter of Acts, where Peter and the other apostles were ordered by the Sanhedrin not to teach in Jesus' name. Even though the Sanhedrin wanted them put to death, their reply was, "We must obey God rather than men!" (v. 29). With no thought either to his job security or personal safety, O'Neal and five other officers set out on a mission of mercy. They kicked in doors and rescued sixty people, including six brought out on stretchers loaned by the fire department. In any other situation this sixteen-year police veteran would not have defied orders, but he felt it was his personal duty to help those unable to help themselves.

> Peter and the other apostles replied: "We must obey God rather than men!" Acts 5:29

After the hurricane, with no other place to go, Robert's wife and their children went to live in Baton Rouge with Robert's sister. The hurricane was over, but it brought great hardship to officers and their families. With looting, confused and hurting citizens, and all the other aftermath of the storm, officers had to work long, hard hours, placing personal needs after police responsibilities.

O'Neal's life reads like a novel. A former Marine gunnery sergeant, he had served in Desert Storm. Before that, he had gone through a bitter divorce. After Desert Storm, his ex-wife told his son and daughter he had been killed in that conflict. Not long before Katrina, his son met Robert's brother in a store, recognized him, and asked his uncle, "How did my daddy die in the war?" That brought about a joyous reunion of Robert and his son.

If you were to ask Robert why he took such a risk at the height of the storm, he would tell you he simply was "doing my duty." But to those for whom he risked his life, he was an angel of mercy!

KRISTINA'S WORLD

Andrew Cowan
Royal Canadian Mounted Police

(IN 1948, Andrew Wyeth painted a young woman crawling on the ground in a treeless field toward a gray house on the horizon— *Christina's World*. The woman, Christina, had an undiagnosed muscular deterioration that paralyzed her lower body. In 1971, another young woman, my Kristina, came into the world with what later would be diagnosed as cystic fibrosis (CF). This is an inherited chronic disease that affects the lungs and digestive system of about seventy thousand children and adults worldwide. On September 3, 2007, Kristina died at age 36, the average life expectancy of CF patients.)

A man got up, got the kids ready, and headed to church. Another day of juggling things with his wife in the hospital, getting ready for the coming week with a new school year about to begin. After church he headed to the hospital for the afternoon, which extended into the night. During the night things went sideways, and forty-two hours later he went home to bed as a single parent and widower, wondering at what had just happened.

I had dealt with other people in similar situations, but this was different. On the way home from the hospital I prayed for the right words to share with our two children. For the first time in many years I didn't know what to say or what to do. Through those early days there was only one set of footprints in the sand: God was carrying me and our children through. But at the end of the day and the end of the road, we Christians have hope and joy in being reunited.

Many had prayed and believed healing would come, but God had other plans—"the big picture." His plans included many small mercies that I have seen only in hindsight. At Kristina's memorial service, her nurses commented they had never seen anyone with end-stage lung failure pass away in such peace. The most amazing thing I ever heard came from a non-Christian officer who attended the service and observed, "It was more like a celebration or a party, not a funeral. How do you go on with all that has happened?"

One day as I questioned things, I found this Scripture passage Kristina had written on the kitchen bulletin board some time before her death: "And the God of all grace, who called you to his eternal glory in Christ, after you have suffered a little while, will himself restore you and make you strong, firm and steadfast. To him be the power for ever and ever. Amen" (1 Peter 5:10, 11).

Dedicated to Kristina: daughter, sister, wife, mother, and best friend (1971–2007).

GILBERT WAS WRONG!

Robin Oake (Ret.)

Chief of Police, United Kingdom

IN THEIR operetta *The Pirates of Penzance*, Gilbert and Sullivan wrote, "A policeman's lot is not a happy one." Gilbert was wrong. Even though in my 42 years of policing I saw and experienced many unhappy occasions, for the most part I have to say "mine was a happy lot."

I was and am a committed Christian believer. The night before my swearing in, a senior constable told me, "Nail your colours to the mast, Robin," meaning not to be shy admitting I was a Christian. The Police Service can be a difficult and sometimes lonely place for an active Christian, but the fellowship of men and women who are followers of Christ is so rewarding. I knew policing was my calling, and that as a Christ-follower I never would be ashamed or shy about my faith amongst colleagues and senior officers. On duty, I might have a real opportunity to speak about Christ whenever it was the right time.

> Fear the LORD your God as long as you live by keeping all his decrees and commands.
> Deuteronomy 6:2

Early on, my wife-to-be gave me a pocket-size Bible. Throughout the years, without exception, I always carried it in my left breast pocket. It

306

was well-used, especially on duty, for personal reading, helping people in grief, or using the Scripture to introduce someone to the Lord Jesus. I often would put a tract on a food tray or take the opportunity to listen and talk to prisoners, again without forcing my faith on anyone. That small Bible also served another purpose: I can remember several occasions when it prevented serious injury to my ribs. Once it took the brunt of a blow with a scaffold pole from a violent man I was attempting to arrest. Another time, a mental patient wielded a chisel which went through my pocket and stopped on the Bible's cover.

I always have been keen and enthusiastic to speak about the hope I have as a Christian, but very careful not to intrude or force the issue. There were doubts and times to keep my mouth shut—I was a police officer first of all. There were times when I should have spoken up and shied away from unseemly conversation. I am nowhere near perfect, I don't have all the answers, and my attitude did not always reflect that of Christ.

From my first day on the job until the last, my "colours were nailed!" Throughout my career, I was faithful to the Lord and tried to serve him well. Perhaps policing "is not a happy lot" for a nonbeliever. But for me, Gilbert was wrong!

SEPTEMBER 5

STEPHEN

Robin Oake (Ret.)
Chief of Police, United Kingdom

IN 2003 my son Stephen was murdered by an Algerian who was convicted of making the deadly toxin *ricin*. Stephen was a detective constable in Manchester.

I was so thrilled and proud that as a Christian young man, Steve felt called by God into the Greater Manchester Police. He made the decision on his own initiative in collusion with his wife and family rather than involving me. I knew how much he thoroughly enjoyed his policing—on the beat, in Traffic Patrol—and eventually in Special Branch, which was his real forte. We kept in close touch, of course, and shared many experiences. I was always glad to help where I could, and give advice and encourage him.

It was a dreadful shock when he was murdered. It devastated the family and also his many colleagues, not only in Special Branch but in the wider Force, as well as among police officers throughout the country. Steve's bravery was much in evidence at the scene of his death. By his actions, although fatally stabbed, he protected three colleagues. Though they, too, were stabbed in the melee, Steve took the brunt of the killer's blows, thereby saving their lives. His and their actions also prevented a terrorist group's proposed use of this deadly toxin to kill thousands of people. He literally laid down his life for his friends.

> You meant evil against me, but God meant it for good in order to bring about this present result, to preserve many people alive.
>
> Genesis 50:20 (NASB)

And, as the Bible states, what man meant for evil, God turned to good. Steve's courageous witness, on- and off-duty, was something to behold; his sporting and musical talents were admired by many, especially when he and his wife led worship at their church. His infectious humor still brings smiles to our faces. He was a character, full of fun and yet so serious about his work. My wife, our daughters, Stephen's widow, and I will miss him until we meet again in heaven. Still, I never will regret that he followed me into policing and gave his life for others.

SEPTEMBER 6

A DIFFERENT TYPE OF BATTLE

Officer William J. Cox

Grand Junction, CO, Police Department

A WOMAN HAD requested officer assistance, and I went. From what Dispatch said, it sounded like a mental health issue might be involved. But then we often don't know what to expect on a call.

The location was a local "safe house" for women who have been victims of domestic violence. I knocked at the front door and then rang the bell; no response to either. At the back of the house I heard women's

308

voices on a second-floor deck. I looked up and asked the ladies if "Sally" (not her real name) was there. Moments later a woman came out the back door and walked over to me. She appeared frightened, looked down at the ground, and spoke rather hesitantly. I got the impression that however frightened she was, she was even more afraid I wouldn't believe her! Finally she asked if I believed in good and evil. After telling her yes, she said there were two women there who openly practiced witchcraft. They were Wiccans!

When she and those women were in the common area of the house, she overheard them talk about casting different spells on her. One spell in particular would cause her to be permanently blind. She said, "I don't feel safe here spiritually." She also wondered if their use of evil could cause her physical harm. As we talked, I learned that she was a Christian who understood evil. She also felt alone, threatened, frightened, and vulnerable. She knew of spiritual warfare, but felt "unarmed" and unsure how to protect herself.

> No king is saved by the size of his army; no warrior escapes by his [own] great strength.
> Psalm 33:16

I quoted from Ephesians 6:11, 12: "Put on the full armor of God so that you can take your stand against the devil's schemes. For our struggle is not against flesh and blood, but against the rulers, against the authorities, against the powers of this dark world and against the spiritual forces of evil in the heavenly realms." After more conversation and teaching on how to call on God for his protection, she felt more at peace, and was more confident about going back into the house.

Not all law enforcement is fighting "bad guys we can see." That is why each day I try to go on duty properly outfitted and armed—with the equipment and training my department provides, and the spiritual armor God has given. I thank God for both!

THE SWITCHEROO DIDN'T WORK

Detective/Sergeant Ingrid Dean

Michigan State Police

FIELD TRAINING days over, I was patrolling on my own. Over my radio I heard, "Be on the lookout for an older model Chevrolet, Michigan plate XXXXX." I'm only half-listening. "Driver pulled out of ABC Bank after attempting to send a bomb through the money-chute at a drive-up window!"

Now I was listening more closely. *The teller sent the bomb back to the driver!* I thought, *Wow, that was a smart move!*

My "gut feelings" told me to head toward the bank, so I did—feeling "every bell and whistle going off." Seeing a car turn into a motel parking lot, I pulled in behind it then drove out another exit, pretending I'd taken a shortcut. I looked at the license plate. *Yep, that's the car, all right!* I remembered not to key my radio with a bomb nearby, as I might detonate the bomb. So I used my walkie-talkie: "Central, I have the vehicle in sight; it just pulled into the Sierra Motel." With that, I waited for the backup unit. When it arrived, we pulled up behind the suspect, who had gotten out of his car and was standing by the driver's door.

I looked at the license plate again . . . the numbers were different. I was thinking, *My first day on patrol and I've misread the plate; this isn't the right car!* I was also thinking, *How can I minimize my mistake and not look so bad in front of this seasoned officer?*

I got out of my car. The veteran officer looked at me and said: "This is the car, isn't it? But the plate is different."

> When the people of Gibeon heard what Joshua had done to Jericho and Ai, they resorted to a ruse. Joshua 9:3, 4

I managed to squeak out, "I think so," but I was thinking, *How could I mess up so badly and see numbers that aren't there? They'll think I'm a nut!*

To my astonishment the backup officer confronted the guy and said, "You are under arrest!" I was horrified! This could be false arrest. Then through the car window we saw the bank bag, and the backup officer said: "There's our evidence!" Our search of the vehicle revealed cocaine, scales . . . and the original license plate! Bad guys can switch plates in seconds!

I believe in divine grace: When you do the best you can, God takes care of you. Somehow the backup officer read my mind. He smiled and told me, "Never second-guess yourself on this job. If you saw it, you saw it. Trust yourself. Trust God. When you really make a mistake, you'll know it."

I felt like the rookie I was as I stood there listening to him, but he was right—"In God We Trust."

SEPTEMBER 8

"WE WILL HELP!"

Captain Paul Lee (Ret.)*

Chattanooga, TN, Police Department

AS SOON as the tee-shirts were ready that FCPO had made up for the Gulfport Police Department, another board member and I took them to Gulfport. After clearing innumerable traffic check points in areas ravaged by Hurricane Katrina, we reached Gulfport. There we found police officers from all over the nation working. Everyone was busy, yet no one complained. Gulfport Police Headquarters had been destroyed in the storm and they were working out of temporary offices. Even so, and on top of everything else they had to do, the department was feeding all the volunteers in a makeshift cafeteria.

After introductions, we began to hear stories of sheer horror, courage, gallantry, and integrity. One officer and his family were forced into their attic, and then onto the roof through a hole they made. They clung to each other for survival for all ten hours of the storm. In the nearby community of Pass Christian, the storm surge pinned officers down in their own building. They shot the windows out, made a human chain and went to the library next door. There, on the second floor, they tore out computer cables to tether themselves to a brick column as the waters rose. We heard story after story of miraculous survivals as well as tragic deaths. The magnitude of destruction and loss, and of cleanup efforts already underway, absolutely could not be described!

Even before going to Gulfport, we knew FCPO would mount an effort to help police and other first responders rebuild their homes and their lives. After seeing the situation first-hand, we were even more committed. Unlike police officers in other states and cities who abandoned their posts, those on the Gulf Coast of Mississippi stood their ground at the risk of their own lives. In total mental agony they waited for the storm to begin, battled through it, and were back on the streets even before it was safe. Their motto is "to protect and serve," and that's what they did!

> Suppose a brother or sister is without clothes and daily food. If one of you says to him, "Go, I wish you well; keep warm and well fed," but does nothing about his physical needs, what good is it? James 2:15, 16

On our drive back to Chattanooga I couldn't help but think, *When citizens need help, they call the police. But when the police need help, whom do they call? They're pretty much the end of the line.* Even though FCPO is not a large ministry, we were going to answer their call. I didn't know how, what, or how much; I just knew that was what God wanted us to do.

*Former president, Fellowship of Christian Peace Officers-USA (FCPO)

HERE AM I. SEND ME!

Officer Rick Wolfe

Hamilton County, TN, Sheriff's Office

"THEN I heard the voice of the Lord saying, 'Whom shall I send? And who will go for us?' And I said, 'Here am I. Send me!'" (Isaiah 6:8). Ever since Hurricane Katrina had struck a few days earlier, this verse had been going through my mind. What happened in the early morning hours a couple of weeks later finally gave me the answer.

It was past midnight on my night shift assignment, and I'd just answered a faulty alarm call. While I was checking it out, the desk officer called me on the radio, asking me to come to the department when the alarm was cleared. When I quizzed him as to why the urgency, all he could say was, "I can't tell you!"

Of course, my first thought was, *Who has registered a complaint against me, and why?*

He said it wasn't anything like that; it was a "good thing."

Arriving at City Hall Rotunda I saw the police and fire chiefs, city council members, and other equally influential community citizens. *Why are they here?* I wondered.

Then a police captain from another shift said they were putting together a "strike team" to go to the Gulf to help maintain security in the aftermath of the hurricane, and would I go?

I had been keeping up with the horrible conditions in the area—the looting, gunfights, and lawlessness—and my first reaction was, "Let me think about it," especially since it was to be at least a two-week commitment! He responded by saying they needed to assemble the team that night and needed my decision right then and there!

> Then I heard the voice of the Lord saying, "Whom shall I send? And who will go for us?" And I said, "Here am I. Send me!" Isaiah 6:8

Then the Scripture verse from Isaiah hit me like a freight train! The captain again asked for my decision, and my only thought was "Here am I. Send me!" The only way to describe my feelings at that moment is that they were surreal, humbling, and with a sense of honor. I felt as if I was in the very presence of the Lord, realizing he had been preparing me for that one moment for several days. I am grateful to have gone to Mississippi and been able to help out other agencies in their time of need; it is an experience I never will forget. I am even more grateful that God's hand was in my being selected to go.

SEPTEMBER 10

COURAGE UNDER FIRE

Officer Dennis Dorr (Ret.)

Sumner, WA, Police Department

THE DATE was September 11, 2001. Like the rest of the world the folks in Sumner—a quiet little town in the shadow of Mt. Rainier—were trying to make sense of the terrorist bombings of that day. Shortly after noon we received word a man was shooting at cars and pedestrians downtown and now was in front of City Hall, where the police department is located. Going to the door I could see him in the middle of the street with a pistol in one hand and a rifle in the other. Just then he raised his rifle and fired at a passing car. I radioed my position and the scenario to Dispatch, then ran out the front door.

Heading with drawn pistol toward the suspect, I yelled at him to drop his weapons. At this he turned and pointed both at me. Again I told him to drop his weapons, and started squeezing the trigger on mine. Just then I saw two civilians directly behind the subject; for fear of their lives I could not shoot but had to take evasive action. I actually heard the click of the hammer as he tried to shoot me, but no shots rang out. With that he began running toward downtown. Another officer and I paralleled him by running in the alley, coming out on the street just ahead of him. He had thrown himself on the sidewalk, arms extended with a weapon in each hand.

> But the eyes of the LORD are on those who fear him, on those whose hope is in his unfailing love. Psalm 33:18

We disarmed and cuffed him, then took him to the department. We later found that the .30-30 lever-action rifle had not fired because he had not levered another bullet into the chamber, and the 9mm pistol had a "stove-top obstruction" (spent cartridge stuck in the top of the slide). With two weapons to kill me, it is inconceivable the suspect failed in his efforts! As the result of his wanton actions he was convicted and put in prison.

By God's grace, both my life and the lives of innocent bystanders were saved that day. For anyone, especially a police officer, not to realize that God watches over us at all times, is unbelievable. Even though I'm now retired I still thank the Lord daily for his care through the trials and tribulations of my thirty-year policing career!

SEPTEMBER 11

TO HELL AND BACK AT GROUND ZERO

William L. Glennie, PhD, Badge No. 8893

Arizona Department of Public Safety

THE MORNING of September 11, 2001, I received a telephone call from my son Michael, a Phoenix Fire Department engineer, informing me of the World Trade Center tragedy. Turning on the TV, I stared in disbelief at the video of the two buildings collapsing.

A myriad of thoughts and emotions competed for my attention as I tried to control my feelings. With twenty-six years of chaplaincy and law enforcement experience, I knew I would be needed. After receiving permission from my two senators in Washington and my department, flight arrangements were made and I flew to Newark, New Jersey. (Keep in mind this was during a time when all flights had been suspended.) After credentialing and a few hours' sleep, I went to Ground Zero early the next morning. Words are inadequate to describe the collapsed buildings or the incredible stench.

For the next ten days I spent twelve hours a day working with the Port Authority Police and Firefighters on top of the collapsed towers. I would pray and counsel, and sometimes give last rites over a person's remains. It was horrible. Even my twenty-six years of dealing with highway tragedies did not equip me for what I saw on top of the 'pile' of steel. Sometimes the coroner had to dismember the body because a twenty-ton beam was lying across it. There were other times when we would only find a pair of firefighter's bunker pants and turnout coat with a number stenciled on it.

> He will wipe every tear from their eyes. There will be no more death or mourning or crying or pain, for the old order of things has passed away.
> Revelation 21:4

The weather was cold and rainy, but it did not stop the recovery effort. As firefighters and police officers were changed out each hour, I would greet them with a smile or a handshake. Sometimes they would say, "I don't know how long I can do this, Chaplain."

One day I accompanied a young widow through the tangled steel to see where her husband was buried in the stairwell in Tower Two. She looked so much like my daughter (who is married to a firefighter) that I "lost it" and started to weep. The young widow reached over, took my hand, and asked, "Are you okay?" God must have been in that encounter because, just for a moment, we bonded in the spirit of her loss.

OUR OPPOSING NATURES

Chief Chaplain Alvin Kass

New York, NY, Police Department

IN JEREMIAH 17:9, God says, "The heart is deceitful above all things and beyond cure." Yet in Ezekiel 36:26 God also says, "I will give you a new heart and put a new spirit in you." Those verses represent the extremes of man's nature—evil and good—and the line that divides them was never more clear than on September 11, 2001.

In my forty-four years of service as an NYPD chaplain, the 9/11 attack on the World Trade Center dwarfed all I'd ever experienced. At Ground Zero the smoke was so thick it seemed like the middle of the night. The sight was sickening; it was a veritable war zone. It was incredible to think those Twin Towers were no longer standing.

From Ground Zero I went to a nearby high school, where exhausted police officers and firefighters took time out for a brief respite. The pain and anguish of the ordeal could not have been more evident. They were worried about their colleagues, and couldn't understand how anyone could do

> The eternal God is your refuge, and underneath are the everlasting arms.
> Deuteronomy 33:27

such a terrible thing. Then it was on to St. Vincent's and Bellevue hospitals to visit the injured. At St. Vincent's a young police officer cried uncontrollably; he couldn't comprehend what he had seen. Family members of Trade Center employees needed comforting, but having been to Ground Zero, it was difficult to encourage them about the fate of their loved ones.

Then I was called to police headquarters, where I stayed until nearly 3 a.m. Together with other department chaplains, we tried to offer strength and comfort to families of officers not accounted for. On the Friday after the disaster, I spoke at an interfaith service at headquarters. Throughout that awful week and the many that followed, our faith in God, along with the strength we drew from each other, is what brought us through the ordeal.

Yes, we have two natures. As a police department chaplain, I often have seen both of these at work. On call 24/7, I work with people of every race, religion, color, and creed, counseling them in times of stress, both personal and professional. I thank God for the strength he gave me to be of service during those terrible days, and I pray it will never happen again.

ADAPTED FROM "A BRIEF RESPITE FROM HELL"

Lieutenant Stan Kid

Malverne, NY, Nassau County Police Department

(Written September 13, 2001) "I spent last night and most of today digging through twisted steel, cement chunks, airplane parts, and personal belongings. The only way to describe it is like hell. Even in daylight, Ground Zero is somewhat dark due to the smoke and dust—plus the awful-smelling air. I thought of a Batman movie, with its eerie, gothic, dark view of Gotham City. It is also a construction site—heavy equipment beep-beeping and roaring, and hard-hat workers everywhere—like one of those excavations in the city with windows cut in the plywood walls so you can watch the crews at work.

"My five men and I joined many others who were removing debris and seeking survivors or bodies. In addition to first responders and military personnel there were also civilians—union men and women: carpenters, engineers, plumbers, steelworkers, electricians, construction workers—and the Salvation Army. Teens volunteered to bring food, water, fruit, and candy. We all worked together in impromptu teams seeking both the living and the dead.

> Yea, though I walk through the valley of the shadow of death, I will fear no evil: for thou art with me; thy rod and thy staff they comfort me.
> Psalm 23:4

"At one point a firefighter began screaming frantically; he and two Marines thought they saw a hand waving from a partially toppled building. Apparatus was brought and firefighters went up in a bucket. One firefighter kept screaming, 'Hurry up!' No use, it was just a bit of insulation blowing in the breeze. We all moved on, disappointed.

"This morning a construction worker cried out, 'We have two!' The roar of the crowd was deafening! Calls went out: 'Water!' 'Back boards!' They made their way up the line. 'We need a canine unit!' Labs were brought, followed by medical personnel. The feeling was incredible! In an hour they were brought out—in bright orange body bags. I can't begin to describe the disappointment and terrible silence. The bags were passed down the same line as the equipment had gone up, as tenderly and carefully as if

317

they had been living souls. Before my day was over, we got five firefighters out from under the rubble. Only two walked out on their own. Whether living or dead, each brought inexpressible emotions.

"The men and women who worked after 9/11 are true heroes, and I'm so very proud to have worked alongside in their very substantial shadows. Hundreds upon hundreds came together with no concern for occupation, race, color, sex, or creed. We saw each other as brothers and sisters, all dealing with an unthinkable tragedy . . . and we kept going until the job was done."

S E P T E M B E R   1 4

A COP, A GUN, AND GOD

Bob Martin (Ret.)

New York, NY, Police Department

NYPD Detective Pete Moog is tough as nails. A linebacker for Seminole State College (OK), as an officer he helped the NYPD football team win several national championships, as a player and later as coach.

The morning of 9/11, Pete and his partner responded to the Trade Center complex shortly after the second (South) tower was hit. They were to set up telephone lines for temporary headquarters at the site. As they headed toward the World Financial Center to tap into the building's telephone lines, they heard a loud explosion; it was the South Tower coming down. As Pete recalls: "I started to run, but the black cloud of debris caught me and tossed me into the air. I landed about thirty feet away, trapped in debris under a pedestrian walkway with fires all around me. There were about fifteen of us cops and firemen.

> "Not by might nor by power, but by my Spirit," says the LORD Almighty.
> Zechariah 4:6

"We banged on the glass wall behind us, hoping to break it so we could escape the smoke and flames. The window was strong, and I was running out of hope. I'm thinking, *This might be it, my time has come,* and I said a quick prayer: 'If I have to go, God make it quick . . . and tell my dad I will soon be with him.' Suddenly I heard three shots. A fellow officer used his Glock 9mm to shoot a hole in the glass large enough for us

318

to get into the building. My partner was still outside so, after taking a few deep breaths, I and three cops went to look for him. We didn't find him, but we did dig out a firefighter from the debris. Just then the North Tower came down. The debris cloud caught me, and threw me into an underground parking garage. Going outside again I saw a female lieutenant face down in the grass. She had a large chunk of cement embedded in her head and two large shards of glass sticking out her back. I carried her down to the Hudson River, and put her on a boat taking injured people across the river to a hospital in New Jersey (she survived). I didn't find my partner.

"Eventually I reported to the 1st Precinct Station House, and found my partner safe there. He and I looked for survivors over the next twenty-four hours, but found none. Most who were in or near the towers as they came down were dead. If it had not been for the hand of God working through a cop and his gun, I might have been one of them."

SEPTEMBER 15

PRAYER LIST ON A HARD HAT

William L. Glennie, PhD, Badge No. 8893
Arizona Department of Public Safety

ONE DAY at the Trade Center site I was asked by the battalion chief to help with some of the families who had come to view the site. As we talked and prayed together, a stately, middle-aged couple told me they had lost two sons in the towers. Their third son was kneeling in front of them in prayer so I knelt down, put my arms around him, and asked God to uphold him and his parents. As they left I mentioned God's promise in the Bible that says, "To be absent from the body, [is] to be present with the Lord" (2 Corinthians 5:8 KJV). Also: "Greater love has no one than this, that he lay down his life for his friends" (John 15:13). They smiled, gave me a hug, and left with gratitude.

Many of the first responders were from the East Coast and had heavy Bronx-type accents. As I approached the pile each morning the men would say, "Good morning, 'Fadda,' are ya goin' to bless me this mornin'?" At that I would stop and pray with them before going to the recovery area.

One night, after debriefing a fire captain, I told him: "I will pray for you each day."

After giving me a look of doubt at my sincerity, he said, "Let me sign your hard hat to remind you."

I answered, "Okay!" When others saw his name, they, too, wanted to sign my hard hat. It now is covered with their names and their numbers, and I pray each day for them.

> He heals the broken-hearted and binds up their wounds.
> Psalm 147:3

As much as I longed to be home with family and friends in familiar surroundings, I had mixed emotions about leaving the men on top of that steel pile. Even though years now have passed since 2001, the thoughts and memories remain of the sorrow caused by that great tragedy, not only for the families of those who died, but also for those who so carefully sifted through the rubble. May God in his great compassion give them a sense of his presence through the remainder of their lives and into eternity.

SEPTEMBER 16

NOTHING LEFT

John M. Wills

Federal Bureau of Investigation

DEAN'S PULPIT was a steel staircase leading to a trailer. A makeshift microphone taped to a copper pipe and an FBI raid jacket for his vestment was what Dean Kavouras, the FBI police chaplain, would be using. He would be leading a prayer service for the agents who toiled in that sacrosanct Pennsylvania field in the days after that terrible Tuesday we've come to remember as 9/11. This Sunday would be the families' first visit to the crash site, and the Red Cross would assist in facilitating the viewing. However, the FBI would be conducting the prayer service.

In the days before, another FBI agent and I had stood at the apex of the hill, looking down across the expanse of yellow wild grass and a grove of trees. The autumn colors of gold and green against the azure sky gave a look of serenity to the Pennsylvania landscape, marred only by the charred hole in the ground where the aircraft had entered. I had turned to Steve and asked, "Where is the wreckage?" We both found it hard to believe the big jet that had been United Airlines Flight 93 could have disintegrated into millions of minute fragments. We looked down and saw men and women from assorted federal agencies, digging in the charred earth on their hands and knees, engaged in the *sacred act* of recovering the human remains of those who had perished. Meanwhile, at a nearby National Guard facility, more of the Lord's work was underway. Dental records were being compared, DNA samples taken and preserved, bone fragments and pieces of burnt flesh prepared for later identification. Grisly work for sure! This total focus on the task is how cops protect their sanity; it's all that keeps them from screaming and running from the room, unable to face the reality of the evil that causes one man to destroy another.

> God is our refuge and strength, an ever-present help in trouble.
> Psalm 46:1

The service began. There were handouts for readings and hymns, even an organist. The ceremony was as solemn an occasion as any church could offer. Participation was voluntary for the 150 agents in attendance, but nearly all of us were there. Differences in religious leanings didn't matter that day; the Lord was clearly there guiding us in our duties when we needed him most.

SEPTEMBER 17

THE CROSS STILL STANDS

Reverend Dean Kavouras, Chaplain

Cleveland Division Safety Forces
Federal Bureau of Investigation

AT THE crash site of United Airlines Flight 93, I dare say the Pennsylvania State Police preached a truer Gospel than any other person on scene. After the crash they erected a 16-foot-high cross made of two sturdy 8' x 8' beams, and draped it with a white shroud. I was told that when one person objected, a trooper told him, "We're in charge, and that's how it is." That cross still stands.

The cross is a reminder of the blackest, most unjust, and most tragic death in all of history, that of the innocent Son of God. It is also the reminder of humanity's finest hour, for on that cross the price of all the sins and guilt and curse of all mankind—from Adam to the last person born—was paid. On that cross death and hell were conquered. In Christ, God opened His loving arms so "everyone who believes in him may have eternal life" (John 3:15).

321

We were told the "official service" could not include references to the Bible or Christianity. But in the shadow of those two pieces of wood, I preached the Word to a number of people. Many of the airline's personnel were brought from the family site to the crash site to pay their respects. They looked at the memorial, the pictures, and the mementos. After they received an explanation of the work going on, I asked if they would like to join in a prayer. We began with the Twenty-Third Psalm in its entirety, along with 1 Peter 5:6–10. Together, all prayed The Lord's Prayer.

One trooper was overtaken with grief. I talked with him and told him Christ died on a cross like the one before us. He paid the price for the sins of the world, and on Easter Sunday rose from the grave. I told him all who put their hope in Jesus will likewise rise to everlasting glory. No psychologist, politician, or financial wizard can make sense out of that, but there is no other hope and no other message in all the world that can save us. I quoted and explained John 11:25, 26, where Jesus says, "I am the resurrection and the life, he that believes in Me, though he were dead, yet shall he live, and he that lives and believes in Me shall never die" (KJV). I explained the everlasting covenant of peace God has with all who believe in Jesus. While the flowery orations of the world may soothe people's psyche for a few minutes, only the Word of God as found in Scripture can heal their souls and restore to them some modicum of peace. God help us in our foolishness!

> For the message of the cross is foolishness to those who are perishing, but to us who are being saved it is the power of God. 1 Corinthians 1:18

SEPTEMBER 18

HE TURNED HIMSELF IN

Lieutenant Michael Gates

Pineville, LA, Police Department

FEW THINGS upset the public more than a rash of home invasions. "Is he in my area? Am I safe? What are the police doing to protect us?" When that happens in any community it creates tension among the citizens, the media, and especially law enforcement people.

Recently a young man went on a rampage in our area breaking into homes and stealing guns. At one point we booked him and his associates at the jail, but before he could be put behind bars he slipped out of his handcuffs in the booking area and escaped. This led to a weekend of terror. He broke into several more homes, stealing guns. At one point an officer spotted him with a stolen pistol in his hand, but the suspect escaped before the officer could stop him.

As Sunday night was turning into Monday morning he made his way to Marksville, Louisiana. There he stole a vehicle, leading officers on a chase through their city and then making his way back to central Louisiana. Officers spotted and pursued him again, but he ditched the car and escaped. Later in the morning he was back in Pineville, successfully eluding our officers in their hunt for him. The behavior patterns he exhibited led us to believe that if we did catch him, someone might be wounded or killed in the process. There was a lot of praying going on that day!

> "The thief comes only to steal and kill and destroy; I have come that they may have life, and have it to the full."
> John 10:10

Tuesday I was in a training session in the building where the police department is located. We broke for lunch and I was walking alone to my vehicle in the parking lot. Just then a vehicle pulled alongside me with the young fugitive as a passenger in the car. He said he was tired and hungry and was turning himself in—no chase, no fight, no injuries. God led him right to our door. Some folks may call it "luck," "good timing," or just plain "coincidence." It was far more than that—it was God at work!

HAVE DONE WITH FILTHY LANGUAGE

Bill Hubbard, Executive Police Officer
Taos, NM, Police Department

HERBERT, your mouth is filthy! I read in a book one time that what comes out of your mouth comes from your heart (Matthew 15:18). Is your heart as dark and disgusting as your mouth?"

Herbert was mad, violent, out of control, and had a *very* filthy mouth. Whether it was the amount of alcohol in him, the bump on the head he got when he wrecked his car, the cops who showed up to arrest him, or a combination of all three was hard to tell. The jail wouldn't take him until he was cleared medically, and it took three of us to wrestle him out of the patrol car and into an ER treatment room.

Once there and cuffed to a bed, his tirade continued at the top of his lungs. Herbert cussed us, the hospital staff, other patients, and anyone else who walked past his cubicle. I took a break while the other two officers put up with him, then it was my turn to stay. That's when I asked him about his heart. My comment had the desired effect: He paused for a breath while his pickled brain tried to process what I'd said. It was like flipping off a switch; Herbert just stopped.

> But now you yourselves are to put off all these: anger, wrath, malice, blasphemy, filthy language out of your mouth.
> Colossians 3:8

After thinking for a moment, he started to cry, "You sound just like my dad!" Within moments he was a tame man. I sat on the edge of his bed and spoke to him from God's Word, having as much conversation as I could through his alcoholic haze. For the next hour he was like a lamb, and not a vile word came out of his mouth. He was even kind to the ER staff! When his treatment was complete, Herbert walked out of the ER without our having to place a hand on him, and without saying a word. At the jail he even thanked the officers who booked him, saying they had been kind. The officers who saw his remarkable transformation still don't believe it, and they credit me with diffusing the situation.

Hebrews 4:12 says, "For the word of God *is* living and powerful, and sharper than any two-edged sword, piercing even to the division of soul and spirit, and of joints and marrow, and is a discerner of the thoughts and intents of the heart." I diffused nothing that night—the power of God's Word made the difference. Never discount the power of the Bible for providing the perfect solution!

"I NEED DIRECTIONS, SIR"

Anonymous

I WAS WORKING in the Prisoner Transport Unit, picking up arrested subjects from all over the county, when I was dispatched to a local high school. There I picked up a 17-year-old arrested by the school resource officer (SRO) for breaking into a car on campus.

The student was a clean-cut, young African American teenager who didn't seem to fit the mold of the typical teen burglar. He was nicely dressed, polite, and well-spoken. As the SRO and I walked him out to my transport van, we talked to him about what it would take to put this incident behind him and stay out of trouble. We explained that once he turned 18 a felony arrest like this possibly could limit his options for educational opportunities and careers.

In the van and headed toward the Juvenile Detention Center, I planned to pick up another young offender. During the trip he asked me something, but the noise level was too high to hear him very well. I turned down my police radio and asked him to repeat what he said. I was shocked at his question: "Sir, can you tell me how I can know the right path to take in life?" I was surprised by two things: the seriousness of the question he asked, especially since we'd only met ten minutes earlier, and that a young African American teenager would ask an older white police officer such a significant question.

> How can a young man keep his way pure? By living according to your word. Psalm 119:9

Almost immediately I recognized this was a God-given opportunity to reach out to this young man with the Gospel.

I knew we would arrive early at the place where I was picking up the other juvenile so I told him, "As soon as we stop I'll come back and give you the answer," and that's what I did. He listened intently as I went through the truths of God's holiness, man's sin, Christ's death for sinners, and our need to repent and trust Christ. He didn't make a profession of salvation that day, but it was exciting to be used by God to share the Gospel. It was clear this young man was seeking a way to escape from the path he was on, not knowing that the problem he and every man must resolve is the sin that, without Jesus, will eternally separate them from God. In the world of law enforcement most criminals live in open rebellion against God, his law, and the police officers who are his ordained authorities. However, God can soften even criminals' hearts, making them willing to listen and providing opportunities for believers to share the life-changing Gospel.

PTSD CHANGED MY LIFE

Special Agent James A. Gunnels

U.S. Department of Homeland Security

WHEN THE Alfred P. Murrah Federal Building in Oklahoma City, Oklahoma, was bombed in 1995, I had no idea how it would change my life. Then, as now, I worked with the Federal Protective Service, and I was dispatched to Oklahoma City the day it happened. For the next week we worked 'round the clock, providing perimeter security. A week later, a moment of silence stopped all work at 9:02 a.m. The enormity of the situation hit me hard. At that moment my world caved in: I was emotionally, physically, and spiritually exhausted. I was diagnosed with acute Post Traumatic Stress Disorder (PTSD) and sent home. To this day, my wife says the man who came home was "not my husband."

Though I received Christian counseling, I wanted to speak with a police chaplain. As part of my counseling I returned to Oklahoma City with the counselor about a week later. One night during that trip I woke up about 2 a.m. and went back to the scene by myself. There I was overwhelmed by grief and sat down in the street sobbing. Then a golf cart pulled up with a police chaplain from South Carolina. I told him he was just who I needed to see. We spent the rest of the night praying and working through some issues. That helped a lot, but the whole experience was so horrible it took me a long time to re-stabilize my life.

> I fell to the ground and heard a voice say to me ... Acts 22:7

About five years later I felt a direct call to be in ministry as a police chaplain. I took all the training available, and now am used to train at our national academy in Crisis Intervention and Law Enforcement Ethics. I know the bombing changed my life radically, sort of a "Damascus

326

Road" experience (Acts 9). I am very grateful for the outcome, especially when I see so many who have come back from war zones, been diagnosed with PTSD, and no longer are productive members of society.

Though I wasn't into anything "bad," I had gone through a "long, dry spell," and certainly wasn't close to God at the time. It's almost as though he had to hit me in the head with a 2x4 to wake me up. I felt like he was saying to me, "Jim, if you don't learn it this time, we probably are going to have a face-to-face chat." Because of what I went through, God is able to use me in a way he never could before, and I am fulfilling a greater purpose in my life.

SEPTEMBER 22

HE WAS PREPARING FOR ME

Officer Bob Rice

New Jersey Critical Incident Stress Management (CISM) Team

MANY PEOPLE wonder where God was September 11, 2001, but I don't: He was preparing a place for me. When I went to Manhattan three days after the bombing, it was my first trip to "The City," even though I only lived 96 miles away. To be effective in helping fellow public safety employees cope with the horrors they were living through, I was taken on a tour of Ground Zero. My first impression was a lasting one: I hope I never have to see anything like that again! Not only was the carnage overwhelming, but I was also out of my element—my CISM training was secular, and I was working with chaplains. *Not good,* I thought.

I was raised in a nominally religious home and exposed to various beliefs over the years, but nothing "took." At Ground Zero, working with three Christian chaplains, God made my spiritual condition clear: I was lost and on my way to hell. Under their influence I began to change gradually, starting with my filthy language. Next came my "heart" infidelity. When one of the chaplains saw me looking lustfully at attractive women, he asked me to name my favorite and least-favorite food choices. I told him "prime rib" and "chicken nuggets."

He said, "Think of your wife as 'prime rib' and those women as 'chicken nuggets.'" You may laugh, but it helped turn my thoughts to where they should be.

327

Bob Rice at Ground Zero

One day I wanted something to read, and a chaplain gave me the Gospel of John. When he asked what I thought, I said I didn't understand it. He said, "Ask God to help you." When I asked how, he said, "Just talk to God like you would a friend." (He also suggested that I not use foul language!) When it came time for the chaplains to return home, we all were in tears. As one left, he named a chaplain who had just come into town, and told me to ask him to "finish what I started."

I knew something was happening in my heart, so the next day I sought out the other chaplain. As we talked I realized I needed Jesus in my life. So I prayed then and there to accept Christ as my personal Savior and Lord. That began a transformation that culminated in the salvation of both my wife and my son. But that didn't end the story. Eight years later I became "one of them"—now *I'm* a chaplain, too!

> I fell unto the ground, and heard a voice saying unto me, Saul, Saul, why persecutest thou me?
> Acts 22:7 (KJV)

SEPTEMBER 23

DOING UNTO OTHERS

Deputy Michael Davenport, Badge No. 496
Oklahoma County, OK, Sheriff's Office

LIKE MANY law enforcement (LE) officers across North America, I responded to the need for additional LE personnel in the aftermath of Hurricanes Katrina and Rita. "All hands on deck" were needed to deal with looters, floating caskets, running search-and-rescue, and manning checkpoints in St. Bernard Parish (New Orleans), Louisiana. Unlike many officers, I needed permission from more than one agency. As president of the Integris Federal Credit Union, I needed permission from my board of directors. They were concerned about management issues in my absence, as well as the fact that this would not be a "fun and games" mission.

The board was partially swayed by two major events in Oklahoma: Timothy McVeigh's senseless bombing of the Alfred P. Murrah Federal Building, and an unusual F-5 tornado that wreaked havoc on so many homes and businesses. In both instances, the overwhelming support we received from law enforcement and other first responders around the country made a real difference. We had an obligation to practice "The Golden Rule."

For nine days I was part of a twenty-five-member LE contingent which went first to St. Bernard Parish, then to Houma and Dulac, Louisiana. We were at Grand Isle as Hurricane Rita approached, and Dulac after the levees broke. We didn't know what to expect, only that we were doing the right thing.

As a reserve officer, one might think my obligations are less than a full-time officer's. I disagree. I am like a National Guard member who makes a commitment to serve our country in time of need. This was a major national disaster, calling for an unusual number of additional LE personnel. Perhaps for me the clincher was a conversation I had with my 12-year-old son about setting a good example when called upon. I had a responsibility to God, my son, and the mission. That's pretty strong incentive for anyone!

> Each of you should look not only to your own interests, but also to the interests of others.
> Philippians 2:4

THE WAREHOUSE

Trooper Caleb A. Williams

Texas Highway Patrol

THE TASK after any major story is the same: clean-up, fix-up, and paint-up. In the aftermath of Hurricane Katrina, that task was enormous! Immediately following the storm, we felt great despair and a sense of isolation from the world. But God heard our prayers and cries for help, and began to send us support from all over the world. In place of an overwhelming sense of loss, we now felt that God was in control. Police officers and supplies came in from all over North America to help us rebuild and regain our lives. Unfortunately, we had no place to keep supplies and tools, and we lacked a staging point for the rebuilding operation. What had been an ideal vacation and retirement destination on the Gulf Coast was now more like a war zone. Not only did we face winter weather coming on, but thievery was also a constant problem.

One morning as another officer and I were praying together, we remembered a large airplane-hangar type warehouse inside the Gulfport Airport grounds. It had been damaged in the storm, but was completely fenced in. We didn't know the airport management, and feared they would not give us access to such a valuable structure in a secure area. But after we had prayed about it and discussed it, we decided to just ask. To our surprise, the Lord opened the door! Without hesitation, they said it would be great for us to use it. One whole side of the warehouse had been blown away by the storm. After getting a "cherry picker" lift, we

330

climbed up the building and enclosed the side with tarps. It was a lot of work with just a few to help, so we questioned how much we should enclose.

The warehouse was really large, and we thought we wouldn't begin to fill it. However, since God had given us the building, we agreed we should not limit him by doing a halfway job. That was a very wise decision. Within a week the entire warehouse was filled and materials were stacked out-

> Ask and it will be given to you; seek and you will find; knock and the door will be opened to you.
> Luke 11:9

side, just waiting to come in. In spite of our little faith, the warehouse served for many months as a place where police and fire personnel were able to get the help and supplies they needed to rebuild their houses and their lives.

SEPTEMBER 25

"CALLING ALL CARS . . ."

Officer David Willard
Clackamas County, OR, Sheriff's Department

RECENTLY the autistic young man had received instruction in how to use the city bus system, and this was his maiden voyage. Though he was 19, he had the reasoning of a fifth-grader. We had been searching for him more than two hours, utilizing two K-9 units and thirty-five patrolmen, with the air unit on standby. Portland, Oregon, is a large city with more than 300 square miles of metro area covered by our transit system, and all the cops, dogs, and aircraft were getting nowhere.

Suddenly I was aware I had not employed the greatest search power at my disposal, our Lord. At that I bowed my head and prayed, "Father, please forgive me for not realizing the power you have in my life every day. You know we are looking for Brandon, and his mom and family are very concerned and frightened. Lord, I do not know where Brandon is, but I know that you do. If it be your will, please tell me where to find him." As I lifted my head, one intersection came clearly into my mind. I believe it came from the Holy Spirit. It was the convergence of three transit lines, a large six-way intersection with about nine bus line stops. It was about ten miles from my location, and opposite the direction Brandon should have gone. I asked my sergeant if I could go there to check out my hunch, and he approved.

It was about 40 degrees and getting dark, so I hurried. In less than ten minutes, I was there . . . and so was Brandon! He told me his feet hurt, that he was tired and very hungry! After placing a call to his mother and advising Dispatch, I took him to a nearby Burger King. He was a good customer that night, consuming three Whoppers, a large order of fries, and two pints of milk! When he finally was full, I took him home. Both he and his mother were born-again Christians, and I was able to share with her how God had shown me the way. I told that to my sergeant—not a believer— who suggested I not spread that story around too much! That was too bad. Perhaps if more people realized the joy of a relationship with God and the power of prayer, this world would be a much better place!

> [God] answered their prayers, because they trusted in him.
> 1 Chronicles 5:20

KILL OR BE KILLED!

Officer Joshua Brewer, No. 674

Chattanooga, TN, Police Department

IN 2002 I was a CHP (California Highway Patrol) officer just transferred to a new and unfamiliar area. It was dusk when I observed a car leaving a residence known for illegal drug sales. The driver was not wearing his seatbelt, a violation in California, so I activated my lights and siren and attempted to stop the vehicle. Instead, the chase was on as the driver sped west on historic Route 66, weaving in and out of traffic at speeds in excess of 100 miles per hour!

About twenty minutes later the driver entered a small, isolated, lake community, racing down residential streets at speeds faster than 60. Being unfamiliar with the area, I was forced to slow down and lost sight of the vehicle as it crested a small rise. When I reached the top of the rise, I was surprised—the road split into a "T" at the edge of a lake. Ahead was a vacant lot and a cloud of dust, but no suspect! From behind a nearby real estate office I thought I heard the hissing of a fractured radiator, but nothing was there—no car, no suspect, nothing! It was natural gas escaping from a broken gas line. When I looked at the lake, I saw a male adult swimming away from shore. He, too, was unfamiliar with the area and had "taken the plunge" at high speed! I called for him to swim to shore, but he began to tread water instead. Soon he tired, went down, came up, went down again, came back up, and then went down for the last time. When rescue divers located his body about an hour later, they found he had been in possession of drugs and a loaded revolver.

> Let the beloved of the LORD rest secure in him, for he shields him all day long. Deuteronomy 33:12

When we told the victim's father of his son's death, he said he was not surprised, that the son had been in prison and had said if the police tried to arrest him, he would "kill or be killed." That's when the reality of the situation set in! In law enforcement, it's not *if* you are faced with a life-or-death situation, but *when*. The criminal element is "in the driver's seat," and very easily can "get the drop" on an officer. Many times in my career I have felt that if it were not for the hand of God being on me, my days on earth would surely have come and gone. I believe such was the case that day!

SEPTEMBER 27

JAMES

Lieutenant Jeff Braley
Hamilton Township, OH, Police

THE FIRST time I met James he was lying in a ditch; his right leg had been severed and was lying above his head. He also had a hole in his right lower back larger than a softball. At the time I believed that all my fellow officer, Chris Wall, and I could do was stay there and comfort him until he died.

His father's car had conked out and, being 16 and strong, he had gotten out to push the vehicle. It was dark, and another juvenile had driven up too quickly and hit the back of his car. After being shoved under the car, he was thrown into the ditch where we found him. As medics worked hard and family arrived, James looked up at Chris and me and asked, "Are you saved?" He spoke of the love of Christ, and his only other concern was for the other driver. He focused on expressing concern and love for us all while we waited for him to be airlifted to Miami Valley Hospital in Dayton, Ohio.

I continued to call the hospital asking about him and always got the same response: "He's hanging in there."

A few days later I went to the hospital, partly for the investigation, but mostly just to see him. He awoke for only a short time, but I remember being overcome by hearing him say to me, "Hang in there; I know God has very special plans for you." I knew it was by God's hand he had survived.

Sometime later it was a very slow incident day on the street, and I was in the office. Our clerk came to me and announced, "There's someone up front who wants to see you." By her smile I knew something was going on. When I opened the door I could not believe my eyes; there sat James with his brand new prosthetic leg. We spoke of golf and many things, but his message was one of joy, gratitude, and the love of God this young man possessed. I now have been to his high school graduation and a family party afterward. My memory of that day will forever be his smile and the love for all he continued to express.

> Be strong and courageous. Do not be terrified; do not be discouraged, for the LORD your God will be with you wherever you go. Joshua 1:9

As a Christian officer, every day of my career I rely on my faith and the grace of God. Never have I met anyone who exemplified faith, courage, and love more than James. He truly is a strong soldier for Christ.

IF WE HELP SAVE A SINGLE LIFE

Sergeant Galen Smidt

Sioux Falls, SD, Police Department

A BUSY SUMMER was coming to an end, and I was looking forward to some quieter months ahead. It was Friday night, September 28. I was home preparing for a relaxing weekend when my phone rang at 9:30. The shift supervisor told me there had been a fiery crash with fatalities, and was requesting our crash reconstruction team. It had been a busy year of fatalities, and the callouts were becoming wearying. However, even after

334

15 years' experience, I had an uneasy feeling this accident was going to be different.

After making necessary calls, I went to the scene of a head-on crash involving a sports car and a full-size pickup truck. The car had exploded into a fiery inferno on impact, killing two teenagers inside. Their burned bodies were still in the car. As I examined them and authorized their removal, I couldn't help but think of my two teenage boys and grade school daughter back safe at home. Just then the parents of the deceased 15-year-old girl arrived unexpectedly on the scene. One of my officers attempted the impossible task of trying to console them. As difficult as it is to deliver a death notice to parents at their home, it is absolutely devastating at the scene of a crash—especially one as gruesome as this. Of all the accidents I've worked, I always will carry the sight of those charred remains in my memory.

> You will keep him *in perfect peace,* Whose *mind* is *stayed* on You, *Because he trusts in You.* Isaiah 26:3 (NKJV)

After that horrific incident, my traffic team used the experience to initiate a Careless Teen Driving Presentation. It since has been given to thousands of students. We may never know how successful we have been, but if we have prevented even one major crash, that will have made a difference.

We're supposed to be "tough," but accidents like that one greatly affect law enforcement officers. Unfortunately, the job causes far too many divorces, alcoholism, and personal problems because officers don't know how to deal with shocking incidents. My team and I handled this one by turning it into a positive training tool. But the real secret to surviving the job is to *make God Number 1* in your life. Through perseverance and his grace, that's what my family and I are committed to do.

SEPTEMBER 29

MY PASSIONS GOT THE BEST OF ME

Sergeant Cameron Grysen

Houston, Texas, Police Department

WHEN YOU'RE working, a patrol officer is never "off duty," even on break. I had just gotten coffee at a "stop and go" when a young man rushed in, saying a domestic fight was going on in an apartment

335

behind the store. He said "hurry," because he thought the suspect was going to kill her! I got the apartment number, called for backup and hurried to the scene.

The woman's screams made it easy to find the apartment. The door was open, and inside I saw a man standing over a woman with a child in her lap; both of them were covered in blood. The man held a plate, ready to throw it when I made my presence known with some "non-biblical words." There is no better way to raise the passion of a police officer than to injure a child, and my "passion meter" was going full-tilt!

Having gotten his attention, he turned, looked at me and immediately threw the plate – at me! Even though I side-stepped the missile, his action pushed my passion meter into overload! To make matters worse, he charged at me full-speed! I stood my ground, moving just before he reached me. Then I swung at him with my flashlight, connecting at the rear of his skull. He dropped like a ton of bricks. As I hand-cuffed him, I found he had a knife in his hand! Definitely, not a nice guy! After calling an ambulance for the victims, I examined the mother and child. Fortunately, the child had not been cut but was covered in his mother's blood, and her wounds were not life-threatening cuts.

> ...say "No" to ungodliness and worldly passions, and live self-controlled, upright and godly lives in this present age. Titus 2:12

After a "stitch up" session at the hospital, my prisoner got a ride to jail. On the way there, he told me had "had it coming," and thanked me for keeping him from doing something even more serious than he did. I was feeling a little bad about not controlling my passion, but justified my actions, knowing things could have been a lot worse if I hadn't hit him like that. Before arriving at the jail, he and I had a little "come to Jesus" talk, and a lecture on not abusing women and children. And when it was all over, I asked the Lord's forgiveness for letting my passions get the best of me!

LIFE IS UNFAIR

Deputy Nathan Bickerstaff
Ellis County, TX, Sheriff's Office

OFFICERS IN law enforcement see unfairness from all perspectives—if not on the streets, then in the career itself. Too often, what cops see as the most unfair is what we find inside our own agencies. However, problems arise when we view ourselves as victims. We can get caught up in both past and present circumstances, and end up with a negative response—anger. Of course, that anger has to be directed at something or someone else.

If we direct anger toward others, offenses follow. If we direct it inward, we enslave ourselves. Guilt often follows anger, which is followed by depression. We feel bad; therefore, we try to find "things" to compensate for the bad feelings. Addictions

> The Lord is my helper; I will not be afraid. What can man do to me?
> Hebrews 13:6

often arise at this point, for they are "things" in which we bury ourselves to cover negative feelings arising from thinking life is unfair. Then you hear the preacher on Sunday morning telling you to love, be faithful and be kind and forgiving, and we want to know, "What world does *he* live in?" It certainly isn't ours!

The next question we ask is, "If God is good, why does he let unfairness happen?"

That's when I turn to Scripture, for it is full of stories about life not being fair. Take Elijah. He was living for God, yet the queen demanded his death. We see this all the time when police get killed simply because they were at work "doing their job." Then there's Jonah. He didn't want to preach to the bad people of Nineveh, but God made him do it. We have to be "civil" to criminals who spit on us, curse us, kick and scratch and shoot us if they get the opportunity. And who could forget Job, or David being chased by Saul, or a host of other "good guys" who had to endure? As cops we ask, "Where is justice?" How can we have confidence in God when life seems so unfair?

The Bible doesn't promise a life free of pain, difficulties, or loss. But it does say in Hebrews 13:5, 6, Jesus will be our companion on the journey. If we never had a problem, we would never need God. Sometimes when life seems unfair I have to practice praising God instead of concentrating on the negative. No, life isn't fair, but it's worse without God. Personally, when I find myself sinking into a pity party I go back to Jesus: He always gives me the perspective I need!

TREASON!

Drucilla Wells, JD, Supervisory Special Agent (Ret.)
Federal Bureau of Investigation

(Drucilla Wells, JD, worked twenty-one years with the FBI. She worked violent crime, narcotics, and organized crime, and spent her last nine-and-a-half years as a behavioral analyst (profiler) in the FBI's National Center for the Analysis of Violent Crime.)

M Y PRIMARY motive for joining the FBI was a desire to serve my country by stopping those who oppressed, robbed, and hurt others. The FBI is all about serving. It's about loyalty to a concept of justice and right. We are taught that FBI stands for Fidelity, Bravery, and Integrity: *fidelity* to the country we serve, the Constitution, and the laws of the land; *bravery* that, at times, requires stepping into difficult and/or dangerous situations; and *integrity* to do the right thing, regardless of the cost. *Treason* is an abomination to FBI agents.

After the September 11 terrorist attacks, I encountered traitors when I assisted with detainee interviews in Guantanamo. I found it difficult to understand how Americans could aid and abet a group that sought to annihilate the United States. However, in the course of my career I encountered a more disturbing form of treason—when an FBI agent betrayed his country, the FBI, and his co-workers. Money was usually not the reason. More often the agent felt unappreciated, treated unfairly by the Bureau or deserving of more respect. There was anger, bitterness, resentment, and envy of those who got better assignments or the desired promotion or transfer. Yet how could they turn from loyal service to treason, choosing self over country? It was beyond comprehension—at first.

> Then he called the crowd to him along with his disciples and said: "If anyone would come after me, he must deny himself and take up his cross and follow me."
> Mark 8:34

Then I realized I have the same flaw. I should be committed to serving God, to putting his purposes and will above my own, to pouring myself out for the Kingdom. Yet—through open rebellion or silent treason in my heart—I repeatedly betray him. I shift my affections and loyalty from God and his kingdom to self and my kingdom. My wants, desires, anger, bitterness, and envy keep me from loving others as I should—as I am commanded to do. Isn't the shifting of my allegiance from God to self as much an act of treason as any traitor betraying his country? My own heart condemns me. As the prophet Jeremiah says, "The heart is deceitful above all things and beyond cure" (Jeremiah 17:9).

GOD PICKED THE SUNDAY

Marius Bordeanu
Romanian police officer

WHEN WE got married, I explained to my new bride that she would spend many hours alone because of my schedule and the demands placed on a police officer. After our marriage, she began attending a ladies' Bible study and accepted Christ as her Savior. I was greatly pleased with the dramatic change in her, but resisted her requests to attend church. I said you cannot be a policeman and a Christian, not with the people I deal with and decisions I have to make! As her continual requests became "nagging" I got angry and said, "Okay, I will go to church *once*, but never ask me again. I will pick the Sunday." She reluctantly accepted that, but asked the ladies at the Bible study to pray for me. The day finally came when I said, "This is it. I will go to church with you this morning, but remember our agreement." What I didn't know then was that *I* didn't choose the day, *God did!*

> Preach the Word; be prepared in season and out of season.
> 2 Timothy 4:2

She was very excited as we dressed and went to church. Being a cop, I looked over the crowd to see who I'd arrested! Then I saw on the platform a uniformed policeman from America! He told of his decision to accept Christ, and how the Lord helped him be an honest man of integrity as he carried out his duties. He gave several examples of how the Lord gave him wisdom and helped him in some very difficult policing situations.

I spent that afternoon in tears thinking about his testimony. That officer proved that a man could be both a policeman and a Christian! Under deep conviction, I took my wife back to church that night to hear him again. The policeman was speaking elsewhere that night, but I listened intently to the pastor's sermon. At the end of his message I went forward and accepted Christ as my personal Savior. I have been faithful to my Lord ever since, and now am a deacon.

When our church started another church in a village not far away, the pastor asked me to preach there. As I preach each week, my hunger in knowing how to "rightly divide the Word" in my sermons has continued to increase. I know God has called me to preach, and my earnest desire is to be ever more effective as a witness and a preacher.

IS OUR WORK ALWAYS HUMANITARIAN?

Sergeant Robin Sexton
Michigan State Police

IS ALL police work "humanitarian," or is some of it just something no one else will or can do? To me "humanitarian" suggests an act that is thought out and done for a purpose, like inoculating children in Africa for polio. Police work is different. We never know what we'll be called on to do, or what response will be required.

When I went into policing I was only 17. A van had rolled, collapsing the top, and the driver was pinned inside. My partner was too large for the crushed entry, so I was selected to crawl in and check for life signs. I didn't mind, because I like being involved in everything—it's my favorite thing about the job. The driver had suffered massive head trauma with blood everywhere, but he was alive and very drunk. We could not free him, and had to wait for the fire department. His throat and mouth continually filled with blood; this hindered his breathing, and he would lose consciousness. Until help arrived and he could be cut out, I had to lie there on my belly, turning his head to drain the blood. Every time he regained consciousness, he would try to fight, and hit me. Then I would have to back off till he needed to drain again. When I finally came out, just about everything from my waist up was soaked in blood.

The driver lived, pled to DUI, lost an eye, and ended up with a deformed face. I ruined a uniform, and for the first time questioned life and death. I know the Bible says God determines the days of our life even before we are born (Job 14:5), but I still am amazed at why some live and some die. There is some contradiction between fragility and a minor issue that causes death in one, compared with the seeming indestructibility of the human body and spirit in another, where a major problem barely causes a comment.

> Then Jesus said to them, "I ask you, which is lawful on the Sabbath: to do good or to do evil, to save life or to destroy it?" Luke 6:9

In this case, the man's life was saved, but did I perform a humanitarian act? Did living give him time to rethink life and seek God, or did he become bitter and curse his Maker? I'll never know. I simply was the only one small enough to crawl into that mangled van, and I've accepted the fact that God set it up that way.

OCTOBER 4

THE SOPHOMORE JINX

Officer Pete Bone

Carpentersville, IL, Police Department

SOMETIMES, during an officer's "sophomore year," he or she can get a feeling of entitlement. We're in our second year, have "been there and done that," are working on our own and handling an impossible job all by ourselves. In our arrogance we can see everybody as an idiot. We have life all figured out, an attitude which can permeate both work and home life. Unfortunately, that year can be "jinxed!"

As a high school senior I wanted to be a cop, so I got my college degree in Law Enforcement. While awaiting acceptance as an officer I worked at an outdoor theatre. One night, walking four abreast with fellow employees to our parking lot, we were run down by a drunk driver. One friend was killed, and my right leg snapped in half. After many months of surgeries and rehab, I was more determined than ever to attain my goal. Finally, a department northwest of Chicago hired me!

As a rookie I had a strong sense of right and wrong with a true desire to serve and protect. I looked for every opportunity to demonstrate my new police knowledge and authority. I married my fiancée, bought a home, and life was complete. Then the "jinx" struck! I began to take my wife for granted, even treating her like people on the street. I viewed life through a secular prism. Eight years later my wife decided I didn't love her and asked for a divorce; I was stunned and devastated.

Through the next six years we kept in contact, watching each other go downhill. My life spiraled out of control with binge drinking, gambling, and severe depression. Several times I sat with a gun in my mouth, feeling suicide was a valid option. Finally God brought back into my life a longtime friend who had become a Christian. During the times we met over the next several months, he subtly shared Christ's message of redemption and salvation. About this same time I learned that my ex-wife had become a Christian, and she invited me to attend her

> Therefore, if anyone is in Christ, he is a new creation; the old has gone, the new has come!
> 2 Corinthians 5:17

baptism. We began to attend church together and I, too, surrendered my life to Christ. We remarried in 2006, no longer sophomores but a couple matured by Christ. My life at work also changed as I exchanged my "secular prism" for a Christian one. As hard as it sometimes is, I now try to view each person as a special creation by God. He has made *me* a new creature!

OCTOBER 5

I CAUGHT THE BALL

Officer Jamie F. Kopinetz
Hummelstown Borough, PA, Police Department

WHAT BEGAN as a typical Thursday became one of the most horrifying days in my career: a 12-year-old girl was drowning in the community pool; I was only thirty-eight seconds away! My quickest access was blocked by a "cherry picker" truck with guys working in the air, so I grabbed my defibrillator and sprinted the two hundred yards to the pool. I arrived just as the lifeguards pulled her out of the water.

As I started CPR, I remember looking across the pool and seeing faces of friends—adults and kids—some seeing death too early in life. I tried so hard to save her, to save Elizabeth. I prayed fervently for God to let her live and give her strength back. After the medics arrived, we worked a long time before finally getting a pulse; she was alive, and we put her in the ambulance. I was trembling so badly I could hardly write my report. I pulled my car into a small cluster of trees and prayed and wept. I've never prayed so hard for anything in my life.

The hospital where they took her is a world-class trauma center. When I went to check on her, it turned out she was epileptic and suffering from seizures. They did everything they could, but after a week the family and doctors removed her from life support and she died. From my perspective, the only good thing was that she was an organ donor who helped others live. At the viewing all I could say was "I'm sorry," and started to weep. Her parents helped me, saying they knew I did all I could, and that God needed Elizabeth more than we did.

> "Well done, good and faithful servant."
> Matthew 25:23

That day upset me so much. Did I do CPR right? Of course—I've taught hundreds of people how to perform CPR over the years. Could I have responded quicker? Thirty-eight seconds is pretty fast! Still, there was doubt in my mind and heart. One day a friend asked me, "Do you ever watch football?" I said yes. Then he said, "Sometimes a player makes an unbelievable catch and runs it in for a touchdown. In spite of that, the team might still lose the game. You caught the ball and did everything you could. She was taken to a world-class trauma center. If the doctors there could not save her, then she could not be saved. The important thing is: The game was lost, but you caught the ball!" That gave me peace. I was "in the game and caught the ball," but God is in control, not me!

OCTOBER 6

CHRISTIAN POLICE MINISTRIES*

Chaplain Grant Wolf
Chattanooga, TN, Police Department

CHRISTIAN police ministries have been in existence at least since 1883 when the Christian Police Association (CPA) was established in Great Britain. Also headquartered in England is The International Christian Police Fellowship, a worldwide affiliation of police ministries.

In North America, the Fellowship of Christian Police Officers (FCPO) represents a large number of Christian officers in Canada and the United

States. Other well-known ministries include International Cops for Christ, Peace Officers for Christ International, and Ten-Four Ministries. In addition to these, there are a number of organizations for police chaplains. The largest is the International Conference of Police Chaplains (ICPC), with a worldwide membership. Another is Peace Officer Ministries (POM), which serves as a chaplaincy resource for officers, chaplains, police agencies, churches, and communities.

A number of effective ministries have developed around police personnel with a zeal for Christ. In Colorado, Detective M. C. "Mike" Williams has a thriving local and e-mail ministry called the Centurion Law Enforcement Ministry, and Iowa DCI officer Don Shreffler has for many years hosted an annual retreat for Midwestern officers. Florida sheriff's deputy Mike Dye wrote *The Peacekeepers Bible Study*, which has engendered a loose network of study groups throughout the United States.

> These all continued with one accord in prayer and supplication. Acts 1:14

When they take an oath to "protect and serve," law enforcement officers automatically place themselves on the side of truth and justice. If they are students of the Bible, they know that God instituted our criminal justice system in Genesis, chapter 3, when he called court into session, meted out the first criminal sentence, and established policing with the cherubim and flaming sword. In Romans 13 they learn that police officers are "ordained of God" (v. 1 KJV) as servants for good.

Because of constant job reassignments, shift changes, and other pressures, many find regular participation in their home church difficult. Like the first-century church, they stay connected with God and fellow Christians in small-group settings. These ministries complement the local church, providing a Christian resource to officers seeking closer fellowship with God.

*Check the Internet for Web site addresses.

CAN I BE A WITNESS?

Anonymous
Texas police officer

L AW ENFORCEMENT officers become very angry when they feel justice has been thwarted. Whatever the reason—unwarranted accusations of racism or any other form of "political incorrectness," attorneys who find "loopholes in the law" to get their client off the hook, or many other ploys—we feel that justice thwarted is "a slap in the face."

In this instance, I was investigating an accident when another investigator called me to his sector seeking my expertise. An officer had been directing traffic around an accident when a driver defied his order. As the officer reached into the man's truck to get the key, the driver started to drive off. At that, the officer shot the driver. The truck swerved into a nearby house, and the driver was severely injured. The reason given by the officer for shooting was that the driver was

> The LORD loves righteousness and justice.
> Psalm 33:5

about to run over his supervisor. This scenario just didn't add up, so I sought more information. A tow truck driver with no reason to lie had seen the incident. He told me a different story, which lined up with the evidence.

Even though the shooting officer was known in our department as "a hothead," Homicide assumed his story was correct. The officer still was charged in a state court, but received a "not guilty" verdict. Then, because the driver was gay (how could the officers have known that?), a pressure group got involved and the case went to federal court. At this point the supervisor was named as "a co-conspirator." Homicide accused him of inconsistencies between his verbal story at the scene and his written statement afterward. Therefore, both the officer and supervisor were charged with conspiracy to deprive the victim of his rights. During the trial, every officer who had worked in the district that night was subpoenaed, but not me. I was not at the scene "officially," and my name was not on any of the reports.

I called the attorney representing the officers saying I had been at the scene and needed to be subpoenaed. It wasn't that I wanted to testify, but I felt the true facts of the case would not be given. The attorney said everyone who was going to be subpoenaed had been. I was not on the list; I hadn't been there, I was told! (Interestingly, TV file video from that night clearly showed I was there.) Consequently, I never testified, and both officers spent time in federal prison. There is no doubt in my mind that the shooter gave a false account—that the supervisor was innocent! Justice was thwarted. God was not in it.

ANGELS UNAWARE

Sergeant David M. Greenhalgh (Ret.)
Delta (Vancouver, Canada) Police Department

ONE SUNNY Tuesday I was on patrol dressed like a businessman and in an unmarked car. I found myself in an area of upper-class homes with a few houses for sale. In a hurry to reach my destination, I had started to pass a parked sedan with a Realtor's "Open House" sign on its roof. For no reason I found myself pulling over, getting out of the car, and walking to the door. I recall saying out loud, "Why am I doing this?" At the door a well-dressed older female realtor welcomed me, and I began touring the vacant new house with her.

In the process she began to recite her troubles—with her daughter, other family, her work, her life! Periodically she said, "I don't know why I'm telling you this," then continued to pour out her heart. Finally I realized God had prompted the stop, and I needed to respond. She said she was a believer and would let me pray for her. Her eyes welled up with tears of gratitude as I did, and I left thanking God for the opportunity to minister to her.

The next Sunday after church my family and I passed that way, and saw the car with the "Open House" sign in front of the same residence. We stopped, got out of the car, and walked up the drive. The Realtor was saying goodbye to prospective buyers when she saw us. Recognizing me, her jaw dropped wide open as if she were frozen in shock. I asked her, "What's wrong? You look as if you'd seen a ghost!"

After a long moment she spoke. "When I met you Tuesday I thought God had sent me an angel. I never thought I would see you

> Do not forget to entertain strangers, for by so doing some people have entertained angels without knowing it.
> Hebrews 13:2

again." I assured her I was no angel. Then her full story came out. On Tuesday when we prayed for God's comfort she was in great anguish over all her troubles. She told me that in the five days since, God had begun to answer many of her concerns.

I've always thought the Scripture about "an angel unawares" (Hebrews 13:2 KJV) described something that might happen to me. But I never thought God ever would use me as the angel!

A DOMESTIC LIKE NO OTHER

Sergeant Dawn Higgins

Indianapolis, IN, Metropolitan Police Department

IN FAR too many instances, the Christmas season seems to exacerbate family problems. A few years ago it happened in my own family: My then brother-in-law took my sister hostage at gunpoint, along with their four- and six-year-old children. A female friend, also an officer, was with me when I learned of the situation. We drove immediately to my sister's house and called for backup.

Mercifully, we were able to get the children out of the house. "Per the book," my friend took them and ran for cover while I entered the house, gun in hand. My sister was sitting directly in front of my brother-in-law, who was pointing his gun at her. She told me

> Now choose life, so that you and your children may live.
> Deuteronomy 30:19

he already had fired once. Though I had been a police officer for nineteen years and am a trained crisis negotiator, my training seemed to go "out the window." After all, this was my *sister!* My "negotiation" quickly dissolved into each of us demanding of the other, "Drop your gun!"

Miraculously, my sister saw an opening and escaped to a bathroom. This seemed to be a turning point, for in moments my brother-in-law put the gun to his head and said, "It's over tonight!" In situations like this, everything around you seems frozen in time. Sharply focused on him, I detected a small movement of his wrist! He was about to pull the trigger, and a bullet would go searing through his head. Unless I stopped him, he would kill himself in front of me. My shot hit him in the stomach, causing him to fall. But while falling he began shooting, hitting me four times—not the ending I'd hoped for! He hit me in my left calf, twice in my left knee, and once in my left arm. In spite of a tendon transfer in my hand, I still have numbness and nerve damage. We both received emergency treatment, and he ended up in prison for a period of time.

Many have said they either would have let him kill himself, or I should have killed him. However, I did not entertain the thought of death for either of us. In that moment I chose hope, and I chose faith. I was confident then, as now, that God was not done with us yet. I believe that God wanted us both to survive so his plan for our lives could be fulfilled. Even today, the Lord's plan continues to be revealed.

OCTOBER 10

A STRANGE TWIST

Reverend Dean Kavouras, Chaplain

Cleveland Division Safety Forces
Federal Bureau of Investigation

ABOUT 9:30 a.m. my phone rang. "I've found your business card and $21 in front of Walmart."

I thought, *This has to be a hoax, something's not right; I haven't been to Walmart in more than a week.* "Thank you, but just keep it," I told the man. "I'm 45 minutes away, and you'd have to wait too long." Then I got suspicious; was he trying to set me up for a robbery?

I spoke to a detective who heads up a robbery detail in that district. He said to call the man back, and see if we could meet in a couple of hours. When he said yes, the detective and I were even more convinced. I put on a "wire," drove there in my car with a detective following, and a marked car some distance behind us. Nearing the meeting place, I called the man, who directed me to his pickup truck. When I arrived he exited his vehicle, and handed me the money, business card, and a bank deposit slip! I was surprised, but still suspicious. I thanked him, offered a reward (which he declined), and left. As he was leaving, the marked car pulled him over, ran his information, and found he was clean. But why was my card with that money? My plan was to go to the bank marked on the deposit slip, find out whose money it was, and return it. When I wrote my next chaplain's report, which goes to many people, I mentioned the incident. Funny thing, the money belonged to one of my readers!

A pastor I'd just met had been to Walmart. On leaving the store, he accidentally dropped his bank deposit slip with my card and the $21. The money was his! After he read my report he sent this e-mail: "You won't believe this, but the money is mine! Do with it as you may, but that is amazing! You gave me your card yesterday!"

My first call was to the man who had returned it. He was as amazed as I, and relieved that our suspicions had been cleared up. Even more amazing, he had been laid off from his job, badly needed the money, waited two-and-one-half hours to return it and wouldn't take a reward. Then we stopped him and eyed him as a potential criminal! The Scripture says, "In Him we live and move and have our being" (Acts 17:28). I do not know this man's relationship with God, but I do know his heart!

OCTOBER 11

"WE NEED YOU"

Chaplain Terry Hallman

Law Enforcement Chaplains of Tuscaloosa County, AL

AFTER MY abdominal surgery one Monday, the doctor said, "No driving for five days." As badly as it hurt just to take a deep breath, I didn't have a problem with that!

But early Thursday my phone rang. It was the chief deputy. After answering with a weak "hello," I heard him urgently say, *"Chaplain, we need you!"* With a shaky voice he told me a deputy's six-year-old daughter had just died, and the family was at the emergency room!

All I could think was, "Lord, help me, I have to go!" With my wife's help I dressed, then drove to the hospital.

The hospital's law enforcement parking area was filled with sheriff's cars. Hurriedly I entered, and quickly found the deputy and his wife. On the table was their beautiful daughter, her face still in the repose of death. When the deputy saw me he rose to his feet and made his way toward me with tears streaming down his face, collapsing onto my shoulders. We wept and prayed together, then I stood by their side until the child was taken away.

Back in the family waiting room were a host of caring comrades in arms, waiting, praying, and showing their support for their brother and fellow officer. Though three hours had passed, and I was weak and drained, by the grace of God I had been able to be there for this family and my department during their most tragic time. I was praising God for allowing me to be his ministering servant. Most of us chaplains serve without pay, and feel honored to do so.

In this age of so-called "separation of church and state," there are some who question whether governmental agencies should allow chaplains. In spite of protests like that, our courts have determined that people in high-stress work—like law enforcement personnel and the military—need "spiritual succor and support." Walk a few days in any chaplain's shoes, and you soon come to understand why. We think of the term "protect and serve" as relating to sworn officers; my job also is to "protect and serve" these fine men and women as they deal with the stress in their lives.

> Like the coolness of snow at harvest time is a trustworthy messenger to those who send him; he refreshes the spirit of his masters.
> Proverbs 25:13

"HAVE MERCY ON ME, A POOR SINNER!"

Constable Merv Tippe (Ret.)
Regina, Saskatchewan

IT WAS A cool fall evening in rural Saskatchewan, and I thought it would be a quiet shift. After a stop at the local café for coffee, I was back in my car and decided to patrol some rural roads. Before long, Dispatch advised me of a red pickup truck stolen from a community about forty miles south; the police there felt it might be coming my way. The incident had happened much earlier in the evening, so I really didn't expect it to show up. However, about that time I exited a rural road onto the highway back to town and noticed vehicle taillights ahead of me. Speeding up, I got close enough to determine it was a red pickup truck, perhaps the one we were seeking. When I radioed in the license number, it came back confirmed.

As we entered town, the vehicle sped up slightly. I then activated the light bar, but the driver of the truck appeared to ignore me, turning down a side street. Even after I activated the siren a couple of times, the truck continued on until he pulled into a yard. I drove up behind him and was about to radio in the stop when he got out of the truck, reached back in, and pulled a rifle off the rack in the back window.

That's when I said out loud what I call my arrow prayer: "Lord Jesus Christ, have mercy on me, a poor sinner!" To this day I am not certain what really happened, except the next thing I knew I was standing in front of the fellow with my .357 Magnum revolver tucked up under his nose. I heard myself saying, "Put that gun on the ground or your next thought will be your last!" The last thing I recall before that was reaching for the handle of the patrol car door. It was as if I had been translated by the Lord to right in front of the thief with my revolver in his face. There was just no way I could have opened the door, gotten out of the car, unholstered my weapon, and run the twelve to fifteen feet to where he was. I arrested, cuffed, and charged him with the theft of the truck, which was later returned to its rightful owner.

> In all your ways acknowledge him, and he will make your paths straight. Do not be wise in your own eyes; fear the Lord and shun evil. Proverbs 3:6, 7

As a result of my physical encounter with him, the next day my right upper chest was bruised near the shoulder, and my shoulder was extremely sore. Once again the "arrow I shot" hit its mark; God had been merciful and spared my life!

OCTOBER 13

STAR WARS FOR REAL

Sergeant Jonathan Milne
New Zealand Police

YOU SEE many strange sights in a police station, but you don't expect to see a Star Wars Storm Trooper. Dressed in the outfit was a large Polynesian man, arrested a week prior for having intimidated children at a local school. We had seized his light saber, helmet, and uniform, and he wanted them back. He also wanted to show us the features and value he placed on the articles. In my darkened office, he demonstrated his light-saber movements accompanied by button-activated voice commands. My staff was amused by the exhibition; senior management was not! We decided he was a low risk to be a repeat offender, and made decisions concerning what services he needed. Little did I know his demonstration would be useful within the month!

> Hold on to instruction, do not let it go; guard it well, for it is your life.
> Proverbs 4:13

Two weeks later, while I was off duty, I was called to assist in negotiations with a mentally ill man. He was considered to be a danger to himself and others after he had attacked police and mental health staff with a large metal sword. He was in the house with a sword in each hand, and the negotiator was trying to communicate with him through an open door. Imagine my surprise when I saw he was wearing a Storm Trooper helmet like the one I'd seen demonstrated in my office! However, this man was armed for battle, refusing to acknowledge or respond to any of the attempts to communicate with him.

I prompted the primary negotiator to ask the subject about the functions on his helmet. It worked! For the first time the man nodded his head and communicated. When asked to push one of the buttons on his helmet, he pushed the one with a recorded voice that said, "Oh, oh, I think this is going to end badly!" Fortunately, it didn't! Shortly thereafter the subject threw down both swords and was taken into custody.

I had to ponder my prior "helmet training session" so close before that threatening, real-life situation. I have never again dealt with anyone in a Star Wars outfit, and there was no connection between the two men. Certainly God was in it, preparing me for later to prevent harm to others. It was a great reminder to pay attention to seemingly insignificant things; we never know when they will be useful!

OCTOBER 14

GOD BUILT THE HOUSE

Sergeant David M. Greenhalgh (Ret.)
FCPO Reconstruction Coordinator*

ONE SATURDAY afternoon in October, Lieutenant Greg Herman walked into the office I'd been assigned in the temporary quarters

353

of the Gulfport, Mississippi, Police Department. Katrina had reduced Greg's house to nothing but sticks holding up a roof. Even though the mortgage still had to be paid, he felt all was lost—it would have to be bull-dozed!

In my spirit I felt it could be rebuilt, so we sat together and wrote down what was still useable: foundation, septic system, driveway, framing, plumbing, some of the ceilings and wiring, and the roof. Approximate value: $60,000! Greg and I believe this was a "rolling revelation" from God, as neither of us had any construction experience. Now we needed someone who did! An experienced carpenter who'd come to the stricken area to volunteer his services confirmed our thinking. Youth for Christ volunteers spent three separate days removing all the debris from his house and property, and God began providing miracles. A Chicago cop repaired the roof so we could work under it. A church in Colorado provided a heating and air-conditioning unit. A contractor repaired the plumbing and wiring, and supervised the reconstruction. A wonderful crew of Canadian cops worked non-stop for ten days doing most of the rebuild. The house frame had shifted, and God provided the heavy equipment needed to move it back. Because of Greg's 6'9" height, special doors were needed. A Florida donor had hand-carved doors built to order and delivered them to the home. Another donor furnished the siding. By the time Greg and family moved into their beautifully restored home, it was better than before, and vividly demonstrated God's love and mercy. The smile on Mrs. Herman's face said it all: God not only provided the house, he also healed her family's hurt from feeling they had lost it all.

> Unless the LORD builds the house, its builders labor in vain. Psalm 127:1

I kept the back of the police report where we made our notes that Saturday so long ago. A contractor would view our jottings as quite simple, but to Greg and me it was a profound revelation from God.

*After Hurricane Katrina, retired Canadian police Sergeant David Greenhalgh spent nearly eighteen months on the Gulf Coast, coordinating efforts of the Fellowship of Christian Peace Officers-USA (FCPO) and FCPO-Canada in rebuilding dozens of homes for first responders and support personnel.

QUALITY TIME TOGETHER (NOT!)

Kristi Neace*, wife of Officer Richard Neace
Union, MO, Police Department

WE NEEDED quality time together, so my officer husband suggested I ride with him for part of his shift. I thought, *Sure, I'll see what he does for a living and, besides, it'll be a romantic two-hour ride under the night sky.* Boy, was I wrong!

> "Do not be afraid or discouraged, for the LORD God, my God, is with you." 1 Chronicles 28:20

Within minutes we were dispatched to a purse "snatch-n-grab" at the bowling alley. Then came the biggie: Another officer in pursuit of a fleeing robber called for backup. In a flash we were off into the dark night, lights flashing and sirens blaring. As we neared "g-force speed" down a secluded road, the other officer radioed that the suspect had turned around and was now heading in the opposite direction. With that, my husband "flipped a U" and sped like mad the opposite way. As for me, I was praying in a loud voice to spare us from any oncoming traffic or an unsuspecting deer that I knew might jump out in front of us any second. Once wasn't enough for my husband; three times he made a U-turn hoping to head off the robbery suspect. Finally, we topped a hill and saw a phalanx of emergency equipment: squad cars, fire trucks, ambulances, and so forth. The suspect had lost control of his car and plowed into a guardrail. In the process he ran another vehicle off the road and down an embankment, trapping the people inside. Fortunately, God definitely had been in control, for the people were not seriously injured and the man was caught.

We stopped, my husband got out to do his duty, and I tried to dislodge my fingernails from the dashboard! Even though my nerves were shot, I tried to regain my composure before he got back in the car. I was hoping that might be the end of our "quality time," but off we went across town to a domestic call. After a few more calls, I informed Rick that though I thought he was completely wonderful and heroic, that I had to make a trip to the little girl's room, and that would be the end of our "quality time" ride-alongs! I thank God there are trained officers like Rick who can handle the pressure and the stress; I could never do the job!

*Author, *Lives behind the Badge*

"ALL RISE. OYEZ, OYEZ, OYEZ!"

Anonymous

WITH THESE words, a scene is played out each workday in courtrooms across America. For officers serving as court bailiffs, it's not like being on a set used in filming *Perry Mason*. It is a place with great risk, as was demonstrated in Atlanta in March 2005 when a sheriff's deputy, a judge, and a court clerk were killed at the Fulton County Courthouse.

As a bailiff, I inspect the courtroom, jury room, judge's bench and chamber, beneath pew benches, everywhere—before the courtroom opens for its session. Before unlocking the courtroom doors I pray and ask God for alertness and wisdom and for a hedge of protection around all. After "All Rise. Oyez, oyez, oyez" is pronounced, the judge enters, and the spectators are seated.

Jurors may think the defendant is not in custody, but he or she is wearing an invisible leg brace under civilian clothes. My unarmed backup sits near the defendant, off to the side, ready in case the defendant attempts an escape. As lead bailiff I sit at a desk facing the courtroom, armed and ready to respond quickly to any problem. Like a Secret Service agent I constantly scan the perimeter, for my job is to protect the judge. Nobody can approach him without permission. If someone attempts to harm him, it is my job to "take a bullet" for him. Before that could happen, I would try to get the judge off the bench and to safety. Together, my backup and I are responsible for the security of all in that courtroom. When incarcerated witnesses are called, extra officers are needed as guards. Many prisoners have a steely, blank look in their eyes, their mean expressions conveying inner turmoil that could signal a ticking time bomb waiting to explode. The tension is very real.

> Blessed are they who maintain justice, who constantly do what is right. Psalm 106:3

At the end of the day my backup bailiffs escort the defendant out of the courtroom and into the lockup. The jurors are dismissed and escorted out of the building. I stand armed next to my judge, and escort him off the bench safely into his chambers. Then I dismiss the people in the courtroom through alternate exits. Everyone is safe this day, and justice has prevailed. Again I pray, "Thank you, God." Tomorrow, there will be another case, another story, and more prayer!

PRAISE GOD, I FINISHED MY SHIFT!

Officer Randy

Baltimore, MD

DURING MY first two years on the job I was working patrol on evening shift and developed a bad headache. When I asked my sergeant if I could go home early, he said we were short-handed and asked me to stick it out. So, not feeling so hot I continued with my duties.

I saw a driver commit a traffic offense, pulled him over, and asked for his driver's license. When his out-of-state license came back "suspended," Dispatch assigned another unit to back me up. When it arrived I had the vehicle towed, arrested the driver ("Lee"), and took him to the station for processing.

> Blessed is the man who does this, the man who holds [justice] fast.
> Isaiah 56:2

During the booking process I dropped hints about the condition of his spiritual life. He reacted positively, and asked me to share the Gospel with him. I told him we could talk outside the station after I took him to the district court commissioner for a bail hearing.

As we left the building he again asked me about the Good News of Jesus. I was encouraged by his eagerness, for I was just as eager to share as he was to hear. Between the station and the courthouse, I did share the Gospel with Lee, and he prayed to receive Christ right there in my police car. Praise God! That was a better cure for my headache than aspirin ever could have been; my headache was gone!

After Lee got out of jail I contacted him and invited him to church. I was newly married at the time and had only my new pickup truck. After that, my wife and I decided that if we were going to take folks to church with us, we needed a different vehicle; we traded the truck for a sedan. We took Lee to our church until he was able to visit a church within walking distance of his home. But he wasn't the last to ride in that sedan.

When I think back about wanting to go home early that night, I find new meaning in the Scripture passages that encourage us to persevere in spite of hardship. Also, in 1 Corinthians 3:6 the apostle Paul writes, "I planted the seed, Apollos watered it, but God made it grow." I believe that in Lee's case others had come before me, God had worked on his heart, and I was just fortunate enough to be there at harvest time! I've learned it isn't important whether I'm planting, watering, or harvesting—what is important is to stay in the game and be part of the process!

"WRECK ON THE SKYWAY"

Officer Elfego J. Gallardo, Jr.
Chicago, IL, Police Department

NOTHING prepared me for what I saw that wintry morning on the Chicago Skyway! I was finishing up a crash report when I noticed a toll-road service truck parked on the shoulder, its driver struggling to remain upright. I also saw a huge fuel spill with debris everywhere, so I activated my lights and blocked a lane of traffic. With hollow voice the driver told me he had been working outside his truck when a car came from out of nowhere and hit it hard. With glazed eyes he said, "I thought I was going to be hit and die!"

When I asked where the car was, he pointed down the road about a quarter of a mile. I saw the vehicle piled up against the median wall with hazard lights flashing, and sprinted there as fast as I could. The driver probably was in urgent need of medical attention so I radioed dispatch. An eighteen-wheeler had stopped, and its driver was looking into the wreck through the front passenger window. Rap music was still blaring in the car, and I saw a male slumped to the right, motionless. The truck driver asked, "Did you see his head?" What I saw horrified me. The entire front cabin area was soaked in blood, as was the driver's body. His skull was cracked open with blood pouring from the wound, and his face was virtually unrecognizable.

I stood there motionless, no thoughts, just in complete dismay, then I called Dispatch again—"Uh, squad . . . I'm no doctor, but I think this driver is no longer with us."

While I secured the scene my heart was racing and my tongue quivering inside my mouth. Gratefully I accepted the midnight sergeant's offer, "Go home, I'll write the report for you."

> "I heard the crash on the highway But, I didn't hear nobody pray." Roy Acuff, 1942

358

Chicago Police car

As I drove home, that terrible scene kept replaying itself in my mind. How tragic for the motorist and his family! Thinking of all the tragic events God has seen down through the ages I asked, "Can I endure many more accidents like this?"

In a still, calm voice the Lord reminded me he had called me into law enforcement, and his calling is honorable. None of what I experience—including my thoughts—goes unnoticed by his eyes. As I neared home he brought this psalm to my mind: "You will not fear the terror of night, nor the arrow that flies by day, nor the pestilence that stalks in the darkness, nor the plague that destroys at midday. A thousand may fall at your side, ten thousand at your right hand, but it will not come near you. You will only observe with your eyes" (Psalm 91:5–8).

SHOULD A CHAPLAIN BE A SNIPER?

Officer/Chaplain J. R. McNeil, Badge No. 279

Pinellas Park, FL, Police Department

THINK ABOUT it for a moment: The officer is 43 with only three years' experience as an officer, and qualifies for the SWAT team . . . as the sniper! You may think the sniper position goes to an old, fat guy who's too out of shape to move quickly, but that wasn't the case. He could run, jump, endure, and sweat with the best of them. He shot paper targets until he could hit the mark consistently anywhere from up close to a couple of hundred yards away . . . and he could take the shot accurately after exhausting physical exertion. One more thing—he was the department chaplain, and he was me!

Pinellas Park SWAT team

360

In most police circles, SWAT is *the elite team*! It is comprised of officers with regular job assignments who put in hours of extra time to be ready when "the call" comes! The sweat and stress require almost superhuman stamina, and if tapped for the team, you're almost "in heaven." But, you ask, "Why would an ordained chaplain be the sniper, since he's the guy with the high-powered rifle who has the bad guy's head in the crosshairs, just waiting to be told to pull the trigger and send him into eternity?" I had to ask and answer that question myself. How could a man of God be able to execute a living, breathing, human being and then go home to a hot meal with his family?

> "For I myself am a man under authority."
> Matthew 8:9

All officers must be ready to use deadly force if the situation calls for it. With the following exceptions, being a sniper is little different from other responsibilities cops are required to carry out: When we are activated, we know the situation must be bad or deteriorating; Since a sniper may not be able to see the imminent threat, he must be ready to respond on command; Finally, like any other officer, the sniper will have to live with the outcome.

Think about this: Who is better equipped to answer the call than someone who respects that all humans are made in the image of God? I want to honor God in everything I do, even if it includes taking the life of a killer to save other innocent lives. Who is better qualified than someone so serious about the awesome responsibility that that person works and trains harder and prays seriously without ceasing? My goal is to be God's instrument wherever he leads me, and that's where he placed me for five years. Thankfully, I never had to take a life. But if asked to do so, I would have carried out the command under God's authority.

OCTOBER 20

MAKING HIS MARK

David Laumatia, Senior Sergeant
New Zealand Police

IN NEW Zealand we call "graffiti" artists "taggers," and the act of doing it "tagging." This particular night a tagger had "made his mark," then disappeared swiftly when he saw me approach in my police car. He sought the cover of darkness around the corner.

Not to be bested by him, I called for a dog unit that tracked him to a building where he had apparently tried to hide himself. Across the road from the graffiti, a male was sitting in the backseat of a car. When questioned, he played dumb and said he was just "waiting for a friend." But the spray paint on his hoodie and empty spray can at his feet gave him away.

Back at the station, I questioned him as to the direction of his life. Other than being deeply into rap music, it appeared this 20-something young man lacked drive and direction in his life. In my opinion, he was headed for a life of death and destruction.

> Choose you this day whom ye will serve; . . . as for me and my house, we will serve the LORD.
> Joshua 24:15 (KJV)

As I continued speaking to him, the Holy Spirit began to convict him of the sin in his life, and he soon became a blubbering mass, with tears upon tears. He told me his mother was a Christian, and that she'd been praying for him for quite some time. After I challenged him about his lifestyle, I took him home to her. Once there, I began speaking to her about the things of God. Until then her son had been very polite, but suddenly he became quite hostile and looked like he wanted to kill me! From the look in his eyes I realized Satan had a grip on him. The power of God came upon me and I boldly said to him, "I know who you are." His mother and I began to pray fervently, and after a short time he snapped out of it—but he could not explain what had just happened to him.

Before leaving, I reminded him he needed to make a decision: Either follow God, or serve Satan. Returning to my car I began to ponder what sort of mark he would make on the world: Would he live a life of foolishness and self-destruction, or become a godly man who served the Lord? The choice was his!

OCTOBER 21

A MILLSTONE SITUATION

Jason J. Everett.
Rolling Meadows, IL, Police Department

DRUG ADDICTION affects everyone: the addicts, their parents and siblings, law enforcement, the community, and, in Tyler's case, the addict's children.

362

The couple met in an inpatient rehab clinic, and had been released at the same time. They stayed together to help each other "stay clean," then cemented the relationship with a child—Tyler. When I met the family, he was two-and-a-half. The first time I was involved, they had left him at home alone.

Over time I arrested them many times: the girlfriend for battery on the boyfriend, the boyfriend for battery on the girlfriend, and so on. Then there were the arrests involving alcohol: driving drunk with a suspended driver's license, driving drunk with a revoked driver's license, criminal damage to property, public intoxication, and open alcohol. They always were intoxicated with alcohol and marijuana. My main concern was for Tyler.

As a Christian and a parent, I could not understand their lack of care and concern for him. Before the parents' relapse into drugs had progressed too far, I would find both Tyler and the home environment clean and neat. But as time went on, Tyler would be dirty and bruised, clothed only in a diaper, and living in a trashy home. In my last contact with this family the home was completely trashed. Tyler's body was black with dirt, and he was covered with bruises. He said he was hungry, and I found he had eaten three cigarettes left on the floor by his mother. Finally, after I had made multiple calls to Child Protective Services, Tyler was taken from his parents and given to his grandparents.

Situations like this are very troubling for law enforcement personnel, especially Christians. We believe in the family unit as being the backbone of society, and we hate to see it broken up. We want to see parents living out God's love in their home, and we know that a child's image of God relates to what they see in their earthly father. We hate it when we have to separate children from their families, but do so in order to protect them in their innocence. Tyler deserved better than he'd been receiving from his parents.

> "If anyone causes one of these little ones who believe in me to sin, it would be better for him to have a large millstone hung around his neck and to be drowned in the depths of the sea."
> Matthew 18:6

THE BACK ROOM

Bill Hubbard, Executive Police Officer

Taos, NM, Police Department

HOW MANY Christians would say the best place to "connect the dots" with an unbeliever is "the back room of a police station"? That's where it happened with Floyd and me.

After spending time in federal prison for dealing dope and stolen guns, Floyd was making a conscious effort to turn his life around. He had a job, was in a stable relationship with his longtime girlfriend, and was even being "Dad" to their two toddlers. He was in handcuffs this time for unpaid traffic tickets he had collected in another part of the state, and was waiting for his mother to come and pay his fines. Floyd worked, and he was looking for child care. As we brainstormed resources I innocently asked, "Do you belong to a church?" thinking there might be some help there.

He said he didn't and here's why: "I don't know what to believe! For eleven years, I have asked everyone I could how to know which religion is right. I've talked to Muslims, Buddhists, Hindus, and others, even read the Koran and some of the Bible. No one could answer my question and tell me which one was right."

> Preach the Word; be prepared in season and out of season; correct, rebuke and encourage— with great patience and careful instruction.
> 2 Timothy 4:2

I'm not the brightest Christian behind a badge, but I realized we had gone from "child care" to a "Holy Spirit" opportunity! I told him, "The truth is in the empty tomb. All the rest—Muhammad, Confucius, Buddha, you name it—are still in their tombs. Jesus isn't, his tomb is empty. Floyd, it you want to beat heroin, alcohol, or any other habit, you talk to those who have conquered it. If you want to learn about life and death, you follow the only One who *beat death!*" We shared and prayed together for quite some time, then together we went over a copy of *The Truth* (Pocket Testament League) that I had with me.

As Floyd considered what I had said, it sank into his heart and tears welled up in his eyes. "I've asked this question all my life, but no one gave a good answer. Now, I get it from a *cop!*" There, in the back room of a New Mexico police station Floyd found "the way and the truth and the life" (John 14:6) and became "a new creation" (2 Corinthians 5:17).

If anyone asks you the best place to help a nonbeliever "connect the dots," just tell that person "anywhere." Tell that person to just do it when God makes it clear through the Holy Spirit the time is right!

NOT ALL STORIES END WELL

Detective Corporal M. C. Williams
Colorado

MAHNOMEN County, Minnesota, Sheriff's Deputy Chris Dewey had wanted to be a law enforcement officer since early childhood. Two years after achieving that goal in 2005, Chris married his high school sweetheart, Emily. Not quite two years later, in 2009 Chris responded to a "shots fired" call, where he was ambushed and shot in the head and abdomen.

In what many consider nothing short of a miracle, Chris survived and was airlifted to Fargo, North Dakota. After five days in intensive care, he progressed well enough to be flown to Craig Hospital in Englewood, Colorado, for intense rehabilitative physical therapy. Unfortunately, his promising recovery came to a grinding halt after a series of progressively difficult medical complications. He required numerous surgical procedures that left him speechless and partially paralyzed. Nearly a year after being shot, Chris was flown back home to Minnesota to continue his rehab.

Through it all, Emily remained steadfast at her husband's side while trying to remain optimistic. Both Chris and Emily understood that God sustained them in the face of a daunting and uncertain future. As committed Christians, they believed God had a purpose in allowing Chris to survive. Their faith was bolstered through the power of prayer. Many Christian law enforcement personnel—sworn and civilian—came alongside them with prayer and other support. God answered those many prayers by strengthening the Deweys' resolve and helping them *stay the course*, regardless of what the future might hold (2 Timothy 2:1–10, Philippians 3:13, 14).

Sadly, this is not an "all's well that ends well" story, for Chris passed away in

> Blessed are those who are invited to the wedding supper of the Lamb!
> Revelation 19:9

365

August, 2010. Rather, it is the story of a godly servant-warrior and a loving and faithful wife who "stood by her man" with God's help and through the power of prayer. It also is a story of Christian officers coming together for a wounded brother. Finally, it is a call to be "ready," for none of us knows what the future holds. If you have not placed your faith and trust in Jesus, Emily joins me in urging you to say yes to Christ today!

CIVILIANS: THINK BEFORE YOU SHOOT!

Sergeant Cameron J. Grysen

Houston, TX, Police Department

THE APARTMENT manager had moved to Houston from a small town, and taken a job at a rundown complex in the inner city. Not only was she having severe culture shock, but she also had to deal with gang members selling drugs on the property. When my partner and I went to see her, she said there were two culprits, and one had a gun. When she said she recently had purchased a pistol, that got our attention!

We explained the Texas laws about shooting at a person: She had to be in fear for her life or protecting someone. Just then, one of the suspects walked by her office window. After we arrested him for trespass and public intoxication, the second suspect, armed, came around the corner. He took off running and my partner went after him while I took the prisoner to our car. Then I realized, *I don't have a key to the car!* I needed to help my partner, but what to do with the prisoner?

> "You have heard that it was said, 'Eye for eye, and tooth for tooth.' But I tell you . . ."
> Matthew 5:38, 39

I asked a security guard to watch the prisoner while I helped my partner. I hadn't gone far when I heard shots behind me. Thinking my partner might be in trouble, I started running toward the sound . . . and into the security guard! I asked him, "Who's watching the prisoner?"

He said the apartment manager had gotten her gun, and told him to go help us.

I thought, *Oh, boy!* Returning to the prisoner, we found he had been shot twice in the legs by the manager. When I asked what happened, she said he tried to run so she shot him. I was thinking, *That may not have been such a great idea,* but was happy to have not lost the prisoner! With help from other units and a helicopter, my partner caught the other suspect, so we achieved our goal.

After the injured suspect left in an ambulance, we called Homicide. Considering the circumstances, they didn't send anyone out, but told us to write a concise report. We did as they asked, but again took time to clearly explain Texas gun laws. After an overnight stay in the hospital, the suspect was discharged to jail the next morning. Fortunately, a grand jury later "no-billed" the apartment manager, for which I was most thankful. God's laws in the Old Testament called for swift and firm retaliation for criminal acts, but we must remember we live in the age of grace and are subject to the laws of the land. My counsel? Civilians, think twice before you shoot!

OCTOBER 25

THE LOST IS FOUND!

Officer Marian Reed

Houston, TX, Independent School District Police Department

THE PRINCIPAL called because she suspected that one of her students was a missing child whose photo she had seen on a poster. She had compared the photo with the student, and felt there was a match. After meeting with the principal, I searched for additional information in the National Center for Missing and Exploited Children database. Sensing this was the missing girl, I contacted the sheriff's office in the county where the case originated to see if the case was still open. It was!

With additional information from the sheriff, I picked up the child's enrollment folder from the school. From a copy of the father's driver's license, I was able to verify the child resided with him. The child's first name had been altered on the enrollment document, but not the middle and last names. I again contacted the sheriff, who confirmed that the child had been abducted by her father. Then I phoned the Houston Police

Department's (HPD) Missing Persons Office, and told them the child was not at school that day.

In checking the child's attendance record, I found to my concern that she had missed several days of school. I had the principal call the father to inquire about the child's absences, and he said he was coming to school the next day to withdraw her. Fearing he was preparing to flee with her, I called HPD back to warn them of the urgency. They discovered that the father, who had abducted the child from South Carolina, had several city warrants, so they were able to locate him and take him into custody before he could run. The child was recovered unharmed and taken to Child Protective Services for transfer back to South Carolina to be with her mother. At that point, a "hold" was placed on the father for felony kidnapping.

> "Whoever welcomes one of these little children in my name welcomes me." Mark 9:37

I feel blessed by God to work in a school environment, and know that the Lord watches over me and those little ones. What a joy it was to help in this situation where justice was served and a young girl was reunited with her mother!

OCTOBER 26

SOMETIMES WE FEEL INVISIBLE!

Sherry Layne, School Patrol Officer
Hamilton County, TN, Sheriff's Office

THERE USED to be a segment on the *Carol Burnett Show* in which she felt invisible—that folks noticed and spoke to those with her, but acted as though she weren't there. Sometimes we feel that way as school patrol officers.

My partner and I have had more than one close call on the Pike, where we work. Even though the protective gear we are issued is very visible, some drivers speed by as though we are not even standing there. We often are asked if it is worth taking the chance every day of getting hit. Our response is, "Yes, the children are worth it. The life of a young child just beginning in this old world is priceless. We never know but that God places us in harm's way just to protect his little children."

One day my partner was motioning for a truck to stop, but he proceeded forward as if she wasn't even standing there. She said that when she got hit it was as if the Lord's mighty hand had lifted her up

> As a father has compassion on his children, so the Lord has compassion on those who fear him.
> Psalm 103:13

into safety to keep the accident from being more severe than it was. She felt that God had lifted her around to the side of the truck after she had been hit on her hip. The blow was so severe that her right ankle and foot swung backward until her heel almost touched the back of her head. She still can't figure out how her hands landed on the hood of the truck and she was able to catch herself from falling. Needless to say she was in shock!

I radioed Dispatch to let them know we needed a unit to assist us, and Dispatch wanted to send the EMTs. She simply refused, saying, "I think I'm okay." When the shock wore off, it was found she had complications with her ankle and knee, but that didn't deter her. In a few days she was back at work, standing with me on the Pike.

We know in our hearts and minds God has a protective shield around us so we can see to the safety of his little ones. We understand that accidents can happen, but we both know our eternal destination if it does. Our daily prayer is, "Lord, keep your children safe in all our school zones; they are just innocent bystanders."

I KEPT OUR RULES BUT BROKE GOD'S!

Sergeant Cameron J. Grysen
Houston, TX, Police Department

ONE GOOD thing about night shift is time off during the day to play golf. Four of us had the same days off, and would play after our last shift of the week. Someone would go before sunup to reserve our tee time. Since it was dark, he'd look for golf balls in a creek by the eighteenth hole, using our high-powered flashlights to make them visible. We had two

369

rules: You shared your bounty with the others, and you kept your mouth shut; we didn't want it getting back to the chief!

One June night when it was my turn, I found more than a dozen balls. I put them in a plastic bag and started back to my car when a "burglary in progress" call came. It wasn't far from the golf course, but I was on my lunch break and not dispatched. However, just in case they needed help, I threw the golf balls in the back seat and headed that way.

About then, the first unit radioed that the suspect had left the store, and they were in foot pursuit. They were going south from the store, and I calculated where they might end up. Reaching that point I stopped, cut off my lights, and was getting out of my car when the suspect literally ran into it. He was winded and gave up quickly. I handcuffed him and radioed to ask what they wanted me to do with him. I was told to bring him back to the burglary site, so I stuffed him in the backseat of my car. Opening the back door, I discovered to my horror there were golf balls all over the seat and floor. I tried to ignore them, but the suspect asked what it was all about. I told him I didn't think there were any golf balls back there, which left him confused! Later, the primary officer told me the suspect couldn't stop talking about all the golf balls in my car. In keeping with my vow of secrecy, I told him I thought the burglar had hit his head or something— there were no balls! Then it hit me: I had lied and practiced deception!

> So I strive always to keep my conscience clear before God and man. Acts 24:16

There's an old saying: "Be sure your sins will find you out." I don't know if those sins ever came to light, but God kept them alive in my conscience. It seemed humorous at the time, but it was no testimony for a Christian!

I AM AN EXPLORER*

Clif Smith

State of Washington

LAW ENFORCEMENT Exploring is a worksite-based program for youth ages 14 to 21, designed to give insights into a variety of career opportunities in the field. It is affiliated with Boy Scouts of America and

Learning for Life. About five years ago my dad went through our local police department's Citizens Academy, and heard about the Explorers. It is a free program, and sounded interesting, so I got involved. Dad went on a "ride-along," and I did, too. After that, I was hooked. Now I am 20 and currently the highest-ranking Explorer in our group. I supervise events, coordinate meetings and training, handle disciplinary action, assist new members with paperwork, and help in the efficient operation of our group of fourteen young adults.

One of our jobs is to assist with officer funerals. We provide additional perimeter and interior security, and help with putting up and taking down displays and such. At a recent funeral, the officer's killer was still on the loose, so there was much more security than usual. We had bomb-sniffing dogs in the parking areas, and armed officers with the Explorers. Since I am a senior Explorer and was in full Class A uniform, I was stationed inside. The officer had been cremated, and after the service, Explorers helped form the honor guard as the urn was carried out by the family. Then we helped carry flowers to the reception hall.

> "Keep all my decrees and all my laws and follow them. I am the LORD."
> Leviticus 19.37

Before the service, some of the medics and firefighters had been talking about the suspect who had killed the officer. They had a description of the car he'd driven, and were told he might be trying to destroy it either by fire or ditching it in the water. After the service, I was with a group of officers who said the guy had been found and shot, but they didn't know if he was dead or alive. It was just good to know he had been captured.

I thank God for the fact my dad went through the Citizens Academy, and that I learned about the Explorer program. Eventually I want to become a police officer working with Narcotics or the Gang Unit. Romans 13:1–6 says police officers are ordained by God, and that they are God's ministers to do good. That's the kind of career I want to have!

*For more information on the Explorer program, go to http://www.learningforlife .org/exploring/lawenforcement/, http://en.wikipedia.org/wiki/Law_Enforcement_Exploring or http://www.policeexplorers.us or contact a local law enforcement agency

HOW LONG DO YOU
WANT TO LIVE LIKE THIS?

Officer Mark Dennis

Franklin, LA, Police Department

AS A RURAL pastor and reserve sheriff's deputy, I had two platforms from which I could spread the Gospel. What better way to serve the Lord than to share Christ with crack addicts, burglars, and others who broke the law in one way or another?

While patrolling one Saturday night I saw an old pickup truck traveling only 15 miles per hour with no visible license plate or working taillights. There were three males in the vehicle, which I pulled over.

I had never met the 21-year-old driver, but had heard his name and knew he'd been in trouble before. He had no license plate, no insurance, no registration, and several vehicle violations. He claimed he had purchased the truck from a teacher at the local high school, and was driving it home to fix it up. He had no bill of sale from the teacher, so there was no verification for his story. When I questioned the other two boys they told me the same story. Sizing up the situation and knowing the area, I went to the Lord in prayer as to the best solution.

> A word aptly spoken is like apples of gold in settings of silver.
> Proverbs 25:11

I called the young man aside, asked him if he realized the next day was Sunday and would he be going to church. He said no. I reminded him of his past violations and asked him, "How long do you want to live like this?" I told him I could write half-a-dozen tickets and have the vehicle towed. However, I believed his story and wanted him to learn something from the incident.

I told him I would follow him home and not issue any tickets if he promised he would attend a church of his choice the next morning. When he promised he would, I asked if he was telling the truth. He responded, "Yes!"

About two years later a family visiting my church asked if I remembered pulling the young man over, and gave the details of the situation. I told them, "Yes, I think so." They then told me the young man had come to their church the next morning and given his life to Christ. They said he couldn't get out of his mind my question, "How long to you want to live like this?" He knew it was Jesus speaking through me and decided "enough was enough." He accepted Christ's call, and was made new. Now, two years later, God was calling him into youth ministry. Praise God!

EMBARRASSMENT AVOIDED

Anonymous
Indiana Police Officer

AS A RESERVE officer, part of my duty was transporting prisoners from the county jail to the town court. A prisoner one evening was a lady who had been arrested for domestic battery. She was the only female, so I put her in the front seat away from the men in the back. She began telling me how glad she was that neither "Officer X" nor "Officer Y" had arrested her because she would have been so embarrassed. When I asked why, she said because she went to their church and knew them and their families. That was interesting, because I am a preacher, and both attend where I preach. I knew she had only been there twice in her life, both times because family members practically made her go.

When I asked her which church, she named where I preach. Several thoughts and comebacks ran through my mind, but I stifled them all. I was dying to ask her what she thought of the preacher! Even though I was dressed in full uniform, I thought perhaps the crosses on my collar might give me away, but they didn't.

Three weeks later, our congregation celebrated its anniversary with a picnic on Sunday evening. There she was! I angled my way over to her and said, "It's great that you can be here tonight." If her look could have been captured on video, I'm sure it would have won a prize. For the next two Sundays she attended morning worship. The second Sunday she responded to the invitation, and rededicated her life to the Lord.

In my varying roles as reserve officer, preacher, and chaplain, I meet people in all kinds of situations. Some people, even in the

> May the words of my mouth and the meditation of my heart be pleasing in your sight, O Lord, my Rock and my Redeemer. Psalm 19:14

373

worst of circumstances, are just looking for a reason to think about their life and make a decision to turn toward God. She and I have never talked about her embarrassing moment, and I'm glad I didn't further embarrass her. Our words have the ability to build up or tear down. Regardless of who we are, we have the power to influence others with our words—positive or negative. I may sometimes forget, but I try to keep two things in mind: Everyone with whom we interact is created in the image of God, and everyone is a potential child of God.

FINAL REST

Lieutenant Sean A. Gill

Macomb, MS, Police Department

(SEAN GILL is a watch commander who often expresses his thoughts in poetry ["From Aaron's Pen"]. This poem was written after a car/train crash in his area in which three children, ages 2, 12, and 17, were killed. None of them was buckled up, and the 17-year-old girl driving was trying to beat a train. That sort of accident is almost as hard on law enforcement as it is on families and friends of those who lost their lives.)

Final Rest

Dispatched, a crash is the call.
Arriving on scene, scattered is everything.
All that we can do, we do the best,
The report started, information gathered,
the scene handled accordingly, noting
everything's point of final rest.
We continue, the information processed,
the report showing everything's
point of final rest.

From Aaron's Pen

While patrolling, I have a tendency to internalize, replay, and reprocess in my mind past events, stirring the thoughts and the emotions. Going through that process one morning, the thoughts of what happens after a fatal crash came to mind. The call is dispatched; we arrive and take in the scattered scene, noting everything's point of final rest. The scene is processed accordingly. Information on the report sadly notes everything's point of final rest, including the bodies.

> But they will have to give account to him who is ready to judge the living and the dead. 1 Peter 4:5

While thinking about the incident I also thought of all the different crime scenes to which we respond, always noting the point of final rest of everything at the scene. Then God spoke to me, reminding me that even though everything gets moved from the scene, nothing is ever at its point of final rest.

Most people passing a cemetery would say, "This is a loved one's point of final rest." Yet God has spoken; the grave will not be our body's point of final rest. For all will stand before him one day and be assigned, some to eternal glory and some to eternal damnation.

MY DREAM JOB

Officer Andrea Brandt
Dallas/Ft. Worth, TX, Airport Police

I T MIGHT not be for some, but being a police officer is my dream job! At 27 years old I had a college degree, a wonderful boyfriend (now my husband), and a decent job. Life was going well except for one thing—I didn't have fulfillment at work or a sense of purpose. An aunt, an uncle, and many cousins of mine have been peace officers, and are the heroes in my life. That, plus the common bond we have in Christ, makes for joyful family occasions. I had thought for years about being a cop, and after much prayer I decided to apply—I know God called me to it!

It was a long process, but the day finally came when I was hired by the *Dallas/Ft. Worth Airport Police Department.* Our force of several hundred officers is greater than that of many good-size towns, and we deal with an incredible variety of circumstances. At the beginning of my police career, my uncle gave me this advice: Learn, help someone, and have some fun! It is amazing how these words of wisdom have worked out in practice. I quickly realized the craziness of police work—fun times, scary times, and the joy and sadness seen every day at a busy airport.

> Give proper recognition to those widows who are really in need.
> 1 Timothy 5:3

One evening while I was directing traffic, a little white-haired lady who works in the terminal's golf shop needed help starting her car. As I walked her to her vehicle, I learned her name and found out she was 80 years old! She told me she and her husband had been golfers, and he had recently passed away. She had worked in the golf shop for years, and still needed to keep busy. We talked about how wonderful her marriage had been, and she told me to enjoy the times my husband and I would have together. Ever since that night I have checked on her, even inviting her to join my entire family for Thanksgiving dinner. Later, my husband and I helped her move.

Yes, policing is my dream job! Through it, God gave me the special opportunity to meet someone I might never have known otherwise. In turn, she has become a special friend. What an awesome responsibility we have as officers!

BATMAN WAS NO ROBIN!

Captain Travis Yates

Tulsa, OK, Police Department
Director, Ten-Four Ministries Inc.

THERE'S A man running back and forth on top of our high-rise wearing a Batman cape!" The call came when I was a patrol sergeant, and when my officers arrived, sure enough, it was true! Many floors above street level a man with a cape was running around the edge of the building, and the wind was blowing hard. Knowing how hard the wind can blow in Oklahoma and seeing his cape billow out, I was concerned the man either would make a misstep or be blown to his death before we could take action. There was only one thing to do: I asked God to protect the man and to help us rescue him before it was too late.

> A wise man fears the LORD and shuns evil, but a fool is hotheaded and reckless. A quick-tempered man does foolish things, and a crafty man is hated.
> Proverbs 14:16, 17

It seemed as if it took forever to get to the top, but when the elevator doors opened I was met by a veteran officer and good friend. "Sarge, here is what we have. The man is too far out on the ledge for us to reach him. The only thing we can do is talk to him whenever he runs past." I asked the officer if he had any ideas. "Yes. See those pillars? We could try luring him close enough to grab him as he runs by, pull his arms through the pillars, and then handcuff him to them."

I thanked him and the Lord for his suggestion and approved the plan with one contingency: I wanted to be the one to grab for the subject. I didn't want anyone else to bear the burden of missing the subject only to see him fall to his death. "God, help me to save this man's life."

Within seconds the man started running again. At just the right moment I reached through the pillars, grabbed his arms and held him as tightly as I could to the pillars. Quickly another officer came to my aid and handcuffed him.

By God's grace, we successfully prevented the man from falling to his death. Of course, he now was handcuffed to the top of a multi-story building, hanging feet first and we had no way to get him off the ledge. Thankfully, God made firefighters with fancy ropes and pulleys! Batman didn't fly that day!

A DEAD SPOT SAVED OUR LIVES

Sergeant Vito Ancona

Lisbon, ME, Police Department

THREE VILLAGES make up the town of Lisbon: Lisbon, Lisbon Center, and Lisbon Falls. I was the only unit patrolling that night and was working with a reserve officer. I was in the Lisbon Falls area when we received a call that three males had walked into a Mom-and-Pop convenience store in Lisbon Center and forcibly stole some beer and snacks. The owner of the store got both the license plate number and a description of the vehicle.

Very soon I saw the vehicle approaching, and could tell by the license plate it was the right vehicle, so I told my reserve officer to call it in. We pulled the vehicle over in a lot next to a gas station. My reserve radioed in the stop, then jumped out of our car, and told the three occupants to get out of their vehicle. For some unknown reason we had stopped in a "dead radio spot," and the dispatcher didn't copy. I was partially out of the vehicle when the dispatcher again asked for my location. As I leaned in to grab the mike I noticed movement in the other vehicle. Floodlights from my unit illuminated that car, and it appeared someone in it was trying to either hide something or get something from under the seat. Sensing danger I realized that only the driver and right front passenger had exited the vehicle, and the man in the car could be a problem!

> For the Lord watches over the way of the righteous, but the way of the wicked will perish.
> Psalm 1:6

Quickly I exited my vehicle, drew my weapon as I approached the vehicle and yelled, "Your hands better come up empty when you put them out or you won't live to see tomorrow!" He must have thought my reserve was the only officer, because when he jumped he almost hit his head on the roof of the car.

We handcuffed and searched all three men and the vehicle. The driver, a convicted felon, was sitting on a stolen German Luger, taken in a burglary. Under the seat I found a loaded .357 Magnum with two-each lead, hollow point, and armor-piercing bullets. In the backseat were a loaded shotgun and two loaded rifles. One had an illegal knife and another a "coke kit." My responding to the dispatcher's request and see-ing movement in the car probably saved our lives. I know it was God watching over us and the instincts he gave me that kept us alive that night.

MY UNINVITED GUEST

Lieutenant Dennis E. Nail

Martinsville, IN, Police Department

ON A NOVEMBER evening my wife and daughter had gone to town. Shadows and darkness cast the light aside, and the stage was set for an uninvited guest.

For the preceding month I had been dogged by the media and poli-tics—all because I had dared express my opinion regarding the 9/11 attack on New York City, our nation's moral decay, and the relentless criticism of Christian values. It seemed on that autumn night, everything came to a head. As I sat on the living room floor, an evil spirit as real as anything made of flesh and bone entered the room. He took a seat beside me, said he could understand my loneliness, and he felt my inner gut-wrenching misery. He instructed me on the way out: Just take the .357 from the kitchen cabinet, walk out into the woods, and end the frustration by taking my life. At first I honestly began to reason with this unholy guest. He was so convincing, so reassuring. But how could this be? As a Christian, how could I dare take my own life?

> I will say of the LORD, "He is my refuge and my fortress." Psalm 91:2

I fell down and called upon the Lord . . . and I heard God's voice. He told me I was bought with a price and belonged to him. My life was not mine to take. He told me he knew what it was like to be deserted by friends, for he, too, had been tempted by the same tempter who was wag-ing spiritual warfare right in my living room. God reminded me he had suffered for my salvation, and that I was going to be all right. I can't explain what I was feeling at that moment, but I could feel his presence as he wrapped his arms around me—comforting, reassuring, and pro-tecting me. He told me everything was going to be fine. Immediately the room seemed to take on a glow. I prayed, opened my Bible, and read some passages—everything was in his hands.

Since then I approach those who attempt suicide with a whole different outlook. For most, no one is present when they attempt to take their lives. They always seem to do it when nobody else is around, no family members or friends. If they don't have Jesus, they have no one. Jesus is a friend who is *always* there, even during the most severe test of faith. He is our strength and refuge. "Why are you downcast, O my soul? Why so disturbed within me? Put your hope in God, for I will yet praise him, my Savior and my God" (Psalm 42:11).

I TOOK THE FALL FOR HER

Officer Elfego J. Gallardo Jr.

Chicago, IL, Police Department

PUT IT down, put the club down!" She responded by advancing toward us with a golf club in her hands "at the ready" and no indication of obeying our command.

It was a warm summer evening, and we'd been told "there's a crazy lady swinging a golf club at people and hitting cars as they drive by." Rounding a corner, we saw her striking the frame of a bus-stop shelter, screaming obscenities and yelling at people who came near her. When she didn't put the club down, we drew our weapons and again gave our verbal command.

By this time, people came from all over the neighborhood and were screaming, "Don't shoot her! Don't shoot her!" This put us in a hard spot. Except for pulling back ever so slightly when we drew down on her, she gave every indication of hitting us hard with the club.

A sergeant arrived, and pointed his taser at her. When she did not respond he fired, but only one projectile stuck. I was thinking, *Now what?!* About that time my partner pulled out her canister of OC (pepper) spray and directed it into the woman's eyes. As she turned her face, I took the opportunity to tackle her to the ground. As we came down, I put my hand behind her head to absorb the impact before she hit the pavement. Unfortunately, several officers who had gathered

> You will see the distinction between the righteous and the wicked, between those who serve God and those who do not. Malachi 3:18

must have thought they were playing football, and I felt their weight upon me and the woman. In the process, I suffered a serious injury to my hand and wrist. I got up, pulled the club from the woman's hands, and she was taken to a hospital that provided mental health services. I also went to the hospital for treatment and saw her there, now apologetic and nonconfrontational. I thought, *What irony! She gets off "scot-free," and here I am with a serious injury!*

My decision to protect her was made in a split second, on the spot and under mounting pressure. Some of my fellow officers thought I was crazy to bear the burden of injury in place of this woman. Many months after—with my wrist still hurting—I sometimes had similar feelings! Yet, I believe the Holy Spirit was beside me throughout the whole incident, and that the Lord's will was done. Others might have handled it differently, but I'm just thankful to God the situation ended favorably and the disturbance was quashed. Our motto is "to protect and serve," and that's what I did that night!

NOVEMBER 6

CRUSHED IN SPIRIT

Chaplain Pat Tosch

King County, WA, Sheriff's Office

HE WAS known as the Green River Killer. Gary Leon Ridgway recalls killing between forty-eight and fifty-three women in King County, Washington. He pleaded guilty to forty-eight counts of aggravated murder in the first degree, making him the most prolific, convicted serial killer in the United States.

November 6, 2003, the courtroom was jammed with the families of his victims. After he received a life sentence without possibility of parole, one member of each victim's family was allowed to speak to Ridgway. Most of the women who spoke then would go to the restroom and cry. As a female police chaplain, I was there to comfort them. All but one of his victims had been a prostitute. I knew that in helping these women deal with their emotions, I had to be led by the Lord; he would have to guide me in what I said.

The youngest victim had celebrated her 15th birthday two weeks before being murdered. After hearing what the family had to say, it was obvious she never had the chance to mature and turn her life around

382

before it was too late. When her older sister spoke, she said both of them felt safer on the street than at home, for there was "another monster" there. At the time of the younger's murder, the older sister was 17. She had found a safe house with only one bed, so there was no room for her sister. She felt

> The LORD is close to the brokenhearted and saves those who are crushed in spirit.
> Psalm 34:18

responsible that her little sister was left alone out on the streets, and had been living with guilt and pain for years. After learning the circumstances, I realized it was not that simple—she had no choice.

Just as it is said, "There are no atheists in a foxhole," I was led by the Lord to say that when that monster Ridgway put his hands around her sister's throat, her sister cried out to God to save her. She may never have known God, but he knew her—her heart, her circumstances, and her prayers, even before she prayed them. I am so grateful we have a heavenly Father who can see beyond our circumstances, meet us where we are, and save us in the moment.

NOVEMBER 7

"NO OSCAR FOR THIS ACTOR"

Sergeant Zac McCullough, No. 835

Chattanooga, TN, Police Department

IF YOU'VE ever doubted the Bible when it says we learn from adversity, don't! (See Romans 5:3.) My experience is living proof that "pain equals gain"! As a longtime Christian and student of the Bible I've always tried to follow "The Golden Rule," but sometimes it's difficult when you're dealing with "bad guys" or "good actors."

On this November day I caught up with a thief who'd just stolen jewelry from a store and tried to duck into the ER of a local hospital to escape being caught. No such luck for him. After a brief chase I corralled him, slung him to the ground, cuffed him, and put him into the back of the patrol car. When the suspect told me his shoulder was hurting, I believed it from the large scar he had from a previous surgery and because of his rough capture. In my "compassionate mode" I took him to the hospital for x-rays, where the cuffs had to come off. This was a *big* mistake—criminals *never* should be trusted!

383

After the x-rays the perpetrator complained of pain and nausea, and asked to go to the bathroom to vomit. Coming out of the bathroom he said he was about to pass out. In my naivety, I offered to get him a wheel chair. While he was "bent over in pain" I discovered he not only was a thief but a very good actor; with his swift upward kick to my groin the fight was on! This ex-Marine did his best to kill me, but my adrenaline took over. Finally, with the aid of a couple of other officers and hospital personnel, he was subdued and on his way to jail. I was treated at the hospital for a broken nose and fractured cheek bone, receiving thirty staples and thirty stitches in my head to close the wounds. For his efforts, the "bad actor" was sentenced to seven years in prison.

> Behold, I send you forth as sheep in the midst of wolves: be ye therefore wise as serpents, and harmless as doves.
> Matthew 10:16 (KJV)

This was the first time anyone had actually tried to kill me, and was the "wake-up call" I needed. The experience taught me not to substitute compassion for street smarts. Since then I've bulked up, improved my tactical skills, and become a member of the SWAT team. Of the many lessons I learned that day the most valuable is this: God *was* and *is* with me, but he expects me to do my part!

NOVEMBER 8

PRAYING ME THROUGH!

Bill Hubbard, Executive Police Officer

Taos, NM, Police Department

COPS ARE people, too! We mow lawns, run errands, and fix leaky faucets—typical family and homeowner's stuff. This particular Saturday I was to drive my elderly father some distance to a fellowship breakfast, while my wife planned a weekend "reading and prayer" retreat in a condo in southern Colorado. God had other plans for me.

At 5 a.m. the telephone rang. There had been a Halloween drive-by homicide—a 19-year-old girl had been hit by a high-powered rifle round through the window, killing her instantly. From descriptions received, we associated the crime with two known gang-bangers. Marked units from three agencies spread throughout the county. At daybreak, I called my dad—no trip. He'd heard it all before . . . his son is a cop.

As the day dragged on the scene was photographed and evidence tagged and collected. Personnel from the medical examiner's office came to take charge of the body.

With their scene work complete, the crime scene team packed up and headed to the office to tag and book their evidence, then start on the paperwork. That is, all but me. Something inside me said to "check out an address in the boonies where the suspects might be," so I headed in that direction—alone. Stupid me!

We were pretty sure the suspects had headed south to the Big City two hours away, but I didn't want to make that drive if it wasn't necessary. It didn't hurt to look, though! Unbelievably, in the middle of nowhere, I found the main suspect walking down a dirt road! As I "cuffed and stuffed him" all I could think about was, *Where is Number 2 with his high-powered rifle?* With Number 1 handcuffed and in my back seat I called for help, took cover, and waited for backup. When they arrived we rushed a nearby trailer and found Number 2 asleep in a back bedroom.

While a deputy was typing up a warrant to search their hideout, my cell phone rang. It was my wife: "I've been reading my book and praying for you!" I explained what had happened, and we compared the times of her prayers; she had been praying for me at the *exact time* I had found and taken down the prime suspect! There was *power* in Debbie's prayers, even though she was praying about the trip with my dad.

Do I believe in the power of prayer? Yes! As it says in Mark 11:24, "Whatever you ask for in prayer, believe that you have received it, and it will be yours."

I COULDN'T HELP HIM!

Jason J. Everett.
Rolling Meadows, IL, Police Department

WHEN TWO women are fighting in a motel parking lot, guess who they call! This time, I was the lucky guy. The two had a mutual boyfriend, and were feuding over him. One was screaming for the unfaithful boyfriend to help her kill his other "girlfriend!" When I arrived, one woman was waiting at the front desk, while the other was nearby. The two women were self-admitted heroin users and prostitutes who followed each other from one motel to the next and from town to town.

As for the boyfriend? He found me by opening his motel room door when I walked by. He asked, "Can I talk to you?" He said he'd only been the homicidal prostitute's boyfriend for about three days and had no intention of stepping into the fight; he'd had enough of the police and jail. Besides that, he was watching the girlfriend's son while she plied her trade. I radioed for another officer to come, then asked the boyfriend if I could look around the room to make sure there were no further issues. After he let me in I found the usual items a heroin user keeps close to him and another older male, sleeping. I awakened him from his drunken stupor, and made him wait outside while we made a thorough inspection of the room.

> "Let the little children come to me, and do not hinder them, for the kingdom of God belongs to such as these." Luke 18:16

The prostitute's 5-year-old son was asleep in one of the beds, and I gently pulled down the covers to inspect his bodily condition. I froze: The gangly little boy dressed in Batman underwear was a double for my son, Ross. Seeing me tense up, the other officer was going to remove the child from the room, but I stopped him. The boy was warm, had no injuries, seemed well-fed, and showed no signs of long-term abuse. In other words, we had no evidence that could be used to rescue the child from the horrors of his current environment. Our hands were tied.

Having concluded the investigation, we set the two female combatants free. However, I spoke at length with the mother of my son's "doppelgänger," urging her to be the kind of mother a child should have. But in the end, I was forced to leave the motel without helping the child. My only available recourse was to write a report of the incident and pray for God's holy interdiction in the boy's life. "Father, since we are worth more than sparrows, please care for this little boy and let him learn about you. Amen" (Luke 12:6, 7).

"MADE IN HIS IMAGE"

Mickey Koerner, former deputy
Polk County, IA, Sheriff's Office

WHILE A jailer, I saw many prisoners come and go—some with cocky attitudes, some contrite, and some just beaten down with no life in their eyes. I had one encounter that changed the way I look at inmates—and people in general—forever. He was being discharged from jail, ready to re-enter the free world, and he left an impression that's lasted for more than twelve years.

As he collected his paper bag of belongings my first thought was, *What a waste!* He was wearing cutoff jeans with a cord belt, no shoes, and no shirt. Restaurants and bars would have rejected him, but the jail took him. As that thought went through my head, I heard a still, small voice say, "Yes, but I love him." It was God speaking to my hard heart about my judgmental attitude.

It is so easy to be judgmental. Officers in uniform are watched and sometimes looked up to by our neighbors, our church, and nearly everyone. That gave me quite an arrogant attitude. *What right do folks like him have to ignore the rules of society, perhaps do harm to others, and then end up in jail—making folks like me have to care for them?* My eyes started to well up with tears when I realized my sin was just as ugly to God as this man's crime was to society. "Do you have evil thoughts?" asked Jesus. "That's just as bad as murder!" Do you have something against your brother and harbor a grudge for years on end? That becomes your sin, not his (Matthew 6:15).

> For all have sinned and fall short of the glory of God, and are justified freely by His grace.
> Romans 3:23, 24

I escorted the young man to the front of the building and out of the jail. Though I never saw him again, daily I have remembered his face, my thoughts, and what God said to me twelve years ago. We all are made in the image of God—what a wonderful gift! God thinks and talks; we think and talk. God is relational; we relate to things, people, and animals. God cares for us in physical, mental, emotional, and spiritual ways, just as we care for family and friends in these same ways. He reminded me that as a deputy sheriff working in the jail I was to see people and inmates as he did: made in his image. It is my God-given duty to honor him in that manner.

THE NIGHT OF TERROR

Chaplain Kenneth H. Dalke

Turner County, SD, Sheriff's Department

IT HAPPENED after dark on November 11: A natural gas pipeline exploded at more than seven thousand pounds per square inch. The company repair crew, drain-tile installers, and farmers were involved. Many had been leaning over watching the repair when the sound of escaping gas was heard. From down in the hole, the foreman yelled, "Get out of here!" He never made it to safety.

The explosion didn't ignite, but left a huge hole in the ground. Splattered everywhere in the dark cornfield was mangled machinery, broken windshields, and mud. The foreman lay dead fifty feet from where he'd been standing, one man lost an eye, and several suffered respiratory and cardiac symptoms due to natural gas inhalation. After the high-pitched hiss of escaping gas stopped, firefighters in full gear carefully approached the scene to check for air safety.

In the eerie, black night, rescue personnel had difficulty knowing who was involved and where they were. Spouses and family members were fearful for their loved ones. We later learned that earlier in the day the foreman had made phone calls to his wife and daughters telling them, "I love you." Those were his last words to his family. As chaplain and member of the fire department and EMS crew, I was also a member of the rescue crew and discovered his body. Over the next couple of weeks, we worked through Critical Incident Stress (CIS) issues with the professionals involved. However, I was concerned for the five farmers and their wives. Horrific incidents like this often cause people to withdraw from even those they love, so intervention is necessary for restoration.

> You will not fear the terror of night, nor the arrow that flies by day.
> Psalm 91:5

I modified the CIS materials, and arranged a meeting with the farmer couples. We began and ended the evening with prayer. The wives met in one room with my wife, while the men met with me in another. Six marriages, mine included, were brought into closer union through the process. But I found there was still more to come. Two months later my doctor had me take a cardiac stress test, which I failed. The results indicated I should have had a heart attack on that night of terror! Even though I didn't know I was at risk, God had protected me through it all. Praise his name!

"THE RIGHT THING TO DO"

Chaplain Thomas Deal

Orlando, FL, Police Department

WHY DID your church open its doors for this; did an employee go here?" For many in today's "post-Christian era," perhaps that was a legitimate question. For us it was no issue—it was just the right thing to do.

A disgruntled former employee in a nearby high-rise office building had killed one worker and injured five others. The Orlando Police responded quickly, as did I. They shut down the building and traffic in all directions, including busy I-4, which carries thousands of locals and tourists every day. All personnel had to be evacuated from the building, but employees of the firm where the shooting occurred (and their worried loved ones) needed special handling. Where could we take them? In my dual roles as police chaplain and associate coordinator of the Cooperative Baptist Fellowship of Florida, I was able on a moment's notice to connect with the nearby College Park Baptist Church. Without hesitation they opened their facilities, preparing their fellowship hall with tables, chairs, and refreshments. They also asked deacons who were available to come as an added source of ministry presence.

As the day wore on, I was asked to return to the crime scene to comfort the fiancée of the slain employee. We offered our presence, our touch, and our prayers, and helped her connect with her family and rep-

> "I was a stranger and you invited me in."
> Matthew 25:35

resentatives of her faith. Both her mother and the victim's mother had to be called. Her relatives lived four hours away, so victim advocates came to give her emotional support until friends and family could arrive. Their 6-month-old daughter was in day care, and had to be picked up by detectives. We began to talk with the mother about the next steps that had to be taken. Finally the day ended, the suspect was found and arrested, and a semblance of normalcy began to return. But the work of the church was not finished.

Over the next several days, Christian counseling was offered to employees of the firm that was attacked. Then the church opened its facilities for the Critical Incident debriefing sessions that followed, even including a lunch for all who attended. After lunch was over the question was asked, "Why did you do this?"

For us the answer was simple: We offered the presence of Christ at a time when his comforting love was sorely needed. We did it because "it was the right thing to do."

BADGE NUMBER 88

Sergeant Theo P. Helms (Ret.)
Michigan Department of Natural Resources

JUST AS the birth of Jesus was the beginning of Christianity, the birth of my first child was the beginning of my Christian walk. When I started my career in law enforcement I didn't believe in God. After I gave my heart to Christ I thought things would be different . . . but sometimes they weren't. There were times when I didn't "feel" God's presence while I was working, and sometimes I struggled to sense it when confronting dangerous situations. I felt the sting and sadness of seeing officers injured and killed, and I wondered if God really was with me. Was he protecting me, was he my constant guide, was he really there? My answer came in a most unexpected way while doing something I don't like to do—shopping!

Each year my wife and I journeyed to the city for Christmas shopping. After enduring throngs of shoppers and long lines I grew impatient and wanted to go home. I thought we were finished shopping at a popular Christian book store when we got through the checkout line. Then my wife saw something she simply "had to buy"; there was no dissuading her! Grumpy, angry, impatient, and with a headache, I browsed a shelf of books, feigning interest. Almost immediately I saw a book with a policeman's badge on the cover, Badge Number 88—*my badge number!* The book was *The Shield of Faith: Behind Badge 88,* written by Saginaw, Michigan, Police Department Sergeant Donald Dinninger. It was a book for me . . . revealed by God. I picked it up and waited in line to purchase it, the easiest wait in a long shopping line I've ever had.

> Will you never look away from me, or let me alone even for an instant?
> Job 7:19

In the years since, I've read the book over and over. I found accounts of officers who had experienced feelings similar to mine. I was not alone;

390

God had been there all along waiting to reveal himself when I was ready. Today I am still a police officer, and it comforts me to know that God is with me even when I can't sense it. He said, "Surely, I am with you always" (Matthew 28:20), and now I really know it!

SOMETHING TO THINK ABOUT

Officer Mike Dye*

Volusia County, FL, Sheriff's Department

"GO HOME," he yelled! It wasn't our first encounter. He rode a bicycle on my patrol route, and served as a lookout for drug dealers. The area is a lower socioeconomic community, and one that has proved to be a haven for drug dealing, prostitution, and other forms of evil. Most citizens who live there are hard-working, decent, God-fearing people. They just don't have the income to live elsewhere.

With that in mind, this time the Lord put something different in my mind. I stopped and before he could ride away asked him, "Don't you like police?" After he said a firm no, I looked him in the eye and said what was on my heart. "Do you have the joy of the Lord in your heart?" His angry look said it all! My next question came quickly: "Do you read the Bible?" I was amazed when he proudly said yes! "Well, that's good. Have you ever read Romans 13:1–5?"

By now the angry look had been replaced by confusion. "What was that verse again?" Giving him the short "Mike Dye" version, I explained that officers are ordained servants of God, here to do good and not harm to people, and that no one should fear us if they are doing what is right.

He moved his bicycle closer to my car and said, "I've never had an officer talk to me about the Bible before. Thank you, sir." Then I gave him a Gospel tract, and suggested he read it and the Bible verses I'd mentioned. Again I told him that policemen are God's servants on Earth to help out during difficult times. Whether he meant it or not, he agreed.

> "Blessed are you when people insult you, persecute you and falsely say all kinds of evil against you because of me."
> Matthew 5:11

As we parted company I told him, "May God bless you."

He responded with, "And may God bless you, sir!" Only God knows if I made a difference in that young man's life. But he made me wonder how many times I've ignored people who really just needed someone to talk to; how many times the hate and invective they shouted out was actually a call for help, spiritual help.

As officers we have a choice: We can drive on by with our windows rolled up and listening to the radio, or we can stop and engage people. Think about it for a moment: Would your city be better if you and the others in your agency spent more time talking with people—even about their spiritual needs? It's certainly something to think about!

*Author of *The PeaceKeepers: A Bible Study for Law Enforcement Officers*

I STEPPED ON HIS TOES!

Constable Merv Tippe (Ret.)

Regina, Saskatchewan

IN THE academy we are taught to be respectful, say, "Yes, sir" or, "No, ma'am," and "remember you are there to protect and serve." Some situations require a little extra!

When you're the only law officer in a rural town and backup is miles away, you hope to avoid major problems. But one night on patrol I received a dispatch to be on the lookout for a green 1972 Chevrolet. Earlier the vehicle had almost struck another car head-on, and it was felt the driver was impaired.

About an hour later a vehicle matching that description went by me in the opposite direction. I made a U-turn and pulled the vehicle over after a short distance. There were six occupants in the car, and the driver showed obvious signs of having consumed alcohol. There also was a strong smell of liquor emanating from the vehicle.

The driver cooperated when asked to exit his car and get in the rear seat of mine. I asked him for a breath sample, which he agreed to provide. However, he asked if the one person who had drunk mostly Coke that evening could be allowed to drive the vehicle to his residence. That seemed like a reasonable request, but when I went back to his car the five others got out of the vehicle against my commands and encircled me.

When they asked what I planned to do with their friend, I told them. Then one of them said, "There are five of us and only one of you; what if we don't let you do that? You seem to be shaking a little bit, Mr. Policeman, are you afraid?" To be honest, I *was* a little concerned for my safety so I prayed a quick prayer that God would give me words that would convince them to back down.

Looking the spokesman right in the eyes, I stepped forward—stepping on the toes of his left foot—got my nose as close to his face as I felt safe to do and said, "No, I am not afraid, but I do shake a bit when I get mad!"

At that the fellow said to the others, "Let's just get in the car and get out of here!"

Sometimes I joke about that incident, saying, "Only God and the lady who did my laundry know how that affected me!" To say the least, as I walked back to my patrol car I was very relieved the Lord had come through.

NOVEMBER 16

ALL IT TOOK WAS A MOMENT

Officer Mark Dennis
Franklin, LA, Police Department

WAYNE WAS an atheist. A KKK member, he was very gruff, with the personality of a porcupine. One day he bluntly told me, "Jesus didn't have a dad, and you know what that makes him!"

I probably should have kept quiet, but said to him, "I don't have to take up for Jesus' lineage, but on Judgment Day you'll have to answer for that comment!" That didn't sit very well with Wayne and his poker buddies.

About three weeks later I found out Wayne had inoperable cancer and was in the hospital. God seemed to say to me, "Okay, bigmouth, now what will you do?" Even though Wayne hated me, I made up excuses to

393

visit him, saying I was in the hospital to see someone else and thought I'd just say hi. Over time his atheist friends disappeared; they didn't want to see a buddy die. Wayne warmed up to me since the only other person visiting was his wife, whom he liked even less than me.

One day I decided to share the Gospel with Wayne. On the way to his room I met his wife, who kept yelling, "He's gone, he's gone!" Entering his room I found him strapped down, yelling incoherently, and "seeing things." He was out of his mind. I telephoned prayer warriors I knew, asking them to pray with me, beseeching God to restore Wayne's mind. I desperately wanted to talk to him about his need for the Lord.

> Then they came to Jesus, and saw the one who had been demon-possessed and had the legion, sitting and clothed and in his right mind. Mark 5:15

About thirty minutes later I walked into the room and Wayne was back to normal. I almost couldn't believe it! I talked to him about God and the fact that salvation is the same whether we accept Jesus as a child or later in life (Matthew 20:1–16). After hearing that, Wayne and I asked God's forgiveness for his sin, and Wayne prayed to receive Christ as his Savior.

I had another appointment but returned later that day. Again, Wayne was out of his mind. Concerned, I prayed by his bedside, and once again he returned to normal. I asked if he remembered my being there earlier that day and what we talked about. He said yes, and that we had talked about Jesus. When I asked him what Jesus did he replied, "He accepted me." It was so powerful to hear Wayne say that, and to know that God had accepted him as his son. Two days later he died. After being God's enemy all his life, Wayne entered eternity as God's friend.

"TOO BUSY TO HEAR"

Kristi Neace, wife of Officer Richard Neace*
Union, MO, Police Department

IT WASN'T that I didn't care or had no interest; I was just too busy. I usually keep the police scanner on in the background while I work, but sometimes it just sort of "fades into the woodwork." I did hear a patrolman's frantic call, "Help! I need backup," but with two young sons running up and down the hallway, I didn't give it too much more thought.

> For he is our God and we are the people of his pasture, the flock under his care. Psalm 95:7

I do recall thinking "I hope someone helps that guy," but then went back to folding the laundry and putting it away. When you're pregnant with your third child and have two active little boys, life can be distracting enough. I guess God knew I didn't need any extra worries that day, for the "guy" calling for backup was *my husband!*

Rick had been on patrol only a few hours when he happened to pull over "the wrong guy" for a DWI. The fellow was taller and stockier than Rick, had a rap sheet a mile long, and was not about to be taken into custody—that night or any other! He already had made up his mind that if he was going down, the cop was going down, too! As Rick told me afterward, they struggled for what seemed like an eternity. The drunk used brute strength to wrestle my husband to the ground, injuring Rick's wrist and forearm. Eventually the man was subdued and taken to jail, but it was my husband who took the brunt of the frightening episode.

It wasn't until the following morning I learned that the voice on the scanner was Rick's. I believe it was God's hand muffling Rick's voice over the scanner, sheltering me from worry, as the kind and loving Shepherd he is.

*Author, *Lives behind the Badge*

GOD WAS IN THE FIGHT AND FOG

Officer Randy
Baltimore, MD

IT WAS Saturday night, and my partner and I were part of a neighborhood enforcement team. We checked out an apartment where noise, drugs, and underage drinking were weekly events. Through a window we could see a youth drinking alcohol, so we knocked, spoke to an adult, and then placed the boy under arrest. He had an "eight ball" (one-eighth ounce) of cocaine on him. We called for a car to take him to the station and headed there ourselves.

On the way a call came for a "breaking and entering" in progress. The dispatcher had said a male was trying to break into a second-floor apartment from the balcony, and we saw him as we pulled up. I also observed a vehicle at the curb with the door slightly ajar and a male in the driver's seat. My thought was to get the driver's ID in case he was involved, then help my partner, who was refusing to come down from the balcony.

> Contend, O LORD, with those who contend with me; fight against those who fight against me.
> Psalm 35:1

I didn't believe the driver when he denied having an ID, so I felt for a wallet in his pocket. At that he kicked me in the chest, and the fight was on! We scrapped from the front of the vehicle to the side and then to the back of it. Seeing the melee, my partner left the man on the balcony to assist me. It wasn't until a third officer arrived we were able to subdue the driver. We arrested both men for attempted burglary and took them to the station. There we found PCP (phencyclidine, a hallucinogen) on the driver, which explained his superhuman strength! For his effort my partner suffered a fractured wrist (and my uniform was ripped).

Next day in church I was still numb from the incident. I do not recall what the pastor said, but it was good to be in the house of the Lord. Later that afternoon while getting ready for work I noticed my badge was missing—ripped off in the fight and now probably in the wrong hands in that high-crime neighborhood. I thought about the complications of dealing with that, so I prayed. I drove my personal car to the intersection where the fight took place and my badge was lying there, right in the middle of the road! It was very foggy that day, and the fog had made it invisible! Thank you, Lord, for protecting me in the fight and answering my prayers!

DADDY'S LITTLE KITCHEN

Officer Caleb Williams
Gulfport, MS, Police Department

Grant Wolf
Fellowship of Christian Peace Officers (FCPO)

CALEB: Some might call Daddy's Little Kitchen a "hole in the wall," but they were there for us. They gave us a place to meet before Katrina, and they opened as soon as possible after. Before the storm we had planned to charter our new FCPO chapter in November; we didn't let the hurricane stop us. Two months into the cleanup, we were on our way back to normalcy—working regular shift hours and then heading home to work on our own or someone else's home. Destruction was everywhere, but so were helping hands. We were small in number and tired, but buoyed by the hundreds of officers from around the United States and Canada who came to help.

Grant and Ruth drove into Gulfport late that afternoon, and I led them on a quick tour. Finally, we were able to put faces to telephone voices and e-mail messages. Then came our chartering dinner at Daddy's. For a few hours there was fellowship, food, and much-needed laughter. It was the boost we needed, a "second wind." All too soon it was over and we went back to work, but the Lord had planned it. We left with a new spring in our steps.

Grant: In Gulfport, Ruth and I were overwhelmed both by the destruction and the indomitable courage of those we met. No chapter chartering over the years was as poignant as Gulfport. As Caleb prepared the room for the meeting he set an empty place with a plate and upside-down glass. A slice of lemon and sprinkled salt were on the plate. Beside it was a sheet of paper with these words:

Let us never forget our fallen brothers of the badge, never forget what they lived for, what they died for, and who they had to leave behind. They are unable to be with their loved ones and families tonight, so we

> I will praise you, O Lord my God, with all my heart; I will glorify your name forever.
> Psalm 86:12

join together to pay our humble tribute to them, and bear witness to their continued absence.

A slice of lemon on the plate reminds us of their bitter fate. The salt sprinkled on the plate reminds us of the countless fallen tears of families, who also paid the price.

The glass is inverted—they cannot toast with us this night. The chair is empty—they are not here.

In spite of the destruction and decay around us, ceremony, symbolism, and honor for those who had gone before still reigned. Gulfport would rise again!

"SHE DIED TOO YOUNG"

Chaplain Don Hipple

Virginia Beach, VA, Police Department

IT WAS a November evening before Thanksgiving when the call came. There had been a fatality about twenty minutes from my home, and could I come? At the crash scene, officers had lights set up and were doing their investigation. It was a two-car crash in which the driver of a small compact car lost control and hit an oncoming vehicle at about 50 miles per hour. The combined force of the two cars was about 90 miles per hour before coming to a complete stop. The smaller car was crushed in on the driver's side. The driver in the other vehicle had only minor injuries. The sergeant in charge said it would be about fifteen minutes before we could notify the family.

The driver was a beautiful 18-year-old college student. She was running late and was hurrying to get home. An hour before, she was happily enjoying time with a friend; now she was dead. No drugs or alcohol were involved, her air bag deployed, and she was wearing her seat belt—all to no avail. As she lay there, a tarp covered everything except her feet. The image I always will remember was her beautiful feet and neatly polished toenails.

A death notification is difficult for all, including law enforcement. When the father

> He will wipe every tear from their eyes. There will be no more death or mourning or crying or pain. Revelation 21:4

saw me and the fatal crash officer, his first comment was, "Don't tell me Gracie was in an accident."

It was so heartbreaking to have to say, "I'm sorry, but your daughter was killed in a collision not far from here."From then until about 1 a.m. we ministered to him, her mother, and her brother. We answered questions as best we could, then just stood back as they grieved. I knew I couldn't sleep, so I just rode around until 5 a.m.

A few months later I received a three-page letter from Gracie's mother that thanked me because "you really seemed to feel our pain through this loss." Yes, I did, and I still think about it at times. Oh, that we'd never have to do this again, but we will. It's part of our job.

NOVEMBER 21

THE MOUNTIES OF MISSISSIPPI

Andrew Cowan

Royal Canadian Mounted Police

A FEW MONTHS after Hurricane Katrina, a group of Canadian police officers and their chaplain headed south to Gulfport, Mississippi. They took a week of annual leave and paid their own travel costs. The question is, Why? The reason can be summed up simply: As police, we are "family," and dozens of our family members were made homeless by Katrina. For many officers, the hurricane and flood surge left them with little more than the shirts on their backs and no place to live. The problem was compounded in that most families had to evacuate, and the workload was too heavy to give officers time off to arrange proper housing. Without their families, the job was even more difficult.

> If one of you says to him, "Go, I wish you well; keep warm and well fed," but does nothing about his physical needs, what good is it?
> James 2:16

We were struck by the sheer magnitude of the damage. Imagine that a giant hand had simply wiped away or knocked over everything in its path. Shrimp boats were tossed into tree stands, two-hundred-year-old trees were snapped, huge container ships were flipped on the beach, and houses

399

were demolished—some under thirty-eight feet of water. Words or pictures can't accurately describe what happened—you had to see it firsthand.

Our task was to drywall and insulate an uninsured home for a twenty-year veteran of the Gulfport Police Department. Before our arrival, volunteers had removed the moldy drywall and carpet, and all of the ruined possessions, disinfected the house for mold, and dealt with the site cleanup. What we found was a bare house and a jumbled mess of tools, toys, personal possessions, and tree parts in the yard. A week later the yard was cleaned up, the house insulated and drywalled, and some of the priming was done. We couldn't do it all, but we had made a difference. We came as strangers to help, but left as family and friends of many we met along the way.

Within days after Katrina, the Fellowship of Christian Peace Officers-USA (FCPO) swung into action to help first responders on the Gulf Coast. This was well before any federal government aid began to arrive. FCPO-USA, in coordination with FCPO-Canada, solicited funds, materials, tools, and manpower to assist in the reconstruction effort. Many "family members" came. Regardless of their personal beliefs or affiliation, God was in it all. When tragic circumstances and disaster strike, everyone has good reasons they can't go, and I understand that. But as one team member said, "To drop what I was doing, take a week off, and 'just go' was the best thing I have ever done."

NOVEMBER 22

COURAGE IN THE FIRE

Dalmas Otieno, Chaplain

Kenya Police Forces

WHY WE take some of the chances we do is often a mystery. Is it to be a hero? Is it because of a loved one? In police work, sometimes it's just because, "It's my job."

In March of 2010, six-year veteran Kenyan Officer Joseph Kipsang risked his life to secure a G3 rifle from a burning house. In the United States, most would consider losing a G3 a loss, but not worth risking one's life over. In Kenya, it was worth that risk. The G3 is Heckler & Koch's improvement on the German Mauser StuG 45, a common World War II rifle. After it was put into production in 1961, the G3 was so reliable and accurate it was quickly adopted as the standard rifle of many NATO countries. Many versions are now available with add-on grenade launchers, bayonets, and flash suppressors.

> Be merciful to those who doubt; snatch others from the fire and save them. Jude 1:22, 23

The house and rifle belonged to Kipsang's neighbor. When gas exploded in the neighbor's house, the homeowner was unable to enter it. But Kipsang surprised everyone by running into the burning home to retrieve the rifle. He emerged with the G3 in his hand, but was so badly burned his appearance was altered. In recognition of his courage, quick action, and professionalism, Kipsang was compensated and the process of promotion begun. His commanders wanted to motivate him and encourage other officers to emulate his exemplary conduct.

When Kipsang risked his life, he was not a believer. Had he perished in the fire, he would have found himself in the burning fires of hell. However, during his period of treatment and recuperation, he became a believer in Christ. Now he is helping advance the kingdom of God in the Kenyan police force. Even though he was unsaved when he retrieved the rifle, he says it was Jesus Christ who delivered him from the fire. His testimony has encouraged many officers to follow his example and become Christians.

As a police chaplain since 1995, I have witnessed too many incidents where men who were unsaved lost their lives. I praise God for saving Joseph Kipsang *in* the fire and *from* the fire!

NOVEMBER 23

HUMILITY IN ACTION

Dr. Mary Glenn, Chaplain
Alhambra, CA, Police Department

PHILIPPIANS 2:1–11 had always been one of my favorite Bible passages. It describes the sacrificial nature of Jesus and our call to follow his example of servant leadership. For me verse 8—"He humbled himself and became obedient to death"—aptly describes what police officers are willing to do.

When I began serving as a police chaplain ten years ago was when I first saw servant leadership being modeled by many officers. In fact, they have taught me more about servant and sacrificial leadership than anyone else. Even officers who are not of faith understand and espouse servant leadership. On countless occasions, officers have put themselves in harm's way for my safety as I rode with them. As they put on their uniform at the beginning of each shift, they mentally have committed to do what it takes to ensure the good and protection of others.

About five years ago, I was riding with an officer to the home of a woman where I had been before. She was mentally unstable, and her abuse of alcohol had further confused her mental state. When we arrived, she had barricaded herself inside her home and refused to come out. Because she had threatened to kill herself, several officers had been called to the scene. Because of my previous contact with her, I was able to talk to her through the door and build a certain level of rapport. I had convinced her to come out, but when she opened the door and saw all the officers, she came straight for me, ready to take me down. (She realized the officers were going to arrest her and probably take her in for a 72-hour psychiatric hold for testing.) The officer standing next to me immediately put me behind him, making sure I was protected. Then he stopped the woman from harming anyone, including herself. That quick act of response and sacrifice forcefully brought to my mind the selflessness Jesus modeled.

> "Do you want to stand out? Then step down. Be a servant."
> Matthew 23:11 (MSG)

Being a police chaplain is an honor and a privilege. Not only am I able to minister to those who serve and protect me, but the officers teach me daily how to live a more Jesus-like life.

NOVEMBER 24

THANKSGIVING DAY

Jason J. Everett
Rolling Meadows, IL, Police Department

FOOT PATROL in the dark of night can be interesting. Did I say "interesting"?!

When my partner and I turned the corner we happened upon a fight in progress. An accomplished barroom brawler would have been proud of the two male contenders, walking in a slow circle in the small open

402

space in front of their apartment, facing each other with choice weapons: a broken bottle, prongs forward, and a six-inch steak knife to counter it. We ran toward where they were fighting, but before we could arrive they took a couple of slashes at each other, missing wildly. When the offender with the bottle saw us he exclaimed (expletives deleted!) something like, "Thank God!" Then he dropped the bottle and raised his hands.

The knife-wielder took this opportunity to lunge at the unarmed man, missing by inches. I pointed my Glock at the steak-knife holder's chest and told him, "Stop, or I'll shoot." After a look that said it all (as well as more expletives!), he threw his knife at me. I ducked, and it flew harmlessly over my head. (I thought it was a "near miss," but my partner insists it was "well off the mark"—easy for him to say since I was the target!) With that I holstered my firearm and made a running tackle at the would-be knife thrower. Final score: criminals, 0, the law, 2!

> He ransoms me unharmed from the battle waged against me.
> Psalm 55:18

Driving home at the end of the shift, I suddenly was struck by thankfulness for how God protects me and my family, for covering me with the kind of safety a law enforcement officer needs, and for everything with which he has blessed me. Ephesians 1:3 states, "Praise be to the God and Father of our Lord Jesus Christ, who has blessed us in the heavenly realms with every spiritual blessing in Christ," and Ephesians 3:18, 19, says, "May you experience the love of Christ, though it is so great you will never fully understand it. Then you will be filled with the fullness of life and power that comes from God" (NLT 1996). Official Thanksgiving Day is only once a year—for us Christians it ought to be every day!

GOD WORKED THROUGH MY HEART

Detective Mark Copeland
Stanislaus County, CA, Sheriff's Department

WHEN YOU ask officers why they became cops, you'll get a lot of answers. I was a young boy who saw a crime and met a cop who changed my life. I wanted to be like him, so I joined the force when I got older.

As a rookie I didn't know much, but learned a lot on the street. I saw how hard life was on people, their families, and me. I started drinking and going to bars, looking for "something" in my life, but didn't know what. Then, in 1982 I met a friend who told me about Jesus. As I studied and prayed it became clear the Lord was what I had been seeking, so I accepted him as my personal Savior and made him Lord of my life. When he blessed me with a loving, God-fearing wife, and our children came along, it was clear to see he was working in my life. I also felt privileged in my career when he moved me into Homicide, for it was there life taught me so much more.

> You will receive power when the Holy Spirit comes on you; and you will be my witnesses.
> Acts 1:8

Cops see so much violence and pain in life, and many don't know how to deal with it. They end up drinking or, even worse, becoming like the people they arrest. Homicide shows you the seamiest side of life, and it brought me great stress and sadness. I asked God to give me an assignment away from so much violence, and he did—but not what I expected. Instead, I had heart surgery, which required a lot of changes in my life, including leaving Homicide.

Now my work allows me to be with my family more, and have greater interface with people in situations where I can talk about the Lord. A lot of Christians speak of, "God first, family second, work and everything else third." For the most part, peace officers have those in reverse. That's a shame, as cops have a great opportunity to witness to people and tell them about God. He doesn't ask much: just love him, serve him, and tell others about him—it's that simple!

NOVEMBER 26

DO NOT RESUSCITATE

Officer Andrea Brandt
Dallas/Fort Worth, TX, Airport Police

HE'S NOT breathing—come quickly!" When this call came, another officer and I raced to the scene.

We quickly realized the man had passed away, and his wife told us he was a "Do not resuscitate." The wife went on to explain they were flying to Florida for him to enter hospice, but he had died on the plane. I felt so helpless.

She was miles from home and had no family nearby. I thought the situation would be quite awkward, but it wasn't at all. Remarkably enough, she was a retired police dispatcher and felt really comfortable around police officers. I was so sad for her that I prayed right there, asking God for strength to help her through that difficult time. I needed the Lord's presence to be with a woman I had just met, and who had just lost the love of her life.

My workload was such I was able to stay with her for half my shift. I helped her with funeral arrangements and necessary paperwork, and got her food and coffee. I don't remember all the conversations, but found her to be a remarkably strong woman. She said her marriage had been wonderful and even though his death and the situation

> Let everything you say be good and helpful, so that your words will be an encouragement to those who hear them.
> Ephesians 4:29 (NLT)

were difficult, she would get through it. Her strength and composure helped me get through that day.

I believe God's hand was in it all: the death that caused us to meet, my lighter workload that day, and her experience as a dispatcher. Many do not know the extent to which dispatchers vicariously experience what officers go through. I believe that background helped give *her* the strength she needed that day. She and I have kept in touch via e-mail, and later she flew through Dallas/Fort Worth to see and thank me again. In spite of the darkness of that day, God let the "Son" shine through for both of us. God wants us to make a difference in the lives of others, and being a police officer helps me do just that!

NOVEMBER 27

"NO MINORITIES AVAILABLE"

Chief Jimmie Dotson
Houston, TX, Independent School District

WHILE WORKING on my B.S. degree in the fall of 1973, I was listening one day to my car radio when the chief of police was being interviewed. When asked about the department's minority recruitment program, he said they hadn't hired any minorities in five years because they could not find any qualified candidates. I knew this wasn't true, and took it as a personal challenge. As a former Marine and Vietnam veteran, I felt sure I was qualified! I wasted no time applying for a position, and was accepted for the next police academy in April. After serving in many functions and assignments within the department, I was promoted to sergeant in 1982.

The department had gained a reputation as the most notorious major-city department in the United States for not being respected by our minority communities. During that time, those of us who were minority officers were in a dilemma: We were not respected by members of our own communities, as well as by some officers of the majority race. No black officer held a higher rank than sergeant. This changed dramatically in the fall of 1982 when a new mayor appointed the city's first African American police chief. Under this chief's leadership, many more qualified minority members were added to the force. The department went from being one without respect to one that was nationally recognized for its leadership in policing.

> And whatever you do, whether in word or deed, do it all in the name of the Lord Jesus.
> Colossians 3:17

Eight years later our chief accepted the chief's position in another city, and I lost my mentor. About the same time, the IRS notified my wife and me that a legitimate energy-savings tax shelter in which we had invested was run by a fraudulent company. We were told we had eight months to pay a substantial sum in back taxes and penalties. "You can do it," they said, "by cutting out your tithes and gifts."

I believed this would be in violation of the Scriptures and our commitment to the Lord, so refused—we would find some other way to pay the debt. Within six months I was appointed the first African American Assistant Chief in the department's history. This enabled us to pay off the IRS without reducing our giving. Now, years later, I continue to praise God for the opportunities he has given me within policing where I have been able to make a difference for minorities, including Christians who often are demeaned by fellow officers. To God be the glory forever and ever!

COVENANT TRANSPORT

Elsa (Mrs. Jimmie) Dotson

Houston, Texas

GOD, PLEASE give me a sign!" My husband was being considered for chief of police in Chattanooga, and I wanted to know that God was in it. We'd been frustrated at the results of similar interviews in the past because of media coverage, and he had said perhaps it was time to get out of the process. I encouraged him to stay in, for we had prayed about his going elsewhere, and felt we should leave it in the hands of God. So, when the next opportunity came he submitted his résumé only because of what I had said. Before interviews in other places, we had learned all we could about the city, and I always went with him. This time, I had surgery and couldn't go.

The end result was they offered him the job (though we had to wait for two weeks before it was confirmed). Then it hit me! I would be leaving my dying mother, my sick twin sister, the church where we were charter members, my job of thirty years, my friends, and a city I loved. I had to know that this was God's will, so I asked for a sign! I was very specific: I asked to see that city's name *in print right there in Houston, Texas!* "Now, Lord, let's see you do that!"

Soon after, while coming home from work I saw a big white tractor-trailer truck, and noticed the company's name, "Covenant Transport," which had a biblical connotation. Covenant refers to God's promise to his people, and Transport means to carry from one place to another. Then I saw something else on the door: The company was located in Chattanooga, Tennessee—the city where we would be going! I said, "Praise God, we're going to Chattanooga!"

> Let me make just one more request. Allow me one more test with the fleece. Judges 6:39

With that sign I asked God for another favor: "Prepare the city for us!" When we arrived I found that 64 percent of the citizens claimed to be born-again Christians, we found a great church home, and we had many Christians for our friends. I was in a regular Bible study with my neighbors, and my husband was able to have a bold witness on his job. His department actually had a chapel where weekly Bible studies were held, and all the meetings began with prayer.

Was it coincidence that I saw that Covenant Transport truck from Chattanooga in Houston that day? No! God's hand was in it all, and I'm glad my faith was strong enough to ask him for a sign!

"GOD WILL BLESS YOU SOMEDAY!"

Patrol Deputy Jared McCord
Oklahoma County, OK, Sheriff's Office

NOVEMBER 28, 2008, began like any other normal day for me. I woke up, got ready for work, kissed my wife and kids good-bye, and left. Later a call came concerning an accident with injury in Jones, Oklahoma. Going there I was met by Jones officer Lieutenant Kenneth "Kenny" Ray. While he worked the accident, I directed traffic. About thirty minutes later, as I was leaving, he said five words that will stick with me the rest of my life: *"God will bless you someday!"*

Four days later I began to discover what he meant. I received a call that a car had fallen and pinned a man underneath. Another deputy, a city of Luther police officer, and I arrived about the same time. When we saw the car resting on top of a man, we knew we didn't have time to waste. I got on one side with the other deputy on the other, and we lifted the car enough for the Luther police officer to pull the man out. To this day we don't know how we lifted all that weight! Then we discovered that the man under the car was Kenny. Not finding a pulse, we started CPR as fast and hard as we could. We all knew Kenny and wanted nothing less than to save his life. We continued working on him until medical help and a Medi-flight arrived. Finally they said Kenny had a heartbeat and flew him to the hospi-

> Whoever invokes a blessing in the land will do so by the God of truth.
> Isaiah 65:16

tal. Our joy was short-lived, however, for an hour later we were told he didn't make it. I kept asking, *Why? How could God have allowed us to bring his heartbeat back and then let him die?*

At his funeral one of his best friends thanked me for doing all I had for Kenny, but I still didn't understand. As I saw it, I hadn't done anything for

Kenny. Weeks later I saw the friend again and asked him what he had meant. The friend asked, "Did you ever hear Kenny say, 'God will bless you someday?'" When I said yes, he said, "God brought you to Kenny when he was dying and all alone. God gave you the opportunity to help him live long enough for his family to gather around him and tell him good-bye. God blessed you, him, and them with those extra few hours of life."

My day still starts the way it always did, but now I tell people, "God will bless you someday." You never know when you will need to be blessed or whom you can bless.

NOVEMBER 30

DO THE RIGHT THING!

Sergeant Dino Heckermann, Badge No. 3537

Streamwood, IL, Police Department

EXCESSIVE USE of force is a shameful subject for police officers. Many will try to mitigate their actions and not take the opportunity to learn from them. I almost fell into that trap!

I responded to a 3 a.m. residential burglary in progress, just in time to assist other officers in apprehending two offenders. They were under the influence of drugs, had a lot of fight in them, and intended to escape. With three years of police experience under my belt I made sure these offenders would remember not to run from the police again! Next day on my way in to report to my supervisor a senior Christian police officer looked at me and said, "Do the right thing." I shrugged off his comment, not knowing I was being called for an internal investigation.

As my actions of the previous night were being questioned it struck me, *I am a new Christian and have to make a choice: Do I do the right thing and tell the truth or try to weasel out of it?* Choosing the right thing would mean a ten-day suspension. God placed me under conviction, and I admitted my wrongdoing. My heart sunk with regret, not because of the punishment, but because my actions dishonored God.

Later that year I bumped into one of the offenders I had mistreated. Only God could have given me the courage for what I did next, but I apologized for my actions. Here I was in full uniform looking into the eyes of a young man I had mistreated and arrested. I don't know which of us was more astonished!

Thirteen years later while working overtime at our local library I noticed and recognized the same man. He also recognized me, and we began to talk. It soon became apparent that he had become a Christian, and we discussed how the arrest had affected both our lives. By my owning up to my misdeed and God giving me the opportunity to apologize, God used the incident for good, molding our characters for greater use in his kingdom.

You intended to harm me, but God intended it for good to accomplish what is now being done, the saving of many lives.
Genesis 50:20

I remain amazed at how God knew at the time of the incident that two young men—a rookie cop and a delinquent—would come together years later and encourage one another unto love and good works. Though the other man and I walk two separate paths in our influence on others, we are united by the grace of God.

GOD HAD DIFFERENT PLANS

Bill White (Ret.)

Signal Mountain, TN, Police Department

COMPARED TO most, I was old when I entered law enforcement. At age 40 I had moved from Chicago to Chattanooga, left real estate, and become a reserve officer with the sheriff's department. Two years later I became a full-time patrol officer for the Signal Mountain, Tennessee, Police Department, "up the hill" from Chattanooga. I loved my job and the time it gave me to spend with family. Then "bang," the town council instituted mandatory retirement at age 60. After 18 years with the department—six years from expected retirement—I was to be unemployed! One month from my 60th birthday I found myself on the outside looking in!

At first I was devastated. Retirement at any time is an adjustment, but when it comes unexpectedly and you find yourself with only a third of your former income it's even worse! This was not what I had expected and certainly not the direction I wanted my life to take. Having a lot of time off seems great at first, but then reality sets in!

After five months out of work and running down various leads I learned of an opportunity to work for a private company contracted by the Federal Protective Service (Department of Homeland Security). After an exhaustive background check and six-month hiring process, I was back at work—providing security at the Federal Building in my own hometown.

> "For I know the plans I have for you," declares the LORD, "plans to prosper you and not to harm you, plans to give you hope and a future."
> Jeremiah 29:11

The end result? My salary and pension combined are 40 percent more than what I earned as a patrol officer, more than enough to get me debt-free and fully prepared for retirement when it finally comes. Not only that, I am quite happy in my new environment.

At first I thought my forced retirement was a cruel joke. But I've come to realize God was in it all the way. He knew what I needed from every standpoint: income, work situation, less stress, more time with my wife, and more time to reflect on God's greatness. What happened was a blessing from God! It just took me a while to understand that God works wonders, and that he takes care of fools like me. He can point you in a better direction than the one you've chosen for yourself. If you haven't yet learned it, God has his hand in everything we do. Like me, I hope you praise and thank him every day for all the wonderful gifts we receive from him.

"TWO FOR ONE" DAY

Chris Burris

Independence, MO, Police Department

SUCCESS OFTEN is being at the right place at the right time. That certainly was the case in this situation. We'd received an anonymous telephone tip regarding the whereabouts of a burglary suspect. After the tipster said the suspect was in possession of stolen firearms, I gathered as much information as I could and established a game plan with my colleagues. I was highly motivated to catch this criminal!

At the apartment complex where the suspect was supposed to be, I had an underlying suspicion there might be more than what the tipster reported. The female who let us in said the suspect was her boyfriend, and we found him barricaded in the bathroom. We were concerned he might be armed, but my partners and I persuaded him to open the door, then took him into custody on an outstanding burglary warrant.

> Some trust in chariots and some in horses, but we trust in the name of the Lord our God.
> Psalm 20:7

We placed the suspect in a patrol car, and I asked the female what she knew regarding the burglary. She said she knew nothing, but had heard about "a murder-for-hire" plot. That really caught me off guard, so I asked her to tell me more. She said two men had given her boyfriend money and guns to "complete the job," but the boyfriend got cold feet. However, he had kept the money and the guns. She also said the transaction took place in another jurisdiction, not ours.

At the station, I gave this information to agencies who might be involved, including ATF. The agent said he would interview the suspect and let me know what he discovered. About a week later I saw on the news the top story that day: "Two charged in alleged murder-for-hire plot." This was the case I had passed on to ATF! The agent later phoned to say the "two charged" were high school kids who had paid three hundred dollars to have their adoptive parents murdered. When the man I arrested backed out, the kids started looking for someone else. The parents were completely unaware of the plot, and may never have known it came to light from an anonymous phone call involving a burglary suspect!

This incident made me even more aware that what I do is important, and that through my efforts, two lives may have been saved. It also made me realize the extent to which God was in the situation and is in my life without my even knowing it. I thank him daily for watching over me and our community.

FROM "RELIGIOUS" TO "CHRISTIAN"

Captain Bob Kolenda
Overland Park, KS, Police Department

MY RELATIONSHIP with God is important in understanding who I am and how I handled being shot.

About seventeen years ago I found I was "religious but lost." I'd been raised in a "religious" home, went to church schools, and knew all about God, Jesus, and the Holy Spirit. I rarely missed attending church on Sundays, but during the week I don't think anyone who knew me or worked with me would have thought I was very religious. I can't say I was "bad," but certainly "good" wouldn't have fit, either.

I had been led to believe the only people in heaven would be those of my faith. My wife and I were married in my church and attended there for a while as a couple, but then she quit going; she said it didn't meet her spiritual needs.

One day she came home from an aerobics class at a different church and asked me if I would attend a couples' Bible study with

> I have hidden your word in my heart that I might not sin against you.
> Psalm 119:11

413

her. To her surprise I said yes. We had one child and another on the way, and I thought we should do "something religious" together.

The only Bible I owned was a huge coffee-table edition, while Cindy had a *Living Bible*. I knew many of the stories from the Bible, but had never read or reflected on them. As we attended and studied together, my heart and eyes were opened. I discovered songs we sang in church actually came from the Word of God! I started going to that church with her, but mine was so ingrained in me I continued there also.

Through Bible study I gradually came to understand that being a Christian means having a personal relationship with Jesus. Romans 10:9, 10, made a big impact on me. The words "believe in your heart" made me realize my belief hadn't been in Jesus, but in my church membership. Finally, one day I prayed to receive Christ and accepted him as my Savior. I did not have a "lightning bolt" experience, but things in my life changed. My language improved, and I walked away from crude jokes instead of being the one who told the best ones.

I was 30 years old when I went "from religious to Christian." Did it make a difference? You bet! The strength God gives me sees me through both the good and the tough times in my life. Without it, I'm not sure I could have handled being shot as well as I did. God's promises *do* give us strength!

DECEMBER 4

PREPARED FOR THE BATTLE!

Captain Bob Kolenda
Overland Park, KS, Police Department

PREPARATION is key to success in any field, including spiritual. Books, friends, pastors, conferences, the laying on of hands, prayer—all helped me grow spiritually after I became a Christian. I needed it all December 4, 2001.

That day our department had focused on several suspects in a credit card fraud scheme. When the day shift officers needed relief, another detective and I took over. While maintaining surveillance on the prime suspect's apartment, we learned he had an associate with a homicide warrant, who was thought to be headed out of town. However, when our suspect arrived, the homicide suspect was with him. My partner called for backup, and we

414

approached the building. While the forgery suspect tried the door (the locks had been changed), the homicide suspect came down the stairs. I approached the door with my gun at low-ready and yelled, "Police!"

Immediately I heard the distinctive crack of a gunshot, and felt an impact to the right side of my lower jaw. I returned fire and saw him fall to the ground. As the other suspect ran down the stairs, I fired a round at him through a sidelight window. He collapsed into a ball on the steps. I had fired a total of seven rounds. My partner moved up, kept both suspects covered, and called for medical assistance.

> ... all of them wearing the sword, all experienced in battle, each with his sword at his side, for the terrors of the night.
> Song of Solomon 3:8

When the shooting stopped I had an unreal peace about me. This is a peace only God can provide. It is the "peace of God, which surpasses all understanding" (Philippians 4:7 NKJV). I knew I was going to be okay. I also knew without a doubt that if I should die I would see Jesus. I had believed this as a matter of faith and because of God's promise in the Bible. But that night it became more than just faith. It became very real to me.

Within minutes help arrived, and I was on my way to the hospital. Even though I sustained serious injuries, I know God orchestrated everything. He gave me the strength to stay focused until my partner could take over; I did not lose consciousness, I didn't feel pain for nearly three hours, and he kept my mind clear. I was prepared for the battle that night, and for the long weeks that lay ahead.

THE BATTLE BELONGS TO THE LORD

Captain Bob Kolenda
Overland Park, KS, Police Department

THE BULLET that had hit me shattered my jaw, lodged one tooth in the roof of my mouth, one in the bottom, and one on the underside of my tongue, then the expanded .38 slug hit the back of my throat. Instead of blocking my airway, the bullet fragments were inhaled into my lungs. This damaged my larynx and one of my vocal cords, which accounts for my current raspy voice. The small bone to which the tongue is attached was also fractured.

Overland Park P.D. has only two trained paramedics. They just "happened" to be right there to assist me, and with me all the way to the emergency room. I was taken to the best trauma center in the area. An outstanding oral surgeon who usually doesn't practice at St. Joseph Hospital "just happened to be there." He didn't have materials available for an external support device (tube bolted outside my face) so had to use a titanium growth plate, which I've been told is a less troublesome method. All "happenstance"? I don't think so!

Throughout my recovery I felt surrounded by the peace of Christ, and could literally feel the power of prayer inside me. It gave me time to reflect on so many blessings:

That God exists and loves us, and that I know Christ and his peace. All his promises are true—never did he leave me or forsake me. Where would we be without a loving and forgiving God?

A strong wife and supportive family, and the gift of more time to love and care for them.

A wealth of friends and the comfort of prayer, which sustained me.

Doctors, nurses, and amazing medical technology; the surgeon who was able to remove the bullet fragments from my lungs through my trachea.

My voice and a mouth that can chew food!

That God spared the suspects' lives.

The support I received from the community, city of Overland Park, and the Police Department.

Clear thoughts through the ordeal that night.

Encouragement from unusual places.

DEALING WITH A HARD SITUATION

Reverend Dean Kavouras, Chaplain

Cleveland Division Safety Forces
Federal Bureau of Investigation

WHEN THE first companies arrived, the house already was roiling in flames. Heroic efforts had been made, but a 4-year-old—twin to a survivor—could not be saved. The attending officers and fire personnel were grim-faced: The loss of life in any fire is bad enough; the death of a child is very hard to take.

The remaining siblings—three girls ages 7 through 10 and unharmed—were taken to the Metro Health Center, and I went there also. Two trauma teams were working feverishly to save an infant and the other twin. At that point the girls and other family members knew nothing of the deaths of an adult male and the twin.

What came next was informing the family of the deaths and the extreme critical condition of the other two. After the doctor informed the adults and the initial shock wore off, I led those present in prayer. Their

> Comfort ye, comfort ye my people, saith your God. Isaiah 40:1 (KJV)

pastor, a very godly man, had been called, and informed the girls. I was impressed with his gentleness, loving care, and ability to give them a divine perspective on what had happened. As he prayed with them, fire and police officers present reverently bowed their heads.

Then the father of the twins, who as yet knew nothing about the incident, arrived. Once more it was my responsibility to inform him, doing my best to comfort him with prayer and a sense of God's presence.

It had been a ragged night. I thought of Psalm 145:9: "The LORD is good to all; he has compassion on all he has made." Silently I prayed and asked God to comfort, strengthen, and bless those who suffered loss that night, and to be a shield for fire and police officers as they carried out their responsibilities with courage and compassion. Dealing with situations like this is hard, and could not be accomplished without the Lord. I thank him for his presence, and the privilege and honor of being a ministering servant when his children are in great need.

417

SEEKING GOD'S VOICE

Officer Jeanne Assam

State of Colorado

FOR THREE months I had been involved with a small ministry in which I had grown a lot from reading Christian books and the new friends I'd made. However, I felt conflicted about my career: Did God want me to remain in full-time policing, or was he calling me to change my career?

Wednesday, December 5, the couple who lead the ministry held their annual staff Christmas party in their home. I told them of my conflict, and together they suggested I should fast for three days—going without food for the purpose of hearing God's voice. I was uncomfortable at the thought of going that long without food, but I knew I could do it, especially if I was serious about getting direction from God.

Thursday at work I discussed fasting with a co-worker. With Christmas coming and plates of treats everywhere, I considered waiting until after Christmas. Her response was what I already knew in my heart: "Begin immediately." The next day I did, and I believe that is what enabled me to hear so clearly on Sunday.

Saturday was the second day of my fast. I was hungry, but feeling surprisingly good. At the time I was on the security team of New Life Church in Colorado Springs, and had security duty that night. Each year we put on a Christmas production that draws thousands from the area, so officers are needed to direct traffic, answer questions, and be on the alert. When I told the

> Listen and hear my voice; pay attention and hear what I say.
> Isaiah 28:23

team leader I was fasting, he said if I wanted to, I could just stay home and spend time with the Lord on Sunday, the third and final day of my fast.

I woke up early Sunday, thinking I would stay home, read my Bible, and seek God's face. I wanted to spend time alone with Jesus. After several hours of prayer and time with God, I took a break and checked the Internet for news. There had been a shooting 75 miles away in a Denver suburb at the Youth with a Mission facility, and the shooter was still on the loose. Chills ran down my spine: I knew in my spirit that the gunman was coming to New Life. I couldn't call the police and say, "I believe this gunman is coming to my church." But after praying, fasting, and seeking God's voice for three days, I felt sure he was. Quickly I showered and got ready; I had to get to New Life as fast as I could!

DEATH CAME TO NEW LIFE

Officer Jeanne Assam

State of Colorado

BEFORE LEAVING for New Life, I fervently asked God to give me a spirit of power, love, and self-discipline (a sound mind [KJV]) (2 Timothy 1:7). I might die that day, but I was not afraid.

Services were over, but many people lingered longer than normal. About ten minutes after our uniformed, off-duty officers had left with their marked squad cars, all hell broke loose. I had gone to investigate a device outside the front doors and come back inside when I heard a muffled "pop, pop, pop" coming from the East Hallway. Soon it was evident those sounds were loud blasts from a high-powered rifle.

The East Hallway is very busy between and after services. More than 100 yards long and 10 yards wide, it is where people pick up their children and where the special needs room is located. There were more than five hundred people in the hallway and thousands more in other areas in and around the church. I shouted, "Where is he?" and another security team member yelled, "He's coming in the doors right now!"

The gunman carried a Bushmaster AR-15 high-powered rifle strapped to his shoulder. I drew my Beretta 9mm from my jeans waist, ready for whatever action was necessary. I was one hundred yards from him, but closing fast as I sprinted down the hallway. When he pulled open the last set of doors leading into it, I was waiting for him. It was the vision I'd seen back at my apartment: a shooter dressed in black entering the church. I stopped running and walked down the middle of the hall, calmly looking for cover before I engaged him. Three thoughts ran through my mind: I love my job; I'm going to kill this guy; and I may die today.

> Rescue me, O LORD, from evil men; protect me from men of violence.
> Psalm 140:1

419

As he continued firing I raised my weapon, lowered it and prayed again, took seven steps past my cover, and shouted, "Police officer, drop your weapon!" He pointed his gun at me . . . and I fired. Instantly, God's presence completely surrounded me; it was so incredible. When the gunman walked in, I had sensed an evil, demonic power everywhere. Now, I felt the magnificent shield of God's power around me. My bullets passed his in midair. Mine hit him several times, but I was not hit once. He died, and that was the end of a killer's wrong choices. Death attempted to enter New Life Church, but life prevailed.

A full account of Jeanne's testimony and this incident are in her book, *God, the Gunman, and Me.*

CALLED TO BE A POLICEMAN

Patrolman L. H.

Illinois policeman

A S I DROVE into the parking lot, Craig had gotten out of his car and headed for his open trunk. Inside was a loaded revolver with which he planned to kill himself. We had received a late night domestic disturbance call from his wife, and Craig left home after that call. His solution was to take his life. After a conversation filled with screaming, silence, and tears, Craig finally agreed to accept my offer to take him to a hospital. Against department practice, I drove him there myself. After what we'd been through together, it seemed right. At the hospital I proudly walked him into the emergency room, and left him with the professionals. I figured that was the last time I'd ever see him.

Months later I found myself mindlessly driving my beat. I was in one of those funks, wondering why I continued to be "The Police." No matter what I did, it was never enough. Day-after-day we deal with the same crimes, problems, and tragedies—it's never-ending. Perhaps it was time to leave police work.

As I reached a busy downtown intersection filled with pedestrians, I saw a man in a suit crazily waving his arms in the air at me. Pessimistically I thought, *Now what dramatic crisis am I about to get dragged into?* Drawing closer, I saw it was Craig . . . with tears in his eyes and a huge smile on his face. I pulled over. He didn't know my name, but said he'd been looking for me for months. He was filled with joy and enthusiasm! He wanted me to know he'd spent three months in a substance-abuse facility. He was an active member in an alcohol-abuse support group, where he regularly told new members how I saved his life in the nick of time that evening. Life at home with his wife and family was good, and his job was going great. He very much wanted to thank me for those several minutes that changed his life!

> Whatever you do, work at it with all your heart, as working for the Lord, not for men.
> Colossians 3:23

God has a way of reminding us of his presence in our lives. For some it's the song of a bird, the solitude of a mountain valley, or the birth of a baby. For me, it was that "chance" reunion with Craig. Just as I had helped clear up doubt, anger, and confusion in his life, God used Craig to do the same for me. God reminded me I was called into policing for people such as Craig and the others I serve. I still have "ups and downs," but I continue unwavering in the profession to which I was called.

DECEMBER 10

THE ANGEL ON MY DOOR

Scott Israel, No. 1223

CID Juvenile/Gang Investigator
Fayetteville, GA, Police Department

COULD I be dreaming? I had just checked out a shopping complex, so why was I here in a hospital? What was going on? Why was I so groggy? Why were people talking to me and shoving a picture in my face? Why were there little angels pinned all over my pillow? I remembered having a little "fender bender," but what was the big deal?

Without knowing it, my life had changed. Seven days earlier, December 3, 1995, my little fender bender was a major crash in my patrol car. On a county road at 70 miles an hour my car struck a culvert that acted as a ramp, sending the car airborne for 96 feet. After striking the ground it rolled three times and ejected me 86 feet. EMTs treated me at the scene (they had to reinflate my ruptured lung) before I was helicoptered to a hospital. A CT scan showed my bottom jaw broken in two places and jammed into my neck with my bottom teeth! My pelvis was broken in two places, three ribs were fractured (one had punctured my lung), and I had a broken nose. It took two titanium plates screwed into my jaw to hold things together.

No one could believe I was alive. I was told repeatedly that a guardian angel had been watching over me, and they had a photo to prove it! Sure enough, on the driver's door of my mangled car, where paint had been peeled off, was an amazing face, of which you could clearly see eyes, nose, and other features—my "guardian angel." It was the most recognizable thing on the car!

After several weeks of recuperation and physical therapy, I was back at work on light duty with a cane. I could have blamed God or others, or been depressed and disgruntled . . . but I was happy to be alive and back at work. I realized God's plan for my life wasn't finished, and I told him he could use me as his tool in whatever ways he desired. Since that day so much has happened! I've been broken, depressed, discouraged, and challenged, but have also been strengthened, overcome obstacles, and triumphed for God. He has kept me from temptation, used me to influence youth and other citizens, and encouraged me and other officers to become stronger Christians. The crash was a painful ordeal, but God—and my "guardian angel"—brought me through it. Thank you, Lord!

> And we know that all things work together for good to those who love God, to those who are the called according to *His* purpose.
> Romans 8:28

THE MURDER OF FATHER GULAS

Reverend Dean Kavouras, Chaplain
Cleveland Division Safety Forces
Federal Bureau of Investigation

A FIRE IN the rectory of the St. Stanislaus Roman Catholic Church had claimed the life of 69-year-old Father William Gulas. By the time I arrived, the blaze had been extinguished, and the Fire Investigation

Unit was just beginning its grisly work. These special servants of God do what detectives have always done, they speak for the dead. In Cleveland, fire fatalities are treated as homicides until proved otherwise. And why was I there? Part of my duties as a fire chaplain is to remind firemen "God *is* our refuge and strength, a very present help in trouble" (Psalm 46:1 KJV).

Nothing was right about the scene. A daytime fire in a church office, a priest who didn't smoke—no good reason for it all. The firemen found trauma at the back of the priest's head; the fire had not accomplished the masking of an obvious murder. Even though it was a crime scene, I knew enough about Roman Catholicism to understand they would want to anoint the body, so was able to arrange the "when and where" of said rite. The anointing priest was from Poland, had worked with the deceased for three years, spoke broken English, and was terribly distraught. Though my helmet clearly said, "Chaplain," I don't think he realized I was a clergyman. When I made that clear he relaxed, and seemed to find reassurance from the presence of a fellow pastor.

Then he asked me, almost as a plea, would I pray with him and be with him as he anointed the remains? I said yes. I reminded him from Psalm 103:15–17 that, "*As for* man, his days *are* like grass; As a flower of the field, so he flourishes. For the wind passes over it, and it is gone, And its place remembers it no more. But the mercy of the LORD *is* from everlasting to everlasting" (NKJV). Together we went into the deceased priest's office for the anointing ceremony. It was a sacred moment

> The heart is deceitful above all things, and desperately wicked: who can know it?
> Jeremiah 17:9 (KJV)

as parishioners, firemen, and coroner's personnel reverently bowed their heads, prayed the Lord's Prayer, and listened to brief words of comfort from the Gospel.

Two days later they had their suspect, a Franciscan brother. One can't help but wonder why anyone would murder a fellow human, especially a man who'd taken vows to honor God. It's one thing to *say* you honor him—another to have God in your heart.

THE FIRE EXTINGUISHER FIASCO!

Officer/Chaplain J. R. McNeil, Badge No. 279

Pinellas Park, FL, Police Department

IT WAS A cheap motel, the kind crooks seem to frequent when they're on the run. This time it was a deranged man threatening to kill cops or anyone who came near his first-floor room. SWAT was called, and the other sniper and I took our positions. My position had me on the ground, about 100 feet from the only window on the entry side of his room.

With my fixed-power scope, all I could see were the window and the front door. I probably could have counted the man's whiskers if he had pulled the curtains back to see what was outside. We must have lain there, prone, for more than an hour. Except for when a team member left the "hotline" phone by his door and an occasional flutter of the drapes, it was boring! But it gave me time to concentrate my prayers: "God, if you need me to take this guy out to save a life, help me do it just as I've been trained to do—one shot, one kill." I had just finished praying and *Bam!*, it happened! The drapes whooshed open, the window exploded, and a huge red thing nearly filled my scope as it hurtled toward me. It was all I could do NOT to pull the trigger! The suspect had thrown a fire extinguisher through the window, and nearly received a .308 caliber rifle slug in the process! When my heart calmed down, I realized he had broken the window and nothing else. I had maintained my composure, didn't fire, and no one was dead—not the suspect, police, bystanders, or anyone. Whew!

> With us is the LORD our God to help us and to fight our battles.
> 2 Chronicles 32:8

The standoff ended about thirty minutes later. The deranged man realized he had no option other than to give himself up. The SWAT Team leader told us to stand down, so we picked up our gear and walked back to our squad cars. While the news media scurried to make a story out of what little happened, we simply maintained a poker-faced composure to hide our feelings inside. We did what we were trained to do and kept the city safe. And our Guide and Protector through it all was the Lord.

COMFORTED BY A *KAUMATUA*

Paul Miller, Constable PMW291

Whanganui, New Zealand, Police

IN NEW ZEALAND, December is the first month of summer. I was in my first six months of policing in New Zealand after leaving the London police force. Just before Christmas I received a radio call to go to a beach a few kilometers away; a body had washed ashore! At first I questioned if it could be true, or just something looking like a human body. Then I recalled that a week before, a man had been washed out to sea about 80 kilometers away. He had been on a summer holiday, tried to rescue his 10-year-old son from a riptide, but was caught in the same tide. Fortunately, the son had been saved.

That morning, two couples had been walking along the beach when they discovered a body, and were clearly upset. We were in a M ori area, so I asked the sergeant to obtain the services of the local *Kaumatua* to minister to these four and pray over the body. *Kaumatua* are respected tribal elders in a M ori community, and have been involved in that area for a number of years. They are chosen and appointed by their people for their ability to

> The LORD is the everlasting God, the Creator of the ends of the earth.
> Isaiah 40:28

teach and guide both current and future generations. While most M ori think of themselves as Christian, their spirituality is much more centered on the environment as a reflection of God's presence in nature than in western Christianity.

When my sergeant, the *Kaumatua*, and I arrived at the spot, we could see clearly they had found the body of a male. None of the four was associated with any faith, but they said they would like to participate in prayer with the *Kaumatua*. Listening to him that morning, I found his thinking and approach so different from mine it was amazing. Afterward, one of the females said she, too, was quite moved by her experience of the morning. I was just grateful for the recovery of the man's body, hoping it would help bring relief to his family.

About a month later I returned with the man's family to the site where his body had been discovered. As I left them in quiet to grieve together, I quietly prayed to the God of the universe.

MAN OR ANGEL?

Officer Richard Neil (Ret.)

Huber Heights, OH, Police Division

A FULLY SWORN peace officer with arrest powers, a badge, and a gun, I was in my second month of policing. It was winter, and I was working midnights in a small town. I saw a man stumbling down the sidewalk, obviously intoxicated, weaving back and forth between the sidewalk and the road. He wasn't wearing a coat, so I asked if he would like a ride home. Without reason he viciously attacked me, and in two seconds "community policing" became "officer survival!"

The man was 6'4" tall, weighed about 250 pounds, and was high on PCP. That gave him a very unfair advantage against my 5'9" height and 185 pounds. Thinking I was doing a good deed, I hadn't told Dispatch of my contact with him, so no help was on the way. I tried to get something off my belt to defend myself, but rolling around in the icy slush, I was fighting for my life! In spite of police training in defensive tactics and my military background, the PCP made him oblivious to my blows. He tugged at my belt, going for my gun, but grabbed the radio by mistake. I was in big trouble and knew I had to use deadly force quickly! Otherwise he would knock me out, get my gun, and kill me.

> For he will command his angels concerning you, to guard you in all your ways. Psalm 91:11

Continuing to hit with my left hand, I grabbed my .40 caliber Smith & Wesson with my right. As I opened the snap with my thumb, blood sprayed over my face. At first I thought it was mine, but it wasn't—it was his! As he rolled off me to one side, I looked up and saw an elderly gentleman; he had hit the man hard with a flashlight! He reached down, gave me a hand, and, with genuine concern, asked if I was okay. He helped me brush off the slush and snow, and reminded me to call an ambulance for the man and assistance for myself. I thanked the stranger repeatedly, and asked where he had come from. He said he was just passing by, and noticed I needed help.

For a moment I turned to attend to the suspect lying in the snow, then back to speak to my rescuer. He was gone without a trace. I had never seen him before, and have never seen him again. By the way he carried himself, I wondered if he was a retired police officer. Whether he was man or angel, I don't know. I just know he was there in my time of need, mercifully acting as a guardian of God's justice.

JESUS 2, SATAN 0

Detective Brycen L. Garner

Indianapolis, IN, Metropolitan Police Department

AS A YOUNG soldier at Fort Hood, Texas, I was the "on call" investigator one December day. We received a call that a woman refused to exit her bedroom, and was threatening suicide. When I arrived, other military police and emergency personnel already were on the scene. Since there were children running about the house, I felt the situation was not as serious as it was dispatched, but that changed within seconds. Entering the back bedroom, I found a woman in distress with a very sharp, surgical-type blade clutched to her wrist. She had demanded everyone leave so she could do what she had to do. At that moment the only thing that came to my mind was the name of Jesus. Involuntarily I called out, "JESUS!" and almost instantaneously his presence was felt.

> God has come to test you, so that the fear of God will be with you to keep you from sinning.
> Exodus 20:20

Having uttered Jesus' name, I walked in and sat on her bed. After reading her suicide letter, my impromptu plan was to keep her talking to find out what she valued—faith, children, etc. She indicated she had lost faith in everything: Her marriage was failing, she had lost her job, and Christmas was coming, and she felt she had nothing to offer her children. She was experiencing sensory overload. For quite a long time I spoke to her from my heart, trying to give her Christian encouragement. Finally, she gave me the blade, and was taken to the hospital for proper help. I don't know what happened to her later, but Jesus won that battle. He had used me as a vessel to at least temporarily give her hope.

Jesus actually won two battles that day. Essentially, God tested me to see how strong my faith was in him. I came from a Christian home, but was far away from my family and friends. Was young Specialist Garner going to rely on the One I had been taught to trust, or would I take

427

another route? I thank God my faith was and is strong, rooted and grounded in Philippians 4:13: "I can do all things through Christ which strengtheneth me" (KJV).

THE BANK HOLDUP

Captain Matt Prindle
U.S. Security, Dallas, TX

I WORE MY bulletproof vest that day because it was cold and wet with a wintry mix. I was in the bank's break room when the manager ran in screaming, "We're being robbed!"

Drawing my pistol I entered the lobby. Two people were lying on the floor, and two others were running out the door. Thinking the man in front was the robber I ran out behind them, only to find the robber was still inside. Going back inside, my only thought was to protect our customers and employees. Soon I found myself eye-to-eye with the suspect, who had ducked behind a teller's window. He was wearing a mask covered by a hoodie, which gave him a dark, foreboding look. My thought was, *I don't want to be a part of this.*

Backing away I heard a round go off. *Did he just shoot? I don't want to shoot if he didn't.* I started to duck down behind a large oak file cabinet when I heard a voice say, "No, go this way," indicating I was to move to the left. I did, and remember seeing two rounds go through the glass about a foot to my right. Again, "the voice" led me back to the right. Just as I got to the end of the glass wall the robber shot me in the bottom seam of my vest over my kidneys. It felt like something grabbed both my ankles, pulled my legs up to about shoulder height, put its hand on my back, and slammed me into the ground face first.

> I . . . will be unto her a wall of fire round about, and will be the glory in the midst of her.
> Zechariah 2:5 (KJV)

As I rolled onto my right side the robber jumped the counter and was coming at me. I thought, "God, make him go away," and I fired two rounds back. I felt like the Grim Reaper was holding my own gun on me. Then I headed for the banker's desk, hit the hold-up alarm, pulled out my phone and called 9-1-1.

Just as I did the voice spoke again: "Move, he knows where you are," so I ran to a more secure position. Now came the strangest part of my experience: I saw three tall, shadowy figures moving from side-to-side on my side of the counter, protecting me from the shooter!

When the battle ended the robber was dead, and I was taken to the hospital, treated for minor injuries, and released. Others have tried to convince me the voice and shadows were simply hallucinations, but I know they were something else: God was my buckler and shield, a wall of protection to me!

WATCH OUT FOR THE OTHER GUY!

Trooper Thalia Stambaugh (Ret.)

Michigan State Police

BACK WHEN I was in high school and just learning to drive, there was an ad campaign for safe driving with the tag line, "Watch out for the other guy." Of course, that meant other drivers on the road who might do something like pull out in front of you, run a stop sign, etc. The tag line worked: It has remained stuck in my mind.

Twice that slogan "popped into my head" in such a way as to be described only as "divine intervention" or "divine guidance." In 1997 I transferred to Niles, Michigan, and bought a house in St. Joseph, about twenty-five miles north of Niles. Half my drive to and from work was on a two-lane state trunk line, which was usually pretty busy both ways with a lot of semis. Within a month of my move, I was making my morning drive from home to Niles around 6 o'clock. It was fall and dark, and I was thinking about a project and listening to the radio while driving. Suddenly, for no reason I thought, *Watch out for the other guy!* Just then, in the oncoming traffic I saw a flatbed semi hauling rolled steel. It had drifted a good way over the centerline and was coming right at me! I had just enough time to veer partially onto the shoulder and avoid a serious collision.

Just recently it happened again. The slogan just sort of "hit me" before another

> "The Spirit of truth . . . lives with you and will be in you." John 14:17

vehicle crossed the centerline. I believe if it wasn't for the sudden alertness it gave me, I would have been hit. In the Gospel of John, Jesus promised the Holy Spirit, saying he would be our Companion and Guide (Chapters 14–16). I believe in God and the power of the Holy Spirit, and am convinced these overt instances are just a small sample of his constant oversight and direction in my life.

HE WASN'T "BRAIN DEAD"

Dr. Clovis H. Sturdivant, Chaplain
Winnfield, LA, Police Department

WHEN MY son was a teen there were times when I thought he was "brain dead." Or perhaps, as some have said about teens, "They live in a universe of one." Somehow he and I made it through, and now he is a field training officer for a police department in another city. As a police chaplain I am well aware of the pressures on an officer to compromise his faith, so I pray regularly for God's protecting hand on his life. My greatest desire is that he be a godly officer of the law!

One night he telephoned his mother and me to share an experience he had just gone through. One of the chaplains in his department was riding with him on duty, and they had dropped by the station for a moment. Dispatch called my son to the front and asked if he would speak with a man who had just walked into the station. He did, and the man immediately handed him the keys to his car. Here is the story:

> Train up a child in the way he should go, and when he is old he will not turn from it.
> Proverbs 22:6

The man was in town on business and had been drinking. He and his wife were having severe marital issues, so he had decided to take his life by driving his vehicle into a retaining wall near the station. He said that "something" had told him to go to the station (which he was able to see from where he was) and he would find help. My son immediately called the chaplain from the back of the station, and they took the man into an adjoining room to talk. Before the conversation was finished, my son and the chaplain had been able to lead the man to Christ.

In all my years as a pastor and a father, I've never been more proud of my son than I was that night. Neither of us was brain dead when he was a teen. He had listened, and I had followed the Lord's instructions and done what a loving father should: "Impress [God's commandments] on your children. Talk about them when you sit at home and when you walk along the road, when you lie down and when you get up. Tie them as symbols on your hands and bind them on your foreheads" (Deuteronomy 6:7, 8).

DECEMBER 19

REMEMBER WHO YOU ARE!

Special Agent Don K. Shreffler
Iowa Division of Criminal Investigation

EVERY TIME they left the house my kids heard, "Remember who you are!" They knew it meant: "Remember how you've been raised, what you believe, what you've been taught, and, oh, yes, that your father is a cop—don't embarrass me!" It also meant, "Remember you're a Christian." Christians in law enforcement have a constant need to remind each other to "Remember, we are Christians!"

Acting on that premise, years ago a group of Christian officers in Council Bluffs, Iowa, began to meet weekly for lunch and prayer, "to motivate one another to acts of love and good works" (Hebrews 10:24, NLT). Then we decided to see how many Iowa Christian officers would gather for a statewide breakfast. It was such a blessing, we repeated it for two more years. However, we wanted more than just a couple of hours once a year together to relax and openly enjoy being

> Then you will remember to obey all my commands and will be consecrated to your God.
> Numbers 15:40

Christian officers. We didn't have to feel "funny" about praying in uniform in the presence of unbelievers, reading our Bibles openly, or talking about work and life from a Christian perspective! That led us to begin "The Retreat."

When Jesus called his disciples, he took them away from the masses. They needed to be trained, to develop a deeper relationship with him and each other, and to be away from other distractions. I find that significant. These guys didn't have to be on guard for unexpected jabs from a passing Pharisee, or the ridicule of a gaggle of Gentiles. They could relax with their teacher, acknowledge what they believed, be who they were, and maybe take a nap if they needed one. The Lord modeled great wisdom in calling his men out and away then, and that's what we do now.

It is that type of atmosphere God has provided for us these past sixteen years. We get away far out in the woods, smell smoke from the fireplace, pray, build each other up, sing loudly, and eat—a lot! Our registration form says, "For cops, by cops." We are taught by godly men who wear a badge just like us, and we learn and get our batteries recharged. Most importantly, we look around at guys we may not have seen since last year and *we remember who we are, to whom we belong, what we've been taught, and what we believe.*

I will continue to remind my children, fellow officers, and all who claim the name of Christ, *Remember who you are!*

DECEMBER 20

NOT FOR MEN ONLY

Mickey Koerner, Chief Instructor
Utah Valley University

ONCE IN law enforcement, always in law enforcement!" Though my first love is flying, the years I spent as a deputy sheriff in Iowa are still in my blood. That's why I decided to attend a law enforcement weekend retreat held annually by Iowa DCI agent Don Shreffler.

To say that Hidden Acres is a "rustic retreat" would not be an understatement. Knowing that, as well as being a woman and no longer in law enforcement, I was hesitant at first to go. I was assured there would be more ladies there but, when I arrived, it was me and "a bunch of guys." They turned out to be twenty-five of the finest "big brothers in Christ" a girl could ask for, and I couldn't have felt more at home than to be in the robust assembly of our nation's finest from city, county, state, and federal jurisdictions! *What a blessing it was!*

We sang, had wonderful fellowship over meals, and received excellent teaching. Each year Don has godly speakers, including pastors and law enforcement personnel. Their messages go right to the heart of LE needs: getting rid of sin in our lives, growing in Christ, being renewed by our time in the Bible, active prayer life, and fellowship. Don's retreat, and others like it around the country, are designed to spur us on and encourage us in treating law enforcement as our "mission field."

> But if we walk in the light, as he is in the light, we have fellowship with one another. 1 John 1:7

I would encourage all LE personnel living in and around Iowa to contact Don* about attending his next spring retreat. Or, if you live too far away, ask him about beginning a retreat in your area. Regular contact and fellowship with other Christian officers are "lifelines" to the many who deal with the everyday world of law enforcement. Oh, yes, if you are a female, just remember these retreats are for officers—but not for men only!

*Contact Don Shreffler at centurion94@hotmail.com

DECEMBER 21

MY BEST CHRISTMAS GIFT

Captain J. L. Francis
Chattanooga, TN, Police Department

I HAD JUST left the firing range and stopped by the city pharmacy. It was the afternoon before Christmas Eve, the weather was cold and bitter, and there were a million things that needed to be done. At the pharmacy a middle-aged woman had been watching me and I thought, *How can I slip past her?* I walked toward the door, intentionally not making eye contact. She stood back until I was ready to leave, and then stepped into my path and asked if she could talk to me. She started with, "You don't remember me, do you?" I said no, and asked if we could step outside the building. I was still thinking "escape," and outside was a few steps closer to my car in the parking lot! I looked at her name tag ("Janice"), and then her story started.

She shared how just more than five years ago she had broken into a young college student's car. I worked the case, chased and located her, and arrested her in some apartments near the school. Continuing her story, Janice started to cry as she said, "You stopped and prayed with me when

433

you caught me." That night, she confessed to nearly ten vehicle burglaries. The Holy Spirit used that moment of arrest to direct her to a Bible-believing church where she accepted Jesus as her personal Savior. She has been clean five years, now works for the city, and helps others with their drug abuse problems!

> Preach the word! Be ready in season and out of season. Convince, rebuke, exhort, with all longsuffering and teaching. 2 Timothy 4:2

Wow! We stood outside on the sidewalk, hugging, crying, and praising! People passing by on foot and in cars were a bit puzzled! Soon, my hectic schedule and unfinished shopping did not matter! Here the whole reason for Christmas was revealed: God sending his Son to die for us, to save us, and to make a difference in our lives. I couldn't wait to call my wife and share this with her!

DECEMBER 22

STOPPED IN HIS TRACKS!

Officer Steve Huskey

Grand Junction, CO, Police Department

FOR MANY, the period from before Thanksgiving to after New Year's Day is not a season of joyful gatherings and celebrations. Holiday shopping brings out thievery in many forms—purse snatchings, car break-ins, shoplifting, home burglaries, etc. It also brings up old hurts and bad feelings, especially in households torn apart by infidelities, divorce, and remarriage.

On December 22, 1996, I was working as the night shift supervisor for the sheriff's office. An officer in one of our towns asked for assistance in locating and contacting a man who had been in a domestic dispute with his estranged wife.

As a couple of other deputies and I got to the town, I saw the suspect driving his car back in the direction of his wife's house. When I tried to stop the man, he took off at a high speed, leading us on a seven-mile chase to a neighboring town. When we got in the town, I called off the pursuit for safety reasons. However, we continued to check the area for him, and located him on a dead-end road. Another officer was in front of him and had just turned around, so he was blocked both ways.

Realizing there was no way out, the man pulled into a driveway that trapped him even further. After he stopped his car, I got out of mine and ordered him to exit his. He responded by firing a rifle at me. The other officer and I returned fire and found our mark: He was dead. During the investigation that followed, it was determined he probably intended to go back to his wife's house to kill her. Also, the rifle bullet he'd meant for me was found in the dirt where I had been standing.

In debriefing after the shooting, the psychologist told me I would suffer serious side effects from the shooting, but that did not happen. Instead, over all these years, God has given me peace that a bad situation was stopped before it got worse. I have tried to love and serve God all my life, and he has protected me through my twenty-six years in law enforcement. At the Christmas season each year I am reminded of God's grace and mercy for me. It also gives me pause to pray for the children of the deceased man, not out of guilt, but that they will choose to follow Christ rather than the path their father chose.

> Be joyful in hope, patient in affliction, faithful in prayer. Romans 12:12

DECEMBER 23

COPS, CHRISTMAS, AND HONOR

Lieutenant Stan Kid

Malverne, NY, Police Department
(Digested by permission from his original story)

WHEN I first joined the department I knew there would be holidays spent apart from the family. Working on Christmas Eve was always the worst until I learned that blessings come disguised, and honor is more than just a word.

I was a one-man patrol on the 4 p.m.-to-midnight shift Christmas Eve. It was cold and all the holiday reminders simply added to my funk. About 10 o'clock a call came to assist an elderly, terminally ill man. At his home I was greeted by a woman in her 80s. The home was furnished in a style I'd come to associate with older people. The lady led me to a small room where a frail, old man lay in bed with a blanket pulled up to his chin. He seemed barely alive with a breathing that was shallow and labored. The frightened look on his ashen face turned calm when he saw me.

> Precious in the sight of the Lord is the death of His saints. Psalm 116:15

At first I didn't understand the sudden change until I saw the top of a nearby dresser. Among other memorabilia, a photo of a young man in a police uniform caught my eye, unmistakably the man in the bed. When I took his hand I knew why I was there; he was dying and afraid of what lay ahead. He wanted the protection of a fellow cop to escort him safely on his journey. A caring God had answered his call and given me the honor of being that escort.

When my tour ended that night the temperature seemed to have risen and the holiday displays made me smile. I knew I had chosen an honorable profession where people care for one another. I pray that when it is my turn to leave this world a cop will be there to hold my hand.

DECEMBER 24

HOMELESS CHRISTMAS NIGHT

Sergeant Cameron J. Grysen
Houston, TX, Police Department

ANY NIGHT, I'd rather be home with my family and two daughters than out on the street, especially Christmas Eve. It was 1984; I was working Central Patrol on midnight shift, and had spent most of the night dealing with domestic disputes. Now, that certainly puts one in the spirit of "glad tidings of joy!" About 3 a.m. I decided to go to a doughnut shop for coffee and a snack (no comments about cops and doughnut shops— they're the only thing open after midnight on Christmas Eve!). To make matters worse, Houston was having a rare snowstorm!

Walking up to the store I saw a homeless man leaning against the wall. I thought, *Nobody should be like this on Christmas,* so when I came out I brought coffee and a donut. He was very appreciative, so I asked him if I could take him somewhere. He had nowhere to go, but I told him, "You can't stay out here in the cold on Christmas morning." I wasn't going to take him to jail, and suggested a local rescue mission. He didn't give a reason, but said he had been kicked out and banned from going

436

back there as well as the Salvation Army. When I asked if he had a family he said he did, but they wouldn't let him in the house.

I thought, *This guy has been rejected by everyone, and needs to know that Jesus cares.* I told him that Christ, too, had been

> Then Peter said, Silver and gold have I none; but such as I have give I thee. Acts 3:6 (KJV)

rejected by his own people and didn't have a home, either. I told him Jesus will never reject anyone who believes on him and trusts him as their Savior. I reminded him Christmas is when we celebrate Jesus' birth of 2,000 years before, and the reason Jesus was born was to give us all the gift of eternal life—free to all who trust in Jesus Christ.

I wasn't able to give him a home or force the mission or Salvation Army to take him in, so I gave him what I could: the Gospel, a tract, and a ride to the county hospital to spend the rest of the night in the lobby.

DECEMBER 25

CHRISTMAS EVERY DAY

Officer Arlene Ajello-Moffitt

Chicago, IL, Police Department

GROWING UP in the projects, I knew how hard it was for my single mom to take care of me while trying to make a life for us. Now, years later, in Ogden Courts, one of the worst projects in Chicago, I was encountering a similar situation. The father was one of my informants, and he and his family were struggling to make ends meet. The mother made a lovely home in a situation most would call hell. When it was discovered "Joe" might be feeding me information, he was fired by HUD from being janitor in his building. From "almost nothing," the family went to "nothing," with no money for basic needs. I was horrified by how he had been "sacrificed" for doing good. He and his wife are Christians, and did their best to help the community and the police.

It was Christmas, and they were strapped for money. That Christmas happened to be my day off, so after spending an early Christmas with my own family, I said I had to work. I drove my personal car, took no Kevlar and only one gun, and drove into Ogden Courts. Packed in the car were a 22-pound turkey and all the fixings, wine for the adults, soda and a *lot* of chocolate desserts for the kids, flowers for the Mrs., and for the Mr.—good news! I had gone to HUD and the board, fighting for him to get his job back (unbeknownst to him). He was back at work in a week.

> And this is love: that we walk in obedience to his commands. 2 John 1:6

The gangbangers looked at my nice shiny car when I arrived! After wishing them "Merry Christmas," I sternly said, "Don' mess with my car!" They left it alone. After the family hesitantly opened the door, I greeted them with flowers, chocolate, and champagne. When they were over their shock, they helped carry the rest from my trunk. We represented two different cultures and two different mind-sets, but we shared a common belief in God. We laughed and cried, held hands, and said The Lord's Prayer. Then we thanked the Lord for what he gives us every day. We enjoyed a wonderful Christmas together, but it didn't stop there.

I had the privilege of tutoring their daughter. Later, she was accepted into a top boarding school and then a fine Ivy League college. In many ways we became family. The holiday brought us together, but I believe Christmas is every day of the year. It isn't about the trappings, but the birth of Christ and what he brought to mankind: loving, sharing, giving, laughing, hugging, and just being together!

DECEMBER 26

A SPECIAL NEEDS CASE

Lieutenant Herbert Cropp (Ret.)

McHenry County, Illinois, Sheriff's Department

POLICE OFFICERS deal with all levels of society – rich and poor, famous and infamous, very intelligent and those with special needs. "Joe" was a special needs case.

Joe was alright if he stayed off alcohol and took his medicine. But if he neglected one or the other, strange things happened. Once he rewired a farmer's milk house. He has been known to open gates and let cattle out, turn machinery on or run a combine in a farmer's cornfield at 2 am. I often responded to those situations, and in time became the only one who could deal with him. I would call him by name, and we'd talk about his parents, fishing (he liked to fish), and why he should not be doing what he did. Sometimes, a farmer would want him arrested. If there were

438

grounds for that, after helping him "mellow out" I would persuade him to get into my squad car for the trip to jail.

One time he beat up a police chief, and then went to a local tavern. Several officers were sent, but they waited for me as they felt I would be able to talk to him. I went into the tavern and tried to start a conversation, but he ignored me. I knew something was wrong, but still tried to get him to talk even when he started to walk outside. Suddenly he yanked me to the ground and started punching me. The other officers pulled him off, handcuffed him, and took him to jail. I was kind of shaken up by this, as he'd never done anything like that in the many times I had dealt with him.

> Do not pervert justice; do not show partiality to the poor or favoritism to the great, but judge your neighbor fairly.
> Leviticus 19:15

Sometime later I saw him in the courthouse. Almost in tears he took my hand, and said repeatedly how sorry he was. "Please forgive me, Herb. You know what happens to me when I don't take my medicine and drink beer." I was touched by his apology, and we gave each other a hug. Sometime later he was hit by a car and killed. Crazy to say, but I felt like I had lost a long-time friend.

I always felt God helped me with the many problems and people I dealt with throughout my career, but I believe he gave me special grace in my treatment of Joe. His parents always told me how much they appreciated the time I took with him. Our goal in policing is to uphold the law; we do it more effectively when we realize we are dealing with God's children.

TEACHING OUR NEXT GENERATION

Officer Mark Dennis

Franklin, LA, Police Department

WE LIVE in a violent society. Fights and domestic disturbances are a normal part of a police officer's job. An elderly woman and a mentally retarded man in our town were bludgeoned to death with a hammer. The murderers turned out to be 16- and 18-year-old boys.

439

As in too many cases, a godly example had not been set for these boys by their parents, especially their fathers. When children see so-called "adults" cursing, fighting, and being arrested, you have to wonder what they must think. In their minds they must be saying, *So this is what it means to be an adult—cursing, fighting, smoking dope, and disrespecting everyone around you.* As an officer I can tell you that by the time they are 13, 14, or 15 years old, they have it down pat. For many, it is only a matter of time until they too are "adults" who are arrested and sit in a jail cell.

The Bible teaches us that Christian parents are to live a different lifestyle. Deuteronomy 6:5–7 states, "You shall love the Lord your God with all your heart and soul and strength. And these words I command to you today shall be in your heart, You shall teach them diligently to your children, and shall talk of them when you sit in your house and when you walk along the way, when you lie down and get up." (NKJV) In other words, Christian parenting is a daily responsibility.

> One generation will commend your works to another; they will tell of your mighty acts.
> Psalm 145:4

When I told my son about the murders and those responsible, we talked about things he and I do together. He quickly realized the truth of what I said: "Those boys have thrown their lives away and lost their freedom." Joy was gone from their lives. As a police officer I deal constantly with the consequences of sin; as a Christian father I have the awesome task to help prepare my children for godly living. God, help me not to fail!

DECEMBER 28

GOD ANSWERS PRAYER

Detective Ed Valkanet, No. 7344

Chicago, IL, Police Department

WHILE I was working nights on Chicago's North Side, we received a report that a housewife had been kidnapped on her way home from night school. Her husband was frantic.

After some time had passed her captors decided to let her go, and dropped her in a snow bank on the West Side. When we found out where she was, we took her husband to her. As soon as she saw us she threw herself into the snow and began sobbing inconsolably. She had been raped repeatedly and tortured by two men who abused her for hours. Tears came to my eyes as she related the terror and shame she had endured.

> God has revealed it to us by his Spirit.
> 1 Corinthians 2:10

We put her into our car, and I began to ask God to help us find the offenders. We asked her if she wanted to go the hospital or help us find the offenders. She said she had been blindfolded the whole time except once when she was able to partially remove the blindfold. At that time, she saw the outside of the building as well as the street. As she described the street, the Lord instantly gave me the name of West Jackson Boulevard. Incredibly, we literally drove right to the house she described.

She also said the inside of the basement apartment where the crime took place was all red. When we peered through a window, the color was as she described. We gained entry, but no one was home. However, we got the name of the resident and broadcast the information. About ten minutes later, a beat car stopped two suspects in an alley, who turned out to be the perpetrators. The woman identified them, and an arrest was made.

Other detectives who came to the scene were amazed at how anyone could have found the offenders in just a little over an hour; that just doesn't happen! For me there was no question of "why" or "how"—it was of the Lord! The Bible says, "If any of you lacks wisdom, let him ask of God . . . .but let him ask in faith, with no doubting" (James 1:5, 6 NKJV). In faith I asked the Lord for wisdom, and I never doubted the outcome. The Bible also says, "The Lord has made Himself known; He has executed judgment. In the work of his own hands the wicked is snared" (Psalm 9:16 NASB). And that was exactly the outcome in this case!

DECEMBER 29

"ARE YOU JESUS?"

Chaplain Paul Northcut

Cross and Shield Ministries, Russellville, AR

ON DECEMBER 29, 2009, we were about to sit down to supper when a man named "Billy" called. He, his wife, and their two small children—a boy age 3 and a girl 4—were at the Main Street Mission in Russellville, Arkansas. The Mission was closed, but some families temporarily living there said, "Let's call the police chaplain." When I met with

441

them they told me they had lost their jobs and home in Colorado, and were trying to get somewhere, anywhere, that might be better. They had some contacts in southern Arkansas and thought that might be warmer than Colorado.

> Whatever you do, work at it with all your heart, as working for the Lord, not for men.
> Colossians 3:23

Billy told me he and his wife were Christians and had asked God to help them take care of their family. They had taught the children to pray, and all along the way the little girl had prayed, "Jesus, please take care of us." In addition to food, gas, and a place to spend the night, most of all this family needed encouragement.

I called the mission directors and explained the situation—a story we have heard over and over again. The mission would fill their gas tank, so I led them to a station and took care of that. Next I talked to a good friend who owns a catfish restaurant. He said, "Let's get these folks fed. Don't worry about the cost; I'll take care of it." While they feasted on the best catfish in the state, I went down to a motel and arranged for a room. Then it was back to the restaurant to tell them where they would be staying. We prayed together at their table and I put a couple of bills in Billy's shirt pocket.

As I was about to leave, the little girl looked up and, with the sincerity only a 4-year-old can have, she asked, "Mister, are you Jesus?"

Not knowing how to answer it I finally said, "No, honey, I just work for him."

Just as police officers can burn out, sometimes I get tired of ministry—it's called "Compassion Fatigue." But every now and then something like this puts things back in perspective and I remember who I work for and how much he blesses me.

WE DON'T HAVE TO DIE AT 57!

Captain Mark Edwards (Ret.)
Plainfield, NJ, Police Division

AFTER TWENTY-SIX years in policing, it was time to retire. I was nearing 57—the "average age of death" for police officers—and didn't want to die with my boots on. But instead of doing away with stress, I exchanged "job stress" for "family stress." Our daughter moved to Colorado and our son lived in Pennsylvania, so we decided to leave New Jersey for Pennsylvania. I think the stress of clearing out our old eleven-room home, buying a smaller one miles away, and moving led to my brain tumor.

After being treated two months for a sinus infection, I blacked out and ran off the road in my van. A trooper took the report, called a tow, and I had my son come get me. On the way home I blacked out again, and the family decided I should go to the ER. After many tests the verdict came: "He has a walnut-size tumor in his brain, with a 95 percent chance of malignancy."

Immediately a voice within me said, "Don't worry about the cancer thing; that is not your concern. You will have to walk the path, but you will not be alone. I am not done with you yet." My family was concerned, but I never went into the "Oh, no! Cancer!" mode. Word spread, and I was prayed for from coast to coast, and border to border. The phone never stopped ringing! When the nurse saw tears while prepping me, she thought I was afraid. But it wasn't that—I was overwhelmed by the tremendous outpouring of prayer and support!

> I thank Christ Jesus our Lord, who has given me strength, that he considered me faithful, appointing me to his service.
> 1 Timothy 1:12

After surgery, I received radiation treatments to the brain and chemo for the lung and lymph nodes. They were quite trying, but God had told me I would not be alone. Do you recall the hymn "Trust and Obey"? If I could learn to trust a fellow officer with my life and obey my superior officers, surely I could learn to trust and obey the Lord. That's not easy when no one is visible, so we have to step out in faith. We do that by being firmly grounded in the Bible, having a consistent prayer life, and through fellowship with other believers. They accuse me of not behaving like a brain surgery cancer patient. I can't! God's not through with me yet, and I want to increase the average mortality age for officers by living a few years longer!

WHEN THE INMATES PRAYED

Officer Michael L. Smith
Hamilton County, TN, Sheriff's Office

DECEMBER 31, 2005, my 14-year-old son, Michael, was diagnosed with a germinoma (tumor) in the center of his brain. It was blocking the flow of fluid, so a shunt was placed just behind his right ear to help. That day he had three seizures within five to ten minutes of each other, and was hospitalized immediately. After a week in the hospital he was released to come home, and we began making arrangements for surgery at Vanderbilt Hospital in Nashville.

> About midnight Paul and Silas were praying and singing hymns to God, and the other prisoners were listening to them.
> Acts 16:25

I am an officer in the Hamilton County, Tennessee, jail, and knew an inmate in the jail who had turned his life around and given it to Christ while incarcerated. When we learned how serious Michael's situation was I telephoned the jail and asked that this inmate be told of my son's problem and our urgent need for prayer. Thereupon he and several other inmates began to pray for Michael.

On February 6 we took Michael to Vanderbilt. We were at the hospital the next morning at 7 a.m., they began prepping him at 9:15, and surgery began at 11 o'clock. He wasn't taken to ICU until around 6:30 that evening. Through the miracle of prayer and by God's grace, his recovery from surgery took only four-and-one-half days! Over the next four months he went through chemotherapy and radiation, and then was released. Michael is 16 now and in remission.

Not a day passes that I don't thank God for his healing power, the skilled medical staff, and the inmates who cared enough to lift us up in prayer. It's easy to generalize that "all inmates are bad" and, "God doesn't hear their prayers," but as a jail officer I've come to realize that kind of thinking is wrong. I'm reminded of a poem written years ago by Sam Walter Foss: "Let me live in a house by the side of the road, where the race of men go by; the men who are good and the men who are bad, as good and as bad as I."

Thank you, God, for helping me realize you love us all and can forgive even a sinner such as me!

STORY CONTRIBUTORS BY DATE

Adams, Keith – March 15, March 16
Adams, Peter
Ajello-Moffitt, Arlene – December 25
Alvis, James – July 1
Ancona, Vito – August 8, November 3
Angley, Michael – June 3
Arguelles, Becki
Assam, Jeanne – December 7 & 8
Beato, Anthony
Belknap, Mark – July 11
Bickerstaff, Nathan – January 27, February 3,
    June 11, September 30
Blumenberg, Brian – April 8, July 29
Bolt, William – August 18
Boman, Chuck – Preface
Bone, Pete – October 4
Bordeanu, Marius – October 2
Braley, Jeff – September 27
Brandt, Andrea – November 1 & 26
Brashears, Randy
Brewer, Josh – September 26
Burris, Chris – November 29
Cain, Brian – March 18
Campbell, John – January 24, March 21, May
    24, July 24
Carr, Will – July 15
Cava, Mike – August 15
Chamberlain, Scott – June 24
Cochran, Dace – January 26, February 6
Copeland, Mark – November 25
Cox, William J. – February 18, September 6,
    October 8
Cowan, Andrew – September 3, November 21
Cromer, Jon – June 12
Cropp, Herbert – May 4 & 9, December 26
Dalke, Kenneth – November 11
Davenport, Michael – May 6, September 23
Davis, Matt – March 13, August 19
Day, James – April 24
Deal, Tommy – November 12

Dean, Ingrid – April 27 & 28, May 17,
    August 13, September 7
DeGrow, Jeff – January 21 & 22
Del Greco, Gary – February 19
Dennis, Mark – May 21 & 30, June 30, July 31,
    October 29, November 16, December 27
Dickson, David – January 28
Dorr, Dennis – September 10
Dotson, Elsa – November 28
Doston, Jimmie – November 27
Dotson, Marcus – February 7
Duke, James – January 23
Dunn, Randy – February 25
Dye, Michael – February 14, June 2,
    November 14
Eacret, Bucky – June 28
Edwards, Mark – August 17, December 30
Elliott, Harold – January 30
Evans, Dale – July 4
Everett, Jason – February 4 & 29, May 26,
    July 13, August 24, October 21,
    November 9 & 24
Figgins, Linda – April 9
Francis, Jeff – December 21
Gallardo, Joe – October 18, November 5
Garner, Brycen – July 6, December 15
Garretson, Dwight – June 7
Gass, Bob – March 26
Gates, Michael – June 28, August 27
Gill, Sean – January 8, October 31
Gilliam, Vinse – April 4, June 10
Gilliland, Chuck – January 3 & 15, September 2
Gilmour, Steve – May 21
Glenn, Dr. Mary – November 23
Glennie, Bill – September 11 & 15
Greenhalgh, David – January 21, March 17,
    April 1, May 7, July 7, August 12 & 30,
    September 1 & 2, October 14
Grom, Charlie – February 10, April 6
Grubb, Leonard – February 2
Grysen, Cameron – January 6, February 20 &
    24, April 11, May 5 & 18, September 29,
    October 24 & 27, December 24

Grysen, Sheriff Bud – April 17, May 7
Grysen, Mrs. Bud – April 13
Gunnels, James – September 21
Hallman, Terry – July 30, October 11
Hammond, Jim – January 9, February 11
Hansen, Peter – July 20
Harley, Hank – June 6
Harris, Kyle – April 29
Harth, John – June 20
Haskins, Eric – May 8 & 10
Haston, Tiffany – June 1
Hayes, Louis P.
Headden, Phil
Heckermann, Dino – March 5 & 27, May 19,
    November 30
Helms, Theo – November 13
Higgins, Dawn – October 9
Hipple, Don – March 4, May 31, November 20
Hubbard, Bill – January 12, April 3 & 15,
    May 3, June 18, July 17, August 20,
    September 19, October 22, November 8
Huskey, Steve – December 22
Israel, Scott – December 10
Jensen, Thomas – February 22
Kariuki, James – August 23
Kass, Alvin – September 12
Kavouras, Dean – April 7, September 17,
    October 10, December 6 & 11
Keilbach, Todd – January 1
Keller, James H. – May 1
Keller, Michael – August 9
Kid, Stan – September 13, December 23
Koerner, Mickey – June 14, November 10,
    December 20
Kolenda, Bob – December 3, 4 & 5
Kolodny, Chaim – February 26 & 27
Kopinetz, Jamie F. – August 1, October 5
Landles, Jim – June 4
Laumatia, David NZ – January 29, March 2
    & 20, April 30, August 7 & 22,
    November 20
Layne, Sherry – October 26
Lee, Paul – September 8

447

Lerner, Chuck – May 20
Lerner, Lisa – January 7, August 11
Londino, Nick – June 27
Lopez, Adam – June 5
Lowen, Robert – February 16, April 20
Marchese, Michael – February 21
Marquez, Donna – March 19
Martin, Bob – September 14
McClung, Michael – April 19
McCord, Jared - December 2
McCollough, Zac – November 7
McGhee, Gary – August 16
McIntosh, Andrew – May 2
McNeil, J.R. – March 31, April 12, August 25,
    October 19, December 12
Meade, Shawn
Miller, Paul – June 16 & 29, December 13
Milne, Jonathan – July 19, October 13
Mills, Bruce
Moore, Karyl – May 13 & 14
Morse, Debra K. – July 27
Nail, Dennis – March 14 & November 4
Napp, Larry – February 17
Napp, Leilani – March 25
Neace, Kristi – May 15, July 14, October 15,
    November 17
Neil, Richard – July 28, December 14
Newell, Dave – July 9 & 10
Nichols, Jim – March 23
Nielson, John – July 3
Nightingale, Stuart – January 11
Northcut, Paul – December 29
Oake, Robin – September 4 & 5
Oliver, Mark – January 17, February 1, April 26
Olson, Glenn – August 3
Osterquist, David – March 22
Otieno, Dalmas – November 22
Paluszak, Joseph – August 26
Parker, Jonathan – June 23, July 2
Peoples, Thomas A. – May 27 & 28
Petrick, Paul – April 18
Phinney, Craig – March 24
Poel, Randy – January 2

Prestidge, Fiona – April 19
Prindle, Matt – December 16
Purdle, Dave – May 8
Reed, Marian – October 25
Restea, Traian – January 14
Rice, Bob – February 28, September 22
Rich, Randy – April 5, 21, 22 & 23
Rush, Jeffrey P. – January 18
Salo, Jim – February 12, August 28
Schinnerer, Traci – June 17
See, Hetzel – January 5 & 13
Sexton, Robin – October 3
Shewry, Jackson – March 11, July 22 & 23
Shreffler, Don – July 5, December 19
Skov, Susan
Smeltzer, Mark – February 5
Smidt, Galen – September 28
Smith, Clif – October 28
Smith, Martin – April 16, June 21
Smith, Michael L. – December 31
Sphar, Art – February 9, March 8
Spruill, Steven R. – April 14
Stambaugh, Thalia – December 17
Stanturf, Tanya – March 10, May 25, July 25
Stevenson, William – January 10
Stone, Glenn – July 21
Sturdivant, Clovis – July 26, December 18
Tippe, Merv – January 4, April 10, July 18,
    August 4, October 12, November 15
Tomisek, Tim – August 10
Tosch, Pat – November 6
Urgo, Chuck – February 23, April 12
Valkanet, Ed – December 28
Walsh, Bob
Wedel, Trace – March 7, August 5
Weeks, Jesse – August 14
Wells, Drucilla – March 29, July 8, October 1
White, Bill – December 1
Willard, Dave – September 25
Williams, Caleb – March 3, August 29 & 31,
    September 24, November 19
Williams, Gloria – February 15
Williams, Mike – January 20, March 30,
    October 23

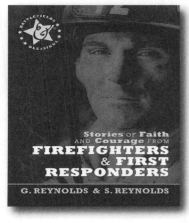